# RURAL AND FARMING SYSTEMS ANALYSIS
## European Perspectives

# RURAL AND FARMING SYSTEMS ANALYSIS
# European Perspectives

*Edited by*

## J.B. Dent

*Institute of Ecology and Resource Management
University of Edinburgh, UK*

and

## M.J. McGregor

*Rural Resource Management Department
Scottish Agricultural College
Edinburgh, UK*

CAB INTERNATIONAL

CAB INTERNATIONAL
Wallingford
Oxon OX10 8DE
UK

Tel: Wallingford (0491) 832111
Telex: 847964 (COMAGG G)
E-mail: cabi@cabi-org
Fax: (0491) 833508

A catalogue entry for this book is available from the British Library.

ISBN 0 85198 914 4

Typeset by Solidus (Bristol) Limited
Printed and bound in the UK at Biddles Ltd, Guildford

# CONTENTS

v

## II: CONTEXTUAL SETTING

## III: ALTERNATIVE PRODUCTION SYSTEMS

# CONTRIBUTORS

*Marc Benoit:* INRA, Station SAD, F-88500 Mirecourt, France

*Joseph Bonnemaire:* ENESAD, INRA-SAD, 26 Bd du Dr Petitjean, F-21000 Dijon, France

*Jaques Brossier:* ENESAD, INRA-SAD, 26 Bd du Petitjean, F-21000 Dijon, France

*John Bryden:* Arkleton Trust, Coulakyle, Nethybridge, Invernesshire PH25 3EA, Scotland, UK

*Javier Calatrava:* Dept Economia y Sociologia Agraria, CIDA, Apdo 2027, 18080 Granada, Spain

*Eduardo Chia:* ENESAD, INRA-SAD, 26 Bd du Petitjean, F-21000 Dijon, France

*Kate Corcoran:* IERM, University of Edinburgh, School of Agriculture Building, West Mains Road, Edinburgh EH9 3JG, Scotland, UK

*Ian Deary:* Psychology Dept, University of Edinburgh, 7 George Square, Edinburgh EH8 9JZ, Scotland, UK

*Ivar Dembovski:* Institute of Rural Development, PO Box 189, EE-2400 Tartu, via Helsinki, Estonia

*Barry Dent:*   IERM, University of Edinburgh, School of Agriculture Building, West Mains Road, Edinburgh EH9 3JG, Scotland, UK

*Werner Doppler:*   Universität Hohenhein, Institut für Agrar - und Sozialökonomie in den Tropen und Suptopen, Postfach 70 05 62, D-70593 Stuttgart, Germany

*Gareth Edwards-Jones:*   Rural Resource Management Dept, Scottish Agricultural College, West Mains Road, Edinburgh EH9 3JG, Scotland, UK

*Andrew Errington:*   Dept of Agricultural Economics, University of Reading, Whiteknights, Reading RG6 2AR, England, UK

*Ruth Gasson:*   York Cottage, Pottery Lane, Brede, Rye, East Sussex TN31 6HB, England, UK

*David Gibbon:*   School of Development Studies, University of East Anglia, Norwich NR4 7TJ, England, UK

*Janice Jiggins:*   De Dellen 4, 6673 MD Andelst, The Netherlands

*Spyros Kyritsis:*   Agricultural University of Athens, Agricultural Engineering Dept, Iero Odos Stz 75, Athens 11855, Greece

*David Leaver:*   Wye College, University of London, Wye, Near Ashford, Kent TN25 5AH, England, UK

*Murray McGregor:*   Rural Resource Management Dept, Scottish Agricultural College, West Mains Road, Edinburgh EH9 3JG, Scotland, UK

*Vagn Østergaard:*   National Institute of Animal Science, Dept of Research in Cattle and Sheep, Research Centre Forum, PO Box 39, 8830 Tjele, Denmark

*François Papy:*   INRA-SAD, F-78850 Thiveral Grignon, France

*Eija Pehu:*   Dept of Plant Production, Faculty of Agriculture and Forestry, University of Helsinki, PO Box 27, 000140 University of Helsinki, Finland

*Penny Perkin:*   Dept of Agriculture, University of Reading, Earley Gate, Reading RG6 2AT, England, UK

*Jim Phelan:*   Dept of Agribusiness, Extension and Rural Development, University College Dublin, Belfield, Dublin 4, Ireland

*José Portela:*  DES-UTAD, 5000 Vila Real, Portugal

*Philip Raikes:*  Centre for Development Research, Gammel Kongevej 5, DK-1610, Copenhagen V, Denmark

*Tahir Rehman:*  Dept of Agriculture, University of Reading, Earley Gate, Reading RG6 2AT, England, UK

*Neils Röling:*  Dept of Communication and Innovation Studies, Wageningen Agricultural University, 6706 KN Wageningen, The Netherlands

*Eduardo Sevilla Guzmán:*  Economia Sociologia y Estudios Campesinos, Universidad Cordoba, Alamenda del Obispo, Apdo 3048, 14080 Cordoba, Spain

*Peter G. Soldatos:*  Agricultural Engineering Dept, Agricultural University of Athens, Iero Odos Stz 75, Athens 11855, Greece

*Colin Spedding:*  Vine Cottage, Orchard Road, Hurst, Berkshire RG10 0SD, England, UK

*Cord Stoyke:*  Institut für Agrarökonomie, Der Universität Göttingen, Platz der Göttinger Sieben 5, D-37073 Göttingen, Germany

*Poul Eric Stryg:*  Dept of Economics and Natural Resources, Royal Veterinary and Agricultural University, Bülowsvej 13, 1870 Frederiksberg C, Denmark

*François Vallerand:*  INRA-LRDE, Quartier Grossetti, BP 8, F-2025 Corte, France

*Hermann Waibel:*  Institut für Agrarökonomie, Der Universität Göttingen, Platz der Göttinger Sieben 5, D-37073 Göttingen, Germany

# FOREWORD

The First European Convention on Farming Systems Research and Extension marked the beginning of an exploration and a sharing. Those of us who have participated in the meetings of the Association of Farming Systems Research and Extension (AFSRE) have got to know each other through our work in developing countries. We know relatively little about the efforts to transform agricultural systems that others have been making in Europe itself. And, owing to the accidents of language and history, those based in the northern and western areas of Europe have had until recently little contact with colleagues in central and eastern Europe and the former USSR, and too little contact with colleagues in the south.

The First European Convention marked the first attempt to bring Europeans who have been applying systems approaches to the problems of Third World agriculture together with those applying systems approaches within Europe. The process of mutual discovery of our diverse experiences is paralleled by the emergence of regional farming systems networks in other parts of the world. In collaboration with the AFSRE, some already are formalized as regional associations, as in Asia; others are more loosely constituted, as in Latin America.

What do we have in common? Beyond the specific applications and models we have developed in particular settings, I believe there are shared values, challenges, concerns and experiences underlying our diversity.

We are first and foremost committed to applying the power of the agricultural sciences to the problems of rapid transformation of farming as a system. Farming systems uniquely combine biophysical and socioeconomic phenomena in dynamic enterprises in which change, both reactive and proactive, is a condition for survival. In particular, we share a concern to strengthen the productivity of smallholder farming systems, as the primary source of livelihood for what is still the larger portion of the world's people.

We have learned that, in order to operationalize a systems approach, it is not enough to build system models and computer simulations of system dynamics. We must engage with members of the rural community, and together explore agricultural reality: in effect, harnessing the power of local, experiential knowledge, mental constructs and values, as well as farmers' experimental capacity, to the strengths of agricultural science.

In moving out of the research station, extension office and the university to work more closely with farmers, we have encountered two challenges, one ecological and one social. The first involves the recognition that the key question is not, or at least not only, 'how do we increase the productivity of agriculture?' but 'how do we sustain the productivity of the natural resources on which all agriculture depends?' The second challenge involves the recognition that there can be no sustainable agriculture, whatever the specific national mix of economic and environmental goals, without sustainable farming communities.

Our individual and collective exploration of these challenges has led us toward two distinctive concerns which serve to define our identity as a like-minded group of theorists, scientists, teachers and practitioners. One is a concern for **method**. The other is a concern for **process**.

There has been in recent years an explosion of interest in methods for working with farmers and other members of rural communities in order to develop agricultural technology and production systems together. We have moved from a somewhat formal and rigid FSR/E method paradigm toward a still-expanding, highly creative, rich and innovative portfolio of participatory methods which engage scientist, extensionist and farmer in joint analysis of problems and opportunities, design of experiments, experimental activity and the evaluation and sharing of results, both in the field and on the research station.

Development of method and exploration of process have gone hand in hand. Much has been learned about the practical steps and procedures required in order to produce reliable and rigorous results, the institutional processes needed to support participatory, field-based systems research and the professional and personal transformations that such a process demands.

The learning of method and process has encompassed a remarkable willingness to reach beyond normal professionalism. It has been accompanied by a spirit which encourages the open exchange of failures as well as successes and which supports critical reflection and peer appraisal of each other's experience of method and process. These characteristics of transparency and risk taking in the practice of our profession are part of our common identity.

However, there is one area in which much still needs to be done. I am prompted to ask whether we are not still undervaluing the talents of women scientists. Is enough being done to provide encouragement and financial support to young women scientists and extension professionals, equal to the opportunities of young male professionals? Certainly at the field level, we have learned that 'participatory' methods are not sufficient to ensure that women farmers, who in some parts of the world are the major producers of food and everywhere play key roles in farming systems, are adequately, or at all, engaged in the formal processes of system development. We have learned also that, whatever the rhetoric about 'whole farm' analysis and development, many, perhaps most, programmes focus on development of the cropping or livestock components, with too little attention paid to the dynamics of intra-household flows of resources, costs and benefits. Only explicit commitment can overcome these biases and shortcomings.

Engagement with method and process in turn has led us to recognize that we cannot, as agricultural professionals, limit ourselves any more to the crop system or the farm system. We are having to deal with systems on a larger scale, involving unsuspected spatial and threshold effects, multi-year time horizons and time lags and a larger range of actors who typically hold divergent views about the nature of the system to be managed.

We have in this dimension of our work begun to move from thinking about working with or facilitating 'platforms of negotiation' towards 'platforms of creativity.' This is leading in turn to another cycle of exploration and innovation in method and process, in order to generate consensus for action, action which is designed to foster mutual learning about how to manage complex agricultural and natural resource systems on scales larger than the individual farm. An important skill here is the joint exploration of the values and properties which those who have a stake in the management of systems desire to see optimized. 'Making visible' the quantifiable values and measurable properties of existing systems and trying out experimental new designs in reality are further important contributions that the system practitioner is making to wider system management.

Complexity, uncertainty, urgency: we are increasingly driven by the political and public fear that time is running out as the chemical loading on global resources increases and the richness of our biological inheritance disappears. As attitude surveys show, an increasing number of people now believe that reductionist, Cartesian science has contributed to the environmental problems of the world. They have little confidence that the same scientific method and research process can contribute meaningfully to the solution. For better or worse, elite scientific decision making among small professional fraternities is no longer wholly trusted or accepted as legitimate by the public at large.

Farming Systems Research and Extension promotes and is allied with a broader resurgence in civic activism and involvement in the search for solutions to compelling human and environmental problems. In my view, it is this broader engagement which alone will ensure good quality decision making and behavioural change at the societal scale as agriculture meets the challenge of the next century. It is in this context that I hope very much that a European group will continue to create ideas and to crystallize experience for others around the world to share.

*Janice Jiggins*
*President*
*Association of Farming Systems Research and Extension*
*1993–1994*

# PREFACE

The farming systems research and extension (FSR/E) approach has been widely used in an attempt to bring about rural change in many developing countries. The approach has been less formally used in Europe, where traditionally the research effort has concentrated on reductionist science aimed at increasing commodity production. It is only recently, with the shift in the emphasis of the European Union agricultural policy from production to the restriction of surpluses, and increasing emphasis on environmental and social protection, that circumstances have emerged which might favour FSR/E procedures. In addition, the significant political changes in central and eastern Europe have led to modification of rural infrastructures and agricultural production. Together these circumstances may provide the opportunity in Europe to question research paradigms adopted in the past and, as part of this, promote the FSR/E approach in Europe. Adoption of the FSR/E approach can be viewed as a way of ensuring that the direction of change is supportive of rural people and the overall environment (biophysical, economic and social) in which they live. It is clear that the methods adopted by FSR/E practitioners outwith Europe will not in all cases transfer exactly into the European rural environment. This book is a first attempt to define the issues of farming systems research as they may be applied within a European context, and is based on papers presented at the First European Convention on Farming Systems Research and Extension held in Edinburgh in October 1993.

Part I of the book examines the conceptual background upon which FSR/E is built and discusses those elements which may be valid for analysing rural systems in Europe based on the experience with FSR/E in developing countries. It is clear that the objective in both cases is to improve the state of the farm household, the business it operates, the community it forms part of and the environment in which it lives by embracing a range of disciplines in a holistic way.

Part II highlights the important changes taking place in rural sectors of European states including the difficult transition that eastern and central European countries are experiencing in moving from a centrally planned to a more market-oriented economy. The increasing role that concerns over the environment are having in the development of farming systems in western European countries is discussed. Finally, attention shifts to an investigation of the link between European Union agricultural policy and the status of farm households and food security issues in a global context.

As western Europe moves out of an extended period of production surpluses and concern for the environment grows, there is an increasing need for the identification of alternative land-use systems which meet both of these issues. Part III highlights some of the options – ranging from the role of organic farming and biomass production, to the role of genetic engineering techniques – which are currently being evaluated. The discussion shows that no single route will be appropriate to meet all the requirements of sustainability.

Change is never easy and negative impacts of rural change in Europe are being felt by farm and other rural households alike. The way in which these households adapt to change will depend on the issues that they face. Change brings with it stress and requirements for new information structures to ensure that the path of change is less stressful. It is becoming obvious that the approaches of traditional science, which concentrate on the farm as a production unit rather than a socioeconomic unit, will need to be replaced. The new research paradigm requires that researchers understand the processes of decision making within farm households and in rural communities. Part IV examines the business and family decision-making processes in farm households and highlights stresses that are occurring as a result of change. There is also discussion of the way in which support services are being withdrawn from rural areas, the changing role of women and the shift to multi-functional households which derive some income from spheres outwith agriculture.

The final section of the book, Part V, attempts to identify the way in which a number of groups within Europe are attempting to develop farming systems research frameworks applicable to European conditions. It is clear that there are major differences of approach. There is an increased recognition that those who have been using resources in rural areas over many years have developed an understanding of the constraints and potentials associated with those resources. This indigenous knowledge, which has been suppressed by the push for improved high science, clearly must not be neglected in the holistic FSR/E context. The French approach to the analysis of rural systems illustrates that progress can be made by adopting a holistic framework including technical issues and socioeconomic and political aspects. However, on-the-ground research which concentrates on observation and analysis also has a number of deficiencies and arguments are made for modelling to integrate the disciplines. In this sense, it is suggested that the development of new methodologies which utilize both quantitative and qualitative data will be fundamental in achieving the appropriate level of integration.

## Acknowledgements

The Editors would like to acknowledge the significant contribution that Janice Hirst and Jane Grandison made in typing and formatting this book.

*Barry Dent and Murray McGregor*

# I

# CONCEPTUAL BACKGROUND

# 1

## FARMING SYSTEMS RESEARCH/EXTENSION: Background Concepts, Experience and Networking

### *David Gibbon*

## Introduction

This chapter reviews some of the evolving themes of farming systems research/extension (FSR/E) over the past 20 years and the development of farming systems networking and associations. Until recently, the development of a farming systems approach within agricultural research systems was primarily the concern of developing country research systems, and the International Agricultural Research Centres (IARCs). There are some important exceptions, notably the work of INRA in France. There are some who would claim that there are many antecedents and that there is nothing new about FSR/E. There are others who would say that the approach is too rigid, top-down and apolitical and that it cannot have relevance for the complexity of developed country agricultural systems. These critics fail to recognize the fundamental principles that lie behind the approach that have been seen to have wide applicability, the evolving dynamic of FSR/E and the great diversity of contexts within European agriculture.

## Agricultural Research: Some Important Characteristics

Formal agricultural research in developing countries has been strongly influenced by western scientific thought and bears many of the characteristics of the physical and biological scientific tradition. Early in the history of agricultural science, in addition to the application of scientific methods, a reductionist approach to problem solving developed and disciplines became clearly defined and proliferated (Arnon, 1989). The focus on commodities was also strong as a result of the colonial political and economic pressure to exploit crops and livestock products which satisfied the demands of growing western industrialized societies (Mansfield, 1950).

The second strong feature of research has been the belief, by research planners and scientists, that formal research and extension are the principal sources of new ideas and technologies that will benefit all farmers. Research and extension institutional structures were developed to support the central source (Biggs, 1990). This approach has failed to recognize the complex manner in which technologies evolve and emerge as a result of many different pressures.

Within many formal agricultural research institutions, the role of social scientists in the design of alternative technologies has frequently been peripheral, although agricultural economists have made major contributions (Collinson's and Norman's early work in Africa, for example). However, the integration of social scientists into the research planning and implementation process has been rare and often difficult owing to a lack of understanding of the potential role from the perspectives of both natural and social scientists (Rhoades and Booth, 1985; Maxwell, 1986). It is possible that this is one of the reasons why so much research output is of little immediate value to the majority of the world's farmers.

Research policy has also had particular biases. Many policies in developing countries have tended to focus on commodity-based commercial agriculture and have supported inputs and marketing of products through a variety of direct and indirect subsidies. Little attention has been given to equity issues, either within or between households, and very few research systems serve the needs of poorer people in the community. Rhoades considers that research has moved through a series of distinct phases since the 1950s – production, economic, ecological and institutional – which have reflected the priority concerns of particular decades (Rhoades, 1989). Sustainability appears to be the current focus of attention (Hart and Sands, 1990), although institutional issues (not becoming important until 1995, according to Rhoades) seem to be increasingly of interest now (Gibbon, 1989; Axinn, 1991).

A problem facing many research systems in developing countries is that their institutional structures and organization were set up many years ago to serve economic and political environments which are very different from those of today. Underfunding, inadequate human resource development and inflexible work planning mean that there is little scope for innovation or the ability to respond to real needs of a range of clients (Trigo, 1986).

The recent concern with resource degradation and environmental quality issues has highlighted the fact that many agricultural research systems are very poorly equipped to deal with these aspects of resource use and misuse. In many countries these issues are often dealt with by different Ministries and often with little integration with related fields.

# Farming Systems Research and Development

Farming systems research ideas have been around for many years in many guises. In the modern era there are a number of key institutions and individuals who have played important roles in raising the profile of the concepts and value of systems thinking. It is these that will be the focus of this chapter.

In Latin America during the 1970s there were a number of projects that had systems components or perspectives – the Puebla Project in Mexico and the Caqueza Project in Colombia. CATIE in Costa Rica and ICTA in Honduras also pioneered work in this area. Later, the International Centres, CIP in Peru and CIAT in Colombia, have made major contributions to the development of systems thinking and farmer needs-sensitive research programmes. CIMMYT has made important contributions in the area of on-farm crop research. Networks and training programmes, often linked to US universities, were also important. A number of donors, notably IDRC, have played a continuing role.

In Africa, systems work, after the pioneering work of Collinson in Tanzania and Kenya, developed separately in west, east and central regions. Networks have emerged to cover these separate regions. USAID had several large farming systems research projects throughout Africa which helped to formulate some of the language and the basic ground rules of FSR/E. Much of this occurred through the USAID support, which was directed through US universities, notable Florida, Kansas, Arkansas, Michigan and Purdue.

In Asia, work on systems followed from some excellent existing local-level research in Thailand, Sri Lanka, the Philippines and Nepal. Work in these areas has continued to be at the forefront of innovation and development in systems work, notably in rapid rural appraisal and participatory approaches.

This major shift in research thinking followed from a general dissatisfaction with the attempts to modernize agriculture, through the transfer of high-input technologies based on single crops, which had been introduced in the 1960s. The development of a more client-sensitive, systems approach to the prioritizing and implementation of research was considered to be essential.

It was felt by many that significant areas of the tropics, notably those experiencing high degrees of climatic and environmental risk, and with relatively low productivity potential, were poorly served by conventional research (Dahlberg, 1979; Shaner *et al.*, 1982). The fact that many millions of people occupied these areas was an additional incentive to pay more attention to them. The move was also accompanied by substantial support from major donors and expectations that significant results could be achieved in a short time (Frankenburger et al., 1989). The International Agricultural Research Centres also gave farming systems research substantial initial support (Dillon *et al.*, 1978).

Although farming systems research approaches have developed through a variety of individuals, institutions and regions, there are a number of key elements that remain essential elements in FSR/E. These are as follows:

**1.** Farming systems research requires researchers to develop a holistic perspective of the real social, economic and political environment of rural communities. Researchers and extensionists need to develop an initial and continuing understanding of the farm, the household, a community or a resource user group as appropriate units of analysis, together with the members of these units.

**2.** A specific client orientation is possible, following the study and identification of differentiated groups of farmers and user groups. This approach has developed because of the experience of conventional research outputs which have tended to favour better-off farmer groups at the expense of poorer rural people, and better endowed areas at the expense of resource-poor or marginal areas.

**3.** As most scientists are trained in one discipline, it is normally necessary to put together multidisciplinary teams (natural and social scientists) for farming systems research to be effective. These teams are required to develop interdisciplinary analytical and operational approaches.

**4.** Farming systems research should focus on the problems and situations identified by and with farmers.

**5.** To be effective, farming systems research is linked to other scientific programmes which can provide specific support and skills to solve particular problems and to extension agencies, planners and policy makers.

**6.** Farming systems research develops in a dynamic, flexible way and continually responds to changing circumstances in an iterative manner.

It is important to recognize that a number of approaches to farming systems research have developed during the last 20 years (Gilbert *et al.*, 1980; Fresco, 1984; Simmonds, 1984). The Francophone and Anglophone approaches are sometimes considered to be somewhat different. However, too much is often made of these differences and many now recognize that there are clear complementarities between approaches (Pillot, 1990). Most are based on the same principles and many programmes have drawn on the most appropriate tools for particular circumstances (see, for example, the FSR programmes at Khon Kaen in northeast Thailand (KKU, 1987)). The incorporation of these ideas from different sources is one of the great strengths of the FSR/E movement.

## Problems of Concepts and Implementation of Farming Systems Research

Despite the very positive approach that developed with the introduction of farming systems research, there have been, and remain, both problems with the limited scope of the original concept and in the ways in which the approach has been implemented or operationalized (Oasa, 1985; Davidson, 1987; Marcotte and Swanson, 1987).

When the concept was first introduced there was an understandable need to develop a clear focus and boundaries of analysis, and to agree on a methodology of research with which researchers and extensionists could work.

This led to two problems. One was the focus on the farm household as the principal unit of analysis. Although this is appropriate in some circumstances, it is not always the case. Other groupings may be appropriate, and there are also important intra-household differences that need to be recognized (see below). A number of writers also placed the farm in the context of a hierarchy, which implies important linkages up and down the hierarchy (Hart, 1982; Conway, 1985). This again is only partially useful, and can lead to some confusion, as there are often linkages between farms and common themes that need to be analysed across farming communities. The Francophone approach to farming systems analysis presents a broad concept of farms as part of the landscape and wider community and also makes an important contribution by stressing a historical analytical approach (Pillot,1990). There is a recognition here that both the farm and the community (however that is defined) are necessary units of analysis.

A second major problem area is the 'stages' approach to implementation of farming systems research which appeared in the early literature and remains dominant in many systems (Norman, 1980; Shaner *et al.*, 1982). This involves a four- or five-stage process of diagnosis, design, experimenta-tion, testing and then dissemination of new technologies. While this has given many researchers an agenda and framework, it has also often resulted in an excessive focus on the initial, diagnostic phase of research. Many research teams have spent far too many resources and too much time on the initial study and collection of information on farming systems, on agroecological zones and on the development of farm typologies, etc., and this has rarely been very productive. With the limited time horizons of projects, researchers have often not gone very far beyond this initial stage before the project closes or changes course. In view of the dynamism of many systems, the delay caused by this excessive emphasis on initial diagnosis can result in proposals and experimental plans that are already out of date or inappropriate by the time they are implemented. There has been a very slow recognition by researchers of the need to consider a dynamic, interactive relationship between researcher, extensionist and farmer, and to initiate activities that support the process of technology development in a variety of ways simultaneously (Thapa *et al.*, 1988).

Yet another major problem area has been the inadequate understanding and analysis of household differentiation, particularly with respect to gender (Jiggins, 1988). This is despite the recognition of the importance of gender many years ago and the incorporation of social scientists into research systems. This positive move has not been developed further as many research systems still have little understanding of the importance of gender analysis, both as an initial step and as an integral activity in research.

Agricultural research institutions remain dominated by the natural sciences and focus on natural science-based problem solving and technology generation. Farmers or potential technology users are still only peripherally involved in research planning or decision making and scientists remain dominated and guided by the prevailing western scientific paradigm. Many of these last problems have arisen from the inappropriate structures created within institutions following the introduction of farming systems research. While some countries have created Farming Systems Research Institutes (for example, Thailand), many have attached farming systems research programmes, units or sections to existing research structures (e.g. Ghana, India, Indonesia), almost treating farming systems research as another discipline or commodity. This approach has also been evident within the context of projects; although many have claimed to have an overall systems perspective, few have been able to develop such a perspective within the prevailing institutional and policy framework.

The other area where farming systems research has failed to have an impact is in agricultural educational programmes, particularly at degree level. Most agricultural educational institutions have developed structures that reflect the proliferation of disciplines which have emerged over the past 30 years. This is true for both developing country and developed country institutions. Staff with established interests are reluctant to make room for what seems to be a new area. A review of the curriculum at Bangladesh Agricultural University in 1986 indicated the difficulties of introducing an FSR course, or modifying existing ones (Gibbon, 1986). A new field or area of study can be accommodated by creating a new sector, provided there is room, but it is very rare that a new concept stimulates the rethinking of the structure and programme of an institution. This has happened at Hawkesbury Agricultural College, Australia (now part of the University of Western Sydney), and it is a model worth close examination (Bawden *et al.*, 1985; Macadam and Sriskandarajah, 1990; Bawden, 1992).

A number of postgraduate courses in farming systems research and development have been introduced in Asia (Weitz *et al.*, 1987), but there is always the danger that by creating a 'new' field, other courses which ought to contain the same fundamental concepts and principles are poorer as a result. Some of the same concerns have arisen from the introduction of special gender courses and agroforestry courses (Gibbon, 1991). Also, there are a number of medium-term or short courses on offer which are designed to reorientate disciplinary scientists. These continue to be in demand and can be found in both developing and developed countries (e.g. the ICRA course in Montpellier and at Wageningen).

Another feature of farming systems research programmes has been the tendency for researchers and their immediate collaborators to imagine that they can quickly develop relevant research outputs that will positively benefit the lives of many rural people. Researchers are only one group of actors within rural areas and it is unrealistic to think that by their actions alone they can have a profound effect on rural livelihoods. It has now been realized by planners and donors that many other agencies that work in rural areas have a better understanding of the priorities, particularly those of poorer people, than researchers and a number of formal research systems now recognize the need to link up with these agencies if they are to be effective in the future (Farrington and Bebbington, 1993).

## Recent Developments and Innovations in Systems Research

These changes have come about against a background of constant adjustment within farming systems themselves and the continuing problem of rural poverty and differential access to resources. Other changes include the growing recognition of the importance of off-farm income, particularly among poorer groups, and the need to broaden the boundaries of farm systems studies to incorporate market influences and a political economy perspective (Biggs and Farrington, 1990). Yet another important influence has been the growing demand for systems of resource management that are environmentally benign and sustainable in biological/ecological, social and economic terms.

### The farmer-first paradigm

A number of writers, non-government agencies and institutions (Chambers, 1983; Richards, 1985; ILEIA, 1990) have supported a strong populist approach to farming systems research based on the belief that alternative or improved technologies can only develop with and by farmer involvement in the whole process. This demands major changes in the attitudes, approach and role of researchers and extensionists (Chambers and Ghildyal, 1985; Chambers *et al.*, 1989) and invites farmers to set the research agenda. Developments of this approach have focused strongly on participation of farmers and the inclusion of farmer knowledge and farmer experimentation in the research process (Haverkort *et al.*, 1991). All this work has had a significant effect on some research systems and projects which have attempted to reorientate their research programmes to incorporate farmers at all stages of the process. Ashby has had some success in involving farmers in varietal selection and evaluation (Ashby *et al.*, 1987). World Neighbors also incorporate farmers into their research and extension activities (Bunch, 1985). Lightfoot's group has developed ways of persuading farmers to represent their farming system and key flows and interactions in novel and interesting ways which greatly assist diagnosis and the design of alternatives (Lightfoot *et al.*, 1989). Many of these ideas are now incorporated into the work of IIED in training for participatory rural appraisal.

In the opinion of the author, the incorporation of farmers into the research planning and priority-setting process has proved to be very difficult in many national research systems, and the major decisions on the strategy and direction of most research programmes remain in the hands of re- searchers. A recent meeting of IIED and IDS at Sussex University (Beyond Farmer First, November 1992) attempted to review the progress made in the previous five years in trying to overcome some of the problems of implement- ing this concept.

### User groups

Other developments have involved the recognition that particular user groups may be a more appropriate unit of analysis of collaboration (Gibbon and Schultz, 1988; Fernandez and Salvatierra, 1989; Worman *et al.*, 1990). This has been an important step forward as it moves away from the rather limiting concept of the farm and nuclear family as the sole unit of study and links with more relevant socioeconomic groupings for further interaction.

### Agroecosystems analysis, RRA and PRA

The techniques of agroecosystems analysis developed by Conway (1985) have been adopted and refined by many projects and programmes and incorporated into rapid rural appraisal (RRA) and participatory rural appraisal (PRA) techniques. These have partly developed in response to the problems created by large surveys – the production of large amounts of information which was rarely utilized in the short term. However, although these techniques are undoubtedly very useful, they should not become a substitute for the collection of valuable baseline data and regular monitoring and interaction with client groups. There is a danger that important features of rural societies may be missed, particularly those associated with differentiation within and between families, and the need to understand within and between seasonal change in farming systems. There is the tendency for very experienced researchers to give the impression that RRA and PRA techniques are the only way to develop research priorities and programmes. This can be a very dangerous assumption for a young researcher to take and can lead to serious mistakes unless there are built-in checks and reprioritizing mechanisms in place. Review and replanning processes are often very weak in many systems (Gibbon, 1989, 1990).

## Equity, gender and social science contributions

Equity issues are not handled well by these techniques, but they have been by those groups who have made a particular study of gender and decision making in rural households (Poats *et al.*, 1988). Much of this work has been carried out by social scientists and those with a particular concern with the role of women in rural development. This important work still remains somewhat marginal to mainstream agricultural research, probably as a result of the slow institutional innovations which have occurred in this area. Agricultural research institutions remain dominated by disciplinary-trained natural scientists who are invariably male. The implications of this fact are rarely discussed seriously (difficult, given the circumstances), but some would suggest that it may lie at the heart of the problems of perception of what science is and how science and technology should serve people, particularly women (e.g. the writings of Capra, Fukuoka, George and Shiva).

## Informal research and experimentation

There have been many useful developments in the art and science of field experimentation and there has been an increasing recognition of the importance of informal research techniques (Biggs, 1980; Chand and Gibbon, 1990; Chand and Gurung, 1991) and of qualitative information and the monitoring of experience (Sumberg and Okali, 1988; Chambers *et al.*, 1989).

## Links with NGOs

A recent development has been the growing interest in the role of NGOs as effective agents for relevant, client-oriented technology generation. This is not to belittle the important outputs from many formal systems, which can be significant, as a recent study of technology generation has shown (Merrill-Sands *et al.*, 1989), but is a recognition that researchers are often few in number and cannot serve all potential clients effectively. A study undertaken by ODI (Farrington and Bebbington, 1993) arises from the fact that many governments now recognize that some NGOs can often operate much more effectively at the community level than formal government agencies, and it makes sense to develop working linkages with them (Berdegue, 1990; Gilbert, 1990). Many NGOs are also working with poor people who have little access to inputs and other resources. Perhaps as a result of this situation, many NGOs are involved with the search for technical solutions which do not involve high external inputs and many are engaged in organic, ecological or biologically based farmer participatory research and development (Baker and Norman, 1990; Haverkort *et al.*, 1991). This work must be of importance in the search for more sustainable solutions for the future and needs more serious support.

## Institutional innovations

Some institutional innovations have been notable during the past ten years, both in research and in education. The analysis of problem areas in research by multidisciplinary groups of scientists and extensionists has been widely accepted. The creation of 'working groups' or 'research thrust teams' and joint interdisciplinary treks are standard techniques used by Lumle and Pakhribas Agricultural Centres in Nepal (Mathema and Galt, 1988; Gibbon *et al.*, 1989; Chand and Gibbon, 1990). The operation of the adaptive research planning team approach was an early development in Zambia which has been a notable success (Kean and Singogo, 1988).

## The problem of conservatism

This very positive work indicates that farming systems research teams are constantly innovating and developing new ways to make research more effective and relevant to people's needs. However, this does not mean that there has been positive change in all agricultural research systems – far from it. There are many institutions, particularly those which are well established and with a strong commodity mandate and disciplinary structures, that have strongly resisted the introduction of a systems perspective, the participation of farmers in the research process and the integration of social scientists into research planning and implementation.

# International Symposia, Publications and the Formation of Associations

The experience gained during the last 20 years of farming systems research has prompted many improvements in the quality and relevance of research. These lessons have been learned through farming systems research projects which have been substantially funded by a variety of international and national donors. There has also been the support for institutional development of FSR in many countries, the activities of the Florida FSSP group (1983–1987), the annual Farming Systems Symposia held in Kansas State University (1981–1986), Arkansas (1987–1988) and Michigan (1990–1992). It is important to recognize that one of the primary objectives of these meetings was to give a forum for young researchers from developing countries to present and discuss their work with fellow professionals from other countries. During these meetings the Association for Farming Systems Research/Extension was formed (in 1989) and a journal (*Journal for Farming Systems Research and Extension*) launched to publish selected proceedings and other FSR/E papers. At the same time there has been an increasing willingness by a range of journals to publish farming systems research findings (e.g. *Experimental Agriculture, Agricultural Systems, Agroforestry Journal* and *World Development*).

Before and during these developments, farming systems research and development activities had and have been in progress in several Francophone countries and particularly in France within INRA. The SAD group have made a very significant contribution to conceptual thinking and the development of a broader, historical and community-based systems approach and some of this work was presented at the meeting on which this book is based. It is also important to recognize that there are several people who have been working in Europe primarily in conventional research systems but with a strong systems approach. Some of this work was also presented at the meeting.

Within the last three years there has been a strong move to regionalize the FSR/E movement, starting with the Asian Farming Systems Association with a meeting in Bangkok in 1990 and a second in Colombo in 1992. The Latin American, North American, African (three) and European Groups are also holding regional meetings and discussing the possibility of setting up regional associations. There will be a major International Symposium in Montpellier in November 1994. Most of the regional groups will meet every other year and the meeting of the International Association for Farming Systems Research/Extension will rotate among the regional meeting locations.

## Future Debates and Directions

The form and role that the International Association will take on and relationships between the regional groups are still under discussion, but it is now certain that the movement has firmly established itself and it is widely recognized by even the most hardened disciplinarian that systems concepts, systems analysis and a farming systems perspective are all necessary parts of both understanding the working of existing farming systems and of developing alternative technologies that may lead to an improvement of the current situation of poor people. Indeed, there is some evidence that the techniques that have been developed and proved so useful in many developing countries may be helpful in the search for more sustainable alternative farming systems in the modern farming sector in Europe.

The international networking of FSR/E researchers and practitioners using modern forms of communication should lead to very positive debate and developments in methodologies (diagnostic techniques, farmer participation, gender analysis, on-farm experimentation, modelling, research integration, etc.) and also prompt a lively debate about the future directions for FSR/E. Many of these issues were discussed at the last International Symposium of FSR/E at Michigan in 1992 and will be brought together in a forthcoming publication, to be edited by David Norman, arising from that meeting.

Educational and institutional innovation and reform and the restructuring of institutional linkages are also areas for further discussion, as are concerns for the present and future needs of rural communities for secure food supplies. The coming together of researchers and planners at this time indicates that there is now a recognition of the interdependence of agricultural production and processing systems at many different levels and a clear interest in the role of FSR/E in contributing to the evolution of more stable land use and livelihood systems.

There is a unique opportunity to pool collective experiences and needs from different starting points in northern, southern, eastern and western Europe in order to make a substantial contribution to the development of more stable systems of production and of policies which will benefit the majority of farming communities in Europe.

## Acronyms

| | |
|---|---|
| FSR/E | Farming Systems Research and Extension |
| CATIE | Centro Agronomica Tropical de Investigaçion y Ensenanza (Costa Rica) |
| ICTA | Institut de Ciencia u Technologia Agricolas (Guatemala) |
| CIP | Centro Internaçional de Agricultura Tropical (Columbia) |
| CIMMYT | Centro Internaçional de Mejoramiente de Maiz y Trigo (Mexico) |
| IDRC | International Development Research Centre (Canada) |
| IIED | International Institute for Environment and Development (London) |
| RRA | Rapid rural appraisal |
| PRA | Participatory rural appraisal |
| NGO | Non-government organization |
| ODI | Overseas Development Institute |
| INRA/SAD | Institut National de la Recherche Agronomique/Systems Agraires et Developpement |
| USAID | United States Aid for International Development |

## References

Arnon, I. (1989) *Agricultural Research and Technology Transfer*. Elsevier, Amsterdam.

Ashby, J.A., Quiros, C.A. and Rivera, Y.M (1987) *Farmer Participation in On-farm Variety Trials*. Network Discussion Paper No. 22, ODI Agricultural Administration (Research and Extension).

Axinn, G.H. (1991) Potential contribution of FSRE to institutional development. *Journal of the Asian Farming Systems Association 1*.

Baker, D. and Norman, D. (1990) The farming systems research and extension approach to small farm development. In: Altieri, M. and Hecht, S. (eds) *Agroecology and Small Farm Development*. CRC Press, Boca Raton, Florida.

Bawden, R.J. (1992) Creating learning systems – a metaphor or institutional reform for development. Paper prepared for the IIRD/IDS Workshop, 'Beyond Farmer

First: Rural People's Knowledge, Agricultural Research and Extension Practice'. 27–29 October 1992, IDS, Sussex.

Bawden, R.J, Ison, R.L., Macadam, R.D., Packham, R.G. and Valentine, I. (1985) A research paradigm for systems agriculture. In: *Agricultural Systems for Developing Countries. Proceedings of International Workshop, Hawkesbury, 1985.*

Berdegue, J. (1990) *NGOs and Farmers' Organisations in Research and Extension in Chile.* Network Paper No. 19, Agricultural Administration (Research and Extension).

Biggs, S.D. (1980) Informal R and D. *Ceres* 13.4, (76), 23–26.

Biggs, S.D. (1990) A multiple source of innovation model of agricultural research and technology promotion. *World Development* 18, 1481–1499.

Biggs, S.D. and Farrington, J. (1990) Farming systems research and the rural poor. The historical, institutional, economic and political context. Paper presented at the 10th Annual FSR/E Symposium, Michigan State University, East Lansing, Michigan, October 1990.

Bunch, R. (1985) *Two Ears of Corn: a Guide to People Centered Agricultural Improvement.* World Neighbors, Oklahoma City, Oklahoma.

Capra, F. (1983) *The Turning Point.* Fontana, Collins, London.

Chambers, R. (1983) *Rural Development: Putting the Last First.* Longman, Harlow.

Chambers, R. and Ghildyal, B.P. (1985) Agricultural research for resource-poor farmers: the farmer first and last model. *Agricultural Administration and Extension* 20, 1–30.

Chambers, R., Pacey, A. and Thrupp, L.A. (eds) (1989) *Farmer First: Farmer Innovation in Agricultural Research.* IT Publications, London.

Chand, S.P. and Gibbon, D. (1990) Samuhik Bhraman: a rapid and appropriate method of prioritising and replanning agricultural research in Nepal. *Journal of Farming Systems Research and Extension* 1(1), 31–55.

Chand, S.P. and Gurung, B.D. (1991) Informal research in Nepal. *Journal for Farming Systems Research and Extension* 2(2), 1–15.

Collinson, M.P. (1981) A low cost approach to understanding small farmers. *Agricultural Administration and Extension* 8, 433–450.

Conway, G. (1985) Agroecosystem analysis. *Agricultural Administration* 20.

Dahlberg, K.A. (1979) *Beyond the Green Revolution.* Plenum Press, New York.

Davidson, A.P. (1987) Does farming systems research have a future? *Agricultural Administration and Extension* 24, 69–77.

Dillon, J.L., Plucknett, D.L. and Vallaeys, G.L. (1978) *Farming Systems Research in the International Agricultural Research Centres.* TAC of CGIAR, Rome.

Farrington, J. and Bebbington, A. (1993) *Reluctant Partners? Non-governmental Organisations, the State and Sustainable Agricultural Development.* ODI, London.

Farrington, J. and Biggs, S.D. (1990) NGOs, agricultural research and the rural poor. *Food Policy* 15, 16.

Fernandez, M. and Salvatierra, H. (1989) Participatory technology validation in highland communities of Peru. In: Chambers, R., Pacey, A. and Thrupp, L.A. (eds) *Farmer First: Farmer Innovation in Agricultural Research.* IT Publications, London, pp. 146–150.

Fukuoka, M. (1985) *The Natural Way of Farming. Theory and Practice of Green Philosophy.* Japan Publications, New York.

Frankenburger, T., Finan, T., De Walt, B., McArthur, H., Hudgens, H.R., Rerkasem, G., Butler Flora, C. and Young, N. (1989) Identification of farming systems research and extension activities: a synthesis. In: *Proceedings of FSR/E Symposium. 1988, Fayetteville, Arkansas.*

Fresco, L. (1984) *Comparing Anglophone and Francophone Approaches to Farming Systems Research and Extension.* Networking Paper No. 1, FSSP, University of Florida.

George, S. (1984) Utopia: the university and the 3rd world. An imaginary cooperation programme. In: van den Bor, W. and Fuller, A. (eds) *Universities and Integrated Rural Development in Developing Countries.* Pudoc, Wageningen.

Gibbon, D. (1986) *FSR in Bangladesh: a Review of the BAU Programme.* Report for BARC, Dhaka.

Gibbon, D. (1989) University involvement in rural development programmes: some lessons from recent experience. Paper presented at Wageningen–Guelph Workshop on IRD, Guelph, October 1989.

Gibbon, D. (1990) *Selective Strengthening of MARIF ATA-272 Phase V. Indonesia.* Report for DGIS, The Hague, May 1990.

Gibbon, D. (1991) *Relevance and Quality of Research in the AFRENA East and Central Africa Programmes: Review and Recommendations.* Report for ICRAF, Nairobi, Kenya, July 1991.

Gibbon, D. and Schultz, M. (1988) Agricultural systems in the eastern hills of Nepal: present situation and opportunities for innovative research and extension. Paper presented at the 8th Annual Symposium on FSR/E, Fayetteville, Arkansas, October 1988.

Gibbon, D., Thapa, H. and Rood, P. (1989) The development of FSR in Nepal: the working group as a focus of interdisciplinary activity. Paper presented at the 9th Annual Symposium on FSR/E, Fayetteville, Arkansas, October 1989.

Gilbert, E. (1990) *Non-Governmental Organisations and Agricultural Research: the Experience of the Gambia.* Agricultural Adminstration (Research and Extension), Network Paper No. 12.

Gilbert, E., Norman D. and Winch, F.E. (1980) *Farming Systems Research: a Critical Appraisal.* Rural Development Paper No. 6, Michigan State University, East Lansing, Michigan.

Hart, R.D. (1982) An ecological systems conceptual framework for agricultural research and development. In: Shaner, W.W., Philip, P.F. and Schmehl, W.R. (eds) *Farming Systems Research and Development: Guidelines for Developing Countries.* CID for USAID, World Bank, Washington, DC, pp. 272–274.

Hart, R.D. and Sands, M.W. (1990) Sustainable land use systems research and development. In: *Sustainable Land Use Systems Research.* Proceedings of an International Workshop, New Delhi, India, 12–16 February 1990, pp. 1–11.

Haverkort, B., van der Kamp, J. and Waters-Bayer, A. (1991) *Joining Farmers Experiments.* IT Publications, London.

Hilderbrand, P. and Piland, P. (1988) *An Inventory of Short Courses and University Courses Related to Farming Systems.* Food Resources and Economics Department, Gainsville, Florida.

ILEIA (1990) *Participatory Technology Development.* ILEIA, Leusden, The Netherlands.

Jiggins, J. (1988) Problems of understanding and communication at the interface of knowledge systems. In: Poats, V., Schmink, M. and Spring, A. (eds) *Gender Issues in Farming Systems Research and Extension.* Westview Press, Boulder, Colorado.

Kean, S. and Singogo, L.P. (1988) *Zambia. Organisation and Management of ARPT Research Branch.* Ministry of Agriculture and Water Development, OFCOR Case Study No. 1, ISNAR, The Hague.

KKU (1987) *Proceedings of an International Conference on Rapid Rural Appraisal.* September 2–5, 1985, Khon Kaen University, Thailand.

Lightfoot, C., Guia, Jr, O. De, Aliman, A. and Ocado, F. (1989) Systems diagrams to help farmers decide in on-farm research. In: Chambers, R., Pacey, C.A. and Thrupp, L.A. (eds) *Farmer First: Farmer Innovation in Agricultural Research.* IT Publications, London.

Macadam, R. and Sriskandarajah, N. (1990) Systems agriculture: the Hawkesbury approach and its implications for farming systems research and extension. Paper presented at the Asian Farming Systems Research and Extension Symposium, Bangkok, Thailand, November 1990.

Mansfield, G.B. (1950) *A Short History of Agriculture in the British Colonies.* Oxford University Press, Oxford.

Marcotte, P. and Swanson, L.E. (1987) The disarticulation of farming systems research with national agricultural systems: bringing FSR back in. *Agricultural Administration and Extension* 27, 75–91.

Mathema, S. and Galt, D. (1988) Samuhik Bhraman: a multidisciplinary group activity to approach farmers. Paper for training course on socioeconomic survey methods, Kathmandu, Nepal.

Maxwell, S. (1986) The social scientist in farming systems research. *Journal of Agricultural Economics* 37 (1), 25–35.

Merrill-Sands, D., Ewell, P., Biggs, S.D. and McAllister, J. (1989) Issues in institutionalizing on-farm client oriented research: a review of experiences from nine national agricultural research systems. *Quarterly Journal of International Agriculture* 3 (4), 279–300.

Norman, D. (1980) *Farming Systems Approach: Relevance for the Small Farmer.* Rural Development Paper No. 5, Michigan State University, East Lansing, Michigan.

Oasa, E.K. (1985) Farming systems research: a change in form but not in content. *Human Organization* 44, 219–227.

Pillot, D. (1990) Francophone and Anglophone farming systems research: similarities and differences. In: *Farming Systems Research and Development in Thailand.* Prince of Songla University, Bangkok, Thailand, 1988, reprinted 1990, pp. 3–25.

Poats, S.V., Schmink, M. and Spring, A. (1988) *Gender Issues in Farming Systems Research and Extension.* Westview Press, Boulder, Colorado.

Rhoades, R.E. (1989) *Evolution of Agricultural Research and Development Since 1950: Towards an Integrated Approach.* IIED Gatekeeper Series, No. 12, IIED, London.

Rhoades, R.E. and Booth, R.H. (1985) 'Farmer-back-to-farmer': a model for generating acceptable agricultural technology. *Agricultural Administration* 11, 127–137.

Richards, P. (1985) *Indigenous Agricultural Revolution.* Hutchinson, London.

Shaner, W.W., Philip, P.F. and Schmehl, W.R. (eds) (1982) *Farming Systems Research and Development: Guidelines for Developing Countries.* CID for USAID, World Bank, Washington, DC.

Shiva, V. (1989) *Staying Alive.* Zed Books, London.

Simmonds, N.W. (1984) *The State of the Art of Farming Systems Research.* World Bank, Washington, DC.

Sumberg, J. and Okali, C. (1988) Farmers, on-farm research and the development of new technology. *Experimental Agriculture* 24, 333–342.

Thapa, H., Green, T. and Gibbon, D. (1988) *Agricultural Extension in the Hills of Nepal: Ten Years of Experience from PAC.* AARE Network Paper No. 4, ODI, London.

Trigo, E. (1986) *Agricultural Research Organisation in the Developing World: Diversity and Evolution.* Working Paper No. 4, ISNAR, The Hague.

Weitz, C., Gibbon, D. and Pelzer, K. (1987) *Farming Systems Development in Asia: Crop/ Livestock/Fish Integration in Rainfed Areas.* Mid-term review for UNDP/FAO, September 1987.

Worman, F., Heinrich, G., Tibone, C. and Ntseane, P. (1990) Is farmer input into FSRE sustainable? *Journal for Farming Systems Research and Extension* 1 (1), 17–30.

# 2

## Farming Systems Research/Extension Approach and the European Context: INRA Experience in Creating a Research Structure for Agrarian Systems and Development in France

### Joseph Bonnemaire

### Introduction

Since the theme of this book can be tackled in many different ways, it is proposed to describe here, as a means of stimulating collective reflection, the experience of setting up the SAD (Agrarian Systems and Development) department of INRA (Institut National de la Recherche Agronomique).

As far as Anglo-American scientific circles are concerned, the FSR/E approach emanates first of all from developing countries (particularly international research centres) and traditionally it is not institutionalized but made up of *ad hoc* project teams for a limited time (Brossier, 1993). The systems approach is nonetheless used in agronomical research in temperate countries, but more often in modelling sector-based biotechnical knowledge than in agricultural professional situations (farms and decision makers).

Given the tradition in French agronomic research, the emergence of the farming systems approach is doubtless more complex and it is interesting to retrace its history briefly, using the experience of the SAD department of INRA. After having described the origins and the rationale of the SAD, the role of this process in the French agricultural R & D system can be more easily understood.

### The Tradition in the Study of Production Systems within the Rural Economy

Production systems taken holistically have been, since the 16th century (Olivier de Serres) and at least until the 19th century (de Gasparin, Mathieu de Dombasle), the subject of traditional studies in rural economics and agronomic science in France. Brossier (1987) notes that, as far as Anglo-Americans are concerned, the development of the farming systems concept is more recent and connected to the work undertaken in developing countries. In the United States, for example, teaching of an extremely disciplinary nature was for a long time in favour of a traditional sector-based approach (disciplinary and top down from the laboratories to the users). This approach was in fact found to be most efficient in developed countries, all the more since over recent decades the United States has based agricultural progress above all on considerable scientific investment, which was focused at first on genetic research: creation of strains and varieties that were highly productive – and highly consuming of inputs – that were simply distributed to farmers afterwards. In spite of Borlaugh and his Nobel Prize, repeated failed attempts to develop agriculture in developing countries finally convinced Anglo-American researchers (the prevalent group in the international organizations) of the future of production systems concepts and of the importance of implementing FSR/E methods that use these approaches for diagnostic assessment (rapid), and for fine tuning and diffusing proposals for improvement aimed towards potential users.

The differences in the agrarian situation and culture between the two sides of the English Channel has existed for a long time and probably explains in part the differences in farm approach which have prevailed in recent years.

In the UK, agriculture has long been more homogeneous, more professional and more elitist than in the Latin countries including France. Small landholders having been eliminated fairly quickly, farmers were much fewer and also better trained. And at least since the first great cattle or sheep breeders and since Darwin, on the large British farms, a community of thought and work has existed directly connected with, on the one hand, the great landowners, and on the other hand, scientific circles and agricultural public services. Enclosures had started in the 16th century under the Tudors, with the development of towns and the beginnings of the cloth industry (the driving force of sheep farming). After a decline of the phenomenon during the entire 17th century following social unrest and the 'Enclosures Edict,' this process of agrarian individualism then resumed and accelerated, especially with the arrival of the industrial revolution towards the end of the 18th century. Hence a class of great landowners progressively prospered in the UK who very often were not only farmers but whose interests concerned the town as much as the country, and who therefore naturally reinforced and enriched all sorts of connections between these two worlds. Very soon great landowners and men of science or public services became used to coming up against each other in the technoeconomic farm system and understanding each other without difficulty. In other words, extension succeeded in passing from the research station to the farm and it is easy to understand why.

In France, the situation evolved differently (Parain, 1956). From the 16th century up until the 18th–19th centuries, the conception of the rural economics of agriculture (inherited from Latin agronomists) remained that of an extremely global system, diverse in its components. Under pressure from the physiocrats and the British agricultural model and also by analogy with developments in industry, emphasis was then placed on the importance of large farms and their vital role in the diffusion of agricultural progress, on the role of capital in agriculture and of profit as an objective, and finally on the need to apply the sciences (in full expansion) to this economic sector in the same way as the others. This trend diminished as a result of the agricultural crisis at the end of the 19th century and the protectionism that was the result. From that moment on, a radical change in approach came about: a new look was given to small landowners who were considered to be an element of social stability and a whole series of theories concerning the social, economic and political advantages of small farms were expounded. Throughout the first half of the 20th century, a choice of policy was made instituting development on a cooperative or mutual basis (credit, insurance, supply and sales): from then on, these structures were supposed to give the same economic advantages to small and large farms alike. Hence, in order to give impetus to agriculture, the emphasis was put on structural and organizational aspects as well as on techniques and science themselves. However, since the end of the 19th century (development of agricultural chemistry and, more recently, development of standard animal quotas and livestock research, etc.), and up to Dumont's 'Trips in France' (1956), sector-specific approaches have been developed in specialized technical areas, these taking diverse directions and yielding diverse results particularly concerning the specialization effort which often accompanies this movement (Geffroy, 1978).

After the Second World War, French agriculture became aware that it needed to catch up with American agriculture, which was held up as a model; small French landowners needed to contribute to the reconstruction of the country with the objective of increasing production whilst diminishing cost (increasing work productivity) in order to satisfy increasing consumer demand and making manpower available for industry. At that particular time, the farm community was much more diverse, more complex and more numerous than in England. As far as agricultural development was concerned, it was impossible to cope with this diversity and to deal directly with the multiple situations involved. In addition, with the help of the agricultural union movement of catholic inspiration (social doctrine of the Church), and repercussions of pre-war ideology concerning the dynamics of progress in agriculture, a rationale prevailed in favour of setting up intermediate technostructures with a view to helping farmers to organize themselves and to help each other through cooptive groups. Most of all, farmers compared among themselves their techniques and their results as demonstrated by examples given to their neighbours. Technical progress and its diffusion, although fed by scientific knowledge, thus remained mainly endogenous to the farming sector thanks to the predominant dynamics of local groups of farmers and, consequently, the farm as a holistic system was always kept in mind.

Hence, small landowners in France were more numerous and had less training than in England, and the majority of them were imbued with catholic ideology concerning productivity (objective: 'feed the world'), which put the emphasis on mutual help and collective action (with an aim to collective social betterment). On top of this, France is the only country with a strongly centralized system among European countries with a 'farming' culture. It was not surprising therefore that, as early as the 1950s and 1960s, France gave priority as a rule to an extension and agricultural development approach that was more 'technocratic' and institutionalized than in the UK, where short cuts for transferring technical knowledge already existed, from where it was created or taught directly to a network of agricultural enterprises which were more homogeneous, less numerous, more technically up-to-date and better inserted into the market economy [cf. the example of the very old organization of the Milk Marketing Board with its (recently contested) privilege for the distribution of small bottles of milk to houses by direct sale].

## Origins of the Department of Research into Agrarian Systems and Development (SAD)

The beginnings of INRA (created in 1946) provided back-up for the reconstruction–modernization of French agriculture with production growth as a clear objective and, as per the American model, a complete trust in research. Research needed to produce techniques that were to be diffused afterwards to an elite group of productivist smallholders, cooperatives and mutualists who would set an example to the groups as a whole. Hence the need to synthesize the knowledge produced, on the farm level, to make this knowledge accessible to the various regional types of agriculture. In order to accomplish this mission, the Ministry of Agriculture added to INRA, the national research institution of a centralized state, a special structure in 1959 to handle the Application of Research to Extension (SARV) equipped with experimental farms for the purposes of synthesis and demonstration.

However, during this period, the close relationship existing between the government of the Fifth Republic and a revived farming profession (progressive replacement of a generation of country squires belonging to the National Federation of Farmer Unions by young, progressive trade unionist farmer leaders from the National Centre of Young Farmers) led the latter to assume responsibility for the extension mission, which soon became 'agricultural development' within the context of laws concerning agricultural goals (1960 and 1962) which stressed economic organization and structure policy and emphasized sector co-management. This mission was financed by parafiscal taxes on products with the aim of redistribution of means among regions, production sectors and types of public. In 1964, the Experimentation and Information Service (SEI), created within the INRA organization, took over from the SARV in organizing the transfer of information endogenous to INRA and in carrying out research on the interfaces insufficiently addressed by the existing disciplines.

Little by little, given the divergence between technical advice and agrarian situations (Dumont, 1956), a need for opening up was felt within INRA scientific circles, composed more and more of specialists. Researchers (many of whom still retained a certain farming culture owing to their social origins and training) became progressively aware of the problem as a result of several types of experience in which marginal areas on the one hand and teacher–researchers on the other played a vital role.

With hindsight, it is clear that a project undertaken by Centre National de la Recherche Scientifique (CNRS) ethnologists and museologists together with INRA livestock researchers and agronomists was an essential initial pluridisciplinary experience: this was the Cooperative Research Programme carried out in 1963–1965 on the high livestock farming plateaux of the Aubrac area in the South Massif Central (RCP Aubrac) (CNRS, 1970). Livestock research and ethno-socioeconomic research were confronted at the time with the breakdown in development of a traditional, very complex production system due to both the economic crisis and the problem of modern techniques. In addition, research took leave of its usual academic methods in keeping a group of researchers in the field who gave precedence to research organization levels with regard to the group involved, rather than to disciplinary programme logic. Their conclusions concerning the capacity of local society to adapt technical progress in a difficult situation whilst preserving its culture were ultimately validated.

However, the French rural economists, like the agronomists, livestock researchers, etc., who were highly implicated in the modernization process, quickly became aware of the other side of this phenomenon revealed by social evolution (Blanc and Lacombe, 1989): difficulties of underdeveloped areas, economic slippage of certain categories of smallholders or of certain production systems, etc. Hence the SEI researchers, upholders of both the traditional INRA research approach and the specific mission institutionalized by the SEI (influenced by questions such as the adoption and diffusion of techniques), undertook as early as the 1960s a series of research projects concerning 'regional potential;' the aim was to find out how technique and environmental diversity affected yield (Deffontaines, 1964, 1967, 1973; Henin and Deffontaines, 1970; Deffontaines and Osty, 1977). Together with economists and livestock researchers close to the teaching profession, these projects focused, as of 1970, on the obstacles to technical progress. They were then quickly directed towards the choices and production conditions of farmers, at first underlining situation and project diversity, and thereafter seen in the context of continuous land areas using the notion of local agrarian systems

(INRA–ENSSAA, 1973, 1977; Petit, 1975; Brossier and Petit, 1977; Osty, 1978a). Hence, in Corsica, the concept of 'system of practices' emerged, making technical and economic functioning plain: the situation consisted of stable practices and variable farm structures! (Cristofini *et al.*, 1978; Deffontaines and Raichon, 1981). In the Causses area of limestone plateaux where Roquefort cheese is produced, genetic and other researchers working at the Toulouse research centre were faced with the constraints of system intensification compared with the constraints of enhancing land areas of great contrast, and with the problem of the connections between the logic of different disciplines and pluridisciplinary programmes.

At INRA, different experiences were being refined and were converging (including in developing countries), creating a pluridisciplinary systems approach for farming activity. Exchanges were developed more and more with other research organizations, particularly those active in developing countries [Centre International de Recherches Agronomiques pour le Développement (CIRAD); Institut Français de Recherche Scientifique pour le Développement en Coopération (ORSTOM)], resulting in similar fields of study. However, the decisive impetus came from the Ministry of Research, which encouraged this movement as early as 1968 by creating successive scientific committees working on a field of study that was ecological at first then more and more socioeconomic and technical (however, with a continuity of methodological thought in the systems' area: Legay, 1986, 1988a,b, 1992; Jollivet, 1988, 1992).

The teacher–researchers of the Universities of Agronomy (Grandes Ecoles) played a decisive role in these initiatives, particularly since they wished above all to train people for action and enjoyed more freedom than the researchers at INRA with its academic constraints with respect to specialized scientific production. They enabled the study of farm operation and typologies to be refined (Petit, 1971; Sebillotte, 1974; Teissier, 1979; Capillon, 1993).

At the same time, under the pressure of teacher–researchers such as Henin and Sebillotte, agronomy itself diversified its approach (up until then mostly chemical and quantitative), making a strong case for aspects such as quality, field observation, physics and, above all, a model integrating different branches of knowledge where the farmer and his decisions had a role to play (notions of crop management sequence and model of yield elaboration) (Sebillotte, 1974). Henceforward, agronomists studied objective-orientated operating systems made up of plant community, soil, climate and human action, together with their interactions.

Familiar with these scientific fields of study and wishing to bring research closer to implementation in areas where a dual problem exists of fighting forest fires (up until then, the main preoccupation concerned wood flammability rather than preventive management of forests) and of livestock farming development in relatively damaged pastoral areas, the French Government decided in 1980 to create two research teams for missions in southeastern

France and in Corsica. These two research teams, faced with the holistic aspects and complexity of production systems, and also with action using a socially accepted FSR approach, found themselves like their predecessors in the newly formed SAD (Vallerand *et al.*, 1990; Hubert, 1993).

## SAD Objectives and Current Research Dynamics

All this scientific thought and experience, together with the necessity of finding an appropriate support structure for certain new research proposals and for certain research teams cramped in existing structures, led the INRA management to create the SAD at the end of 1979 (about 50 researchers; Fig. 2.1). The working commission behind this decision also recommended an organized effort to synthesize knowledge emanating from the different disciplines (Group Bouchet, 1978). The distinction was already well and truly made between synthesis and system. Even now, however, it must be admitted that, within research organizations such as INRA, this necessary distinction and complementarity between syntheses of biotechnical knowledge (traditional mission of the 'upstream engineers' who long worked beside research teams in applied research departments) and research concerning production systems (integrating the different actors in the research objective) are not always understood by all.

The initial field of study of the SAD (INRA–SAD, 1979) was to implement a common research approach concerning the functioning of farms considered to be managed systems (Fig. 2.2): internal coherence, specific objective to be achieved by the project, comprehension through the use of practices, insertion in a local environment and in a system subsector, homogeneous grouping using typologies, and inclusion of spatial and temporal dimensions. Recourse to systems analysis and to modelling, and scientific thought on these subjects, are an element of unity between research levels (notions of scale and integration of levels) and between research teams. In fact, this course of action can be interpreted as a re-enlargement of agronomic science henceforward directed more towards agricultural activity in its geographical, economic and social situation. Study of agricultural activity, starting with the basic unit that one farm represents, led to identification of a guiding principle of research into the systems used, using 'technical facts' (practices and ways of carrying them out) (Gras *et al.*, 1989; Osty, 1990).

An external audit commission (Sautter, 1986) came to the conclusion that SAD work was both original and necessary (INRA–SAD, 1985), at the transition between holistic agronomy and a natural and social science approach; in their opinion, this research in engineering agricultural development seemed to be aiming at a sort of agricultural anthropology. The commission noted, however, a certain hesitation in integrating all the rural data (socioeconomic differentiations taken as a whole, pluriactivity, etc.) and

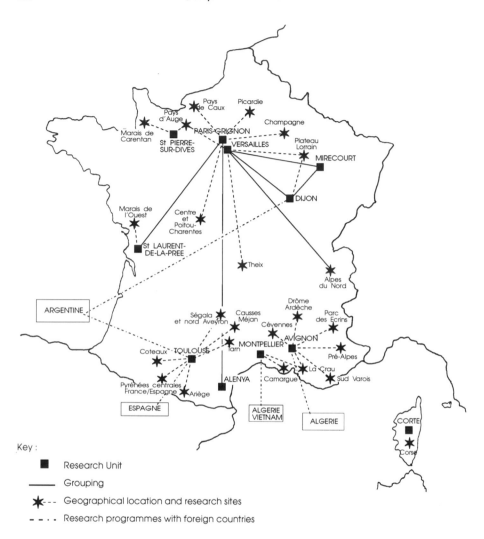

**Fig. 2.1.** Location of SAD units and research sites (from Vissac *et al.*, 1992).

also a certain distance with respect to professional agricultural organizations (enhanced by the term 'development') (connected with the historic division of prerogatives).

Although it has inherited partly from the SARV and the SEI, the SAD refuses to assume the role of simply diffusing knowledge. Over and above objectives relative to application, more or less spatially confined, the SAD ambition concerns method.

The commission was nonetheless aware of the difficulties in activating

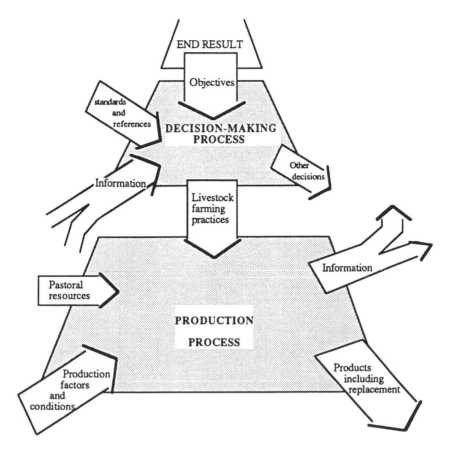

**Fig. 2.2.** Representation of the functioning of livestock farming systems, based on the combination of two complementary models (from Osty and Landais, 1993).

this type of research field comprising interfaces: the real world and recognized disciplines, the vertical (system subsector) and the horizontal (land areas and social groups), the micro level (farm) and the macro level or at least the meso level of the local agrarian system. The commission also noted that connections between disciplines bring institutional partitioning into play but care must be taken not to transpose pyramid-shaped institutional organization charts into the domain of cooperation between scientific groups.

Lastly, the commission suggests that the SAD clarify its scientific jargon and its references to theory, remarking, however, that this is neither a question of lack of imagination, nor an inability to position itself, but simply the stamp of scientific effort applied to a 'frontier:' the SAD is at the transition of agronomy, ecology and social science; it is placed where a local issue meets up with surrounding organizational forces, horizontal meets up with vertical, existing situations meet up with development, research and action (Sautter, 1986). An answer can be found in *Systems Modelling and Agrarian Systems* (Brossier *et al.*, 1990), which establishes the triple epistemological origins of the SAD: Simon and his theory on optimal decision and procedure rationality; Piaget and his constructivist epistemology as a basis of the learning theory; Morin and the paradigm of auto-eco-reorganization in modelling complex systems; all this plus various other pieces of research by epistemologists and theoreticians of systems modelling (e.g. Le Moigne, 1990).

At the end of this first period, the SAD was more directly confronted with the question of its dealings with action and its relationships with the institutions responsible for back-up. These matters came up with respect to system subsectors and rural areas faced with the crisis in production systems, with the needs of industry and with environmental consequences. Postulates concerning comprehensiveness, complexity and the necessary integration of decision makers and their decisions in systems' projections were confirmed.

The current objective of SAD research (Vissac *et al.*, 1992) is to contribute to the knowledge of human activity through the study of the interrelations between ecological, biotechnical and social processes as they affect agriculture and the rural sector:

- goals and activity organization;
- conception and implementation of decisions;
- progress, contents and consequences of productive action.

The farm is central to this research, but is considered more and more with respect to its links with system subsectors or with areas which are specified by the issues that these organizational levels address, and this in the context of changing social demand. The research field concerns (Fig. 2.3):

- production systems and farm operation;
- links between farm supply companies, production, transformation and consumption within the system subsectors;
- dynamics and management of rural areas.

A first type of research work (external diagnostic assessment) concerns the analysis of aspects such as farm structure and operation, performance elaboration and methods for organizing system subsectors or land areas.

The second type of research work (Papy, 1993; Vallerand, Chapter 26) no longer seeks to understand a situation with a view to action, but to produce knowledge about the actual processes of action and organization. Project management by the decision makers themselves becomes the subject of study, in other words providing the means with which the processes behind imagination, creation and innovation control by the actors involved can be understood.

Interconnections between study levels of these phenomena is another

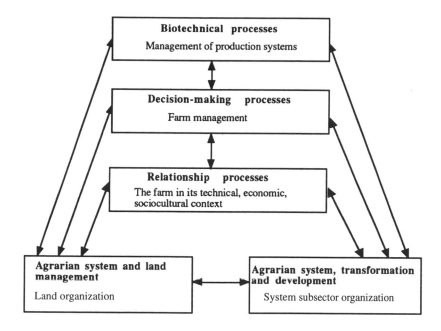

**Fig. 2.3.** Main themes and levels of investigation of INRA–SAD (from Landais, 1992b).

important issue, all the more so since the increasing number of movements between surrounding and surrounded factors has led to the identification of new subjects of study regulating these interactions, for example, herd, forage system and female lifetime performance (connections between problem finding and problem solving).

For all these interconnections involving a specific objective, either real or envisaged, systems modelling plays an essential role; it defines, with respect to the activities under study, a conceptual and methodological framework of a general nature (Landais, 1992a,b) which enables one, at the same time, first to organize all the knowledge necessary in analysing a specific situation and in comparing the different situations involved, and second to have access to the viewpoints held by the different decision makers. Knowledge of these viewpoints is essential in understanding their actions. Changes in these viewpoints always accompany (foresee, explain or justify) new behaviour, which of course is of interest to those carrying out development.

Running through the programmes within this field of study, scientific thought of a more thematic nature is being pursued on subjects such as farming activity and spatial processes, crop systems, livestock farming systems, action research and social elaboration of quality.

# The SAD Department and Agricultural Development

Development is a technoeconomic and sociocultural process which tends to increase the range of possible changes in the systems involved (therefore increasing their capacity to adapt and perpetuate over an unspecified time) and to ensure better control of these changes by local operators (Landais, 1992a,b). Sebillotte (1993) insists on the fact that generalized references are a thing of the past, and therefore that individualization in implementing advice is necessary; hence there are several consequences:

(i)    The need for correct positioning with respect to science, given that farmers should not extrapolate beyond validity limits and researchers should be interested in how their results are used. This leads to innovation being reconsidered as a social process and research organization as a learning process. In fact, technological innovation is progressively added to during its diffusion in the domain for which it is destined. Practising aid to decision making implies, for example, placing the decision maker in the situation of devising a solution with which he agrees, even if this is completely different from what he initially imagined. This is effectively a learning process. This justifies researchers in placing study subjects in their context and contributes to social demand.

(ii)   In order for research to be able to prepare a plan of action, it is absolutely necessary for researchers to have access to economic organizations and to their 'rules.'

(iii)  If agriculture is managed, knowledge of the principles used is required.

In this respect, it can be pointed out with Petit (1993) that development is first and foremost a social change which can only be understood when examined in its entirety, which implies at least three closely linked dimensions: the success of development operations depends in fact on government policy, on institutions determining social group functioning and on the techniques used by producers.

While, or perhaps before, researchers were modifying their ideas, creating a sort of systems approach to farm problems, similar progress was being made in agricultural professional circles thanks to a number of experiences carried out by organizations seeking research references for farms: from the action-research groups working on case models (Rouquette, 1988) to the National Networks for Experimentation and Demonstration which, during the past ten years, has mobilized several thousand farmers and 20–30 professional agronomists.

A certain number of issues that were taken directly to the SAD at its inception (Rouquette *et al.*, 1981) are a fairly good demonstration of the main questions to tackle at the interface of this research field and agricultural development:

(i)     Land organization and the definition of 'farm:' the SAD has always been reticent to set down in a permanent way, for the use of development, either a typology or outlines of 'agrarian systems' or geographical areas incorporating a specific combination of potentialities and handicaps of specific agricultural and non-agricultural socioeconomic forces. Typologies are a function of the objectives and hypotheses set in order to create them. On the other hand, with regard to methods for interpreting diversity in terms of choice of production systems, it is a fact that this matter of typologies has progressively impregnated development activities and that the SAD has made a decisive contribution to this.

(ii)    Creation and organization of references: in spite of valuable contributions to methodology by the SAD, further work and comparative analysis of several organization systems could prove most useful.

(iii)   Farm functioning (internal dynamics): this is without a doubt the area in which SAD work has been most prolific and most productive for agricultural development: formulation of a systems approach, notion of farm 'trajectory,' tools for aid in decision making, etc.

(iv)    Control over changes in agrarian systems and farms over the long term: owing to insufficient continuous presence on the same area of land, the SAD has probably not yet made sufficient headway in this important field of study even if worthwhile contributions have been made (Jest, 1974; Cristofini *et al.*, 1982; Osty and Auricoste, 1989).

(v)     Comparative analysis of development organizations and institutions: after several initial research projects, the SAD, taken up by other objectives, has not pursued this highly political subject, leaving it to more specialized researchers.

(vi)    Adaptation of development activity programmes making them more diverse: the SAD has been highly involved in promoting collective action, but more attention probably should have been given to individual action, and also to comparative analysis.

(vii)   Connections necessary between research, training and action: training situations proved to be a strong incentive for research to refine its results so as to 'produce teachable concepts,' and an excellent occasion for expressing social demand. Action-research practices have spread and have been formalized, the introduction of the action notion allowing, in particular, for the often somewhat rigid institutional barriers to be crossed.

# Future Issues

## *Improved understanding of social demand*

Separations between institutions have not always facilitated communication with the development sector, all the more since the latter often went hand in hand with a vertical approach by system subsector. However, thanks to the contacts established in the field, the SAD has answered a certain number of needs. In the current European context, this research trend can help one to understand more fully the social demand for research, given the renewed complexity and diversity of farming systems (following a period of a trend towards uniformity) and the processes and decisions guiding changes in these systems.

Traditional research into improving techniques was long guided by direct economic interests, but progressively, margins of progress have shrunk and interactions have made the task more difficult. Today, this downstream steering is becoming less and less powerful; on the other hand, progress in biology has become so rapid that henceforward this is the discipline 'attracting' the directions taken by applied research. Steering by direct 'social demand' (even unelaborate and broken down) is being replaced by steering induced by the specific dynamics of upstream fundamental research as much as by overall technical dynamics (from the fertilizer industry through to biotechnological processes by way of the agri-food industry and pharmacology). Also, one can question if the 'justifications' that FSR/E could and can contribute to the technical choices needing to be focused on are still valid and still have an impact on this scientific movement. Nonetheless, coherence has it that it will be on the level of overall farm analysis that debate about the technical directions of agronomic research and the interface with social demand will be addressed, at least in part. This implies maintaining a research field of study concerning farms as complex systems and making sure that this is not cut off from the progress in applied biology, or from the individual and collective preoccupations and practices of the various people involved in development. In order for this manifestly important research field to retain its pertinence, scientific circles and other fields involved in development alike need to make the necessary investment.

## *Interaction with research of a more analytical nature*

At this juncture, the question of relationships with more analytical disciplinary research needs to be re-examined. Within the SAD a certain number of positive experiences have been noted [for example, research work concerning goat grazing on complex plant cover (Meuret, 1989), work on agronomy and aid to decision making for cash-crop systems and work on economics and management]. However, there are reservations as to the results expected of this scientific interaction and potential mutual questioning. For example, it is not easy today to place biology – as was the case 40 years ago – back efficiently into an organized array of usable disciplines in order to answer a social demand. However, this is one of the questions that need solving. In this debate, the problems of formulation, of concepts and methods and of reciprocal scientific recognition of the latter by the disciplines involved represent important and difficult issues. Thus, with the increasing influence of these research fields concerning production systems, together with consolidation and progress of the methods being used, a certain 'disciplinarization' is under way of a scientific practice that was originally fundamentally pluridisciplinary. Also, the disciplines cannot be applied to action.

Progress in complex systems research is, of course, affected by improvements in the tools used but also by increased organization as soon as a partial transition is made from research on specific subjects towards research on projects (transition from a positivist attitude to a constructivist attitude).

### Consideration of the multiple functions of agriculture

This type of approach particularly allows the functions of agriculture to be opened up to aspects other than that of producing. This is essential when strategy is a preoccupation. For example, with respect to livestock breeding, over and above the supply of animal products, a new look is being taken at its role today – even in Europe – in fertilization and pollution, its role in maintaining rural areas, its role in accumulating and preserving wealth, the aspects of prestige and in some cases social power, its cultural and even political role and also its role in play activity and teaching (Bonnemaire and Vissac, 1988). Also, as Sebillotte (1993) points out, the multiple-function aspect of land becomes the necessary setting of all scientific thought, particularly concerning the social needs relative to land use by town dwellers. New forms of social coordination are hence needed (beyond activation of farmers with respect to production systems). In addition, differentiated types of agriculture on the land are being identified more and more: the combination in a given area of different categories of farmers ('industrial,' marginal, polyactive, etc.) varies enormously according to a whole series of local factors.

### Awareness and implementation of farmers' new qualifications

The conditions for practising the farming profession are becoming increasingly complex; also this profession needs to be considered not only with respect to pursuing or beginning farming itself, but also to the collective needs of society as a whole (Hervieu, 1993): needs relative to land area, to product quality, to relationships with nature, among others. The FSR/E approach, which integrates project diversity, situations, practices and results, can aid in clarifying the future configuration of this profession, for society as a whole and above all for the farmers themselves. Their higher level of training needs to be taken into consideration, which means recognizing their capacity to choose (Sebillotte, 1993), making the question of aid to decision making still more complex (sector-based specialized services but also partnership for overall advice).

Further, evolution is rapid concerning the land area and system subsectors, and the new CAP has not made the situation any simpler. This new CAP establishes the principle of massive recourse to subsidies, in compensation for lower prices, and above all maintains criteria for attributing subsidies (hectares, heads of livestock) that are fixed and fairly neutral as to the level of adaptation of systems of land management to product and quality elaboration. The tendency is thus to freeze skills and the lack of them, competence and incompetence. More imagination and initiative will be necessary to incorporate this type of constraint into real holistic farm projects and into a framework of agricultural and rural development policy with its three dimensions – the human element, land areas and products and functions. It can be noted here that traditional extension has up until now dealt with the means and results of change, leaving it up to those involved to formulate the objectives of the changes required and the initiatives needed to carry them through. It will be even more important to have models and tools to aid decision making that do not 'simplify' the farm, for farmer action and advisory action are becoming steadily more elaborate with regard to objectives, initiatives and practices.

### Definition of the expanded networks involving farmers

New decision makers involved today in agricultural development need to be taken into consideration, such as local communities, water agencies and associations defending specific interests (Sebillotte, 1993). A new awareness regarding rural problems has been noted, for example, on the regional level, and the FSR/E approach can be useful in sensitizing and enlisting the cooperation of regional authorities and in facilitating their involvement.

The farm is not the only place where the farmer works out solutions and where he necessarily implements them; in addition, his solutions affect his environment, and particularly the ways other farms or decision makers act (Darre,1985). It can be said that the agroecosystem is being extended. This takes us back to the problem of micro-social mediation, around which numerous operational bodies can be mobilized (associations, various groups, etc.) that exist in the field but on which research has had, as yet, little effect.

## *Consideration of farming activity and environmental management*

The emergence of environmental protection and management as affected by agriculture brings the interests of society to the fore, in addition to local and holistic aspects (requiring connections between organizational levels). In requiring compatibilities between several often contradictory goals, the environment also raises the question of social coordination including with new operators. 'Society takes back nature and the land' (Sebillotte, 1993); the farmers are no longer alone in their involvement in rural areas but their production systems have the most impact on them.

## *Development of quality: a social reality as well as a technical and commercial reality*

The research work on farms carried out by the SAD has also led to progress being made on quality, a particularly sensitive subject for the future. Work is under way on product description rather than its inherent characteristics. Raw materials are not without effect on, and closely linked to, farming activities. Quality, for the consumer, has an intrinsic dimension (product characteristics) but also an external and socioculturally important dimension (production technique, production environment, cultural images, etc.). This takes us back to system subsector organization and to negotiation between the decision makers concerned.

## *Renewed approach towards organizations involving production systems*

The traditionally mechanistic notion of the system subsector stressed functional coordination centred on the product, to the detriment of strategy and decision-maker organization. Understood as a 'meso system,' this notion allows the phenomena of competition and cooperation to be analysed and to introduce means of coordination between decision makers, so organizing exchange and reducing uncertainties and organization costs. The 'meso system' takes us back to the notion of a 'common destiny' elaborated by decision-maker strategy and which can be other than the product alone (i.e. product quality, regional identity) (Valceschini, 1990). It should be noted that, as far as quality is concerned, the notion of 'Appellation d'Origine Contrôlée' establishes a link between the vertical and horizontal approaches to development. Scientific thought relative to certain forms of extensive livestock farming (Landais and Balent, 1993) benefit from being considered in this way since, if the commitment of producers and organizations (economic and development) cannot be directed more towards added value (including integration of new functions), our forms of extensive livestock farming risk becoming uncompetitive compared with those used in other areas or countries enjoying more favourable conditions.

All these aspects lead us to point out that the principle determining factors of agricultural evolution are exterior to it. Research on production systems has remained too centred on a field of study internal to agriculture; for example, general economic policy measures and overall social and cultural dynamics are often placed in an 'environment of the system' and included in the approach in a vague way. An effort must be made better to interconnect these macro levels with analyses on the farm level. Also, regulations, and legal and fiscal aspects which are currently evolving and becoming more important, probably need to be better integrated into the analysis of production systems. Building an FSR/E approach on an intermediate (meso) scale is an essential issue. This is useful for example in understanding the roles of new decision makers, or even animal breeds (Vissac, 1992) in certain contexts, and as an organizing concept for a development model on the regional level. All this is necessary in order to understand the evolution of an agrarian area. It is therefore essential to make progress simultaneously on several professional scales and to interconnect them properly.

With a commendable view to diversifying themes, the tendency in the past was to diversify development structures as and when new missions came up. Today, however, most of these structures have no other choice but to return to centring on the farm as a whole taken in its individual context (Sebillotte, 1993) and the proliferation of these structures is no longer justified, especially in a period of budgetary restriction. A common field of study on production systems and development can make this unavoidable restructuring process more pertinent just at a time when economic groups of all kinds are tending to concentrate on their 'basic professions.'

# Conclusions

On a more general level, organized and up-to-date production systems research can reinforce the coherence of R & D processes and constitutes a means of directing and promoting agronomic research. Thus, given the progress of biology and the new research fields it generates (INRA, 1993), together with cultural changes in a scientific community often increasingly removed from farming activity, the specificity of agronomic research still defined by target plant and animal species loses its pertinence. Comprehension of phenomena alone should not be the exclusive aim of INRA research either, but rather it is the resulting effect of knowledge gathered on the initial subject (herd, field, food product, forest, lake, etc.) taken as a whole with its specific practices and uses that constitutes the bottom line for evaluating the relevance of innovation. Therefore, from INRA's point of view, three directions need to be pursued. First, regarding the on-going study of life sciences, specific problems raised by interacting groups of individuals need to be analysed. Second, so as to grasp better the new interests vital for agricultural production, agroindustry and the management of rural areas, together with the intense and changing nature of their constraints, a special effort needs to be made concerning 'contextual sciences' (i.e. production systems approach centred on decision makers rather than on products). Third, in order to create operational methods, the cooperation of 'integrative sciences' needs to be enlisted, including land and renewable resource sciences, or those relative to fine tuning crop management sequences and managed productive systems, more flexible in dealing with the double constraint of productivity and respect for the environment (INRA, 1993).

Currently, a strong need is being expressed on the part of society at large for making a new start in building man–nature relationships, intelligible to all concerned and coherent with their vision of the world. For example, maintaining biodiversity constitutes an ethical, cultural, socioeconomic and political issue which concerns society as a whole, and in which farmers have a vital role to play. Owing to their professional experience, farmers can be active in the concrete process of establishing a rapport with the plant and animal world that satisfies both reason and ethics. For example, this experience can activate exchange between man and animal within a livestock farming process; it allows farmers to argue that the ethics of living organisms and the environment cannot be created 'in the name of the rights of nature,' but in the name of the rights of all men to have access to nature inasmuch as they respect it (Hervieu, 1993). This essential cultural link is affected by the shared understanding of what an agricultural production system really is, together with its functioning, its insertion in an environment and its dynamics. This common theme shared by farmers and those responsible for society as a whole serves as a reference for a complete and systemic vision of farming activity. The farmers can thus participate in elaborating an up-to-date ecological philosophy, and find a new sense in and coherence to their profession, and in perceiving their function more clearly, they can more easily formulate strategy (Hervieu, 1993).

The SAD department approach calls certain traditional extension models into question to the advantage of a constructivist systems approach, resulting in FSR of a 'second order' (Russell and Ison, 1993), which holds that knowledge is a product of society and that the real world includes the people involved, their positions and their actions: each operator or observer, through the issues he chooses to handle, effectively specifies the system to be created. Hence, in development action, those involved are not only conveyors of 'exterior' and 'objective' knowledge, but are rather catalysts and conceptualists in a collective creative process in which they fully participate.

As we have noted, it is important here to encourage and stress a research approach rather than a teacher–student type of relationship (action-research systems). As pointed out by Latour (1989), research (especially experienced by certain farmers involved as partners) is much more easy to communicate than science proper ('science is the past stage of research'!). This means recognizing the fact that diffusion cannot be separated from production, and that there is a continuous chain (a process that does not end with research scientists) participating in the production of knowledge and learning: a true network which continually and progressively manufactures, looks after, evaluates and repairs, trains, etc. In fact, agricultural development needs a basic collective research impetus concerning production systems, and it is as necessary to generate know-how, learning and technology, as it is knowledge, in the usual sense of the word.

## Acknowledgements

This work is largely based on the collective scientific thought of the INRA–SAD department, directed by B. Vissac, whom I particularly thank for his stimulating support and suggestions. This text has also been enriched by the comments and experience of J.L. Rouquette and by the discussions I have had with a number of colleagues, particularly C. Beranger, J. Brossier, E. Landais and P.L. Osty, whom I warmly thank for their help.

## References

Auricoste, C., Deffontaines, J.P., Fiorelli, J.L., Langlet, A. and Osty, P.L. (1983) *Friches, Parcours et Activités d'Élevage. Points de Vue d'Agronomes sur les Potentialités Agricoles; le Cas des Vosges et des Causses.* INRA–SAD, Versailles, 55 pp. + maps.
Balent, G. (1987) Structure, fonctionnement et évolution d'un système pastoral. Le pâturage vu comme un facteur écologique piloté dans les Pyrénées Centrales. Thèse de Doctorat d'Etat, Université de Rennes, Rennes.
Beranger, C. and Vissac, B. (1992) Bases théoriques et méthodologiques pour une approche zootechnique globale: le système d'élevage piloté. In: *Colloque d'Étude des Systèmes d'Élevage en Ferme dans une Perspective de Recherche Développement, Saragosse, 11–12 September, 1992.* To be published.
Bibe, B. and Vissac, B. (1978) Amélioration génétique et utilisation du territoire. In: Molenat, G. and Jarrige, R. (eds) *Utilisation par les Ruminants des Pâturages d'Altitude et Parcours Méditerranéens.* INRA, Paris, pp. 481–491.
Blanc, M. and Lacombe, Ph. (1989) Quarante ans d'économie rurale en France. In: Bodiguel, M. and Lowe, Ph. (eds) *Campagne Française, Campagne Britannique.* L'Harmattan, Paris, pp. 125–154.
Bonnemaire, J. (1988) Diversité et fonctionnement des exploitations. In: Jollivet, M. (ed.) *Pour une Agriculture Diversifiée. Arguments, Questions, Recherches.* L'Harmattan, Paris, pp. 92–103.
Bonnemaire, J. and Vissac, B. (1988) Race bovines et modèles de développement. In: Jollivet, M. (ed.) *Pour une Agriculture Diversifiée. Arguments, Questions, Recherches.* L'Harmattan, Paris, pp. 252–267.
Bonnemaire, J., Deffontaines, J.P. and Osty, P.L. (1980) Observations sur l'agriculture en zones défavorisées à partir de recherches sur le fonctionnement des exploitations

agricoles. *Comptes Rendus de l'Academie d'Agriculture de France* 66, 361–375.

Bonnemaire, J., Deffontaines, J.P., Houdard, Y. and Petit, M. (1987) Sistemas de produccion y sistemas agrarios en las colinas del Himalaya del Nepal. *Agricultura y Sociedad* 45, 229–259.

Bonneval, L. de (1993) *Systèmes Agraires, Systèmes de Production. Vocabulaire Français–Anglais avec Index Anglais.* INRA, Paris, 285 pp.

Bonneviale, J.R., Jussiau, R. and Marshall, E. (1989) *Approche Globale de l'Exploitation Agricole.* Foucher/INRAP, Paris, 329 pp.

Brossier, J. (1987) Système et système de production. *Cahiers ORSTOM, Série Sciences Humaines* 23, 377–390.

Brossier, J. (1993) Recherche-système made in USA. *Courrier de la Cellule Environnement de l'INRA* 19, 53–62.

Brossier, J. and Petit, M. (1977) Pour une typologie des exploitations agricoles fondée sur les projets et les situations des agriculteurs. *Economie Rurale* 122, 31–40.

Brossier, J., Deffontaines, J.P., Houdard, Y., Lenoir, D., Petit, M., Prod'homme, J.P. and Vincent, J. (1980) *Politiques Départementales et Pratiques de Développement. Analyse Comparée de la Marne et des Vosges.* ENSSAA/INA–PG/INRA–SAD, Versailles, 119 pp. + appendices.

Brossier, J., Vissac, B. and Le Moigne, J.L. (eds) (1990) *Modélisation Systémique et Système Agraire. Décision et Organisation.* INRA, Paris, 365 pp.

Brossier, J., Chia, E., Marshall, E., Petit, M. (1991) Gestion de l'exploitation agricole familiale et pratiques des agriculteurs: vers une nouvelle théorie de la gestion. *Revue Canadienne d'Économie Rurale* 39, 119–135.

Brun, A., Chassany, J.P., Osty, P.L. and Petit, F.E. (1979) L'utilisation des terres peu productives: Le Causse Méjan. *Recherches Économiques et Sociales. Notes Critiques et Débats* 15, 307–357.

Capillon, A. (ed.) (1989) Grassland systems approaches; some French research proposals. *INRA–SAD, Etudes et Recherches sur les Systèmes Agraires* 16, 218 pp.

Capillon, A. (1993) Typologie des exploitations agricoles, contribution à l'étude régionale des problèmes techniques. Thèse de Doctorat, INA–PG.

Capillon, A. and Sebillotte, M. (1980) Etude des systèmes de production des exploitations agricoles. Une typologie. In: Servant, J. and Pinchinat, A. (eds) *Caribbean Seminar on Farming Systems Research Methodology (Pointe-à-Pitre, 4–8 May).* Guadeloupe, pp. 85–111.

Capillon, A., Fleury, A. and Sebillotte, M. (1973) *Essai pour Dégager les Voies d'Évolution des Exploitations Agricoles de l'Ouest du Morbihan.* 2 vols. INRA, INA–PG, Paris, 219 + 330 pp.

Capillon, A., Sebillotte, M. and Thierry, J. (1975) *Evolution des Exploitations d'une Petite Région: Élaboration d'une Méthode d'Étude.* CNASEA/GEARA, INA–PG, Paris, 35 pp. + appendices.

Cerf, M. and Sebillotte, M. (1988) Le concept de modèle général et la prise de décision dans la conduite d'une culture. *Comptes Rendus de l'Academie d'Agriculture de France* 74 (4), 71–80.

Cerf, M., Papy, F., Aubry, C. and Meynard, J.M. (1990) Théorie agronomique et aide à la décision. In: Brossier J., Vissac, B. and Le Moigne, J.L. (eds) *Modélisation Systémique et Système Agraire; Décision et Organisation.* INRA, Paris, pp. 81–202.

CNRS (1970) *L'Aubrac. Etude Ethnologique, Linguistique, Agronomique et Économique d'un Établissement Humain. Vol. 1: Agronomie, Sociologie Économique, Géographie.* CNRS, Paris, 299 pp.

Couty, Ph. (1987) La production agricole en Afrique subsaharienne: manières de voir et façons d'agir. *Cahiers ORSTOM Série Sciences Humaines* 23, 391–408.

Cristofini, B. (1986) La petite région vue à travers le tissu de ses exploitations: un outil pour l'aménagement et le développement rural. *INRA–SAD, Etudes et Recherches sur les Systèmes Agraires* 6, 44 pp.

Cristofini, B., Deffontaines, J.P., Raichon, C. and de Verneuil, B. (1978) Pratiques d'élevage en Castagniccia; exploitation d'un milieu naturel et social en Corse. *Etudes Rurales* 71–72, 89–109.

Cristofini, B., Deffontaines, J.P., Houdard, Y., Moisan, H., Petit, M. and Roux, M. (1982) *Rambervillers, 10 ans après: Intérêts et Limites d'une Typologie pour Apprehender l'évolution des Exploitations Agricoles*. INRA-SAD, Versailles, 56 pp.

Darre, J.P. (1985) *La Parole et la Technique. L'Univers de Pensée des Éleveurs du Ternois*. L'Harmattan, Paris, 192 pp.

Deffontaines, J.P. (1964) Essai de détermination des potentialités agricoles régionales. *Acta Geographica* 1964, 28–34.

Deffontaines, J.P. (1967) Une méthode de détermination des facteurs techniques limitant la production agricole en montagne. *Fourrages* 31, 36–52.

Deffontaines, J.P. (1973) Analyse de situation dans différentes régions de France. Freins à l'adoption d'innovations techniques. *Etudes Rurales* 53, 80–90.

Deffontaines, J.P. (1991) L'agronomie, science du champ. Le champ, lieu d'interdisciplinarité: de l'écophysiologie aux sciences humaines. *Agronomie* 11, 581–591.

Deffontaines, J.P. and Osty, P.L. (1977) Des systèmes de production aux systèmes agraires. *L'Espace Géographique* 3, 195–199.

Deffontaines, J.P. and Petit, M. (1985) Comment étudier les exploitations agricoles d'une région. Présentation d'un ensemble méthodologique. *INRA–SAD, Etudes et Recherches sur les Systèmes Agraires* 4, 47 pp.

Deffontaines, J.P. and Raichon, C. (1981) Systèmes de pratiques, terroirs, moyens d'analyse d'une agriculture régionale. *Economie Rurale* 142, 30.

Dumont, R. (1956) *Voyages en France d'un Agronome*. Librairie de Médicis, Paris, 485 pp.

Duru, M., Gibon, A., Langlet, A. and Flamant, J.C. (1978) Recherches sur les problèmes pastoraux pyrénéens. In: Molenat, G. and Jarrige, R. (eds) *Utilisation par les Ruminants des Pâturages d'Altitude et Parcours Méditerranéens*. INRA, Paris, pp. 231–253.

Duru, M., Gibon, A. and Osty, P.L. (1986) Pour une approche renouvelée du système fourrager. In: Jollivet M. (ed.) *Pour une Agriculture Diversifiée*. L'Harmattan, Paris, pp. 35–48.

Duru, M., Papy, F. and Soler, L.G. (1988) Le concept de modèle général et l'analyse du fonctionnement de l'exploitation agricole. *Comptes Rendus de l'Academie d'Agriculture de France* 74 (4), 81–93.

Flamant, J.C. (1983) La zootechnie: le contrôle social des populations animales, le contrôle des fonctions biologiques, la maîtrise des systèmes d'élevage. In: *Table Ronde Ethnosciences. Dialogue et Coopération entre Sciences Naturelles et Sciences de l'Homme et de la Société, Sophia Antipolis, 14–18 November*. 15 pp.

Geffroy, B. (1978) L'industrialisation de l'élevage, cent ans d'utopie. L'encadrement professionnel des producteurs bovins et son rôle dans le développement de l'élevage de 1840 à 1940. Thèse 3 ème cycle de géographie rurale, Nanterre, Paris.

Gibon, A. and Matheron, G. (eds) (1992) *Global Appraisal of Livestock Farming Systems and Study of their Organization Levels: Concepts, Methodology and Results. Proceedings of Symposium, Toulouse, France, 7 July 1990*. Agrimed Research Program, 4th Annual

EAAP Meeting, Office of Official Publication of the European Communities, Luxembourg, 510 pp.

Godard, O. and Legay, J.M. (1992) Entre disciplines et réalité, l'artifice des systèmes. In: Jollivet, M. (ed.) *Sciences de la Nature, Sciences de la Société; les Passeurs de Frontières.* CNRS, Paris, pp. 243–257.

Gras, R., Benoit, M., Deffontaines, J.P., Duru, M., Lafarge, M., Langlet, A. and Osty, P.L. (1989) *Le Fait Technique en Agronomie.* INRA and L'Harmattan, Paris, 184 pp.

Groupe Bouchet (1978) *Réflexions et Propositions du Groupe 'Recherche et Développement.'* Rapport Interne, INRA, Paris, 55 pp.

Henin, S. and Deffontaines, J.P. (1970) Principe de l'étude des potentialités agricoles régionales. *Comptes Rendus de l'Academie d'Agriculture de France* 8, 463–472.

Henin, S., Feodoroff, R. and Gras, R. (1960) *Le Profil Cultural. Principes de Physique du Sol.* SEIA, Paris, 320 pp.

Hervieu, B. (1993) *Les Champs du Futur.* François Bourin, Paris, 173 pp.

Houdard, Y. (1993) *Agriculture dans les Hautes Collines du Népal Central.* INRA, Paris, 291 pp.

Hubert, B. (1987) Problèmes posés par la mise en place de systèmes sylvopastoraux en région méditerranéenne française. In: Hubert, B. and Etienne, M. (eds) *Contribution du Comite Français,* Séminaire MAB Dehesas, 30 March–4 April, Madrid, pp. 63–78.

Hubert, B. (1993) Comment raisonner de manière systémique l'utilisation du territoire pastoral? In: Gaston, A., Kennick, M. and Le Houerou, H.N. (eds) *Proceedings of the IVth International Rangeland Congress, Montpellier, France, 1991,* Vol. 3. CIRAD, Montpellier, pp. 1026–1043.

Hubert, B. and Girault, N. (eds) (1988) *De la Touffe d'Herbe au Paysage. Séminaire Viens (France), 13–14 Janvier.* INRA–SAD, Paris, 336 pp.

INRA (1993) *INRA 2000, le Projet d'Établissement de l'INRA.* INRA, Paris, 90 pp.

INRA–ENSSAA (1973) *Conditions du Choix des Techniques de Production et Évolution des Exploitations Agricoles. Région de Rambervillers (Vosges).* Etude No. 4. INRA–SEI, Versailles, 119 pp + appendices.

INRA–ENSSAA (1977) *Pays, Paysans, Paysages dans les Vosges du Sud.* INRA, Versailles, 192 pp.

INRA–SAD (1979) *Eléments pour une Problématique de Recherche sur les Systèmes Agraires et le Développement.* INRA, Paris, 114 pp + appendices.

INRA–SAD (1985) *Bilan du Département (1979–1985). Vol. 1. Rapport Général.* INRA–SAD, Paris, 112 pp.

Jest, C. (ed.) (1974) *L'Aubrac. Dix Ans d'Évolution: 1964–1973.* CNRS, Paris, 152 pp. + appendices.

Jollivet, M. (ed.) (1988) *Pour une Agriculture Diversifiée. Arguments, Questions, Recherches.* L'Harmattan, Paris, 336 pp.

Jollivet, M. (ed.) (1992) *Sciences de la Nature, Sciences de la Société. Les Passeurs de Frontières.* CNRS, Paris, 589 pp.

Jouve, Ph. (1984) Le diagnostic agronomique: préalable aux opérations de recherche-développement. *Montpellier, Les Cahiers de la Recherche–Développement* 3/4, 67–76.

Jouve, Ph. (1988) Quelques réflexions sur la spécificité et l'identification des systèmes agraires. *Montpellier, Les Cahiers de la Recherche–Développement* 20, 5–16.

Jouve, Ph. (1990) L'expérimentation en milieu paysan: démarches et méthodes.

Montpellier, *Les Cahiers de la Recherche–Développement* 27, 94–105.

Landais, E. (ed.) (1986) Méthodes pour la recherche sur les systèmes d'élevage en Afrique intertropicale. *Actes de l'Atelier de Mbour, 2–8 Février, Maisons-Alfort.* IEMVT–CIRAD/ISRA, Etudes et Synthèses de l'IEMVT No. 20, 733 pp.

Landais, E. (1987) *Recherches sur les Systèmes d'Élevage. Questions et Perspectives.* INRA–SAD, Versailles, Document de travail, 75 pp.

Landais, E. (1992a) Système d'élevage: d'une intuition holiste à une méthode de recherche, le cheminement d'un concept. In: *Comm. Colloquio Mesoamericano Systemas de Produccion y Desarollo Agricola, Mexico, 19–30 June 1992,* INRA, Versailles, 19 pp.

Landais, E. (1992b) Tendances actuelles des recherches sur les systèmes d'élevage: exemples de travaux du département 'systèmes agraires et développement' de l'INRA. *Cahiers Agricultures* 1, 55–65.

Landais, E. and Balent, G. (eds) (1993) Pratiques d'élevage extensif. Identifier, modéliser, évaluer. (Ouvrage collectif.) *Etudes et Recherches sur les Systèmes Agraires et le Développement.* INRA–SAD, Paris, Numéro Spécial 27, 310 pp.

Landais, E. and Deffontaines, J.P. (1989) Les pratiques des agriculteurs. Point de vue sur un courant nouveau de la recherche agronomique. *Etudes Rurales* 109, 125–158.

Landais, E., Lhoste, P. and Milleville, P. (1987) Points de vue sur la zootechnie et les systèmes d'élevage tropicaux. *Cahiers ORSTOM, Série Sciences Humaines* 23, 421–437.

Langlet, A., Flamant, J.C., Molenat, G. and Osty, P.L. (1978) Les parcours des Grands Causses ; contraintes et possibilités techniques d'une mise en valeur par l'élevage ovin. In: Molenat, G. and Jarrige, R. (eds) *Utilisation par les Ruminants des Pâturages d'Altitude et Parcours Méditerranéens.* INRA, Paris, pp. 257–334.

Latour, B. (1989) La science est le passé de la recherche. *Pour* 122/123, 13–21.

Le Bail, M. and Caneill, J. (1992) Agronomie et qualité des productions végétales. *Colloque SFER: la Qualité dans l'Agro-alimentaire,* Société Française d'Economie Rurales, Paris, 6 pp.

Le Bail, M. and Valceschini, E. (1990) Qualité des produits agricoles et coordination dans les filières agro-alimentaires. *Economie Rurale* 198, 41.

Legay, J.M. (1986) Quelques réflexions à propos d'écologie: défense de l'indisciplinarité. *Acta Aecologica/Aecol Gener.* 7, 39–398.

Legay, J.M. (1988a) Méthodes et modèles dans l'étude des systèmes complexes. In: Jollivet, M. (ed.) *Pour une Agriculture Diversifiée; Arguments, Questions, Recherches.* L'Harmattan, Paris, pp. 14–24.

Legay, J.M. (1988b) Contribution à l'étude de la complexité dans les systèmes biologiques. In: Demongeot, J. and Malgrange, P. (eds) *Biologie et Économie. Les Apports de la Modélisation.* Série d'Économie Appliquée, No. 34. Institut de Mathématiques Économiques et Librairie de l'Université, Dijon.

Legay, J.M. (1992) Les moments théoriques dans la recherche interdisciplinaire. In: Jollivet, M. (ed.) *Sciences de la Nature, Sciences de la Société. Les Passeurs de Frontières.* CNRS, Paris, pp. 485–489.

Le Moigne, J.L. (1990) *La Modélisation des Systèmes Complexes.* Dunod (AFCET), Paris, 178 pp.

Meuret, M. (1989) Feuillages, fromages et flux ingérés. Thèse de Doctorat, Faculté des Sciences Agronomiques de Gembloux, INRA–SAD, 229 pp.

Meynard, J.M. and Sebillotte, M. (1989) La conduite des cultures: vers une ingénierie agronomique. *Economie Rurale* 192/193, 35–41.

Morin, E. (1977, 1980, 1987) *La Méthode. Vol. I: La Nature de la Nature; Vol. II: La Vie de la Vie; Vol. III: La Connaissance de la Connaissance.* Editions du Seuil, Paris.

Morlon, P. (1992) *Comprendre l'Agriculture Paysanne dans les Andes Centrales (Pérou–Bolivie).* INRA, Paris, 522 pp.

Osty, P.L. (1974) Comment s'effectue le choix des techniques et des systèmes de production? Cas d'une région herbagère dans les Vosges. *Fourrages* 59, 53–69.

Osty, P.L. (1978a) L'exploitation agricole vue comme un système. Diffusion de l'innovation et contribution au développement. *Bulletin Technique d'Information du Ministère de l'Agriculture* 326, 43–49.

Osty, P.L. (1978b) *Le Causse Méjean 4. Elevage et Éleveurs en 1975.* INRA, Versailles, 196 pp.

Osty, P.L. (1990) Le fait technique en agronomie. Points de vue et questions sur quelques concepts. In: Brossier, J., Vissac, B. and Le Moigne, J.L. (eds) *Modélisation Systémique et Système Agraire. Décision et Organisation.* INRA, Paris, pp. 19–28.

Osty, P.L. and Auricoste, C. (1989) Une image des élevages du Causse: évolutions récentes (1975–1983) et questions pour l'avenir. *Annales du Parc Nationale des Cévennes* 4, 15–54.

Osty, P.L. and Landais, E. (1993) Fonctionnement des systèmes d'exploitation pastorale. In: Gaston, A., Kennick, M. and Le Houerou, H.M. (eds) *Proceedings of the IVth International Rangeland Congress, Montpellier, France, 1991,* Vol. 3. CIRAD, Montpellier, pp. 1137–1146.

Paillotin, G. (ed.) (1993) *Recherche et Innovation: le Temps des Réseaux. Rapport du Groupe 'Recherche, Technologie et Compétitivité' de Préparation du XIè plan.* Commissariat Général du Plan, La Documentation Française, Paris, 160 pp.

Papy, F. (1992) Agriculture et environnement: des éléments de réflexion. *Courrier de la Cellule Environnement de l'INRA* 19, 81–85.

Parain, C. (1956) Un mot du vocabulaire de synthèse historique: agriculture. *Revue de Synthèse* 77 (1), 43–54.

Petit, M. (1971) Recherche sur les obstacles au progrès fourrager. *Fourrages* 47, 163–188.

Petit, M. (1975) L'adoption des innovations techniques par les agriculteurs. Plaidoyer pour un renouvellement de la théorie économique de la décision. *Pour* 40, 79–91.

Petit, M. (1993) Recherches agronomiques pour le développement. *SADOSCOPE* INRA–SAD, Paris, No. 66, 7 pp.

Piaget, J. (ed.) (1967) *Logique et Connaissance Scientifique.* Encyclopédie de la Pléïade. Gallimard, Paris.

Rouquette, J.L. (1988) Les problèmes que pose aujourd'hui la production de références techniques. 2. Un travail au niveau des systèmes d'exploitation. Le cas de l'Aveyron. *Comptes Rendus de l'Academie d'Agriculture de France* 74, No. 4, 51–57.

Rouquette, J.L. *et al.* (1981) *Les Rôles Possibles du Département de Recherches sur les Systèmes Agraires et le Développement INRA dans le Cadre d'une Politique de Recherche de Références et d'une Politique de Développement Engagées par la Profession Agricole.* Conseil Départemental de l'Agriculture de l'Aveyron, Rodez, 16 pp.

Russell, D.B. and Ison, R.L. (1993) The research–development relationships in rangelands: an opportunity for contextual science. In: Gaston, A., Kennick, M.

and Le Houerou, H.N. (eds) *Proceedings of the IVth International Rangeland Congress, Montpellier, France, 22–26 April 1991*, Vol. 3. CIRAD, Montpellier, pp. 1047–1054.

Sainte Marie, C. de, Prost, J.A., Casabianca, F. and Casalta, E. (1992) La construction sociale de la qualité: enjeux autour de l'appellation contrôlée Brocciu Corse. In: *Colloque SFER: la Qualité dans l'Agroalimentaire. Société Française d'Economie Rurale, Paris, 26–27 Octobre*, 14 pp.

Sautter, G. (ed.) (1986) *Commission d'Audit du Département de Recherches sur les Systèmes Agraires et le Développement (SAD). Rapport Général (Juin 1986)*. INRA, Paris, 56 pp. + appendices.

Sebillotte, M. (1974) Agronomie et agriculture. Essai d'analyse des tâches de l'agronome. *Cahiers ORSTOM, Série Biologie* 24, 3–25.

Sebillotte, M. (1978) Itinéraires techniques et évolution de la pensée agronomique. *Comptes Rendus de l'Academie d'Agriculture de France* 11, 906–914.

Sebillotte, M. (1979) Analyse du fonctionnement des exploitations agricoles; trajectoire et typologie. In: INRA–SAD (ed.) *Eléments pour une Problématique de Recherche sur les Systèmes Agraires et le Développement*. INRA, Paris, pp. 20–30.

Sebillotte, M. (1989) *Fertilité et Systèmes de Production*. INRA, Paris, 370 pp.

Sebillotte, M. (1991) Some concepts for analysis farming and cropping systems and for understanding their different effects. In: *Proceedings of the 1st Congress of European Society of Agronomy, Paris, 5–7 December 1991*. INRA, Paris.

Sebillotte, M. (1993) *Avenir de l'Agriculture et Futur de l'INRA*. INRA, Paris, 139 pp. + appendices.

Sebillotte, M. and Soler, L.G. (1988) Le concept de modèle général et la compréhension du comportement de l'agriculteur. *Comptes Rendus de l'Academie d'Agriculture de France* 74, No. 4, 81–93.

Simon, H.A. (1981) *Science des Systèmes, Sciences de l'Artificiel*. Dunod, Paris.

Teissier, J.H. (1979) Relations entre techniques et pratiques. *Bulletin INRAP* 38, 1–19.

Teissier, J.H. (ed.) (1986) Espaces fourragers et aménagement; le cas des Hautes Vosges. INRA, Paris, 228 pp.

Valceschini, E. (1990) Exploitation, filière et mésosystème. In: Brossier, J., Vissac, B. and Le Moigne, J.L. (eds) *Modélisation Systémique et Système Agraire. Décision et Organisation*. INRA, Paris, pp. 269–282.

Valceschini, E. (1992) la qualité des produits alimentaires dans une économie de marché. In: *DEMETER 92, Economies et Stratégies Agricoles*, ouvrage collectif. Colin, Paris.

Vallerand, F., Casabianca, F., Santucci, P.M., Prost, J.A., Bouche, R., Casalta, E. and Vercherand, J. (1990) Dynamisation d'un système agraire régional par l'organisation. In: Brossier, J., Vissac, B. and Le Moigne, J.L. (eds) *Modélisation Systémique et Système Agraire. Décision et Organisation*. INRA, Paris, pp. 283–296.

Vallerand, F., Casabianca, F., Santucci, P.M. and Bouche, R. (1992) Apports du concept d'organisation dans une recherche/action sur des systèmes d'élevage méditerranéens. In: Gibon, A. and Matheron, G. (eds) *Global Appraisal of Livestock Farming Systems and Study of their Organization Levels: Concepts, Methodology and Results. Proceedings of Symposium, Toulouse, France, 7 July 1990*. Agrimed Research Program, 4th EAAP Annual Meeting, Office of Official Publication of the European Communities, Luxembourg, pp. 21–44.

Vissac, B. (1978) *L'Animal Domestique Révélateur des Relations entre une Société et son Milieu.* Dépt Génétique Animale, Jouy-en-Josas; INRA, Paris, 24 pp.

Vissac, B. (ed.) (1985) *Bilan du Département Systèmes Agraires et Développement (1979–1985).* INRA, Paris, 2 vols, 112 + 205 pp.

Vissac, B. (1986) Technologies et société: l'exemple de l'amélioration bovine en France. *Culture Technique* 16, 176–187.

Vissac, B. (1988) Histoire agraire, mouvements et rythmes de l'élevage. In: Hubert, B. and Girault, N. (eds) *De la Touffe d'Herbe au Paysage. Séminaire, Viens (France), 13–14 Janvier.* INRA–SAD, Paris, pp. 313–336.

Vissac, B. (1992) Livestock farming systems research/developement/action; from the developed to the developing countries. In: *4th EAAP Annual Meeting, Madrid, 13–17 September.* Commission on Animal Management and Health, 15 pp. + appendices.

Vissac, B. (1993) Société, race animale et territoire; entre les théories et l'histoire: réflexions sur une crise. *Natures Sciences Sociétés* 1, No. 4, 1–12.

Vissac, B., Hubert, B., Baudry, J., Casabianca, F., Deffontaines, J.P., Langlet, A., Papy, F. and Pluvinage, J. (1992) *Plan à Cinq Ans du Département (1992–1996).* INRA–SAD, Paris, 29 pp. + appendices.

# 3

## FARMING SYSTEMS RESEARCH/EXTENSION IN THE EUROPEAN CONTEXT

### Colin Spedding

## Introduction

The question as to whether FSR/E has anything to offer in the European context depends upon the definition of the terms.

If FSR is the application of a systems approach to farming systems, then it is difficult to see why it should be any less relevant to European farms than it is to others. Indeed, it can be argued that a systems approach is fundamental to the study of all systems and goes far beyond farming. Much therefore depends upon definitions and, as in so many discussions, it is *not* adequate to behave as though we all know what the terms mean and further definition is not needed.

There is a further question, and perhaps a more important one, as to whether it is any longer satisfactory to consider farming systems by themselves, as if they stood alone, in some way isolated from other parts of life – whether, indeed, they can be regarded as independent systems, or whether they are really subsystems of much larger systems.

The question of definitions will be examined first.

## A Systems Approach

A systems approach in my terminology (Spedding, 1988) is one which requires that the system to be studied/understood/improved/repaired/copied be identified and described in a way that serves the purpose. Description has to include content (components, interactions, subsystems), boundary, inputs and outputs and some reference to the context in which the system operates. My definition of a *system* is 'a group of interacting components, operating together for a common purpose (or at least in a coordinated way), capable of reacting as a whole to external stimuli: it is unaffected by its own outputs and has a specified boundary based on the inclusion of all significant feedbacks.'

Descriptions may be best represented by models, since these have a clarity and coherence that non-model descriptions may lack. This does not exclude the possibility of word models, but these cannot easily portray coherent pictures of dynamic systems.

My preferred definition of a *model* would be wide: 'an abstraction and simplification of the real world, specified so as to capture the principal interactions and behaviour of the system under study and capable of experimental manipulation in order to project the consequences of changes in the determinants of the system's behaviour' (Spedding, 1988). Modelling is thus one of the techniques or tools that a systems approach may employ. Such tools are used as and when appropriate and are thus enabling rather than in any way limiting.

Any application of a systems approach that is tied to particular techniques is to that extent limited and it is then legitimate to ask whether it is relevant to a particular situation (or region, such as Europe).

A crucial question, then, is whether FSR/E is so characterized by limiting techniques.

## FSR/E

FSR/E is not always regarded as being the same as a systems approach: sometimes it is seen as in opposition to it.

Simmonds (1985) recognized three subcategories of FSR/E, as follows:

- FSR *sensu stricto*, is the study of farming systems *per se*, as they exist; typically, the analysis goes deep (technically and socioeconomically) and the object is academic or scholarly rather than practical; the view taken is nominally 'holistic' and numerical system modelling is a fairly natural outcome if a holistic approach is claimed.
- New farming systems development (NFSD) takes as its starting point the view that many tropical farming systems are already so stressed that radical restructuring rather than stepwise change is necessary; the invention, testing and exploitation of new systems is therefore the object.
- On-farm research with farming systems perspective (OFR/FSP) is a practical adjunct to agricultural research which starts from the precept that only 'farmer experience' can reveal to the researcher what farmers really need. Typically, the OFR/FSP process isolates a subsystem of the whole farm, studies it in just sufficient depth (no more) to gain the necessary FSP and proceeds as quickly as possible to experiments on-farm, with farmers' collaboration. There is an implicit assumption that

stepwise change in an economically favourable direction is possible and worth seeking.

All of these appear to be unnecessarily restrictive and it is hard to see why, for example, a study aimed at making changes in a system cannot also contemplate the development of a new system. In my view, a wider systems approach is actually required for both. In any event, it is necessary to recognize Checkland's distinction between 'hard' and 'soft' systems (Checkland, 1981, 1990).

### *'Hard' systems*

'Hard' systems are those involving industrial plants characterized by easy-to-define objectives, clearly defined decision-taking procedures and quantitative measures of performance. Such systems tend to the mechanical, although biological systems are often of this kind (e.g. those represented by a single individual). Highly developed agricultural systems (e.g. battery hens) are also at this end of the range.

The more intimately people are involved as part of a system, however, the less appropriate this view becomes.

### *'Soft' systems*

'Soft' systems are, by contrast, those in which objectives are hard to define, decision taking is uncertain, measures of performance are at best qualitative and human behaviour is unpredictable.

In 'hard' systems, it is possible to focus on problems and endeavour to find solutions. In 'soft' systems, matters are rarely, if ever, so straightforward. In both kinds of system, however, it is still the case that 'improvement' is sought.

## Improvement of Agricultural Systems

The ultimate purpose of the study of agriculture is directly, or indirectly, the improvement of agricultural systems. Agricultural education, research, development and extension are primarily directed towards this end.

Improvement may be brought about by one of three main methods:

1. advice on component changes;
2. adoption of innovation;
3. copying.

All of these can be encouraged by 'extension' activities.

Systems thinking requires that advice on a component change should be related to the functioning of the systems as a whole. If it is not, the operator (e.g. the farmer) has to depend on his or her own judgement as to whether the advice offered will actually benefit his or her system. This, in turn, has to be based on a knowledge of how the system operates.

Pioneer farmers will often try out ideas that are new to farming practice, though they may well have emerged from R & D programmes. Sometimes, of course, such new ideas originate within practice. All involve some risk and this can only be minimized by testing the ideas on some kind of model. This may be done by the farmer, using a very simple mental model. In any event, it should be recognized that the content, detail and level of sophistication of a model will vary according to whether the purpose is to operate, repair or invent new systems.

The extension or spread of new ideas and systems is commonly achieved by copying what others are doing, apparently successfully.

The main problems are the following:

**1.** Judging that the system to be copied is, in fact, 'better,' based on the evidence available and the period (of years) from which it is derived, and the range of soil types and weather conditions experienced, etc.
**2.** Since the operator's farm may well differ in important respects from that from which ideas are to be copied, it is necessary to judge the relevance of the ideas to the copier's situation. For example, how similar do the copier's crops and animals have to be for ideas to be successfully translated?
**3.** A major problem is knowing *exactly* what to copy. Clearly, many of the details are trivial (e.g. a tree in the middle of a grazing system), but it is hard to judge what is *essential* in a system. This, of course, is precisely what modelling is about and perhaps the only way of testing essentiality of components is to put them (and only them) into a model and see if it gives the same answers as found in the real world. (I pass by the question of how 'same' is to be assessed and with what precision the answer has to be expressed.)

I have long argued that the process of improvement has to start with two questions:

**1.** What is the system to be improved? (Spedding, 1988).
This requires the construction of some kind of model in order to provide an adequate description. It is here that systems techniques have their place and a great deal is now on offer.
**2.** What constitutes an improvement?
An improvement may hardly seem to need agreement, but it is a great mistake to suppose that every operator of a system actually wants the same things. Farmers (in developed countries) will readily agree that they want to maximize their profits but, on further examination, they never do – except within a whole range of constraints, just as no-one wishes to increase output without regard to the inputs employed. However, many farmers prefer to incur less work, to

reduce risk or to gain other satisfaction than making money.

So it turns out to be by no means obvious what will strike a particular farmer as an improvement. It is even less obvious that whatever he selects would necessarily be the choice of his wife or his children or the nation. Worse still, whatever beneficial outcome may result, it may not be the only outcome and there is therefore a balance to be struck, not only between costs of production and the resulting benefits, but also between the benefits and the disbenefits of output. Common examples of such disbenefits are various forms of pollution and, depending upon when the cost of dealing with it is met, the overall balance will look different to different people. An extreme example of this, especially in developing countries, is the fact that help rendered to one farmer puts him at an advantage over his competitors – often his neighbours – so an improvement to one system may actually worsen competitor systems not the subject of any planned change.

Hence one of the unforeseen effects of the initial change may be a disbenefit even when it resulted in an improved system.

## Relevance to Europe

The approach that I have been discussing should be relevant to the improvement of *all* farming systems (and beyond).

Whatever definition is used for FSR/E, it has to be directed to the improvement of farming systems and, since the operational units in agriculture have the properties of systems (hard or soft), the approach is appropriate.

Farms in Europe may differ from farms in other parts of the world but they also include a great variety of farms, varying in size, intensity of use of land, labour and capital, and also in their soil, climate and topography. Within this range, there are some very small farms (near subsistence), some very large businesses and a great many farms operated by part-time farmers. If there were techniques especially relevant to farm types, it is unlikely any one would serve such a variety of different cases. There will equally be many similarities between some of them and farms found in other parts of the world.

It is possible, however, to discern two features that are particularly relevant to European farms. These are rapid technological development and public concern about the environment.

## Technological Development

Based on advances in molecular biology, it is becoming possible to engage in genetic manipulation and thus the acceleration of genetic change.

Transgenic animals may not only be more productive, they may also produce new products, such as compounds of value in human medicine. These developments may mean radical changes in some components that will need to be interpreted in terms of whole production systems. Gene transfer in plants may confer pest and disease resistance without recourse to agrochemicals.

All these possibilities raise public concern about animal welfare and the environment, both issues that go beyond the farming system.

Concern about animal welfare centres on two issues. The first relates to the methodology employed – whether any of the techniques involved reduce the welfare of the animal. The second concerns objections to the possibility of producing animals that are physically impaired in some way, as with pigs with a predisposition to arthritis.

There are also more fundamental concerns about 'unnatural' interference, the insertion of genes from one species to another, which might even affront some religious principles, and the use of human genes (even as copies) into animals used for food.

There is great potential for good in these developments, but it is the public concerns that may affect their acceptability.

## Public Concern about the Environment

This is already resulting in legislative control of the use of sprays and fertilizers, just as concern about animal welfare has resulted in legislation that limits the ways in which animals can be reared, transported, marketed and slaughtered.

There are worries that the pollen from genetically modified crops could transfer to other plants, such as weeds, their resistance to herbicides resulting in uncontrollable weed infestation.

It is difficult to reassure people who are concerned, simply because no-one can be 100% sure that these possibilities can be ruled out. So people may object to new technology either as consumers, refusing to buy products that have involved genetic manipulation or irradiation, or as citizens worried about the environmental or welfare consequences.

The point about all these issues is that they represent outputs that produce feedback effects on the system itself. This breaches my definition of a system and implies that what is defined as a farm system may be too narrow in the future. No system can be regarded as completely described if it takes no account of public reaction to its processes and products (including pollution), where this is powerful enough to change the system, by legislation, social or economic pressure.

## Future Systems

There are similar arguments from an economic standpoint, but it has always been hard to argue that the outputs of any one farm alter the economic framework (e.g. resulting in a lowering of product prices). There are stronger arguments that the whole food chain should be considered as one system, because of the interactions between farm and the food industry that now processes most of the farm output.

The strongest argument, however, for a wider definition of systems is probably the need to take account of interactions with the environment and public opinion. There is no reason to suppose that this is unique to Europe, but it is certainly more marked there than in many other parts of the world.

## References

Checkland, P. (1981) *Systems Thinking, Systems Practice.* Wiley, New York.

Checkland, P. and Scholes, J. (1990) *Soft Systems Methodology in Action.* Wiley, New York.

Simmonds, N.W. (1985) *Farming Systems Research. A Review.* World Bank Technical Paper No. 43, World Bank, Washington, DC.

Spedding, C.R.W. (1988) General aspects of modelling and its application in livestock production. In: Korver, S. and van Arendonk, J.A.M. (eds) *Modelling of Livestock Production Systems.* Kluwer, Dordrecht, for the CEC, pp. 3–9.

# 4

# THE ROLE OF FARMING SYSTEMS RESEARCH/EXTENSION IN ENCOURAGING LOWER USE OF NON-RENEWABLE RESOURCES IN FARMING

*David Leaver*

## Introduction

Intensification in agriculture is usually associated with an increase in the use of non-renewable resources. This has been the general trend over the last 50 years in Europe as the quest for self-sufficiency in food production has been positively pursued. In the EC, the resulting surpluses of production, the high cost of disposing of these on the world market and the high cost of direct subsidies to farmers have brought about recent modification to the Common Agricultural Policy (CAP). The transfer of farmer subsidies from units of output to area payments and setaside in the arable sector, plus the output quota systems and extensification inducements in the ruminant livestock sectors, are all indications of a new deintensification direction. Increasing environmental legislation concerning pollution from farms, landscape maintenance and building controls are further pressures on the agricultural industry to find alternatives to further intensification of agriculture.

The role of farming systems research and extension (FSR/E) in the transition to a less intensified agriculture can at this stage only be speculative, as this methodology is not well developed in Europe. Research funding has been dominated in recent years by a major support for basic science notably in the field of molecular biology. It is presumed that in agriculture this knowledge will 'trickle down' through applied research and development and ultimately be applied at farm level. Whilst this may subsequently prove to be correct, historically most innovations in food production have occurred at or close to farm level. The science behind such innovations has tended to be researched afterwards.

As FSR/E is concerned with agricultural development at the farm level and as it is concerned with a holistic approach dealing with the economic, environmental and social aspects of the farm, it would appear to be a more appropriate approach to bringing about change in agriculture than the science-driven approach.

Farming systems with lower external inputs of non-renewable resources will increasingly be a priority for the future. Conventional, science-driven, reductionist research and technology transfer will play a part in such developments, but an interdisciplinary approach as in FSR/E must have an important role if we are to avoid the pitfalls of the past.

# Which Non-renewable Resources?

The inputs to farms which consume non-renewable energy resources are mainly in the form of farm mechanization, mineral fertilizers and chemical pesticides. On livestock farms the purchase of feed inputs also represents an indirect use of non-renewable resources used to produce, process and transport the feed sources to the farm.

The relative importance of farm mechanization, mineral fertilizer input and chemical pesticide input in developed and developing countries is shown in Table 4.1. This shows that mechanization plus mineral fertilizers account for over 90% of the energy consumption on farms.

In the USA and Europe, commercial energy going into farm mechanization has plateaued and may decline in future as a result of output controls.

**Table 4.1.** Use of commercial energy for inputs (%) (from Stout, 1990).

|  | Developed countries | Developing countries |
|---|---|---|
| Farm mechanisation | 64 | 29 |
| Mineral fertilizer | 35 | 69 |
| Chemical pesticide | 1 | 2 |
| Proportion of total used worldwide in agriculture | 73 | 27 |
| Nitrogen | 86 | 93 |
| Phosphorous | 9 | 6 |
| Potassium | 5 | 1 |
| Proportion of total used worldwide in agriculture | 59 | 41 |

Larger, more efficient machinery and greater field sizes have assisted this trend. Of the inputs into fertilizer production, about 90% is utilized in the production of nitrogen fertilizer, the remainder being mainly for phosphate and potash fertilizers. Most nitrogen fertilizer is produced from natural gas, and is therefore a large user of non-renewable energy. The recent changes in CAP policy are leading to some decline in fertilizer use. In the UK there was a 10% decline in the use of N, P and K fertilizers between 1991 and 1992, and agrochemical sales have dropped by a third in the last decade.

Natural resource degradation on farms is not as great a problem in temperate areas as in tropical areas, where high temperatures, seasonally high rainfall and vulnerable soils increase the risk of degradation when farming practices change. Nevertheless, soil erosion is a problem in some temperate regions where intensive farming is practised and also where trees are removed from slopes. Although some natural resources are potentially renewable over time, the loss of biodiversity of flora and fauna resulting from farm intensification remains a problem.

## The Role of Conventional Research

Conventional (reductionist) research by its nature is not directly innovative on farmers' behalf. It tends to be innovative in developing new methodologies which allow knowledge to be advanced. Nonetheless, such knowledge is concerned with knowing 'more and more about less and less'. Such knowledge may have application at some time in the future, but the probability of an innovative success occurring is low for most scientists.

One approach of applied research is to examine input/output responses in order to predict on farms the outcome of input decisions. This type of research, for example fertilizer input/cereal yield responses or concentrate input/milk yield responses, is carried out under controlled conditions. The objective is to draw up quantitative prediction models which have farm application. This approach suffers from a lack of information on interactions between different inputs and on site to site variations in response and therefore it has high errors of prediction. It also neglects the environmental implications of the inputs and outputs and the social implications of such changes in management. Such research can therefore at best be considered to be imprecise and at worst completely misleading, when used for extension purposes.

Two examples are given below which indicate how conventional research can lead to the wrong answers in practice and to an overuse of non-renewable resources.

*Example 1*

The nitrogen (N) fertilizer recommendations for grassland in the UK are based on the results of harvested plots on different soil types and in different rainfall regions (Morrison *et al.*, 1980). The N input/grass harvested response curves show an average of over 20 kg dry matter output per kg N fertilizer input. In contrast, however, the response to N fertilizer on farms is only about 8 kg dry matter per kg N (Leaver, 1991). The reason for the difference is that the research leading to farmer recommendations was carried out on mechanically harvested plots of newly sown perennial ryegrass. On farms, however, a high proportion of the grassland is less responsive as it is permanent pasture and also nutrients are recycled (about 80% of N eaten is excreted in the faeces and urine). Grazing is less efficient than mechanical harvesting, owing to treading and to rejection of fouled areas, and at low N fertilizer inputs legumes fix atmospheric N to replace fertilizer N. Therefore, there are a large number of reasons why the response of grassland to N fertilizer input is much greater under controlled experimental conditions than under commercial farm conditions.

A consequence of these N recommendations derived from this research is that large amounts of N are wasted. It has been estimated from systems studies (Leaver and Fraser, 1989) that only 12–15% of N brought on to intensive grassland dairy farms in the form of fertilizer and feed goes off the farm in meat and milk. The remainder is lost to the air or to groundwater or is incorporated into the soil organic matter. The environmental implications of this N surplus are greater losses of ammonia and nitrous oxide to the air (the former is associated with acid rain and the latter is a greenhouse gas) and losses of nitrate into groundwater. Apart from these environmental implications, the economics of N fertilizer use on grassland have rarely been studied. In a most comprehensive study (Forbes *et al.*, 1980) carried out on commercial farms, it was found that although N input was significantly and positively correlated with stocking rate and the amount of grass utilized, it was also positively correlated with fixed costs. The correlation between N fertilizer input and profit was consequently zero.

It can be concluded that the use of conventional research methodologies to devise recommendations for farmers has resulted in recommending an over-use of N fertilizer and hence an over-use of a non-renewable energy resource. This has both economic and environmental implications at farm level and a resource use implication globally.

*Example 2*

In dairy cow nutrition, a large body of research has shown that when a forage is offered at a daily amount to satisfy maintenance requirements and concentrates are fed to satisfy the requirements for milk production, there is a curvilinear response to concentrate input. Also, a greater response in milk yield per unit of concentrates occurs with cows of high yield potential compared with those of low (Broster and Thomas, 1981). These findings have formed the basis of feeding recommendations with the core element being that milk yield should be monitored for individual cows and concentrate inputs adjusted accordingly. This led to complex methods of feeding, using automatic milk yield recording at each milking and computerized feeding at in-parlour and out-of-parlour feed stations, utilizing automatic recognition of cows wearing transponders around their necks.

However, research on feeding methods 10–15 years ago began to question the need for such sophistication (Leaver, 1986). Comparisons were made between similar groups of cows fed concentrates individually through transponder-controlled feeders according to their milk yield level or where all cows were fed the same daily amount of concentrates (flat rate). The cows had *ad libitum* access to grass silage, which is the most common forage system found on farms. In ten such comparisons, the sophisticated feeding method never out-produced the flat-rate method and on average the milk production from the flat-rate system was slightly higher.

The explanation for the similarity of production on the two feeding systems is that the forage was offered *ad libitum* and not at maintenance level as in the earlier experiments. Under *ad libitum* forage feeding conditions, the milk yield response per unit of concentrates is similar for high- and low-yielding cows. Thus, the earlier research carried out under controlled atypical farm conditions provided the basis for flawed recommendations to farmers, leading them into large investments in equipment and time.

These two examples illustrate how reductionist research with too narrow a focus can lead to the wrong conclusions when applied to a farm system. This can result in the large over-use of non-renewable resources (N fertilizer in Example 1 and equipment in Example 2). If FSR/E had been applied to these questions of technology inputs to farms, the economic, environmental and social implications of the inputs and outputs would have been examined under farm conditions. These were largely ignored in the two examples, where the emphasis was placed mainly on the input/output relationships of the technologies under controlled experimental conditions.

## The Role of FSR/E

The nature of the FSR/E approach is both holistic and participatory. The holism includes the consideration of environmental and social aspects of farming systems and also economic aspects. Also, the approach considers interactions between these aspects at household, farm and community levels. The participation involves working closely with farmers in identifying constraints and research priorities and where necessary implementing on-farm research together with the farmer. An understanding of the needs and motivations of the farmer is essential.

Motivations for farmers to change may include the potential for increased income and profitability, but for many farmers, life style, less physical work and status are strong influences on which technologies are chosen and used. This participatory approach is important not only in developing sustainable production systems at farm level but also in influencing policy makers in agriculture through feedback to them of information on the constraints being applied to farming systems and their effects on farm households, local communities and local environment

## Use of Non-renewable Resources and Farm Size

The balance between labour input and mechanization changes with farm size. Normally, farms increase in size over time in an attempt by farmers to increase income through scale and also to reduce overhead costs per hectare.

A reduction in energy input per hectare may also result. Table 4.2 confirms the effect on overhead costs in relation to power and machinery, with costs per hectare declining with increased scale at least up to a certain farm size. In contrast, paid labour costs per hectare increase with increasing farm size and as a consequence the total of power, machinery and paid labour costs is fairly similar for farms of different size. The explanation is that on small farms there is a greater proportion of unpaid family labour per hectare. This is of greater importance on livestock farms than arable farms.

Increasing from a small to a larger scale of farming is the normal trend in agricultural development, and satisfies many of the needs of farmers, especially for greater income, less physical work and probably greater status in the local community. The greatest risks associated with such expansion are

**Table 4.2.** Power and machinery costs and labour costs per hectare (£) (from Nix, 1993).

|  | Dairy farms | | Cereal farms | |
|---|---|---|---|---|
|  | Under 50 ha | Over 100 ha | Under 100 ha | Over 200 ha |
| Power and machinery (A) | 370 | 285 | 240 | 195 |
| Paid labour (B) | 180 | 275 | 85 | 115 |
| Unpaid labour | 370 | 65 | 145 | 35 |
| A + B | 550 | 560 | 325 | 310 |

over-gearing of the business and having inadequate management skills for the larger scale operation. FSR/E is one supportive approach which will examine such economic and social factors at the individual farm level.

This conventional model of agricultural development, of increasing farm size, increasing mechanization and reducing labour input, is rarely challenged. However, the positive relationships between scale and efficiency of resource use only apply up to a certain level. The increase in farm scale above the optimum for efficiency is to enable the farm business to generate more total profit and not profit per hectare. In the EC, where subsidy income (especially in the arable and dairy sectors) is related to scale, there will continue to be a strong incentive to increase in size to generate more subsidy (and productivity) income.

The trend towards larger farms utilizing high external input technologies will only be curtailed or reversed if subsidies are switched from production to environmental management initiatives with a sliding scale of payment according to farm size. Charging the true cost of non-renewable resources and of pollution arising from external inputs to the farmer would also reduce inputs.

A further bias is the strong emphasis of research and development on input technologies for the resource-rich farmer. Very little research in Europe is directed at the problems of the smaller farmer, presumably owing to the belief that he/she will soon be out of business. The problems of small farmers are different from those of large farmers. The high mechanization (energy) cost per hectare is one question which requires examination on small farms. The FSR/E approach is an ideal methodology for such studies, both in identifying constraints to the farm, prioritizing the research required and carrying out the research in close relationship with the farmer. Unfortunately, there is little prospect of switching research priorities to solving farmers' problems as opposed to scientists' problems whilst 'agricultural research structures of national and international organizations are driven by bureaucracies under political direction' (Dent, 1990) and whilst these structures are dominated by scientists who have little empathy with farmers.

## Reducing Non-renewable Resource Use on Farms

The non-renewable resources which pose the greatest problems of sustainability in farming practices are set out in Table 4.3.

A significant swing away from using high levels of these inputs in the EC seems unlikely, however, as long as farm products are heavily subsidized (which encourages higher inputs) and the full input costs (including the cost of environmental degradation) are not paid.

Nevertheless, a systems approach should identify where some of the present practices are uneconomic (e.g. N fertilizer application to grassland)

**Table 4.3.** Non-renewable resource inputs used in agriculture: their potential problems and some solutions.

| Inputs to agriculture | Potential problems | Solutions |
|---|---|---|
| Power and machinery | Reliance on non-renewable energy | Alternative energy sources<br>Increase efficiency of use<br>Reduce operations |
| N fertilizer | Reliance on non-renewable energy<br>Pollution | Use of rotations<br>Use of organic manures<br>Use of legumes |
| Pesticides | Reliance on non-renewable energy<br>Pollution<br>Human health | Use of rotations<br>Use of resistant crops<br>Integrate pest management |
| Grain fed to livestock | Reliance on non-renewable energy<br>Intensification contributing to pollution and animal welfare problems | Use of by-products<br>Use of pasture/forages<br>Outdoor systems<br>Deintensify housing |

and begin to develop alternative approaches which are more sustainable through utilizing reduced levels of non-renewable resources. The possible solutions outlined in Table 4.3 require an interdisciplinary approach both to develop appropriate technologies and to examine the environmental and socioeconomic implications arising from the new systems.

# Conclusions

Farming systems research and extension has the potential to reduce non-renewable resource use in agriculture, as it can examine the complex interactions between climate, soil, plant, animal and humans under farm conditions which conventional research cannot. The over-use of N fertilizer on grassland resulting from a conventional research approach is one such example. The research failed to take into account the influence of the animals in the system, especially the effect of recycled nutrients. The holistic approach of FSR/E should also lead to finding solutions to problems more quickly owing to its participative nature in working closely with the people who have the problems, namely farmers. Conventional reductionist science is a necessary part of the overall science strategy, but if it is to be of benefit to agriculture, the results must be tested within a farming systems context.

One criticism of farming systems R & D is that like much other research, it is often methodology driven rather than objective driven. It is important that appropriate methodologies are chosen after the problem to be solved has been clearly identified. This could mean the use of static or dynamic survey analysis, on-farm research, farmlet studies, institution reductionist research, desk-top farm management analyses or simulation modelling. All are valid components of systems research. A further criticism is that too much emphasis is often given to system analysis without the research group being involved in how to change the system for the benefit of farmers and agriculture in general.

Agriculture is a high user of non-renewable resources, especially power and machinery, and nitrogen fertilizer. There is a strong need to institute research programmes which address the question of how to reduce such inputs by developing farming systems which can be considered sustainable. This is an important step within the major question of how to produce enough food globally to feed the rising world population without degrading the natural resources of the planet.

# References

Broster, W.H. and Thomas, C. (1981) The influence of level and pattern of concentrate input on milk output. In: Haresign, W. (ed.) *Recent Advances in Animal Nutrition – 1981.* Butterworths, London, pp. 49–69.

Dent, J.B. (1990) Optimising the mixture of enterprises in a farming system. In: Jones, J.G.W. and Street, P.R. (eds) *Systems Theory Applied to Agriculture and the Food Chain.* Elsevier, Amsterdam, pp. 113–130.

Forbes, T.J., Dibb, C., Green, J.O., Hopkins, A. and Peel, S. (1980) *Factors Affecting the Productivity of Permanent Grassland. A National Farm Study.* GRI/ADAS, Hurley, 141 pp.

Leaver, J.D. (1986) Systems of concentrate distribution. In: Broster, W.H., Phipps, R.H. and Johnson, C.L. (eds) *Principles and Practice of Feeding Dairy Cows.* Technical Bulletin No. 8, NIRD, Reading, pp. 113–131.

Leaver, J.D. (1991) The role of fertilizer nitrogen in the 1990's. In: Mayne, C.S. (ed.) *Management Issues for the Grassland Farmer in the 1990's.* BGS Occasional Symposium No. 25, British Grassland Society, Hurley, pp. 140–150.

Leaver, J.D. and Fraser, D. (1989) A systems study of high and low concentrate inputs for dairy cows. Grassland production and utilisation over four years. *Research and Development in Agriculture* 6, 183–189.

Morrison, J., Jackson, M.V. and Sparrow, P.E. (1980) The response of perennial ryegrass to fertiliser nitrogen in relation to climate and soil. *A Report on the Joint ADAS/GRI Grassland Manuring Trial GM 20.* Technical Report No. 27, Grassland Research Institute, Hurley.

Nix, J. (1993) *Farm Management Pocketbook,* 23rd edn. Wye College, University of London, Ashford, 216 pp.

Stout, B.A. (1990) *Handbook of Energy for World Agriculture.* Elsevier Applied Science, Barking, 504 pp.

# II

## CONTEXTUAL SETTING

# 5

# Farming Systems Approach and its Relevance for Agricultural Development in Central and Eastern Europe

## Werner Doppler

## The Current Situation in the Former Centrally Planned Countries of Central and Eastern Europe

The process of transition from a centrally planned communist to a market-oriented democratic country has a number of common features which create problems in agricultural development. This can be summarized for countries in central and eastern Europe as follows.

According to the Institut für Internationale Wirtschaftsvergleiche (1993), central and eastern European countries have lost 70% of their economic power since 1989. Only Poland and Hungary can expect an increase in gross domestic product by 1–2%, while the Czech Republic is expected to be at the point of moving from negative to positive growth. Russia and the Ukraine will have a further decline of GDP of about 15%. This is associated with extremely high inflation rates of 60% in Poland, 165% in Rumania, 192% in Russia, 35% in Hungary, 58% in the Czech Republic and 480% in Bulgaria in 1991. A further factor is that before 1989, 25–35% of the national workforce in these countries were employed in the agricultural sector. This has decreased dramatically, leading to a high rate of unemployment in rural areas. These developments have resulted in the following consequences:

**1.** The financial resources available at national level for agricultural recovery programmes are extremely limited and at farm level virtually no investment capital is available. Investment capital is urgently needed to finance the transition of land and other resources to private owners and to finance new and additional resources and inputs. This is associated with relatively high interest rates.

**2.** A high unemployment rate, together with a reduced income for large social groups, has led to a general decline in the purchasing power for agricultural products. As a consequence, market conditions for farmers in the rural areas have not improved and are often worse, while in urban areas the demand for agricultural products continues to increase. This highlights the need for improvements and development of marketing and transportation infrastructures.

Administrative and institutional changes have created a vacuum in very important parts of the agricultural sector. This is especially relevant in the following areas:

**1.** The need for strong private farmers' organizations and a rural lobby to inform politicians and society about the economic situation facing farmers, and to urge policy makers to improve the economic conditions for private farmers. This is even more important since the relevance of agriculture, in the view of society as a whole, has declined compared with other sectors such as industrial production.

**2.** Private or public extension services for private farmers were non-existent at the beginning of the transition period. In addition, the financial resources and extension staff experienced in disciplines such as private-oriented farm management and marketing, needed to establish an efficient extension service, were and still are limited. Experience in private farming obviously differs between the countries but is, nevertheless, a basic problem.

**3.** Private marketing organizations need to be established to collect, process, store, transport and market agricultural products and to provide farmers with farm inputs. In central European countries the process of establishing such organizations is currently going on, but the same process has yet to begin in eastern Europe.

In the past, most of the agricultural resources, especially land, were not owned and cultivated by private people (there were exceptions, most notably in Poland and to a lesser extent in the Czech Republic). During the period of transition from a centrally planned to a market economy, ownership of land will be passed to private entrepreneurs. This process will be slow and has not even started in some countries. During the period of transition there will be a lack of:

**1.** a clearly and precisely defined legal framework and of institutions which are in a position to ensure quick transfer of the resources to private hands; the rural sector is characterized by political and administrative deficiencies in areas such as rights to ownership and compensation of former owners;

**2.** financial sources for farm businesses and households to allow them to use the resources at their disposal efficiently and to allow them to reach a position from which they can meet minimum repayment schedules;

**3.** an efficient extension service in addition to a low level of farmer and extension staff knowledge to allow an efficient and rapid transition to the new market-based economy.

The potential for introducing more innovations in farming systems has improved since 1989 owing to improved information about external and international innovations and to a greater motivation of farmers as a consequence of the privatization. However, the reality of the situation is that innovations are only being adopted slowly; if at all. The main bottle-necks are as outlined above (lack of clear tenure, access to credit facilities and an efficient extension service and low levels of farmer knowledge) plus the high risk involved in implementing technologies which have not been tested in the local conditions, and lack of economic returns in some years due to changing market conditions within the country and internationally (especially in relation to the European Union market).

The transition period has created a radical change in the structure of farming systems (Table 5.1). This is of relevance in the following areas:

**1.** The tendency in the transition phase to shift from large-scale farming to medium- and sometimes small-scale family farming requires a radical change in decision making in terms of the setting of objectives, use of farm resources,

**Table 5.1.** Selected indicators for central and eastern European agriculture (1990) (from Werner, 1993).

| Indicators | Poland | Hungary | Czech Republic | Bulgaria | Romania | USSR | Russia |
|---|---|---|---|---|---|---|---|
| Cultivated land ($10^6$ ha) | 18.7 | 6.5 | 6.7 | 6.2 | 14.7 | 557.5 | 222.0 |
| Private farms: | | | | | | | |
| Land ($10^6$ ha) | 11.2[a] | 4.0[b] | – | – | – | 12.0[a] | 7.0 |
| Farm size (ha) | 6.0[a] | 5.0[b] | – | – | – | 25.5[a] | 43.0 |
| Yield (t ha$^{-1}$): | | | | | | | |
| Maize | 49.1 | 40.9 | 34.7 | 29.6 | 27.6 | 36.3 | 17.0[c] |
| Wheat | 39.6 | 51.9 | 54.2 | 43.8 | 32.1 | 22.4 | 18.0[d] |
| Potatoes | 197.9 | 167.6 | 187.0 | 103.6 | 85.1 | 109.5 | 116.0[d] |
| Labour ($\times 10^6$) | 4.4 | 4.8 | 0.9 | 4.1 | 3.0 | 25.8 | 10.2 |
| Self-sufficiency (meat) (%) | 103.0 | 142.0 | 104.0 | 114.0 | 103.0 | 96.0 | – |

[a]1993.
[b]1993, about 40% in part-time farming.
[c]All cereals.
[d]1992.

farm and household organization, marketing of products and procurement of inputs.

**2.** An extreme specialization in agriculture within a country and also between countries in central and eastern Europe has created monocultural farms specializing in cattle, cereals, etc. This approach to farming is highly sensitive to market changes and fails to capitalize on the favourable impacts associated with mixed systems, e.g. transfer of soil fertility between crops. Specialization of production meant that members (employers) of a 'farm' had highly specialized knowledge. This meant that experience in managing a whole farm is missing.

**3.** Markets have changed. New marketing channels are needed and international markets will have to be explored. A new relationship between farms and marketing organization is required and has to be established.

**4.** Private part-time farming and gardening played an important role before 1989 in some countries such as Poland and is currently a stepping stone for private development in agriculture. These forms of production often supply fruits, vegetables, eggs, broilers and wild animals to markets.

The examples discussed above show that there are some similarities between a number of the countries discussed, but in others there are still significant differences. Even within countries differences can be very substantial, as for example between high potential zones such as Györ, Csongrad and Veszprem (Hungary), western and southern Bohemia (Czech Republic) or Poznam, Wroclaw and Lublin (Poland) as compared with other areas.

The question that I will attempt to answer in this chapter is that given the general state of the agricultural sector in central and eastern Europe (as described above), to what extent can a farming systems approach contribute to the solution of these problems?

## The Farming Systems Approach and its Potential

The farming systems approach provides the philosophy, the concept and the strategy for developing and introducing solutions to problems at farm-household and village level. It consists of two components, a holistic and a behavioural component.

### *The holistic component*

The holistic approach is based upon knowledge and experience in systems theory and upon the existing practical knowledge and experience of the local people concerned. Such a holistic concept comprises a systems view which includes the following (Table 5.2):

**1.** The *interdependences and complexity* of the farming systems approach

**Table 5.2.** Definition and description of various stages of the farming systems concept.

| Definition | Holistic approach | | Behavioural approach | |
|---|---|---|---|---|
| | Complexity | Sustainability | Decision making | Farmer's participation |
| Stage I<br>No farming systems concept | Production, commodity approach | Static (current state), no sustainability | Single problem, single objective | No participation |
| Stage II | Production systems | Current state as compared with future ideal stage | Multiple problems and objectives, defined by the researcher | Participation in extension programme |
| Stage III | Resource allocation, whole farm approach | Past dynamics and ideal stage in the future included | Multiple problems and objectives and priorities of families and extension | Participation in researcher-managed on-farm research |
| Stage IV | Farm-household system | Past dynamics, optimization of future development and sustainability | Target groups' objectives combined with objectives of the society and extension | Participation in researcher- and farmer-managed on-farm and in-household research |
| Stage V<br>Ideal farming systems concept | Farm-household system in the socioeconomic environment | Past dynamics, long-term future simulation of development and sustainability | National and target groups' problems and multiple objectives determine research and extension | Participation in on-station, on-farm, in-household research and evaluation as well as in extension |

includes not only the farm, but also household and off-farm activities and considers as central the decisions made by people (e.g. farm families). The farm/household/off-farm activity complex is an instrument. Individuals or families make decisions concerning this complex according to their objectives which result from their view about their problems under the physical, economic, social and cultural conditions given. Such a view overcomes the single commodity, single problem and single objective strategy. Following the decision-oriented farming systems approach, the area of activities will be selected according to families' needs. This guarantees that all those fields which are of relevance and motivate the farming population to improvements will be investigated. Besides production, such fields could be resource conservation, storage and losses, home processing, food security, food preparation in the household, water provision for the household and health care. In addition, the holistic approach will also include families' external relations with their community and their demands for developing, testing and evaluating organizational, social and administrative innovations such as establishing and institutionalizing farmers' cooperation (e.g. through farmers' associations, marketing cooperatives, machinery pools), organizing families (e.g. self-help groups) or in training the rural population.

**2.** The farming systems approach is a *dynamic approach* which serves to understand past development better, to explain why systems have evolved the way they have, to analyse the long-term impact of indigenous solutions to problems, to determine the reasons for failure of concepts and actions for solutions to problems, to obtain information concerning the problems and objectives of individuals, families and communities and to measure the long-term impact of future actions and strategies. This will result in the definition of long-term priorities for action aimed at solving problems which include the indigenous forces and their potential for solving problems and the priorities of the target group.

The dynamics of past and future development in the analysis of farming systems includes an understanding of socioeconomic stability and sustainability. This has two dimensions: (i) seasonal fluctuations in farm, household and off-farm activities due to conditions such as rainfall, market supply and demand, storage losses and sickness and (ii) long-term sustainability, which refers to the potential and sustainable performance of resource use by farms, households and off-farm activities to conserve, or improve, the living standard of the people.

### The behavioural component

The behavioural approach takes into account the objectives and values of the target groups (farmers) and other conditions relevant for decision making. This approach includes the following (Table 5.2):

**1.** The *structure and responsibility of decision making.* Analysis and forecasting of decisions in farm families and at village level are characterized by the decision-making process and the underlying objectives of the decision makers. To understand and explain the decision-making process in a farming system, information and analytical knowledge is needed about:

(a) who (one person, the family, the clan, the village or community, key persons in the village, the tribe) makes decisions in a family about farm and household management and family issues, and the processing and marketing of products, and at communal and regional levels about social and village issues and the allocation of regional resources;

(b) what are the interpersonal and social linkages in decision making, for instance the relationships within a family concerning such questions as the role of men, women, children and old people, the relationships within the society of a village or clan concerning such things as the role of village chiefs, tribal chiefs, priests, traders, money lenders, landlords, extension service and foreign experts and the relationship to culture concerning, for example, taboos, social norms and customs and rules;

(c) who benefits and in what way they benefit from any change or from unchanged situations and what the chances and consequences are of taking away these benefits.

The objectives of decision makers form the basis for decisions. Analyses of these objectives will therefore have to include questions such as:

(a) what is the relationship between needs, objectives and motivation of farmers and families?;

(b) what are the objectives, the structure of multiple objectives and their relationship within a family, between families belonging to the same farming system and to other interest groups?

**2.** A *participative element.* Since the decisions of people (individuals, families, village societies, etc.) are central to the decision-oriented farming systems approach, their behaviour is also of central importance. This requires the involvement of farmers in testing, evaluating and selecting possible solutions (innovations). Adopting such an approach ensures that innovations have been proved under farmers' conditions, which in reality means under conditions of scarcity of resources, rising costs, changing environmental conditions and policy and market irregularities. Using the experience of local people to find solutions which are considered suitable by farmers can transfer information quickly to farmers and increase their motivation for adoption. The approach, therefore, overcomes the top-down concept and gives room for a bottom-up strategy or elements of it to be developed.

An ideal concept helps to clarify the definition and the objectives of the concept, but has to be seen under the conditions of the real world. The farming systems approach is meant to move towards an ideal situation and concept. In reality, the approach may never reach the ideal situation but the stages involved in moving to that end-point have been defined in Table 5.2.

## Contribution to Agricultural Development in Central and Eastern Europe and Institutionalization Needs

### Possible contributions of the farming systems approach

There are a number of areas where the potential of the farming systems approach could be utilized to improve agricultural development in those central and eastern European countries which are in transition from centrally planned to free market economies. These are:

**1.** The suitability of the approach to determine the optimum strategy for private farms with respect to farm size (land ownership, renting of land), capital investment (machinery, buildings) and diversification of production and marketing (typical problems of the transition period).

In terms of the transition period, the following observations can be noted: (i) privatization of land leads to smaller farm sizes; (ii) the need for suitably sized machinery and buildings for the smaller and diversified farms, which requires a large financial investment by the private farms; and (iii) a higher degree of diversification of agricultural production in one farm including livestock and crop mixtures. The introduction of the farming systems approach can solve the problems associated with these developments, but also offers the possibility of determining the consequences of change within a framework of policy impact analysis. The most relevant areas where a farming systems approach would provide guidance are in determining:

> **(a)** the optimum size of family farms under different conditions (minimum area for long-term sustainable income and living standards); this could help in allocating land (ownership, land markets), and in defining credit facilities and the terms associated with that credit;
> **(b)** the optimum mix of small- and large-scale farms and of full- and part-time farming related to industrial development and employment in rural areas;
> **(c)** the level of mechanization under different cost and price scenarios and labour availability in rural areas; this will have an impact on employment in villages, on credit requirements, on intensity of production and on the type and volume of agricultural products sold in markets;
> **(d)** suitable pricing policies and the need for subsidization in the short- and long-term, and the consequences of such policies on farming systems development, market supply and demand and national budget.

**2.** The suitability of the approach to take into account the close relationship between farm, household and off-farm activities in addition to the external associations with the surrounding communities such as a village.

In the newly emerging private family farms, households and off-farm activities are much more closely related and play a considerable role in farm families' decision making. Off-farm jobs and hence part-time farming may increase in the future. The objectives of these families differ from those of the former state farms and show a mixture of maximization of farm and family incomes, ensuring liquidity, and in some countries the provision of a subsistence supply for the family with respect to food, water, housing, clothcs, health, education and relieving the drudgery of work. Social aspects are also of relevance. The decision-oriented farming systems approach, where farm, household and off-farm activities are considered as a system in which families or family members decide according to their multiple objectives, is highly suitable for the emerging family farms as described above. The farming systems approach therefore can be used for analysing farming systems development and to better understand and explain why change is occurring in a particular way and, as a result, determine possible new paths for improvement based on farmers' views.

**3.** The suitability of the approach to develop, test and evaluate (in cooperation with extension agents) innovations in agricultural production, resource economics, processing, storage and marketing in cooperation with farmers.

The liberalization and privatization of the agricultural and related sectors has increased the possibility that innovations (solutions to farmers' problems) can be developed, tested and offered to farmers by an institution or private company. Farmers who demand such innovations will only accept new ideas or buy the new innovative technology, or organizational concepts, if they believe that they will benefit from it. A liberal market for innovations tends to prefer solutions which match the farmers' hierarchy of priorities. Both private companies and public extension services will therefore include and influence farmers' views with respect to the relevance of innovation. Participation is one of the most efficient strategies to ensure that the farmers' readiness to adopt offered solutions is high. This has a direct impact on the efficiency of extension services and on the economic benefit of private companies.

The participative element of the farming systems approach considers farmers as a part of the research and extension programmes. Their contribution to the development and evaluation of technical, organizational, social and administrative innovations allows extension services to offer solutions which are more appropriate to farmers' problems. This will include a wide range of technical innovations in production, processing and storage, and also organizational innovations on the farm (farm management knowledge), with marketing of agricultural products and in the procurement of the means of production – including credit. Farmers' associations, cooperatives, machinery pools or self-help groups might have to be developed in those situations where farm families cannot cope with their problems on their own.

**4.** Suitability as an instrument for extension and farmers' participation. Private or public extension services for private farmers were completely missing at the beginning of the transition period. There is an urgent need to establish an efficient extension service and to recruit extension staff experienced in disciplines such as private-oriented farm management or marketing. The farming systems approach cannot contribute to the establishment of an institution, but can be the basis for the training of needed staff. With respect to training, the same applies for marketing organizations in the agricultural sector and the farmers themselves.

**5.** The suitability of the approach as an instrument for policy impact analysis. Farming systems-based policy impact studies provide policy makers and administrators with information about farmers' reactions to alternative policies. In the transition period there is a specific need for such evidence in developing policies related to land ownership, credit facilities and use of investment capital, market conditions and training of farmers (e.g. in farm management).

Besides these main areas in which the farming systems approach can contribute to improvement of family farms, there are a number of beneficiaries and related benefits associated with adopting the approach. These are summarized in Table 5.3.

### *Institutionalization of the farming systems approach*

The application of the farming systems approach can be an individual issue, but can also be accepted as a general strategy for dealing with agricultural development in a country. If such an approach is to be introduced and adopted within institutions then there is a need to ensure that the approach is institutionalized. This is especially important if the approach is to be applied in all relevant organizations contributing and dealing with farming systems development. The most relevant subsectors and institutions are as follows:

**1.** *Agricultural and rural development faculties at universities:* Curricula require adjustment to incorporate multi- and interdisciplinary courses and provide the linkages to extension services and farmers so that students experience the problems of application under practical conditions. The introduction of a farming systems approach at universities would lead to the provision of systems-trained academics, extension staff in public and private extension, research staff in universities and national research centres and administrators in ministries and similar institutions.

**2.** *Public and private extension:* The introduction of the farming systems approach to regional (or even country-wide) extension services is one of the major preconditions for an efficient use of the approach. It requires reorganization of the extension service so that several disciplines (as long as there are

**Table 5.3.** Beneficiaries and benefits expected from and introduction of the farming systems approach.

---

A sustainable increase in the living standard of the farm family because the solutions being offered are:
- better adjusted to their situation;
- targeted at those problems they give highest priority;
- leading to an improvement in the farmers' knowledge and experience due to active participation;
- contributing to the reduction of risk and their dependence on other persons and institutions leading to an increase in social security;
- contributing to the conservation of the resource base of the family.

Research institutions and extension services:
- staff who better understand the complexity of the farm-household system and its values and the priorities of farmers and their decision-making processes;
- adoption rates as a criteria for the success of research and extension will increase and hence improve the efficiency of extension provision.

Regional administration:
- easier administration of a single but complex strategy in a region as compared with several different but simple strategies;
- rural deficit analysis sets priorities for regional activities.

National policy decision units:
- improvement of the information base through policy impact analysis showing the consequences of actual or potential future policies at micro and regional level;
- reduction of risk as policy impact analysis provides a warning instrument for future crises and/or the impact of no policy decisions.

---

no general systems experts available) act in a team searching for solutions to problems and discuss these with the farmers. Such an organization initially requires a high degree of discipline and team work. In addition, cooperation with other institutions, such as universities and research centres, is important. In reality, it is often found that research and extension are found in two different institutions which are often independent of each other. A common feature is that under such conditions, research institutions tend to have their own extension component, and extension institutions their own research component. Therefore, resources are usually not used at an optimum level of efficiency.

**3.** *Administration:* The acceptance of the farming systems approach in ministries and other similar institutions is relevant, since decisions to introduce this approach at a national level are made here, and the use of the results of farming systems policy impact studies will have to be accepted here if they are to contribute to more realistic policy decisions. Staff training is required to familiarize them with the potential of the systems approach.

# Constraints and the Future Outlook

The introduction of the farming systems approach in central and eastern European countries during the transition from centralized to market-based economies is facing severe constraints and these constraints may reduce the future level of penetration of the approach.

## *Constraints*

**1.** To introduce the farming systems approach would require a large number of staff who have experience with this approach. None of the countries experiencing change is in a position to provide enough local staff. Since external staff cannot be provided in such large numbers and will not be accepted by those countries, there is no realistic chance of generally applying the farming systems approach immediately for handling the typical problems of the transition period. Even the introduction of the farming systems approach as a long-term strategy would require external support in the form of staff and financial resources. It is likely that such support will only be provided on a limited scale within the next 8–10 years, therefore reducing the chances of the adoption of country-wide farming systems programmes within this period.

**2.** The introduction of such an approach requires the support of the existing institutions.

**(a)** The existing universities within the countries can act as a starting point. Within these institutions there are a number of staff who support the adoption of a farming systems strategy based on private farming. Universities can be expected to show the highest degree of readiness to accept the concept and it is for this reason that the introduction of the farming systems concept should start there.

**(b)** Existing institutions for agricultural extension will have to follow a completely different strategy. Before they are able to develop innovations and train farmers, the extension services require reorganization and a new philosophy. The political and administrative problems involved in establishing or reorganizing existing institutions indicate that a period of 2–10 years is needed before efficient and experienced organizations and staff are available. In central Europe the period can be expected to be shorter than in eastern European countries. Once the extension services are well established, comprehensive training programmes for extension staff will be needed. In many countries the current situation does not allow such a strategy to be started because there is a lack of manpower, financial resources and political will to establish new, or reorganize existing, extension services.

## Future outlook

At present the only realistic chance for a general introduction of the farming systems approach is by embedding the concept in university teaching and research programmes. This will require international cooperation and some training. It can be expected that the adoption of farming systems approaches will occur slowly over a period of time, ranging from a few years in countries such as Poland, the Czech Republic or Hungary, but taking much longer in eastern European countries. The introduction of a farming systems-oriented extension service as a country-wide strategy might be realistic in a few cases within the next 10 years, but again the process will require a much longer time horizon in eastern Europe. Such a realistic view is more relevant than looking at the introduction of the farming systems approach from any idealistic point of view.

# Further Reading

Bedu, L., Martin, C., Knepfler, M., Tallec, M. and Urbino, A. (1987) Appui pédagogique a l'analyse du milieu rural dans perspective de développement. In: *Documents Systèmes Agraires*. Department Systèmes Agraires du CRAD, Montpellier.

Doppler, W. (1993a) *Application of the Farming Systems Development Concept in Development Projects*. Technical Paper, Farm Systems Management Series, No. 5. FAO, Rome.

Doppler, W. (1993b) Contribution of the farming systems approach to regional food security and rural infrastructure. In: Thimm, H.-U. and Hahn, H. (eds) *Regional Food Security and Rural Infrastructure. Proceedings of an International Symposium*, Vol. I. LIT-Verlag, Münster, Hamburg.

Doppler, W. and Maurer (1993) Farming systems development in academic training. In: *The Institutionization of Farming Systems Development. Proceedings of a Technical Meeting at FAO, Rome*. FAO, Rome.

FAO (1990) *Farming Systems Development – Guide-lines for the Conduct of a Training Course in Farming Systems Development*. FAO, Rome.

FAO (1992) *Applying a Farming Systems Perspective to Agricultural Development*. FAO, Rome.

Friedrich, K. and Hall, M. (1990) Developing sustainable farm-household systems: the FAO response to challenge. In: Seepersal, J., Pemperton, C. and Young, G. (eds) *Farm Household Analyses, Planning and Development. Proceedings of a Regional Workshop*. University of the West Indies.

Institut für Internationale Wirtschaftsvergleiche, Vienna, various reports; cited by Werner (1993).

Schrader, J.V. (1993) Optionen für die Agrarpolitik osteiropäischer Reformländer. Privatisieren und dem Wettbewerb aussetzen? *VDL Journal* 4, 8–10.

Tripp, P. and Wooley, J. (1989) *The Planning Stage of On-farm Research: Identification Factors for Experimentation*. CIMMYT, Mexico D.F., Mexico and CIAT, Cali, Colombia.

Werner, M. (1993) Entwicklungstrends in der osteuropäischen Landwirtschaft. Bruchlinien trennt die Reformstaaten. *VDL Journal* 4, 4–7.

Wolff, H.-P. (1992) *Training Program on Farming Systems Approach in Ethiopia*. Mimeo, Hohenheim.

# 6

# INSTITUTIONALIZATION OF AGRICULTURAL EXTENSION IN ESTONIA: Appraisal and Prospects for Development

*Ivar Dembovski*

## Background Information

### Current role of agriculture in the Estonian economy

Estonia comprises 4.5 million ha of which 32.2% was agricultural land and 44.7% was under forests in January 1993. Of the agricultural land 78.5% was arable and the rest under natural pastures (Vanatoa, 1993). In 1992, the total population was 1.56 million with over 28% of the total population living in rural areas (Ministry of Agriculture of Estonia, 1992).

In 1990, agriculture provided approximately 12% of employment (Ministry of Agriculture of Estonia, 1992) and in 1992 accounted for 12% of the gross domestic product, having declined to this level from 19.6% in 1989 (National Statistics Board of Estonia, 1992). During the first quarter of 1993, agricultural products comprised 20.1% of total Estonian exports and 13.3% of total imports (Aasmäe, 1993; Anon., 1993a) with 65.3% of agricultural production being exported during the first two months of 1993 (BNS, 1993).

### Agricultural policy orientation and agriculture since the restoration of independence

Since the restoration of independence during the period 1989–1991, the government has been preoccupied with reforms in all major aspects of life in Estonia. In agriculture, the land reform and the agricultural property reform were started in 1992, with the aim of returning land and property to its former owners, or their descendants, and establishing private ownership of agricultural enterprises. Collective and state farms are being reorganized into new enterprises that are generally smaller in size and typically have a business structure of a partnership, limited company, cooperative or a sole trader (family farm). In many cases the new enterprises consist of individual self-contained production units of the former large-scale farms. Family farms are being established in parallel to the reform of large-scale farms, often on the basis of farms that existed before World War II. The developments in the structure of farming systems in Estonia between 1939 and 1992 are illustrated in Fig. 6.1.

By the beginning of 1993, the reorganization had started in most of the large-scale farms and approximately 100 collective and state farms (out of the total of 360) had been reorganized into over 1300 new enterprises by the spring of 1993 (Leetsar, 1993). Data are not yet available about the size of the post-reform enterprises. The new enterprises include not only agricultural production, but also enterprises that provide services to producers and rural communities (warehouses, workshops, transport enterprises, construction, central heating, shops, child care, etc.). These services have also been established on the basis of the various units of former large-scale farms.

The establishment of family farms started in 1988, somewhat earlier than the agricultural reform. The number of family farms has increased to over 8500, as can be seen in Fig. 6.1. In December 1992, the average size of a family farm was 25.6 ha, of which 11.1 ha was arable land. In January 1993, the family farms made use of 8.5% of total arable land (Eesti Vabariigi Pôllumajandusministeerium, 1993).

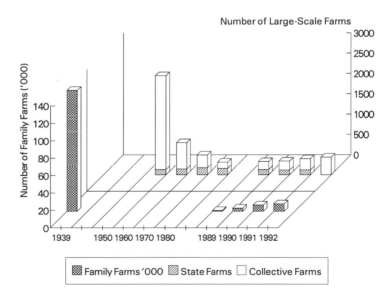

**Fig. 6.1.** Changes in the structure of farming systems (Estonia 1939–1992). Note: data for collective farms for 1992 includes state farms. (From Järvesoo, 1978; Ministry of Agriculture of Estonia, 1992; Eesti Vabariigi Pôllumajandusministeerium, 1993.)

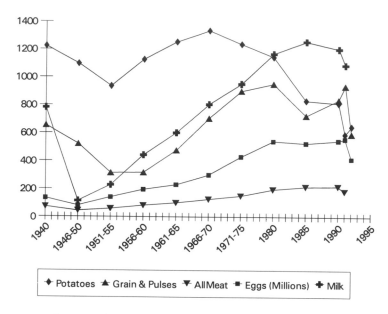

**Fig. 6.2.** Annual output of main agricultural products in Estonia (thousands of tons). (From Järvesoo, 1978; Ministry of Agriculture of Estonia, 1992; Eesti Vabariigi Põllumajandusministeerium, 1993).

There has been a considerable decline in agricultural output since 1990. Figure 6.2 illustrates the long-term trends in the output of main agricultural products in Estonia.

The recent decline in output has been caused mainly by two factors:

**1.** collapse of the markets for agricultural output, unreliability of supplies of inputs and a deterioration of the ratio of prices received for produce to inputs;
**2.** the temporary disintegrating influence of the radical reforms in agriculture because the new production and administrative structures do not yet function and as the managers of the old structures, being insecure about their future, have not been interested in making efforts to maintain production.

The difficulties of Estonian agricultural producers and food-processing enterprises have been deepened by exports of agricultural produce to Estonia from other countries at dump prices.

The productivity of agriculture in Estonia before the beginning of the reforms was significantly lower than in the neighbouring countries of Sweden and Finland, where the climatic conditions are comparable. The weighted average crop (barley, oats, rye and potatoes) yield per hectare in Finland was 140% and in Sweden 223% of that in Estonia on the basis of 1988–1989 harvests. The average annual milk yield per cow in Sweden and in Finland was over 150% of the yield in Estonia (USCIA, 1992). According to the Ministry of Agriculture of Estonia, productivity has declined further since 1988–1989.

The number of people employed in agriculture is declining as the new private agricultural enterprises are more conscious of the effective use of labour and as the demand for foodstuffs has reduced owing to the low purchasing power of the population. According to the Central Bureau of Statistics, agricultural jobs accounted for 52.4% of the total decrease of jobs in Estonia during the first quarter of 1993 (Anon., 1993b).

In this situation, a heated discussion is going on about whether protection and support should be provided for agriculture. On the one hand, the producers are putting pressure on the government to introduce import restrictions and to establish public financial support for agricultural production. On the other hand, the government, which follows a general orientation towards free trade, is reluctant to establish any protectionist measures for agriculture as it would cause an escalation of inflation by increasing the prices of food, which are already high in comparison with wages. In addition, protectionism would create unwanted problems in foreign trade relations. However, even if the political will existed for providing price support, the budgetary constraints in the current economic situation leave very limited resources available for subsidies. The outcome of current discussions still remains to be seen. No clearly expressed long-term agricultural production policy has been agreed as yet. Regardless of whether the free trade policy is continued or whether protectionist measures are introduced, it is in the national economic interests to achieve an efficient agricultural industry.

Given the low productivity of agriculture, the relatively high importance of agriculture in the economy in terms of its share in the GDP, in foreign trade and the provision of employment, and the significance (in terms of size) of the rural population, the agricultural policy makers are facing a need to devise a comprehensive policy that has two main dimensions:

**1.** Agricultural development – achievement of an efficient and competitive agriculture, capable of satisfying domestic demand and producing for export. Such development would improve agriculture's contribution to the balance of trade by earning foreign exchange and also avoiding unnecessary expenditure on imports of agricultural products that can be, and have traditionally been, produced locally.
**2.** Rural economic development and diversification – this should aim to develop non-farm enterprises in order to produce appropriate infrastructures for the post-reform agriculture, to provide employment opportunities for rural people who become redundant in agriculture and to contribute to economic growth in general.

The development of a strong and efficient agricultural extension service can have a significant impact in achieving these goals.

# Conceptual Background to the Institutionalization of Extension in Estonia

It has become increasingly acknowledged by those writing about agricultural extension that within countries, a complex of multiple private and public extension institutions exist. The term 'agricultural extension complex' has been used by Rivera and Gustafson (1991) to express the complexity of issues related to extension activities and institutions. In the context of this paper, the term 'extension complex' will be used to refer to the complex of different institutions that provide advice to agricultural/rural communities within a country.

The extension complex contains a number of elements (specialized extension organizations or extension arms of organizations which have a different main purpose), that carry out extension work to suit a number of different interests, exercised by various institutions/groups in a society. Such elements are created when an institution/group in the society wishes to influence the behaviour of a certain target audience in the group's interests by providing information and knowledge about particular issues or products to that audience. The types of institutions and social groups with potential interests in extension can be clustered on the basis of their motives for providing advice to agricultural and rural communities as illustrated in Fig. 6.3. The interests of different groups can be of fundamentally different natures, for example, broad societal interests (such as concern about sufficient

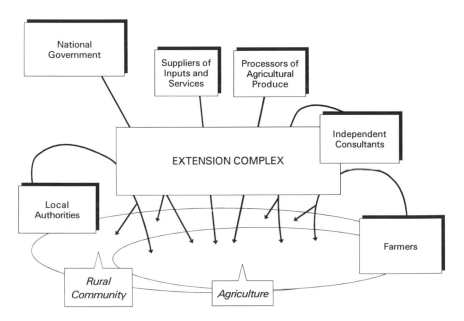

**Fig. 6.3.** Groups of institutions with potential interest in agricultural extension.

supplies of food, overall economic development, improvement of the viability of communities and/or protection of the environment) or private economic interests (such as economic gain of individuals or organizations from increased production or sales).

On the basis of the experience in western Europe, the following types of institutions/groups can be distinguished:

- *National Government and the Local Authorities*, which address the farming community and the rural population with wider national or local interests in mind, although farmers' interests are also mentioned.
- *Farmers* form a special group in the sense that they employ extension workers or consultants in their own interest either directly (group of farmers employing an adviser) or through their own political or economic organizations (associations or cooperatives) in addition to using the extension services provided by other types of groups/institutions.
- *Processing Industries* may direct advisory efforts to farmers in order to ensure a stable supply of commodities of an appropriate quality from farmers. In this case, the advisory work is carried out in the interests of increased profits and competitiveness of the industry itself, but again with the stated parallel goal of achieving farmers' interests.
- *Suppliers of Inputs and Services* may provide advice to farmers on how to make best use of the services and inputs supplied by the organization. The motive is to demonstrate the benefits, popularize the product and thus hopefully to obtain further purchases and attract more customers.
- *Independent Consultants*, in the form of businesses or sole entrepreneurs that provide advisory and information services as a main line of business. The independent consultants derive their income solely from advisory work and their main interest is to sell good-quality advice, relevant to the needs of farmer clients, and thus to maximize their own profits. For this reason, the group of independent consultants is shown in Fig. 6.3 as being partly within the extension complex and not outside as with other groups, for which the provision of advice is an activity in support of the achievement of their other interests.

All of the above groups can operationalize their interests in various organizational arrangements and can be classified accordingly (Rivera, 1988; unpublished work, 1989). The above distinction between interest groups is of an abstract nature but provides a basis for analysis. In reality, the different groups often combine their interests in one organization, for example, arrangements where farmers' associations have government support for running extension services or where farmers set up cooperatives for providing services for themselves, such as marketing, processing, input supply, etc. Over time, the interests of different groups may change from being consistent to being in conflict as the agricultural, economic and social situation evolves. As

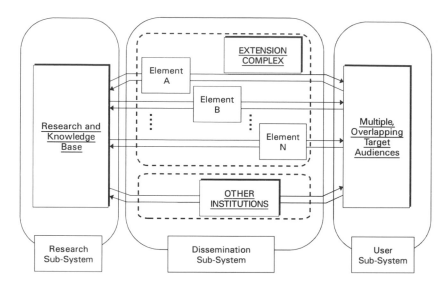

**Fig. 6.4.** The extension complex in the agricultural knowledge and information system perspective. (Partly based on Röling, 1988, p. 201, referring to Nagel, 1980, p. 34.)

a result, the structure of the extension complex will change.

In Fig. 6.4, the complex of extension organizations is placed into the context of the agricultural knowledge system as illustrated in Röling (1988, p. 201). Each element of the extension complex provides a vehicle for carrying a part of the cycle of knowledge- and information-related processes (indicated with two-way arrows in Fig. 6.4), that take place within an agricultural knowledge and information system (AKIS). Such processes include anticipation, generation, transformation, operationalization, transmission, storage, retrieval, dissemination, utilization and evaluation of relevant information and knowledge (Röling, 1988 after Nagel, 1980; Röling and Engel, 1991). It is important to bear in mind that the organizations of the extension complex form only a part of the dissemination subsystem. In addition, other vehicles for the AKIS processes are provided by institutions such as education and media.

During the Soviet period, the dissemination subsystem in Estonia did not contain institutions that are in this chapter referred to as elements of an extension complex. This absence of extension services may be explained (as will be shown below), by the differences between the wider social and economic systems in the former Soviet and western societies. The characteristics of the wider economic and social system have an impact on the institutionalization of AKIS processes by determining several key parameters of the environment in which the AKIS actors operate.

Various producers and other actors have, in an open and dynamic society such as most western economies, an essential need for up-to-date information about the state of the different systems that their activities are related to. Access to such information is crucial to the survival and successful functioning of the actors in a competitive environment. Therefore, in a dynamic society, where the self-regulatory influence of the market is present, a need exists for institutions, such as extension, that continuously provide the actors with information and knowledge vital for decision making. In a centrally planned economic system (such as that formerly present in Estonia), the need for such institutions did not exist as changes were slow, little competition existed and the various actors had little freedom in their decision making. The producers, distributors and input suppliers were all prescribed what commodities, in what quantities, at what prices and to which outlets to produce and/or supply. Even the methods of production (e.g. the time of sowing and harvesting, the production technology) were at times dictated by the authorities. The dissemination of management-related knowledge and information was carried out by institutions such as central planning authorities and the media. Technical information was disseminated in formal education institutions (degree or in-service training courses) or through direct links between research organizations and the large-scale farms.

The recent reforms in Estonian society have brought with them a significant degree of freedom for various actors who now operate in a very open economic environment that is largely determined by market forces. Various agriculture-related actors are experiencing a lack of information about their environment which makes their situation insecure. Therefore, it can be expected that action will be taken to reduce the uncertainty of their situation by setting up mechanisms which help the actors to obtain information on a day-to-day basis, to generate an understanding of the changing environment and to take appropriate action. Such mechanisms can be institutionalized into various extension organizations controlled in the interests of the various groups/institutions as outlined above.

## Appraisal of Sources of Agricultural Advice in Estonia

In 1992, an appraisal of the complex of organizations involved in the provision of advice to agricultural producers in Estonia was carried out. The appraisal formed part of a wider project which had the objective of devising a general strategy for the establishment of a comprehensive nationwide extension service in Estonia. The project was financed by the Ministry of Agriculture of Estonia and executed at the Institute of Rural Development of Estonia (IRDE) under the leadership of the author.

## Methods of appraisal

The situation was analysed in three steps:

**1.** Initially, in January 1992, a one-day rapid appraisal session was organized, with 56 participants from a large variety of institutions concerned with agricultural production, education, research, advice and administration in Estonia. The participants were divided into three groups, each of which concentrated their attention on one of the following three aspects: the existing and potential suppliers of advice, the existing and potential consumers of advice and the current and potential topics of advice. Using the knowledge and experience of the participants, the groups compiled lists of issues/organizations regarding their relevant topics. Thereafter, the groups provided feedback to each other during a participatory workshop relating their findings to those of the other groups, and providing their own perspectives.

**2.** The rapid appraisal session was followed, over the next six weeks, by a series of fact-finding visits to the organizations involved in providing information and advice to farmers in all administrative regions of Estonia.

**3.** As a next step, the project incorporated a series of networking activities including meetings in various institutions and three intensive organization–development workshops (ODW). The three ODWs, held in March, June and September 1992 and lasting three days each, used a method developed at the IRDE, which involves a sequence of participatory workshops with multiple groups and presentation/feedback plenary sessions. The ODWs were primarily aimed at building a consensus among the various institutions (providers and consumers of advice, research organizations, policy makers) about the direction in which agricultural/rural extension in Estonia should be developed. The emphasis in this was mainly on building a national advisory service. The discussions during the ODWs provided further insight into the existing extension arrangements and activities as a by-product.

## Organizations involved in provision of advice

The main conclusion of the appraisal was that the agricultural advisory activities, which had started to develop within a number of different organizations, were in general insufficient because they were underfunded and lacked coordination. At that point, no organization had agricultural extension as its main priority, although a number of organizations provided limited agricultural advice. The sources of advice can be categorized into the following three groups:

**1.** organizations with structural units in all 15 administrative regions of Estonia;

**2.** single organizational structures of nationwide importance that provide advice as an institution or where individual members of staff advise farmers in addition to performing their primary duties;

**3.** experienced individuals who share their expertise with producers (often in the immediate vicinity) either informally or formally for a fee or other kinds of remuneration.

### Category I: organizations with offices nationwide

In the first category, there were four groups of organizations: (1) Agricultural Producers' Unions; (2) Family Farmers' Unions; (3) Departments of Agriculture of Regional Governments; and (4) a network of Training Centres. The precise arrangements, relationships between the organizations and the level of advisory activity varied from region to region. In some regions the organizations worked closely together pooling their resources, but elsewhere rivalry existed. A general outline of these four types of organizations is given below.

The Agricultural Producers' Unions and the Family Farmers' Unions are economic, and to some extent political, organizations of the main groups of agricultural producers: large-scale farms and the agricultural enterprises created on the basis of such farms, in the first case, and the newly established family farms in the second. The two organizations were mainly concerned with obtaining supplies and finding outlets for their members. The advice provided by the Producers' Unions was very limited and confined to information and suggestions regarding marketing and supplies. The Family Farmers' Unions employed advisers with different technical and economic specializations, but much of the advisers' time was spent on obtaining and distributing supplies, state support and credit in addition to actually marketing the produce of family farms.

The Regional Authorities employed in most cases an adviser who had the task of facilitating the agrarian reform by explaining the procedures set for reorganizing state and collective farms. In one region an advisory centre had been established by the authorities with specialists in animal husbandry, arable farming and agricultural economics with a mandate to make their expertise available to all producers regardless of the union to which they belonged.

A network of Training Centres had been established during the Soviet rule, one in each region, for providing in-service and vocational training to skilled workers and middle-level managers of collective and state farms. As a result of the reforms, the demand for such centres in their previous form disappeared, which led to attempts to start providing advice to the new production structures. Owing to financial difficulties, most of the Regional Centres were being closed down or incorporated into one of the above organizational types at the time of the appraisal. The headquarters of the former network had been reorganized into an independent Training and Advisory Centre.

*Category II: single organizations of nationwide importance*

In the second category, a number of specialized and general organizations can be mentioned, that were standing alone in the sense that they did not have any regional or local branches or offices. It was identified that advice was mainly provided on the initiative of individual members of staff, but examples of formal contracts and projects involving institutions and producers were also found. Such organizations include:

*   The Agricultural University;
*   Agricultural and Forestry Research Institutes (including analytical facilities);
*   The Higher School of Agrarian Management, a specialized in-service management training and consultancy institution [the Higher School of Agrarian Management was attached to the Agricultural University in 1993 and is currently known as the Institute of Rural Development of Estonia (IRDE)];
*   Agricultural colleges with different specializations, located in various regions; at one of the colleges a training and advisory centre has been established by the National Family Farmers' Union;
*   Plant protection, plant breeding, artificial insemination and veterinary institutions.

In general, the organizations in the categories I and II were experiencing severe financial difficulties as the funding from the government had been significantly reduced or withdrawn completely. Only the organizations involving newly established family farmers have received some support, but this was not adequate or sufficiently secure for them to set up and develop appropriate advisory services. It was perceived by those who participated in the appraisal that agricultural producers would not have the resources nor willingness to establish and/or maintain a national advisory service in the current conditions as the terms of trade for agriculture have deteriorated considerably. However, the possibility of producers contributing towards the cost of advice was considered as realistic and desirable.

*Category III: independent/individual consultants*

The third category, independent consultants, overlaps considerably with the first two categories of organizations that act to some extent as sources of advice. Such overlap results from the fact that often the members of staff of the various organizations have a private 'practice' in addition to their job-related duties. However, a number of individuals were identified who had no relation to the organizations in the first two categories. For example, the graduate specialists of former large-scale farms and other people with special skills (e.g. computer and engineering skills), who are well known locally, are often approached by the new agricultural enterprises and family farmers for advice and services. In 1990, a database of persons who indicated their willingness to work as advisers/consultants was compiled at the IRDE. Details of almost 100 individuals were recorded. In the spring of 1992, half of them were surveyed to identify whether they were actually involved in advisory work. All those who responded (29) had been providing advice, mostly as a supplementary activity to full-time employment in some other organization. The frequency ranged from a few times a month to ten times a week. The respondents together covered a wide range of topics, including arable farming, animal husbandry, land improvement, accounts, legal issues of establishment of private farms, use of computers, construction and design and heating systems.

### Other sources

No indication was found of advice being provided by input supply organizations or processing/marketing organizations. Such organizations are currently undergoing privatization and reorganization. The processing organizations face a need for technological modernization and are experiencing severe problems in marketing, which result from payment difficulties in their traditional markets in the former USSR, decline in the local demand due to reduced purchasing power of the population and from increased competition from foreign companies. The sales of farm inputs have also reduced as a result of the rapid decline in the profitability and volume of agricultural production. Given this background, it is understandable that the participants of the initial rapid appraisal session identified the supply and processing organizations as potential consumers rather than potential providers of advice.

## Prospects for Development

All the institutions/groups with potential interest in developing advisory activities, identified earlier, operate within an environment created by existing economic conditions and the orientation of government policies. This environment has an effect on the scope that such institutions/groups have for developing advisory activities.

In the Introduction, it was indicated that agriculture is an important branch of the Estonian economy, which is not as productive as it could be. It was shown that agricultural production is currently in decline owing to the loss and contraction of markets, and as a result of the initial effect of radical reforms affecting the ownership and systems of farming. This has caused a severe economic depression in rural areas. It was also clear that an orientation towards free trade is being followed by the government regardless of the pressure from agricultural producers for protection and subsidies.

In this situation, a number of implications arise regarding the prospects for developing extension activities by different institutions/groups with potential interest:

- *The public and the agricultural producers:* it is in the interests of both society at large and the farmers to improve the efficiency of agriculture. Therefore, an arrangement should be reached where advice on issues related to productivity and efficiency in agriculture is financed jointly. In parallel with this, public support should be given to developing the producers' ability to adjust to market requirements and penetrate markets as this would increase the long-term sustainability of agricultural production.
- *The public and the rural entrepreneurs:* the development of non-agricultural economic activities in rural areas is becoming increasingly important in bringing about growth in the economy in general and achieving economic and social sustainability of rural communities. Therefore, extension work relating to business development in rural areas should be supported by the National and Local Governments.
- *Organizations concerned with farm produce* are likely to develop an increasing interest in providing advice to farmers in order to improve product quality and reduce the seasonality of supplies of produce from farms, as this will improve the chances for survival of such organizations in an environment of increasing competition.
- *Farm input supply organizations* cannot be expected to develop a considerable involvement in the provision of advice unless such a move improves their sales, which is unlikely in the conditions of decline in agriculture.
- *Independent consultants:* the scope for the activities of independent consultants will contract if the provision of advice on a free-of-charge basis is established by other organizations, but could increase if a fee-paying organization was instigated.

In 1993, the Ministry of Agriculture of Estonia financed the development, at the IRDE, of draft legislation for establishing the Chamber of Rural Commerce – a parastatal umbrella organization controlled by agricultural, agriculture-related and non-agricultural rural producers. According to the working party which developed the draft, the functions of the Chamber of Rural Commerce would be to: (i) represent the interests of the various rural producers in negotiations with Government and in the development of policy and regulations; and (ii) be responsible for developing and managing the advisory and various information services as well as in-service (re)training of the rural workforce (Kraak, 1993; Tamm, 1993a,b).

At the time of writing this chapter, the draft legislation was in the process of being proposed by the Government for discussions in Parliament. If the proposed legislation is passed, it will be an important step in the development of the extension complex in Estonia. The legislation would clarify the status of advisory services and the mechanisms of government involvement in advisory work. It would also place the advisory activities under the control of users, thus creating an opportunity for developing efficient linkages between the users and research and development organizations.

However, the major constraint imposed by the lack of resources for advisory work still remains. Initial finance should be provided from public funds and it would be desirable to combine national resources with technical and financial foreign aid, which is currently being offered by various donors. Although public and/or donor start-up support is clearly required, the advisory services should be developed with a long-term objective of increasing cost-recovery from users.

## Acknowledgements

The support and contributions of colleagues at the Institute of Rural Development, Agricultural University of Estonia, Tartu, Estonia – Jüri Ginter, Benno Maaring, Meelis Müil, Anneli Parisalu, Valdo Ruttas, Vilja Saluveer and Mati Tamm – who worked as a team in carrying out the project, are gratefully acknowledged.

## References

Aasmäe, V. (1993) Allakäigutrepi kaudu Euroopasse. *Maaleht* 9 September.
Anon. (1993a) Impordi maht riikide lôikes. *Äripäev* 6 September.
Anon. (1993b) Pooled likvideeritud töökohad olid pôllumajanduses. *Rahva Hääl* 167, 26 July.
BNS (1993) Impordikeeld vähendab Eesti pôllumajanduseksporti Euroopa Ühenduse riikidesse vähemalt 18%. *Postimees* 17 April.
Eesti Vabariigi Pôllumajandusministeerium (1993) *Lähtealused Pôllumajanduse Arengukavale aastani 2000*. Eesti Vabariigi Pôllumajandusministeerium, Tallinn.
Järvesoo, E. (1978) The postwar economic transformation. In: Parming, T. and Järvesoo, E. (eds) *A Case Study of a Soviet Republic. The Estonian SSR*. Westview Press, Boulder, Colorado.
Kraak, V. (1993) Majanduskoda – hea vôimalus koostööks. *Postimees* 26 November.
Leetsar, J. (1993) *Agricultural Strategy Until Year 2000*. Presentation made by the Minister of Agriculture of Estonia, Mr Jaan Leetsar, at the Congress of Agricultural Producers of Estonia in Paide, Estonia, 26 March.
Ministry of Agriculture of Estonia (1992) *Agrifacts about Estonia from 1970 till 1991*. Infotrükk, Tallinn.
Nagel, U.J. (1980) *Institutionalisation of Knowledge Flows: an Analysis of the Extension Role of Two Agricultural Universities in India. Quarterly Journal of International Agriculture* Special Issue No. 30.
National Statistics Board of Estonia (1992) *Estonia: A Statistical Profile*. National Statistics Board of Estonia, Tallinn.

Rivera, W.M. (1988) Developing agricultural extension systems nationwide. A structural approach. *Journal of Extension Systems* December, 29–49.

Rivera, W.M. and Gustafson, D.J. (1991) New roles and responsibilities for public sector agricultural extension. In: Rivera, W.M. and Gustafson, D.J. (eds) *Agricultural Extension: Worldwide Institutional Evolution and Forces for Change.* Elsevier Applied Science, Barking.

Röling, N. (1988) *Extension Science. Information Systems in Agricultural Development.* Cambridge University Press, Cambridge.

Röling, N. and Engel, P.G.H. (1991) The development of the concept of agricultural knowledge information systems (AKIS): implications for extension. In: Rivera, W.M. and Gustafson, D.J. (eds) *Agricultural Extension: Worldwide Institutional Evolution and Forces for Change.* Elsevier Applied Science, Barking.

Tamm, M. (1993a) Kas maarahva ja valitsuse vastassesi vôib kasvada koostööks. *Postimees* 1 November.

Tamm, M. (1993b) Maamajanduskoja teeb maarahvas ise. *Postimees* 30 November.

USCIA (1992) *Estonia. An Economic Profile.* United States Central Intelligence Agency, Washington, DC.

Vanatoa, E. (1993) Taimekasvatus 1992. Aastal ja 1993. Aasta esimesel poolel. *Kaubalehe Ärilisa* 6–13 August.

# 7

## Agriculture and Farming Systems: Developing and Implementing Policies under Social, Political and Structural Change in Denmark

### Vagn Østergaard and Poul Eric Stryg

### Introduction

As Denmark is a member of the EC, the economics of Danish agricultural production are very much influenced by the European Common Agricultural Policy (CAP), but specific Danish agricultural and environmental policies have also had a considerable influence on the production conditions for agriculture and the development of farming systems. Initially this chapter illustrates the principal agricultural and environmental political objectives and tools used in recent years. This includes discussion of the major principles of the CAP reform and likely impacts of these reforms on the agricultural structure and production, in addition to the impacts of Danish environmental legislation. This is followed by observations of how farmers have reacted to the policy changes implemented so far and how they are expected to react to future changes. Finally, some mention is made of the contributions that research and advisory services can make in assisting farmers to adapt to the new conditions.

### The EC Agricultural Reform

The CAP was set up to secure European food supply and farmers' income. It has been very successful in achieving its first goal but has been less successful in meeting the requirements of the second. In the 1980s especially, the EC has had to struggle with surplus production and budgetary problems. An increasing environmental awareness has also contributed to doubts being raised about the expediency of the policies pursued to date. On the basis of this, the European Commission presented a proposal of reforming the common agricultural policy in July 1991. After difficult negotiations several points in the so-called MacSharry Plan were changed and European Ministers of Agriculture reached an agreement to implement the reforms in May 1992.

## *Principal factors of the reform*

The major plank of the reforms is that there will be a shift from producer support to compensation on a per hectare basis for a range of arable crops – cereals, oilseeds and protein crops. In addition, the intervention price for cereals will be gradually reduced by 35% over a period of three years to 100 ECU per tonne in 1995–1996. The current mechanisms for cereals (intervention, export restoration, import protection) are to be maintained, but agricultural producers must produce and sell oilseeds and protein crops at world market prices, as the traditional institutional prices will no longer apply. In Table 7.1 the current prices of main crops prior to the reform are presented, together with an estimate of the prices in 1995–1996.

As compensation for the fall in prices, a schedule of hectarage payments has been instituted, but such payments are tied to a proportion of the arable land on each farm being setaside. Payments are also made for the land setaside. Denmark has so far been considered as a single-yield region receiving the per hectare area compensation and setaside payments shown in Table 7.2.

Since the mid-1980s, the cereal price has decreased on average by 3% per

**Table 7.1.** Current prices of main crops before and after the reform (ECU t$^{-1}$).

|                             | 1991/92 | 1992/93 | 1995/96 |
|-----------------------------|---------|---------|---------|
| Cereal, intervention price  | 160     | 155     | 100     |
| Rapeseed, producer price    | 300     | 135     | 133     |
| Pea, producer price         | 226     | 210     | 122     |

**Table 7.2.** Danish area compensation and setaside payments (ECU ha$^{-1}$).

|                             | 1993 | 1994 | 1995 |
|-----------------------------|------|------|------|
| Area compensation payments: |      |      |      |
| 　Cereals                    | 130  | 182  | 234  |
| 　Oilseeds                   | 410  | 410  | 410  |
| 　Protein crops              | 339  | 339  | 339  |
| Setaside payment            | 234  | 297  | 297  |

**Table 7.3.** Calculated 'cereal price' for fodder grain (ECU t$^{-1}$).

|                              | 1992 | 1993 | 1994 | 1995 |
|------------------------------|------|------|------|------|
| Intervention price           | 155  | 117  | 108  | 100  |
| Area compensation payment    | –    | 25   | 35   | 45   |
| Total 'cereal price'         | 155  | 142  | 143  | 145  |

year, due among other things to the stabilizer arrangements. It is clear from the values shown in Table 7.3 that the effect of the current agricultural reform is a stabilization of the 'cereal price,' when this is calculated as the sum of the intervention price and per hectare compensation payments (in this case the payments have been calculated on the basis of the average harvest yield in the base period).

However, the values presented in Table 7.3 conceal the significant variations in the total 'cereal price,' which will occur between individual cereal farmers and between regions. Effectively farms and regions with above-average yields will receive significant reductions in income due to the reform, while farms and regions with below average yields will be over-compensated. This means that there will be a significant shift in incomes between farmers and regions, having a resulting impact on regional land prices and tenancy rents (Stryg *et al.*, 1992). However, work has been initiated to establish a more 'equitable' arrangement, so that the area compensation payments will be more closely related to the productive quality of land.

The values in Table 7.3 exclude the possible losses due to the compulsory setaside of arable land. In 1992–1993, 15% of the arable land devoted to cereals, oilseeds and protein crops was to be setaside in rotation. From 1993–1994 a permanent (non-rotational) setaside of arable land is also possible, but the setaside percentage will then increase to 18% in Denmark (and to 20% in most other EC countries). Under existing regulations, the setaside land must either be left fallow or used for cultivation of non-food crops. In 1992–1993, approximately 205,000 ha or 10% of the basic area were setaside in Denmark. Of the land setaside, approximately 203,000 ha were left fallow, while approximately 2000 ha were used for cultivation of non-food crops (mainly rapeseed).

It has been estimated, based on model results (Rude and Stryg, 1992), that the area setaside in 1995 will constitute approximately 250,000 ha or about 11% of the basic area. As a result of the slippage-effect and increasing harvest yields per hectare, the total production of reform crops is expected to decrease significantly less than the equivalent reduction expected from the setaside land (Stryg and Knudsen, 1993).

The size of the cattle production sector is influenced both by the reduction in the intervention price for butter (about 1% net) and the national milk quota (about 2%), and by the decrease in the intervention prices of beef, which over a period of three years must be reduced by 15%. As compensation for the fall in the price of beef, the payments made for male beef animals and suckler cows have been increased. However, the extent of payments will be limited by a ceiling on the total amount that can be paid out and a limit on the number of eligible animals per hectare. The carrying capacity above which no payment is payable is to be gradually reduced from 3.5 units of bovine animals per hectare in 1993 to 2.0 in 1996.

The agricultural reform is expected to reduce the Danish gross domestic product at factor cost by about 1.5 billion DKK or approximately 7%. The reform is expected to have a marked influence on the holding structure, and if there is any possibility of transferring the setaside obligation and of leaving entire farms fallow, a relatively large number of small farms will probably disappear as independent farms.

### Accompanying measures of the reform

The main objective of the agricultural reform was to limit the supply of agricultural products that are in surplus. Although not the primary objective, the reform process will tend to reduce the environmental strain of agriculture. Indeed, the falling prices of crops will reduce the levels of application of fertilizer and pesticides on arable land. The introduction of more flexible arrangements for leaving areas fallow, especially the possibility of setting aside large contiguous areas on a permanent basis, will bring about considerable advantages for conservation and the environment.

A number of accompanying measures have been incorporated into the reform process which are aimed specifically at reducing the environmental impacts of intensive farming methods on the environment. These are payments which are paid to encourage:

- environmentally friendly practices;
- reducing the use of artificial fertilizer and pesticides;
- conversion to ecological farming;
- a shift from intensive to extensive crop production without rotation;
- for turning previously arable areas into permanent grass;
- a 20-year setting aside of arable land which can be used for environmental purposes.

Other accompanying measures involve changes in the current arrangements concerning afforestation and woodland improvements and the introduction to a scheme whereby farmers can be encouraged to retire early. From 1 January 1994 it will be possible for Danish farmers aged 55 and above to receive a retirement grant of 10,000 ECU annually, provided they sell or lease their farm.

# Environmental Legislation

In recent years, Danish environmental legislation has increasingly restricted the possibilities of Danish agriculture. The Action Plan for Aquatic Environment, the Pesticide Action Plan and the Action Plan for Sustainable Agriculture have been of substantial importance.

## *The Action Plan for the Aquatic Environment*

In 1989, the Danish Parliament, 'Folketinget,' passed a bill aimed at reducing the leaching of nitrogen from agricultural land by 50%. To fulfil this, a number of measures were adopted such as the inclusion of more green fields, changes to fertilizer application and crop rotations and an increased capacity for storage of farmyard manure. In addition, increasing emphasis has been put on information provision and advice from the advisory service on methods of production which help to conserve the environment. A review of the progress of the Action Plan in May 1990 found that a halving of nitrogen leaching could not be achieved through the current initiatives, even if there was full compliance with the scheme. The amount of farmyard manure is the main reason for this and at present there is a push to ensure that Danish agriculture improves the utilization and application of such manures.

## *The Pesticide Action Plan*

The use of pesticides in Denmark grew significantly after World War II and in the period between the mid-1950s and 1984 the use of pesticides increased more than fivefold. Today crop production is heavily reliant on the application of pesticides to combat weeds, diseases and pests. The Pesticide Action Plan was introduced in 1986 with the objective of reducing the use of pesticides and protecting harmless and useful organisms among flora and fauna, on land and in the water. The Plan set targets of reducing the frequency of use of pesticides by 25% and 50% respectively, by 1990 and 1997, compared with the corresponding average for the period 1981–1985.

In 1990 the level of use of pesticides corresponded to the Plan's aims, but the target set for frequency of application was not met (see Figures 7.1 and 7.2 for details).

## *The Action Plan for Sustainable Agriculture*

As the Action Plan for the Aquatic Environment or the Pesticide Action Plan did not seem to achieve their desired aims, it was decided to make an Action Plan for Sustainable Agriculture. In this case the Government proposed that a further set of measures be adopted to achieve its environmental aims, e.g. initiatives to obtain a better utilization of the manure and a reduction of

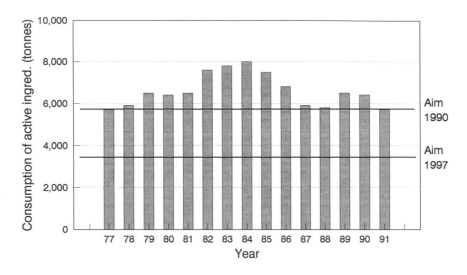

**Fig. 7.1.** Development in the use of pesticides from 1977 to 1991 (Skop, 1993).

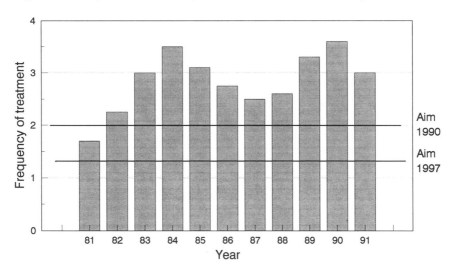

**Fig. 7.2.** Development in the frequency of treatment of crops with pesticides from 1981 to 1991 (Skop, 1993).

artificial fertilizer. As far as pesticides were concerned it was estimated that the target set could probably be attained before 1997, whereas the target for reduced frequency of application was abandoned and an intensified research effort to find solutions was started.

After the presentation of the Action Plan, a Committee of Parliament – the Sustainable Committee – was set up, with the brief of developing a detailed prescription for the Plan. The Committee has proposed increased utilization of nitrogen from animal manures and records of fertilizer application, while at the same time initiating a number of investigations into ammonia evaporation, appropriate stocking rates and alternative recording criteria for the frequency of treatment with pesticides.

Organic farming, which in 1992 comprised only 0.8% of the holdings and 0.7% of the farm acreage in Denmark, has been stimulated by subsidies to the farmer for converting from conventional to ecological production methods. The marketing of organic products was stimulated by introducing an official, Government control and trade mark. The subsidies for conversion are able to be adjusted over time but the reality is that the rate of increase in organic farming has slowed because consumers are not willing to pay the increased price premiums demanded for organic food.

Although the emphasis in encouraging organic agriculture has been on the environmental implications, it is also necessary to recognize that organic production systems have economic and social implications which need to be considered alongside the environmental impacts.

## Farmers' Reactions to the EC Reform

Farmers have changed their levels of production and production systems markedly through recent decades, resulting in new agricultural structures. Rude and Stryg (1992) were able to model expected farmer reaction to the CAP reform and the anticipated impacts on Danish agriculture and the Danish economy. The results showing the changes in numbers of farms over the period 1990–2004 are shown in Table 7.4. They show that there will be a marked reduction in the number of farms within the main farm types and most markedly within cattle farming, where a decrease of 38% is expected.

Table 7.5 shows the expected changes in animal production up to year 2004. The number of animal units (see note under Table 7.5) is expected to decrease by 26% within cattle herds and to increase by 24% within pig herds.

The production of nitrogen within animal manure is expected to decrease by 4%. The acreage used for farming (excluding fallow and marginal areas) is expected to decrease from 2.8 million ha in 1990 to 2.4 million ha in 2004, or a 13% drop caused by CAP but without the effects of the GATT negotiations. In addition, there is likely to be a change in the areas of crops grown with cattle farming shifting towards less fodder beet and grass/clover, towards more small grain crops for silage.

**Table 7.4.** Changes in numbers of farms[a] in Denmark ('000) (from Rude and Stryg, 1992).

|  | Actual figures | Expected with CAP changes | |
|---|---|---|---|
| Main type of farming | 1990 | 1995 | 2004 |
| Cattle (relative) | 26 (100) | 20  (77) | 16 (62) |
| Pig (relative) | 11 (100) | 11 (100) | 9 (82) |
| Cash crop (relative) | 40 (100) | 37  (93) | 29 (73) |
| Total numbers (relative) | 77 (100) | 68  (88) | 54 (70) |

[a]Note: a large number of the farms are not farmed on a full-time basis.

**Table 7.5.** Changes in the number of animals and amount of nitrogen in farmyard manure (FYM) in Denmark (× 1000 animal units[a]) (from Rude and Stryg, 1992).

|  | Actual figures | Expected with CAP changes | |
|---|---|---|---|
|  | 1990 | 1995 | 2004 |
| Cattle (relative) | 1240 (100) | 1035  (83) | 915  (74) |
| Pig (relative) | 860 (100) | 945 (110) | 1065 (124) |
| Other animals (relative) | 90 (100) | 95 (106) | 100 (111) |
| Total numbers (relative) | 2190 (100) | 2075  (95) | 2080  (95) |
| Total N in FYM and deposited during grazing ($10^6$ kg) | 225 (100) | 215  (96) | 215  (96) |

[a]One animal unit equals: 1 dairy cow per year, 3 sows (including piglets) per year or 30 slaughter pigs.

## Research Activities of Importance for Adjustments to Policies

Much research, which can give guidance on the adjustments needed in farming systems as they move to less intensive systems, is currently going on in western Europe, particularly in the northwest regions. The results from randomized experiments conducted on experimental stations concerning, for example, nitrogen (N) input to plant or animal production can be used for calculating the expected consequences of N manipulation on N losses, and also the level and quality of production. These experimental results can to some extent also be used to model the wider consequences of differing levels of N use on the extent of changes that could be expected in land use and animal production at the farm, region or country level. The economic and environmental consequences of less nitrogen use have been analysed and discussed by Rude (1991).

In Denmark, research into farming systems has gone on for a longer period. For example, in 1968 the Multidisciplinary Research in Cattle Production Systems programme was reorganized to fulfil the following overall objective:

> To describe the economy of different systems in cattle production under the existing production conditions and prevailing possibilities of practical farming, as great importance is attached to testing and analyzing the economic influence of new, not well-known production alternatives. Furthermore, special emphasis is placed on an overall consideration, including all components economically relevant to cattle production in the analysis and the demonstration of the applicability of experimental results in practice. On each individual farm efforts are made with the existing possibilities to optimize the production by means of the knowledge of analysis and production techniques available from research and experimental institutions in Denmark and abroad.
>
> (Thysen *et al.*, 1987)

These activities are becoming more and more important as sources of information leading to adjustments in policy. The research methods adopted in this programme are primarily based on system thinking and multi-disciplinary studies founded on studies within commercial farms (the 'real world'). The on-farm studies are both experimental and non-experimental in character. As animal production interacts closely with nature and is influenced by uncontrollable factors (such as climate), it is important that the farm is studied and described from a holistic point of view over a number of years.

Knowledge of non-experimental character is defined here as measurements, recording and description of the 'real world,' which are based on rationality and therefore can be communicated and discussed, whereas non-experimental knowledge can be a base for development of the studied system and/or for formulation of general knowledge. General knowledge can be formulated by classification of the non-experimental knowledge followed by means of appropriate statistical procedures. The final interpretation and generalization should include relevant results of randomized experiments.

It is often seen that there is a larger variation within rather than between production systems. The reasons might be differences in management and the interaction of the management system with production system in a complex way. Consequently, this interaction is studied within case studies (description of production over time) or by monitoring the system, when management systems are developed. Both case studies and monitoring require intensive and detailed measurements and recording on the farm as well as close collaboration between the farmer, the recording staff and the researcher. Furthermore, collaboration with scientists within other disciplines and also local advisers and veterinarians, is also of great importance.

The methods which are extensively used in research into animal production systems are systems thinking and systemic modelling, which are illustrated in Figure 7.3.

The economic and environmental effects of conventional and organic farming have been estimated on the basis of results from commercial farms by Christensen *et al.* (1992), Kristensen and Hindhede (1992), Kristensen and Kristensen (1992), Kristensen *et al.* (1992) and Østergaard and Kristensen (1993) using the methods outlined above. The results of these studies have been communicated directly to farmers, agricultural advisors and politicians and also through annual meetings and the written media.

It is assumed that environmental benefits will be achieved by controlling the N surplus at farm level. Control can be achieved by setting limits on stocking rates, controlling what crops are grown and suggesting prefered rotations, animal feeding practices, amounts and types of fertilizer, the slurry techniques used and when slurry is to be applied (Hansen and Østergaard, 1992).

However, the level of N surplus is the responsibility of the farmers, although they have little control over N deposition from the atmosphere.

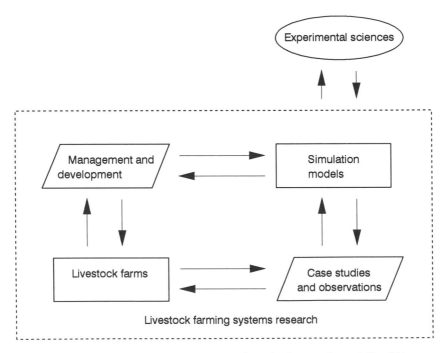

**Fig. 7.3.** Elements and processes in the research method, systemic modelling (Kristensen and Sørensen, 1991).

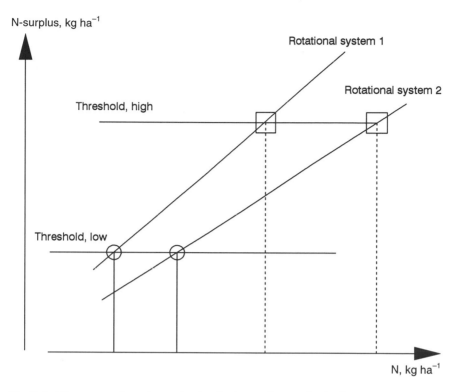

**Fig. 7.4.** Nitrogen surplus at increasing levels of N per hectare by fertilization, including use of slurry depending on feed input at farm level.

Consequently, farmers need to understand not only the movements of N in the short term but also know how it moves in the long term, if they are to manipulate the factors mentioned above leading to a reduced input of N per hectare. Figure 7.4 shows schematically the relationship between N input and N surplus for two different rotational systems controlled by good management. Furthermore, it shows the threshold levels for unwanted pollution at two different localities – by soil type (clay versus sand) and climates. The two threshold levels, high and low, indicate a level of N surplus which should not be exceeded in order to avoid pollution. The level for different localities should be estimated and in combination with the relationship between N fertilization and N surplus for various production systems, it is possible to calculate – for certain conditions – the economic optimum level of N application which would not lead to a serious risk of pollution.

An integrated decision support system for the planning of feed supply and land use on dairy farms (ADAM-H) has been developed by Hansen (1992) and has been used for several analyses, such as computer-simulated effects on the efficiency index, labour input and economic values of manure within livestock production systems (Hansen and Østergaard, 1991, 1992). The results show that beef cattle production can in some cases be an attractive alternative for the protection of natural resources, but it depends on the type of breeds adopted, the reason being that the interaction between the type of beef cattle and production conditions influences the ranking according to the economic result (Østergaard and Andersen, 1992).

## Extension Activities Concerning Implementation of Rules and Production Adjustments

The extension activities are primarily organized by the farmer's own organizations, i.e. the Farmers' Unions and the Smallholders' Unions. The activities are carried out by advisors of the Danish Agricultural Advisory Centre and include services such as calculation and advice about manure storage capacity according to herd size (number of animal units), appropriate techniques for application of manure, the levels of N fertilization for individual crops depending on land, climate, prices, etc., composition of crops within the rotational system and land requirements for appropriate disposal of the farm-yard manure. The local advisory services are assisting the farmers, on an individual basis, to understand the large number of regulations now in place and how to make the optimum adjustments to their production system.

## References

Christensen, J., Olsen, P., Overgaard, J., Østergaard, V., Vester, J., Fog, E. and Mølsted Jensen, L. (1992) *Rapport om Økonomien ved Omlægning til Økologisk Jordbrug (Report on the Economy of Change to Organic Farming)*. Ministry of Agriculture, Copenhagen, 68 pp.

Hansen, J.P. (1992) *ADAM-H – An Integrated Decision Support System for Planning of Feed Supply and Land Use at the Dairy Farm*. Report No. 718, National Institute of Animal Science, Foulum, Tjele, 168 pp (with English abstract).

Hansen, J.P. and Østergaard, V. (1991) *Livestock Production Systems and Use of Slurry. Computer Simulated Effects on the Efficiency Index, Labour Input and Economic Value of Slurry*. Report No. 698, National Institute of Animal Science, Foulum, Tjele, 96 pp (with English abstract).

Hansen, J.P. and Østergaard, V. (1992) Alternative dairy cattle system – computer simulated environmental and economic results related to the use of slurry. *Livestock Production Science* 31, 29–42.

Kristensen, E.S. and Kristensen, I.S. (1992) *Analysis of Nitrogen Surplus and Efficiency on Organic and Conventional Dairy Farms*. Report No. 710, National Institute of Animal Science, Foulum, Tjele (with English abstract).

Kristensen, E.S. and Sørensen, J.T. (1991) Development of sustainable livestock farming systems: methodology and results. Paper presented at the 11th AFSR/E Annual Symposium, 5–10 October 1991, Michigan State University, East Lansing, Michigan.

Kristensen, E.S., Halberg, N. and Kristensen, I.S. (1992) *Organic Farming, Technical and Economic Farm Results 1991–92.* Report No. 714, National Institute of Animal Science, Foulum, Tjele, pp. 138–143 (in Danish).

Kristensen, T. and Hindhede, J. (1992) *Low Cost Systems in Conventional Dairy Production, Technical Economic Farm Result 1990–91.* Report No. 714, National Institute of Animal Science, Foulum, Tjele, pp. 45–104 (in Danish).

Østergaard, V. and Andersen, B.B. (1992) *Beef Cattle – Basis for Choice of Genotype in Suckler Herds with Various Production Conditions.* Report No. 715, National Institute of Animal Science, Foulum, Tjele, 48 pp (with English abstract).

Østergaard, V. and Kristensen, T. (1993) The economic and environmental effects of extensive cattle production systems. Paper presented at the 44th Annual Symposium of the EAAP, 16–19 August 1993, Aarhus.

Rude, S. (1991) *Nitrogen Fertilizers in Danish Agriculture – Present and Future Application and Leaching.* Report No. 62, Institute of Agricultural Economics, Copenhagen (with English summary).

Rude, S. and Stryg, P.E. (1992) Landbrugsreformen og landbrugets miljøpåvirkning (The CAP reform and the impact on the environment). In: *Landbrugsreformen og Miljøet (The CAP Reform and the Environment). Orientering fra Miljøstyrelsen,* No. 5, pp. 15–45 (in Danish).

Skop, E. (1993) *Stofstrømme i Dansk Landbrug og det Omgivende Miljø (Flow of N, P, and Pesticides in Danish Agriculture and the Surrounding Environment).* Internal report, Ministry of Environment, Copenhagen, 30 pp (in Danish).

Stryg, P.E. and Knudsen, M.H. (1993) *Slippage Effect of Set-aside of Arable land. A Study of Rotational and Non-rotational Set-aside in Denmark.* Report to the EC Commission, pp. 23–42.

Stryg, P.E., Madsen, B., Olsen, P. and Groes, N. (1992) *Forslag, Forlig og Fremtid – Regionaløkonomiske Regnestykker for Dansk Landbrug i EF (Proposal, Compromise, and Future – Regional Economic Modelling of Danish Agriculture in the EC).* AKF Rapport, Copenhagen, 148 pp (in Danish).

Thysen, I., Kristensen, E.S., Sørensen, J.T. and Østergaard, V. (1987) *Dairy Cattle Production Systems and Management Systems. Cattle Production Research. Danish Status and Perspectives.* Landhusholdningsselskabets Forlag, Copenhagen, pp. 169–182.

# 8

# OBJECTIVES AND ATTITUDES OF FARM HOUSEHOLDS IN THE REPUBLIC OF IRELAND

## Jim Phelan

## Introduction

The objectives and attitudes of farm families are shaped by the resources they possess or have access to, by past activities and policies that have or are influencing development and by their perceptions of what the future may hold. Therefore, in order to understand the objectives and attitudes of farm households, it is necessary to examine the areas just mentioned. It is also important to look at the importance of agriculture to the national economy.

## Problems in Rural Areas

Life in the rural countryside in Ireland and in several other peripheral areas of the EC where agriculture is important is now under more severe pressure than at any time over the last century. Between 1973 and the mid-1980s the Common Agricultural Policy (CAP) and Regional Fund offered prosperity to rural areas. Great quantities of capital were available to support farming and to raise farm incomes, thus generating a new found wealth in rural areas. Rural infrastructure was developed to reduce the remoteness of rural areas from central markets. All boats were to be lifted by the rising tide.

There is now a growing realization that although the CAP has been successful in promoting the expansion of agricultural commodities and in raising the incomes of some farmers, it has failed to do so for others. The demand for traditional agricultural produce such as beef and milk is declining. Teagasc (1992) reported that Irish per capita consumption of beef in 1980 was 25.7 kg. This had declined by almost one third to 17.3 kg in 1990. The European Commission (1991a) state that reform of the CAP would aim at orienting agriculture more towards the market place. The McSharry proposals show that this plan is being pursued, and additional pressure for these reforms is coming from recent GATT agreements.

Three core problems that affect rural areas not only in Ireland but across the whole of the Community are lack of off-farm employment, low farm incomes and the resulting demographic imbalance.

### Lack of off-farm employment

There is a high dependence on agriculture in Ireland – it employs 15% of the workforce. The Republic of Ireland has a very weak rural industrial base, thus the adjustment from a high dependence on agriculture to a more diversified economy is difficult, especially at a time when 20% of the workforce is unemployed. While one quarter of Irish farmers have an off-farm job, 60% are classed as being underemployed. Off-farm jobs are scarcest in the more peripheral areas. Current efforts at creating alternative enterprises on farms tend to support the better resourced farmers. Getting into such enterprises, be it tourism-related or new enterprises such as mushrooms or deer farming, even with good grants, is beyond the scope of those in rural areas who most need assistance.

### Low and declining farm incomes

The lack of availability of off-farm employment and the high level of underemployment would be of little concern to farmers were it not for the fact that the farm income for the majority of farmers is well below the average industrial wage. Miley (1991) discussed the 1990 National Farm Survey and reported that only 20% of farms earned an income from farming of over £10,000. Low incomes predominated with 60% of all farms having a farm income of less than £5000. A study carried out by Markey *et al.* (1991) showed that income from farming accounted for just 54% of total household income for primary occupation farm households in 1987 in Ireland. However, for over 60% it was their only source of earned income. They also showed that this figure was in rapid decline, having declined from 75% in 1973. This study also showed a significant rise in the risk of poverty for farm households. Some 20% of households were at risk in 1973, and this had risen to 35% in 1987. The risk of poverty for farm households was three times greater than that for the remainder of the self-employed sector and seven times greater than that for the employed sector.

A significant trend being observed is the increasing importance of direct subsidies, i.e. headage payments and premiums. These are now a major factor determining income levels. In 1990, these subsidies accounted for 90% of the average income from sheep farming and 50% of the average income from cattle farming. CAP reform has made these supports more visible. Although there is commitment to them currently, this may not be the case in a few years time.

To compound the problem even further, the last 50 years have witnessed the emigration of the most highly skilled, better educated young people, leading to a demographic imbalance in rural areas. Walsh (1991) reported that 'What used to be called the flight from the land continues. In the 20 years to 1965 over 230,000 went, in the 20 years to 1984 around 200,000; and by all accounts the movement accelerated since then.' Results from the most recent census of population presented by Commins (1991) show that of the 155 rural districts in Ireland outside Dublin, 75% lost population between 1986 and 1991. This was an increase from 29% over the period 1981–1986. As expected, the decline was most severe in the more remote rural districts. The selective nature of migration was highlighted by O'Hara (1990). Old and young people predominate in rural areas and those young people who remain tend to be unskilled and poorly motivated. This finding was reinforced by the work of Walsh (1991), who reported that 'Those who stay [in rural areas] are older and on average worse-off than workers in industry.' There is a continuing decline in the percentage employed in agriculture, not just in Ireland but also in many other Community countries. Throughout the Community, there is a growing realization of the need to preserve the cultural heritage of the various traditions that go to make up the Community. Growth at the expense of the rural areas for many people is simply not acceptable.

## Community Policy and Initiatives

Rural area policy in the Community and particularly in Ireland has undergone a great deal of reorientation in recent years. Ireland has particularly been affected by a reorientation of policy because the rural area policy is funded to a large extent by the Community. Hence it is appropriate in any examination of Irish rural area development policy first to examine Community development policy. Community policy orientation towards rural areas has undergone considerable changes in recent years. This was initially prompted by a number of developments:

**1.** The mounting surpluses and spiralling costs which arose mainly as a result of guaranteed prices for traditional agricultural commodities. Growth in agricultural output in the Community and worldwide during the 1970s and 1980s has resulted in the need to bring policies more into line with market realities. The European Commission (1990) observed that the reduction in output volumes and price support will place a major burden on farmers and leave between 6 and 16 Mha of agricultural land surplus to requirements.

**2.** The realization that price support measures and guidance schemes have not succeeded in bringing about significant development in the more disadvantaged regions of the Community.

**3.** The massive inequity in terms of allocation of the benefits of the CAP between large and small farmers. The European Commission (1991a) observed that there are many rural regions with ageing populations of householders living in relative poverty.

**4.** The realization that the solutions to the problems of rural areas must encompass support for a range of activities besides farming. The European Commission (1991b) identified this realization. It stated: 'The future economic development of rural areas will become increasingly dependent on sectors other than agriculture: tourism, forestry, industry. In some areas, these alternative rural activities will replace agriculture, whilst in others they will be additional.'

**5.** Concern for the rural environment. The European Commission (1991a) observed that in recent decades the rapid growth of intensive farming, the expansion of tourism and the spread of urbanization and transport have helped to give rise to public concern about the environment. In northern parts of the Community, there is increasing concern with water pollution, soil contamination, loss of flora and fauna and changes in the appearance of the landscape. In southern parts of the Community, there are problems of land abandonment, soil erosion and forest fires. Maintenance of a sound ecological balance in rural areas is a vital component of the integrated approach to rural development.

## Irish Policy and Initiatives

In Ireland, in the early years of Community membership, the solution to low farm incomes was simply to increase output and income was likely to increase. As a result of CAP reform, increasing output may no longer be possible and will probably no longer be profitable. According to O'Donohoe (1990): '... whatever the outcome of GATT negotiations, productive employment possibilities in traditional agriculture for all farmers but particularly for the majority in the under 20 ha category will be greatly weakened.'

Other solutions such as agriforestry, rural tourism and alternative farm enterprises are being promoted by the Irish Government. It realizes that traditional agriculture will continue to be the basis for underpinning the rural economy. It considers that opportunities for increasing production are limited owing to CAP constraints. There is scope to increase and safeguard income through the production of higher quality produce and through cost control. Further diversification of the rural economy is necessary and local communities will have to be assisted to pursue development in sectors other than those related to traditional agricultural production. The Irish Government's aim is to create a balance between non-agricultural and agricultural development, so that the rural population will benefit from the overall improvement in the economy through the creation of additional employment opportunities in rural areas and the consequent stabilization of the population. In summary, according to the Programme for Economic and Social Progress (PESP) (1991): 'The Government ... are committed both to the achievement of a more competitive agricultural and food sector and a more diversified rural economy which can provide additional income and employment opportunities.'

However, how this is to be attained has never been clarified. The concept of rural development is not entirely new to Ireland. Thirty years ago the Irish Government found themselves in a situation somewhat similar to their Brussels counterparts over the past five years. Early attempts at implementing a rural development strategy for Ireland began in 1962 with the setting up of the Inter Departmental Committee, to deal with special problems of agriculture in the west. In 1962 the Inter Departmental Committee organized the pilot area development programme. This programme had as its primary aim the development of agriculture in a selected number of disadvantaged areas in Ireland. This was followed in 1963 by the establishment of the County Development Teams, which aimed at bringing closer coordination between the various government departments and local authorities. In 1968 the Small Farm (Incentive Bonus) Scheme was launched to encourage more intensive farm business on small but potentially viable holdings, through the operation of a planned farm development plan.

With the accession to the Community, however, the whole context of national policy formulation was changed. Rural development went out of focus until the mid-1980s. Irish regional policy was reduced mainly to the implementation of regional industrial plans by the Industrial Development Authority (IDA). The CAP effectively replaced national agricultural policies from 1973 onwards.

In the last few years, rural development has again appeared on the Irish policy agenda promoted mainly by a reorientation in EC policy. The direction of national policy similar to that for the Community as a whole has changed from aiming at increasing production and modernizing farms to one of higher efficiency, reduced costs and improved quality with greater diversification.

Perhaps the greatest commitment the government has made to rural development is their setting up of the Integrated Rural Development (IRD) Pilot Programme. The programme, administered by the Department of Agriculture and Food, was put into operation in 12 sub-county areas over the period 1989–1990. A coordinator was appointed to each area which had a population of less than 15,000 persons. Apart from a small amount of money for technical assistance, no funding was provided. The role of the coordinator was to stimulate local groups to develop projects for their own areas.

Irish experience with IRD has been good. In the 12 Irish pilot area IRD programmes, 25 primary agriculture projects and 38 alternative farm enterprise projects were undertaken in the agricultural sector. In the South Kerry pilot area, a shellfish farming project was initiated. In the industry sector, 17 small-scale manufacturing projects were undertaken, e.g. in the South Kerry pilot area a Kenmare Lace Co-op was established. In the service sector, a wide variety of projects were undertaken. These were predominantly of a tourism nature such as the restoration of an old deserted village and an old Royal Irish Constabulary (RIC) barracks, again in the South Kerry pilot area. According to MacGuinness (1991), over 400 jobs were created, of which almost 200 were part-time and over 220 were full-time jobs. Although some progress has been made in the area of rural development, it has not assisted, to any great extent, the indigenous farm population. The benefits that have accrued have mostly assisted those who already have good incomes.

More recent attempts at rural development are based on local initiatives at community level. A number of rural groups have grasped the nettle themselves and attempted to draw up their own development plans for their respective areas. These have essentially been imaginative attempts on behalf of the groups to confront the issues of rural depopulation for their local areas and communities. Most of these projects have taken the form of limited companies or cooperatives, some of which have received Liaison Entre Action de Development de L'Economie Rurale (LEADER) funding. Funds have also been made available for rural development under the Operational Programme for Rural Development (OPRD) and under the PESP agreement. One of the concerns regarding projects to date under various rural development initiatives is the extent to which they have focused on tourism. Over 75% of projects undertaken have had a strong tourism orientation.

## Agriculture and Rural Development

Agriculture is an extremely important sector of the Irish economy. Within the Community, Ireland is one of the most rural and agrarian-based societies. Excluding the Dublin metropolitan region, over 60% of Irish people live in rural areas (i.e. outside centres having 1500 or more persons). Farming is the predominant activity in these rural areas. The basic problem in rural areas in Ireland is therefore a high dependence on agriculture at a time when the importance of the agricultural sector on a European basis is declining. Associated with this are the problems of underemployment and low farm incomes. The lack of any significant impact of rural development initiatives on the farming community also gives cause for concern. Nationally, only about one quarter of farmers are engaged in off-farm employment and the opportunity for expanding this given the current levels of unemployment in Ireland are not good. Hence job retention, be it in agriculture or in other rural industries, is of paramount importance.

## Objectives and Plans of Farm Households

The situation described above is important in understanding farm household attitudes to future development. The following points are noteworthy from research work carried out by the Department of Agribusiness, Extension and Rural Development, University College Dublin, in Counties Louth, a relatively good farming county, and Donegal, a mixed farming county in the north west (250 farms in total):

**1.** Only 4% of farmers in Louth and fewer in Donegal had adopted an alternative enterprise, 18% planned to in the future, but for the majority of them this was a long-term aspiration; the most common reasons given for not investing were cost and the high risk involved.
**2.** Approximately 33% in each county had some person in the household who earned income outside the farm.
**3.** 4% in Louth and 10% in Donegal were in receipt of unemployment assistance, while 9% in Louth and 18% in Donegal were in receipt of small farmers' dole (social welfare).
**4.** Approximately 70% in each county were willing to become involved in a scheme that compensated them for managing the countryside in an environmentally friendly way.

Table 8.1 summarizes the changes that farmers have made over the past ten years and their plans for the next five years. The information shows clearly that most farmers see their future as stabilizing advances made in the past or as a continuation of past trends, although at a reduced rate. The low level of aspiration for off-farm work in rural or surrounding areas reflects the reality, as there is little likelihood of it being available. Although many of these farmers have stated earlier that they would participate in environmental management schemes, they would do so but not if it involved cutting back significantly on current production levels.

The greatest constraints on future development identified by this group of respondents were cash flow (almost 80%), quotas and restrictions (over 25%), high investments (18%) and bureaucracy (8%). Marketing was not viewed as being a significant constraint.

The information from this study shows clearly that farmers view their continued existence as being achieved through carrying on the core business of agricultural production. A study carried out on milk production in County Clare (Mannion *et al.*, 1993) showed how supports could be put in place to allow small dairy farms to participate more equitably in the development process. This is a county that has been the focus of significant rural development efforts recently. The report clearly shows the importance of agriculture and particularly milk production to the rural economy of the county. It quantifies the jobs lost in agriculture and the knock-on effects that the loss of this income had for other employment areas, such as teaching, the

**Table 8.1.** Changes (%) made by farm households over the last ten years and their intentions over the next five years in Counties Louth and Donegal.

| | Past 10 years | | Next 5 years | |
| --- | --- | --- | --- | --- |
| | Louth | Donegal | Louth | Donegal |
| Start or expand a farm enterprise | 72 | 69 | 42 | 25 |
| Start or increase off-farm work | 5 | 5 | 4 | 6 |
| Purchase new machinery/equipment | 74 | 71 | 31 | 24 |
| Increase area farmed | 62 | 42 | 22 | 12 |
| Farm more intensively | 66 | 56 | 21 | 12 |
| Farm less intensively | 6 | 16 | 14 | 9 |

post office and services. The most startling finding is the lack of concern about job losses in agriculture. These losses are to a large extent perpetuated by current policies – policies which very often conflict. For example, the compulsory cuts in milk quota in the county have removed over £4.5 million from the rural economy. Rural development efforts, on the other hand, have contributed £2 million. The conclusions are obvious. The study highlights the need to focus on those in agriculture who have considerable resources and where jobs could be retained if these farmers were facilitated to participate in the development process. The study fully realizes that the population decline in agriculture will continue and that more farmers will be supported through social welfare. However, there is a significant number of farmers who could be retained in productive agriculture at a cost to the state that would be less than other available alternatives. If this is to happen, a stronger political focus must be brought to bear on the role of agriculture in rural development. It must also be remembered that farmers are a key component of the rural countryside. If they leave, big changes will occur and the countryside as we know it today will no longer exist.

## Conclusions

The objectives and attitudes of farm households are shaped by the resources which they possess or have access to, by past activities, by policy and by their perceptions of what the future holds. Income from farming is viewed as their most important source of income and many, particularly those at risk of leaving the countryside, see little opportunity of adding to this income from productive employment outside agriculture or from alternative enterprises. Farmers are willing to practise countryside management, but not if it involves significant reductions in their current level of activities. The diversification of the rural economy will assist some of those farmers in obtaining extra income through off-farm employment, but for a large proportion agricultural production will remain their main source of income. If state support is not directed to those who want to develop and who have significant resources with which to do so, then we shall continue to see a rapid movement to a situation where agricultural production becomes concentrated in the hands of a few. A massive increase in direct income support would be the only way of ensuring viable farm households for the marginalized sector in rural areas. The likelihood of this support being made available to the extent required is highly unlikely. Conflict exists between current policies: some on the one hand are forcing marginalization, whereas others are trying to solve the problem. We need a more comprehensive rural area policy that focuses on the harmonious development of the total resources. A proper typology of rural areas based on total resources is also required, as this would assist in the targeting of specific groups with specific policies appropriate to their needs.

# References

Commins, P. (1991) Rural depopulation: challenge for rural development. *Farm and Food* Oct–Dec, 25–27.
European Commission (1990) *Community Initiative for Rural Development – Leader*. EC Communication, EC, Brussels.
European Commission (1991a) *The Agricultural Situation in the Community: 1990*. Report, EC, Luxembourg, Brussels.
European Commission (1991b) *Communication to the Council and the European Parliament 'Europe 2000: Outlook for the Development of the Community's Territory: A Preliminary Overview'*. EC, Luxembourg, Brussels.
MacGuinness, M. (1991) How did the pilot programmes work? *Irish Farmers Journal* 5 January, Irish Farm Centre, Dublin.
Mannion, P.J. (1990) Problem focused advisory work: why the need? Paper prepared for Workshop on Extension Planning Methods, Poland.
Mannion, P.J., Phelan, J., Kinsella, J. and Kenny, M. (1993) *A Strategy for Retaining the Maximum Number of Milk Suppliers in County Clare*. Department of Agribusiness, Extension and Rural Development, University College Dublin, Dublin.
Markey, A., Phelan, J., McHenry, H. and Caskie, P. (1991) *Study of Farm Incomes in Northern Ireland and the Republic of Ireland*. Third Study Series: Report No. 1, Co-operation North, Dublin.
Miley, M. (1991) *Farm Incomes in 1990*. Teagasc Press Release, Teagasc, Dublin.
O'Donohoe, S. (1990) *Co-operatives and Rural Development*. Preliminary submission by the ICOS Rural Development Committee to the Department of Agriculture and the

EC Commission for a proposal for cooperative involvement as 'Agents' in the implementation of the 'LEADER' programme. 84, Merrion Square, Dublin.

O'Hara, P. (1990) *Agricultural and Food Policy Review.* Government Publications, Dublin.

PESP (1991) *Programme for Economic and Social Progress.* Government Publications, Dublin.

Teagasc (1992) *Irish Agriculture in Figures.* Teagasc, Dublin.

Walsh, R. (1991) The lie of the land: decision time for Irish agriculture. *The Irish Times* 6 October.

# 9

# FOOD SECURITY OR FARM SUPPORT?
## A Sketch of Food Policy in the North and South

*Philip Raikes*

## Introduction

Food security is primarily a matter of income security and of social networks to assist in times of need, rather than of aggregate national food production. Food imports do not necessarily imply shortage and food exports are no guarantee against hunger. Relationships between food production and security of access to food are complex, ambiguous and mediated through socioeconomic and political relationships.

In the North, where very few work in agriculture and even fewer are full-time farmers, this is obvious enough. Those who risk food shortage are invariably those at the very bottom of the income scale, or those who have been abruptly dumped there by civil war or other catastrophe. Most northern countries, other than Japan, feed upwards of half their total grain supply to livestock and still have a surplus for export, often as the unintended result of subsidies.

Food policy in the North has been largely a by-product of farm policy, with food security a useful slogan justifying policies to increase agricultural production with subsidies and tax breaks. (For much of continental Europe, vivid memories of wartime and post-war shortages fuelled this in the first decades after 1945.) These have benefited the richest farmers, increased the capital and chemical intensity of farming and generated huge surpluses to be dumped on world markets. Wage, employment and social security policies have had far greater effects on northern food consumption and security.

In Africa, large numbers of people suffer from hunger and malnutrition, and still larger numbers risk hunger, i.e. lack food security. Foodstuffs are in short supply for whole regions at particular times. One can hardly deny the importance of the links between physical food supply to food security.

However, looking only at the supply of food and ignoring incomes and 'entitlements' is as misleading, and generates incorrect policies. It focuses food policy on increasing aggregate food production as fast as possible, ignoring the distributional effects of how it is produced. Expanding mechanized grain production on large farms may reduce access to both land and jobs among the rural poor, worsening their access to food, even in situations where the food is produced nearby. Of course, food production affects food security, but this includes how it is produced, by whom and under what conditions (political, market, etc.), not just the aggregate amount.

In the South, food policies have also aimed to raise agricultural production through input-based modernization, although often combining this with measures to hold down urban food prices. This plus the cost of modernization, and the institutions to bring it about, have tended to depress farm prices of food grains (helped by low international prices resulting from northern export disposal). It may thus have obstructed as much as helped the development of production, while concentrating benefits on richer farmers at the cost of the remainder and of food security in poor households. Northern policies are an inappropriate model for southern agricultural development, and one whose shortcomings are aggravated by northern dumping on world markets.

In both cases there are signs of serious breakdown under pressure of internal and international forces. FSR/E could contribute to the formation of more appropriate farm policies in both the North and South, if the surrounding political and economic conditions allow, which is far from certain. The focus of this book is European agriculture, but any discussion of food security must consider parts of the world where this is an issue. In the present case, the main southern point of reference is eastern and southern Africa. Some of the themes sketched here are treated more fully in Raikes (1988).

## What is Food Policy?

There is no simple definition of food policy, which could in principle include all policies bearing on the access to food and nutritional status of a country's people. This is probably too broad, but does emphasize one highly relevant point: 'food policy,' as such, is easily 'over-ridden' by policies in other spheres. Macro-economic policy affects income, employment and price levels. Policies influencing the distribution of land and other means of production also affect food security, as do those affecting peace and security, war probably being the major single cause of famine.

If the term 'food policy' is restricted to decisions specifically concerning food and food products, one can distinguish between policies which affect or control the distribution of food and those intended to affect its production, recognizing that many, if not most, policies span this divide. Another relevant distinction is between policies affecting 'normal' consumption and those concerned with relief supplies in the event of famine or to the absolutely destitute poor. One can also sketch out some simple patterns in an extremely rough historical typology.

Control over the disposition of basic staple foods has been a feature of human societies for many thousands of years. Joseph, in the Bible, acting as both early-warning system (his dreams) and food policy advisor to Pharaoh, was one example, but by no means the earliest. His policy advice was standard for the type of society – producers to deliver grain to the ruler's barns as a tribute, some of it for redistribution in the event of shortage. This 'food security policy' was as fair and effective as the ruler and system within which it operated, with very wide variations in the balance between tribute and redistribution. Providing food security would evidently have served to legitimate royal or aristocratic exactions of tribute, but this did not by any means ensure its delivery.

With the growth of towns and food trade, as in preindustrial Europe, it was common for states to impose price controls on foodstuffs sold in major towns and quality controls to stop its evasion through adulteration and short weighting. The purpose was to prevent cheating and speculative price increases in the event of shortage. It was not aimed at improving the food situation of the poor or destitute, for whom begging, the church and local authorities 'provided' with varying degrees of inadequacy and brutality. In wartime, a directly opposite type of 'food policy' came into play, the purpose of which was to deny food to the enemy. The burning of crops by invading armies was more than just wanton destruction, while the central aim of a siege or blockade, from Troy to Sarajevo, is to starve a city's population into submission.

While directly aimed at merchants, food price controls ranged agricultural producers (or landlords) wanting high crop prices against urban consumers wanting cheap food. The landed aristocracy retained the upper hand, notably with regard to protection against grain imports, until industrialization provided a powerful ally for urban consumers. Early capitalist industrialization in Europe was labour intensive with low wages. Staple foodstuffs were a major item of expenditure, so their price was a major component of the real wage and determinant of cost and competitiveness. European settlement of the vast prairie lands of America, Africa and Australia provided the basis for vastly increased production of cheaper grains, once technical developments had increased farm productivity and reduced costs of transportation. This set the urban bourgeoisie and rural landowners directly at odds over the widespread protection of national grain markets. From the mid-19th century, with Britain leading the way, the tariff barriers protecting European agriculture were reduced and grain imports increased massively.

Food security was thus separated from local agricultural production and, except in time of war, the international market replaced price regulation as a means of holding food prices down. In preindustrial societies the harvest was an important economic determinant, and its failure a major cause of economic downturn, as food prices rose, forcing cutbacks in all other forms of expenditure. However, with the development of industry and the international trading system, the impact of any one country's harvest is much reduced. The causes of recession tend to derive from outside agriculture and to be imposed on it, in the form of reduced demand for and prices of crops.

This transformation has since had other dimensions. With incomes rising in the industrial countries, food expenditure takes a far smaller proportion of wages – and an increasing portion of food value is added in processing. Wages have also fallen as a proportion of total value added, so food prices lose their previous economic and political importance and the advanced industrialized countries can reintroduce protection for their much reduced agricultural sectors. However, where preindustrial protection accrued primarily to landlords, with limited impact on output, the new protection affects a radically transformed capitalist agriculture and agribusiness, far more responsive to economic incentives. This was increasingly true from the early 20th century, but accelerated after the Second World War, with an enormous expansion of the application of science, inputs, machinery and credit. This led to some degree of disintegration at farm level, especially of crop and livestock activities. Fertilizer replaced manure and rotations, tractors replaced animal draught and chemicals replaced rotation in weed and pest control. This has been accompanied by increased external integration, most evident in the increasingly common phenomenon of contract farming.

## Food Policy in Africa – Some Similarities and Contrasts

In most African countries, including South Africa, most of the population are forced by low income to use much of their income on basic foodstuffs. Food security is thus a matter of major political importance to a majority of the population.

Much of Africa was colonized by European powers before or during the 19th century, and these brought with them the array of food policies which had been applied at home or in other colonies (India being especially important for British African policy). During the years of European incursion, 'policy' was, as always in war, largely concerned to deny people food by burning crops and blockading supplies. Even once order had been imposed, concern for African food security was normally overridden in settler colonies by concern over the labour supply. Colonial food policy was a highly ambiguous affair, concerned to prevent outright starvation without providing incomes so high or secure that people could avoid going out to work for very low wages. Only where settler sectors were small or absent, as in British West

Africa, was there much encouragement of African cash-crop production. In settler colonies, cash-crop production by Africans was often forbidden outright and markets were totally monopolized by whites. Problems of urban food supply were minimized by controlling influx to the towns. Colonial states regulated the rations of workers on settler farms and plantations and in some cases provided famine relief to areas hit by harvest failure. Far more costly was support to the settler farms which produced most of the marketed grains, involving price support, crop insurance against harvest failure and the exclusion of Africans from markets.

Technical developments changed part of this picture after 1945. Expansion of tractor use largely eliminated the labour shortage which had dominated earlier policy, but with widely varying effects. In Tanganyika, with a small and mostly non-British settler sector, this led to some opening of markets to a few Africans soon after the war; opportunities grasped with both hands by emerging businessmen (with at best ambiguous effects, since a combination of tractors and short-term profit making often led to unsustainable practices and land degradation). In Kenya, the first impact of mechanization and reduced labour needs was a renewed settler offensive against 'squatters' (labour-tenants), which did much to spark off the Mau Mau rebellion. After this had been crushed, some land and opportunities were opened to (selected 'loyal') Africans, combined with land consolidation which took the credit for the ensuing rapid increase in production. (Land consolidation in Kenya is often cited as evidence for the incentive effects of freehold tenure. Judith Heyer and others have shown that removal of barriers can account for the whole increase.) Further opening of markets accompanied land-transfer schemes at independence, and more barriers fell during the following decade. In this process Africans took over the previously white highlands and most cereal production.

In South Africa, this change is yet to come. A burst of African cash-crop farming in the late 19th century frightened whites into rolling it back by edict. The 1913 Land Act prohibited blacks from owning land outside the 'reserves,' then 8% of the land. Subsequent legislation did all that was possible to squeeze out those who already owned freehold land. Efforts redoubled after 1945, and with increased availability of tractors (and subsidies), white farmers mechanized rapidly, sacking and expelling many black workers to the 'homelands,' now increased to 14% of the land (for 86% of the population). The grain marketing system for whites resembles those for settlers in Kenya and colonial Tanganyika. However, where the Tanganyika Farmers Association (TFA) was opened to Africans in 1956 and the Kenya Farmers Association (KFA) in the early 1960s, the South African cooperatives are still only for white farmers.

## *Food and agricultural policy in the North since 1945*

The main factors affecting food consumption and security in northern countries since 1945 have lain outside agriculture, in the combination of economic and social welfare policies which produced the 25–30 year long 'boom' after the Second World War. (A major improvement to British diet occurred under rationing during the War itself, a point widely and conveniently ignored by market enthusiasts.) This set of state-supported compromises between capital and labour raised productivity and real wages, so generating both a rapid increase in overall production and the consumer demand for it. While social welfare payments took care of food security, the consumer-durable 'revolution' was transforming patterns of food consumption and marketing, while freezing made previously perishable foods storable and increasingly palatable. However, despite large increases in meat production and its multiplier effect on the demand for feed grains and high-protein livestock foods, the change in food consumption was unable to keep up with the more rapid increases in food production.

Agricultural policy in most northern countries since 1945 has therefore been based on the massive use of science to increase productivity in farming, subsidies to maintain prices in the face of overproduction and more subsidies to get rid of the surpluses. The subsidies, being based on output and farm size, concentrate some 80% of support on the largest and wealthiest 20% of farms. They have hugely increased mechanization and chemical input use (for examples of over-use, see Leaver, Chapter 4), and so accelerated the inexorable rise of 'minimum economic scale' and the consequent extrusion from farming of successive groups of small farmers. In Europe and the USA, the number of people involved with farming is now well under half the number in 1945 and is still falling.

Internationally, the most important effect of this policy has been the production of huge surpluses and the development of means to dispose of them. Food aid has used food security in the South as a useful justifying slogan, while subsidized exports have helped to change the shape of the world grain market. Before 1939, Europe was by far the world's major grain importer, and developing countries either exporters or self-sufficient. Now the EC is (entirely as a result of subsidies) among the world's major exporters, and the South as a whole has become a net importer of grains.

The basis for this was laid in the USA, the world's major grain exporter. The desperate situation of US agriculture during the Depression of the 1930s led to the setting up of the (State) Commodity Credit Corporation to buy grains at a fixed price and dispose of them outside the US commercial market, via food stamps or exports. [Food stamps provide a specialized form of purchasing power (only for food) which is kept largely separate from commercial markets, since those affected could not otherwise have afforded the food anyway.] Lend–Lease during the War and Marshall Aid after it showed the way, and by the mid-1950s surplus disposal became food aid under PL480. For the following decade, food aid comprised up to half of US grain exports, tapping entirely new markets in the Third World.

This was not a stable situation, since it involved a steady increase in spending on export subsidies. It also set the EC and USA at loggerheads, almost ending in a trade war during the 1980s. The USA was already feeling the budgetary pinch by the late 1960s, when it was the only significant exporter of subsidized grains. In the early 1970s, it aimed to boost commercial exports, with currency devaluation (ending the Bretton Woods currency system) and a major grain deal with the former USSR. This led to a huge increase in grain prices at the peak of famines in Africa. This essentially short-term phenomenon also led to much Malthusian heart-searching about limits to growth and population outrunning food production, even while high prices stimulated a rapid increase in US and EC production (further boosted by the accession to the EC of the UK, Denmark and Ireland from lower protection regimes).

By the mid-1970s, the EC was established as a major world exporter, the world market was back in surplus and the USA was back where it had been in 1972. Since then there have been surpluses of wheat and feed grains and competition to off-load them. The EC subsidizes its exports automatically through the established mechanism; the USA has responded with a variety of programmes, many of them involving mixed deals, with the subsidies sprinkled artfully among them (for example, some wheat, investment in a factory, supply of weapons and (say) training for police 'interrogators,' with varying 'grant elements,' and all presented as 'development aid'). The EC overstepped the mark in the mid-1980s when, seeking to spread the support net wider and reduce the cost of exporting, it subsidized the production of oilseed rape, breaking an undertaking to the USA not to support competitors for soyabeans. This played no small part in initiating the GATT Uruguay Round, itself part of an agreement over protection of the EC frozen chicken market.

Recent years have seen the EC under pressure within and outside GATT to eliminate export subsidies and dismantle the protective system lying behind them. What has emerged from the horse-trading of the Uruguay Round is far less than this, and unlikely to affect world prices significantly in the near future [Gardner (1993) predicts about a 1% per annum increase in wheat and maize prices to the year 2000, 1.5% for beef and under 1% for sugar]. However, it has meant a partial shift in the focus of EC farm support, from crops to farms and (slightly) to smaller farmers. This seems to offer at least some improvement in the prospects for a broader based 'farming-systems-plus' approach to research and extension. This has not affected food security in Europe, although reduction in social welfare expenditures in some countries has led to the re-emergence of homelessness and hunger.

# Northern Food Policy and African Food Security

While the North experienced a rapid increase in food output for stagnating markets, most African countries had the reverse. After independence, urban populations grew rapidly, as did their incomes and political influence. New middle classes increasingly adopted 'international' diets; the urban masses asserted demands for cheap food, supported by industrialists seeking to keep wage bills down. Food demand increased rapidly, as did pressures to keep its price low. Being a matter of considerable political importance, the supply of food to the towns was brought (or kept) under the control of the state, with purchasing agencies having the inconsistent tasks of holding prices down and increasing production. (In Kenya and Tanzania food shortage was not a major problem during the 1960s. Indeed, around 1970 there were pressures in both countries to reduce prices to save the losses incurred on exports.) They sought to overcome this conflict, but in fact magnified it by adopting a highly technocratic policy for modernization, simplified from that of the North. [This grossly oversimplifies a process whose (largely negative) dynamics had been played out for decades between peasants and colonial extension officers.]

Agricultural policy in the North has its problems; the cost and trade rivalry involved in surplus disposal, failure to assist small farmers and the environmental effects of over-use of chemicals. Other problems come into play when this model is used as the basis for technology transfer to Africa.

**1.** *Factor–wage price ratios are different.* In the North wages are relatively high and equipment and inputs are cheap. In Africa the reverse is the case. State policy compounds the difference. Northern countries give heavy subsidies to agricultural sectors commonly amounting to no more than 5% of the population. In tropical Africa, agriculture employs up to or over 70% of the population, and is often the major or only revenue base.

**2.** *Agricultural modernization focuses on individual crop innovations* rather than whole farming systems, and often with insufficient local adaptation in respect of climate, soils, farm size and pre-existing practice. The latter, referred to as 'traditional,' is often ignored, or regarded as an impediment to progress (well known to farming systems researchers, since early examples of FSR emerged in Africa, in direct response to the lack of attention to the whole farm – or parts of it not directly concerned with recommended crops/innovations. Thus, M.P. Collinson, at Ukiriguru in Tanzania in the early 1960s, found 'failure to adopt' certain recommended innovations to be the result of labour constraints generated by the combination of crops grown by small farmers whom officialdom considered only as 'cotton growers'). Innovations are thus often superimposed on systems with which they fit poorly.

**3.** *Input-based agriculture depends on well functioning systems* for the delivery of inputs, credit and services and the collection, grading, processing of and payment for produce. In much of Africa these are either absent or concentrated in 'high-potential' areas (good climate and/or soils, in close proximity to urban or export markets and controlled by white settlers). In many areas roads are impassable during the rains; communications are slow and unreliable; fertilizers arrive after the planting season with monotonous (ir)regularity; produce is not collected or paid for for months on end. All this is especially true for small peasant farmers and in peripheral regions.

Imposing agricultural development programmes on such systems often only makes things worse, especially when, as so often, they involve grants or subsidies which tempt poorly paid officials to corruption and bring sharp political elbows into play. For example, subsidized input deliveries on credit have been a standard of modernization projects, to overcome 'resistance to change' (but also sometimes to make a non-viable innovation economic). Given dependence on agriculture for revenue, an overall subsidy to the sector is out of the question, so subsidies are provided for particular areas or groups of farmers, selected by projects or programmes, and paid for by agricultural producers not included in the projects. Credit and input programmes are channelled through state monopoly crop-purchasing agencies, to allow cross-subsidies and loan repayment by 'deduction-at-source.' The subsidies (plus an involuntary subsidy to those who fail to repay) must be recouped by increasing the marketing margin and reducing the prices paid for crops to producers. Costs by far exceed those of the inputs distributed, as they involve bureaucratic structures and control mechanisms, offices and transport, plus corruption and further mechanisms to control it. It is worth stressing that this is less a matter of incorrect policy choices within the modernization framework than a general effect of this approach to agricultural development.

## Conclusions

The preceding discussion hardly scratches the surface of a complex problem and as a description is clearly oversimplified. However, even at this level of generality, a few conclusions can be drawn.

As in the North, although in different ways, such policies favour the larger and better placed farmers. The more this is the case, the less is the contribution to food security, no matter how large the production increase. South Africa has run a whites-only version of the CAP and produced large export surpluses, while significantly worsening the food security of rural blacks by throwing them out of work and off the land. In the recent drought, its provision for the hungry has been judged less effective than that of Zimbabwe, with one quarter the per capita income. One reason is that 80% of South Africa's 'drought relief' went to indebted white farmers and the banks to which they owed the money (Green, 1993). When Zimbabwe became independent, peasants were, for the first time, encouraged to produce maize, resulting in a burst of increased production. However, most of this came from, and benefited, larger peasants in the better watered north of the country. Zimbabwe has been relatively effective in relieving the effects of food insecurity but less so in providing food security for the poor and landless (this is as much a matter of stagnant employment as anything else). In both Tanzania and Zambia, a series of maize-inputs credit programmes, designed to increase national production, had limited effect on official agency purchases for the towns. In Tanzania, much of what production increase there was went on to the black market, a process which fed on itself as produce diversions reduced official deliveries, raising black-market prices and diverting more produce, etc. Liberalization has meant more visible food production and easier access for those with the money. How it has affected overall production and food security is harder to say. Market-oriented Kenya has ironically been far more reluctant to liberalize grain marketing, recognizing its enormous political importance (see, among others, Raikes, 1994). There have been serious famines and food shortages in the arid northern parts of the country; drought, loss of pastoralist herds and exchange entitlements for them and political repression all having been relevant factors. In all these cases, it is difficult to show any clear relationship between aggregate cereal (and root-crop) production and food security.

While indebtedness and structural adjustment in the 1980s have reduced incomes and so food security, there may (or could) be benefits from the breakdown of much agricultural modernization policy, starved of subsidies and state funds. This has been accompanied by devaluation-induced price increases for farm inputs, which could lead to refocusing in terms of the integration of labour, skills and reduced input levels over whole farms (or broader household) systems. Whether political and economic conditions will allow for this is another matter.

# References

Gardner, B. (1993) *The GATT Uruguay Round: Exports from the Agricultural Super-powers*. CIIR and SAFE, London.

Green, R.H. (1993) Economics of food security. Paper presented at the NCFD Conference on Food Security in South Africa, Johannesburg.

Raikes, P.L. (1988) *Modernising Hunger*. James Currey, London.

Raikes, P.L. (1994) Business as usual – food marketing in Kenya. *Acta Sociologica* xxxiv (1): also CDR Working Paper No. 93.9, CDR, Copenhagen.

# III

## ALTERNATIVE PRODUCTION SYSTEMS

# 10

# ROLE OF FARMING SYSTEMS RESEARCH/ EXTENSION IN GUIDING HIGH INPUT SYSTEMS TOWARDS SUSTAINABILITY

*Javier Calatrava*

## Introduction

Farming Systems Research/Extension (FSR/E) is often associated with low external input farming systems in developing countries, and particularly with the generation of new agricultural technology in family farms with limited resources. Most of the existing literature on the subject is focused on case studies of traditional farming systems in developing countries; studies concerned with the application of FSR/E in high external input systems (HEIS) are not very common. In spite of this, FSR/E has a role in helping to improve the performance of HEIS, particularly in guiding such systems towards sustainability.

The concept of sustainable farming systems is difficult to grasp and its definition is often dependent on the perspective adopted. These difficulties are even greater when the concept of sustainability is applied to high-technology agricultural systems with a high demand for external inputs. Even if sustainability is used in its most generic sense, we must still define the element or elements of the system which we wish to sustain. Moreover, if we are concerned in particular with sustainability as the maintenance of the capital stock, to ensure the system produces satisfactorily in the future it is still necessary to determine whether the objective is one of weak or strong sustainability. In the former case, HEIS usually show a greater capacity for sustainability owing to the effect of replacing natural inputs with artificial ones, in order at least to maintain the system's global capital stock. On the other hand, if the requirement is for strong sustainability, which infers the maintenance of natural capital stock, then HEIS are found to be much more likely to lose sustainability than more traditional extensive systems.

Moreover, if the concept of sustainability adopted is not necessarily anthropocentric (i.e. is measured in terms of energy flows, for example), then in general HEIS are found to be much more fragile than more traditional systems, especially when sustainability is viewed in the medium to long term.

Sustainability is not therefore necessarily related to a particular farming system; the concept of sustainability which is adopted is always related to concern about possible environmental and natural resource limitations which may impede or diminish the functioning of the system in the future. This concern may arise not only in traditional systems but also in systems with a high industrial input requirement. Graham-Tomasi (1991) asserts that there is no reason why sustainability should only be a feature of low external input farming systems, and gives the example of many farming systems situated in marginal areas low in resources, whose level of sustainability is precarious. However, there is no lack of authors (see, for example, Carter, 1988) who clearly identify the concept of sustainability as a characteristic of farming systems with low demands for industrial inputs.

This chapter initially discusses the main features which characterize FSR/E and gives a brief history of the different conceptual approaches to it. This discussion is followed by comments on the circumstances in which FSR/E could be usefully applied to HEIS, using as an example the case of plastic-covered horticulture in southeastern Spain.

## Main Characteristics of FSR/E

Although FSR/E is sometimes regarded as an ambiguous concept, which has various origins, there are a series of features which can be considered as generic and common to the different approaches (Gibbon, 1992). The main generic features of FSR/E are as follows:

- the farming system is taken as the basic unit for research and extension;
- improvement to the system is assumed to be the general goal;
- improvement of the system must be considered within the context of medium- to long-term sustainability (in both ecological and socio-economic terms);
- a significant and detailed knowledge of the system is necessary, for which the analysis of farming systems naturally plays a fundamental part;
- the analysis of systems is not based on conventional techniques but tries first to understand the system and learn from it.

In order that FSR/E is implemented satisfactorily there are a series of desirable requirements which should be met. These are that the approach should be problem solving; adopt a holistic perspective towards the system and its problems; be multidisciplinary; enhance the role of social scientists with respect to conventional research and extension; be highly specific, in the sense that it should basically be client/protagonist oriented; have a dynamic flexibility and be adaptable to changes in and evolution of the system itself; and be implemented within a genuinely participative scheme, not only in identifying the problems, but also in defining the objectives and designing research and extension activities; finally, the role of indigenous knowledge should be enhanced with respect to conventional research and extension.

# What is the Future for FSR/E?

The pioneering studies of farming systems analysis began in the second half of the 19th century, and were primarily concerned with traditional farming systems in Africa, being closely related to the colonial phenomenon. These studies, with a clear anthropological thrust, can be divided into the following three chronologically consecutive stages:

- Studies of traditional farming systems as an 'anthropological curiosity.'
- Analysis of traditional farming systems with the idea of improving them, by means of external technological contributions to the system.
- Learning about systems in order to understand them, to make it easier to collaborate and improve them from the inside. The pioneer of this approach was the Belgian anthropologist Pierre de Schlippe who, in the mid-1950s, defined the farming system as 'a behavioural framework in relation to the land, followed by the members of a rural community' (Schlippe, 1956). Besides taking this basically anthropological stance, Schlippe shows more interest in learning from traditional farming systems than studying them as a result of the curiosity which his predecessors had, even reaching the point, on some occasions, of suggesting that it may be possible to gain something from traditional knowledge which may be of use in improving modern farming systems. For Schlippe, '. . . a series of social and technological norms, derived from experience and a profound knowledge of the natural environment, govern the behaviour of traditional farming system . . .' (Schlippe, 1957). Pierre de Schlippe can be considered the pioneer of the modern concept of systems research, almost two decades before the results of the Green Revolution brought with it the suggestion of a need for avoiding the massive technology transfers of a generic type (Calatrava, 1990).

The approach to systems analysis which is attributed by many authors to having initiated FSR/E evolved from the need to rectify the negative aspects associated with the process of international technology transfer which characterized the Green Revolution. From this emerged the need for research which was undertaken at a local level, specifically aimed at a particular farming system, whilst taking into account the natural environment, and carried out with the collaboration of the farmers involved. Today, new reasons have arisen which support the need for research with a focus on the system.

These reasons, for example, are related to the ecological crisis and the level of environmental deterioration, concern for efficiency and sustainability, a desire to increase food safety standards and to increase farmers' protagonism and a new interest in agroecology (coevolutionary approach).

When considering the future direction of FSR/E, it is necessary to question to what extent and under what conditions FSR/E could become a comprehensive substitute for conventional or formal research/extension. The widespread implementation of systems research in agriculture requires a significant institutional change which, according to the Induced Institutional Innovation Theory (Ruttan and Hayami, 1984), will require changes in the following supply and demand factors:

*Factors which affect supply:*
- Political willingness.
- Negotiation and agreement between corporate interests.
- Social sciences research.

*Factors which affect demand:*
- Technical changes.
- Changes in the availability of inputs.
- Changes in output markets.

The factors which affect demand for FSR/E have clearly been acting in the past few years, requiring significant changes in the objectives and institutions of agricultural research. These factors include, for example, technological changes, scarcity and loss of natural inputs and changes in the markets (internationalization and diversification, appreciation of quality and of natural products, changes in demand and in consumer behaviour, etc.).

Of the supply factors, the first two mentioned above (political willingness and negotiation and agreement between corporate interests) are those which could cause, in the near future, the greatest obstacles to the development of the FSR/E approach. This is because there exist a whole tradition and complexity of interests around conventional research, and scientific policies respond strongly to these interests, not only at a national but also at an international level. Research in social sciences (the third factor) has advanced considerably in the last few years, and the scientific work related to FSR/E has now begun to constitute a coherent theoretical body. However, research on the subject must be continued, in order to reinforce this important institutional supply factor.

It is my view that FSR/E will gradually be implemented in the short to medium term in specific cases in which its necessity is more evident and where conventional research has been able to contribute few solutions, or indeed no solutions at all, to existing problems. Its implementation on a larger scale in the short to medium term is very unlikely because of the problems mentioned above.

## Application of FSR/E to High External Input Systems

The role that FSR/E has in high external input systems will depend on the following factors:

**1.** the efficiency and level of performance of the system in its current state;
**2.** whether the system is a household-dependent system;
**3.** the level of manpower use, i.e. the degree to which the system is labour intensive;
**4.** the degree to which the system is embedded in the sociocultural framework of the community;
**5.** the level of interconnection of the system with the surrounding environment (artificiality of the system); and
**6.** the level of sustainability (both ecological and economic).

The more the system is household dependent, labour intensive and embedded in the sociocultural framework, and gives rise to justified doubts about its sustainability in the short to medium term (factors 2, 3, 4 and 6 above), and the less efficient and artificial it is (factors 1 and 5), the more beneficial the application of a participative systems research to improve it will be, in particular the introduction of the necessary modifications to ensure sustainability.

Figure 10.1 shows that from a static point of view, the systems outputs are a function of the links between the farming system and the environment, the system's inputs and the management of the system in a given institutional context such that:

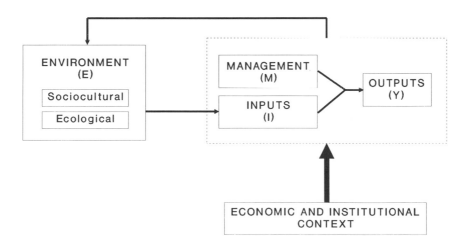

**Fig. 10.1.** Basic scheme of the functioning of a system.

$$Y = f (I, M, E)$$

where $Y$ = the system's output, $I$ = the system's input, $M$ = management and $E$ = environmental context, and for any given environmental context

$$Y = f (I, M/E)$$

The more nearly $(I, M/E) = (I, M)$ is achieved, the higher the degree of artificiality of the system, thus decreasing the sense of taking action with FSR/E.

## The System of Intensive Horticulture in Southeastern Spain

The system of intensive plastic-covered horticulture in sanded soil (soil covered with a layer of sand) was developed on the southern Mediterranean coast of the Iberian peninsula to produce early vegetables. Since its beginnings a quarter of a century ago, this system has been the subject of numerous studies, which approach the subject from different standpoints (see for instance Rueda, 1965; Capdevila *et al.*, 1970; Calatrava, 1982, 1985; Mignon, 1982; Palomar, 1982; Olea, 1985; Berbel, 1987; de los Llanos, 1990; Canero *et al.*, 1992). Figure 10.2 shows that the main locations of this type of horticulture are on both sides of the city of Almeria, the western side being larger in surface area, but together these areas (totalling 16,000 ha) constitute the largest plastic-covered horticultural concentration in the world. Growth of the area of plastic-covered horticulture has been spectacular since its inception in the early 1960s (Fig. 10.3).

The basic technological characteristics of the system are as follows:

- The soil is almost entirely artificial, being formed by a layer of sand and manure, with the original soil barely contributing to the productive process.
- The plastic covering enhances the favourable climatic conditions (mild temperatures and abundant sunshine – over 3000 hours per year) while reducing the unfavourable conditions (high night/day temperature differential).
- The system works on the basis of a substantial use of agrochemicals such as fertilizers, pesticides, flowering hormones and growth regulators.
- The system is labour intensive owing to the constant use of agrochemicals and significant requirements for harvesting.
- Water is an important component in the system because of high evapotranspiration rates and because the area experiences low annual rainfall (< 300 mm per annum) with significant seasonal variation. Water is drawn from large underground aquifers which are currently over-exploited, leading to salt water intrusion; this constitutes one of the most serious problems associated with the current production system.

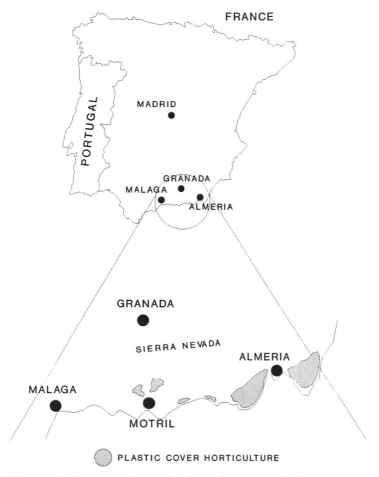

**Fig. 10.2.** Main plastic-covered horticultural areas in southeast Spain.

Surprisingly little is known about the sociocultural impacts of the production system, but the following points illustrate some of the known facts.

- The system is relatively recent, the first sanded crops dating from less than 30 years ago.
- The system was developed in two consecutive stages with a logical time overlap: open-air sanded soil was introduced at the beginning of the 1960s and the plastic covering was added later, in the 1970s. Through time the system has become increasingly intensive, and is now considered to constitute a complete technological package.
- The two most important technological elements of the system, namely the

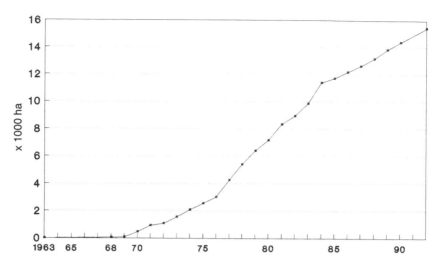

**Fig. 10.3.** Evolution of plastic-covered horticulture in Almeria (Spain) (from Canero *et al.*, 1992).

'sanded soil' and the 'plastic covering,' come from traditional crop techniques found in the local and neighbouring areas. The 'sanded soil' originated from the observation of effects on vegetable crops on the coast of Granada close to the beaches, which became covered with sand when it was windy. The frame for the plastic covering was, and to a large extent still is today, based on the wooden frame traditionally used for table grape growing in the immediate hinterland.

- Thirty years ago, the highly productive area of Almeria was practically desert and sparsely populated, and was colonized with the help of considerable public investment in infrastructure (water management, roads, etc.) and assistance with the initial investment in the preparation for planting.
- The introduction of the production system required an enormous cultural uprooting of the first-generation settlers and led to the emergence of a way of life based on the prosperity achieved by a rapidly generated economic growth, but not coupled with any equivalent social or cultural development.
- The productive system is based almost exclusively on family-type enterprises. The few large commercial enterprises, with some exceptions, have failed.
- At first, the productive system offered high economic rewards. However, it also created a high degree of instability, owing to its dependence on high yields, the time taken between planting and harvest and the prevailing market situation.

• From the beginning, the system presented a low level of sustainability which went unnoticed because of the immediate economic success, which allowed the area to be transformed from being marginally economic to being one of the agricultural areas with the highest income per head in Spain (Calatrava, 1985).

In summary, the production system is an artificial system operated predominantly by families, relying on concentrating large amounts of water, labour and agrochemicals of various types in a semi-artificial soil, protected by a plastic covering, but one in which some environmental elements play an important part. The main objectives of the business are to maximize the output per square metre and produce yield as early as possible.

## The Role of FSR/E in Intensive Horticulture in Southeastern Spain

In the mid-1980s, three situations arose which rang alarm bells and caused worry about the future of production from the system of intensive plastic-covered horticulture in sanded soil:

**1.** A fall in product prices in real terms because of the saturation of the market and growing external competition. This was made worse by increases in real costs, especially labour and energy.
**2.** The major aquifers used for irrigation were becoming exhausted and significant intrusion of salt water was occurring. Salt water intrusion into the aquifers led to the prohibition of construction of new 'invernaderos' (plastic-covered areas of sanded soil used for intensive horticulture) in 1985 without the permission of a local regulatory commission.
**3.** The increasing occurrence of pesticide residues in fruit and vegetables, at levels close to their tolerance level.

Added to these factors is the serious decline in the rate of return that farmers have been receiving on their investment, which had fallen to 10–12% in 1992 (Cañero *et al.*, 1992). This has meant that at current interest rates in Spain the returns generated by the production system are almost exclusively received by salaried employees and family labour. Thus the system currently maintains a well paid contracted workforce, just manages to pay interest due on borrowed capital, but generates minimal business profits. These facts explain why small family enterprises (average 1 ha) continue to operate and the virtual absence of large commercial businesses.

In these circumstances, there are several issues which need to be explored in order to try to improve the socioeconomic and environmental sustainability of the system in the medium to long term, namely reducing production costs and the level of environmental pollution. The following factors, which in many cases are linked to these two major concerns, require further research:

- integrated pest management;
- reduction in the use of fertilizers and pesticides;
- development of water-saving techniques;
- development of new crop varieties;
- the current financial position of the family enterprises;
- analysis of the allocation of resources and technical efficiency; and
- improvement in cooperative efforts in marketing and quality control of inputs and outputs.

At present there are two experimental stations and various extension agencies in the area, although part of the research is undertaken in larger centres situated in other ecological systems with different geomorphological conditions (such as Granada and Cordoba). In general, the research and extension activities which are being carried out in the local area are not of a participative nature. However, some research programmes in which farmers are collaborating have begun, but these still have a conventionally directed focus.

FSR/E has the potential, in these circumstances, to focus research and extension activities to help move the current system towards greater sustainability. However, this potential is limited, first by the very inertia of the current forms of research, which tend to oppose radical changes in focus of their activities and second, by the inertia of the production system itself. Because it has operated on the basis of high inputs and showed high economic returns in the 1970s and 1980s, many farmers do not see sustainability as a serious problem in the medium to long term, although some have become worried by the trends experienced in the last few years. Finally, many of the farmers are reluctant to experiment within their own enterprises because they have developed an underlying confidence in the current systems of production and also because of the high costs which might be borne should the crop be destroyed or produce a lower yield or lower quality product.

Furthermore, one must bear in mind that the search for sustainability would necessarily bring with it significant and abrupt changes in the system's technology, and a focus on the quality as opposed to quantity of the produce, the latter having been the major focus since the introduction of the production system. As a result, an FSR/E framework will have to be implemented slowly and gradually.

# References

Berbel, J. (1987) Analisis de las decisiones en el campo de la horticultura familiar en Almeria: un enfoque multicriterio. Doctoral Thesis, ETSIA, Cordoba.
Calatrava, J. (1982) Los regadios del litoral mediterraneo andaluz, realidad problem-

atica de una agricultura de vnaguardia. *Informacion Comercial Espanola* 582, 67–88.

Calatrava, J. (1985) *La Horticultura Litoral de Primor en el Contexto de la Agricultura Andaluza*. ICE Mars, Madrid.

Calatrava, J. (1990) Los sistemas de agricultura tradicional: las agriculturas ecologicas de siempre. In: *Seminar on Agroecology*. Proceedings Junta de Andalucia, Priego de Cordoba, p. 43.

Canero, R., Calatrava, J. and Castilla, N. (1992) Naturaleza del uso de materiales plasticos en la horticultura bajo abrigo: su influencia en la estructura de costes y en el nivel de rentabilidad. Paper presented at the XII International Conference of Plastic in Agriculture, Granada.

Capdevilla, F., Elena, M. and Calatrava, J. (1970) Estudio monografico del subsector cultivos de primor en la costa granadina. In: *Nuevas Posibilidados del Campo Granadino*. Banco de Granada, Granada.

Carter, H. (1988) The agricultural sustainability issue: an overview and research assessment. In: Javier, E. and Reuborg, V. *The Changing Dynamics of Global Agriculture*. ISNAR, The Hague.

de los Llanos, C. (1990) L'agriculture sous abri du Campo de Dalias. In: *L'Andalousie dans L'Europe: L'essor Du Secteur Fruitier et Maraicher*. Casa de Velazquez, Madrid pp. 21–95.

Gibbon, D. (1992) Farming systems research for sustainable agriculture. In: de Haan, H. and Van der Ploeg, J.D. (eds) *Endogenous Regional Development in Europe: Theory, Method and Practice*. EEC, DGVI, pp. 29–45.

Graham-Tomasi, Th. (1991) Sustainability: concepts and implications for agricultural research policy. In: Pardey, Ph.G., Roseboom, J. and Anderson, J.R. (eds) *Agricultural Research Policy: International Quantitative Perspectives*, ISNAR, Cambridge University Press, Cambridge.

Mignon, C. (1982) *Campos y Campesinos en la Andalucia Mediterranea*. MAPA Coleccion Estudios, Madrid, 606 pp.

Olea, B. (1985) *Empresas Agrarias de Cultivos Intensivos en la Costa del Sol*. Universidad de Malaga, Malaga, 333 pp.

Palomar, F. (1982) *Los Invernaderos en la Costa Occidental de Almeria*. Serie Agricultura, Biblioteca de Temas Almerienses, Almeria, 159 pp.

Rueda, F.Y.J.M. (1965) *Cultivos Enarenados de Hortalizas Extratempranas*. Mundi Prensa, Madrid.

Ruttan, V.W. and Hayami, Y. (1984) Toward a theory of induced institutional innovation. *The Journal of Development Studies* 20, 204–224.

Schlippe, P. de (1956) *Shifting Cultivation in Africa: The Zande System of Agriculture*. Routledge and Kegan, London.

Schlippe, P. de (1957) *Methodes de Recherches Quantitatives dans l'Economie Rurale Coutumiere de l'Afrique Centrale*. Direction de l'Agriculture, des Forêts et de l'Elevage, Brussels.

# 11

## PLANT BIOTECHNOLOGY AND SUSTAINABLE AGRICULTURE

### Eija Pehu

### Introduction

The term plant biotechnology is defined here as the 'integrated use of biochemistry, microbiology and chemical engineering to exploit plant materials and genetic resources for the production of specific products and services' (Mantell *et al.*, 1985). These techniques include cellular level manipulations such as rapid multiplication of plants, disease elimination via meristem culture, *in vitro* storage of germplasm, haploid plant production, somatic hybridization and *in vitro* selection. At the molecular level research is moving very fast to identify genes that could be transferred into crop plants.

Cellular and molecular manipulation techniques can, and already have, shown potential in crop improvement. These techniques are also viewed as a potential means of developing food production systems at a reduced cost to the environment. Interestingly, a recent review on field testing of transgenic plants has shown that the three main focal points of commercial interest in agricultural biotechnology are pathogen/pest resistance, herbicide tolerance and food quality, which account for 80% of the field testing permits issued globally. The remaining 20% cover topics of mainly non-food plant developments (Beck and Ulrich, 1993).

'Contemporary development history has shown that technological change is not deterministic and therefore its evolution can be governed to achieve certain social goals' (Clark and Juma, 1991). It is the scientific community and those setting research priorities who can have a say in the way we apply biotechnology. The high investment cost of biotechnology research, and thus the prominent role of multinational companies in biotechnology research, coupled with patenting legislation to secure the commercial interest of these companies, have had an impact on research priorities. However, recent discussions on the impact of biotechnology have possibly been too negative and to some extent ignored its potential benefits, especially in diversifying economic activities and developing alternatives for crop improvement for sustainable agriculture.

## Plant Biotechnology and Crop Improvement

The development of recombinant DNA techniques and recent developments in genetic transformation methods have made possible the transfer of important traits, such as resistance to pests and diseases, tolerance to environmental stresses, better crop growth, increased carbon assimilation and stimulation of nitrogen fixation. All of these approaches aim at improved food production in marginal areas or with reduced external inputs. However, the extensive introduction of only a few genotypes or varieties with improved characteristics has the danger of narrowing the genetic base of the crop and therefore stability of production. It is also easy to forecast similar developments for intensive cropping systems, such as export crops. The multinational companies, being tightly linked to agroindustry, are keenly interested in the near-market applications of biotechnology. In these cases it is likely that the social dimension of sustainability will not be advanced. Rather, these inputs are likely to be restricted to agribusiness-like farmers, thus widening the gap between poor and wealthy farmers. Again, 'if injustice is the problem, technology is not the solution.'

In spite of the tremendous potential for plant biotechnology to develop varieties for sustainable cropping systems, it is also important to note that our knowledge on the risks involved in the release of genetically manipulated plants is limited. However, this has been recognized by the policy makers and the scientific community, and extensive risk-assessment programs have been initiated and regulations have been imposed for issuing permits for field testing.

In view of the possibilities described above, the 'gene revolution' can have far-reaching positive impacts on crop improvement for low-input agriculture. However, there are issues other than the biological and technical feasibility, such as research priorities and the capacity of different producer groups to utilize biotechnology products. These and other related issues have been discussed by Sasson and Costarini (1991).

### *A short history of developments in plant biotechnology*

Since the 1930s, scientists have developed techniques for growing plant cells in test-tubes. Small pieces of plant tissue are placed in growth medium containing various nutrients and organic compounds, and the tissue starts to proliferate, producing a mass of tissue. In appropriate growth regulator conditions this tissue can be re-differentiated to give a whole plant. This property of regeneration from a cell into a plant is known as totipotency and is the basis of all cellular-level manipulations. Applications of these manipulations can be grouped as follows: rapid multiplication through micropropagation; disease elimination through meristem culture; germplasm storage and transport; production of haploid plants; production of novel genotype combinations via somatic hybridization; and selection of improved cell lines and introduction of DNA sequences by transformation.

In micropropagation, the totipotency of plant cells is used to multiply a particular plant of desired genetic make-up. It is of great economic importance in the production of several root and tree crops, which are normally difficult to multiply. Meristem culture is a technique whereby only the growth point of the plant, called the meristem, is cultured. The advantage of this technique is that it eliminates viruses from the subsequent generations. In combination with micropropagation, meristem culture has become a routine means of producing clean plant material of vegetatively propagated crops. Finally, *in vitro* shoot cultures have proved to be an excellent means for germplasm preservation and, moreover, for transport of genetic stocks from country to country.

Plant biotechnologies have been successfully incorporated into conventional crop improvement schemes. For example, the *in vitro* phase can be used to introduce mutations in the plant genome, thus creating variability for the breeder to select from. This approach has been used in sugar-cane, sorghum, potato, rice and wheat breeding programmes. Somaclonal variants with increased tolerance to environmental stresses have been identified (Scowcroft, 1985).

An immense advantage to plant breeding has been achieved through methods such as anther culture and somatic hybridization. In anther culture, immature pollen grains are developed into plants and will be haploid and thus easier to select. Anther culture has been successfully applied to potato, barley and rice breeding. In somatic hybridization plant cells can be used to develop a novel inter-specific hybrid. This approach is being implemented, for example, in potato, tomato and oil seed rape programmes. The potential of these techniques in improving different crop species is an attractive line of research for variety development for low-input agriculture. The author's research group at the Department of Plant Production is using somatic hybridization to achieve multiple resistance to viruses, bacteria and fungi in Scandinavian potato lines. It is also using an interspecific fusion approach to develop crops that produce insecticides approved in organic farming in Finland.

The fastest moving area in plant biotechnology is recombinant DNA techniques, whereby isolated genes are transferred between organisms. Isolation, cloning, characterization and introduction of DNA sequences back to crop plants are the focus of hundreds of research groups in the world. Hundreds of gene sequences have been cloned so far. For example, insect resistance has been achieved by transforming plants with genes encoding a toxin from *Bacillus thuringiensis* and virus resistance through transforming crops with a viral coated protein sequence.

A large number of the cellular and molecular level manipulation techniques have a great potential to improve crop production in various cropping systems. Decisions relating to the choice of research policy in biotechnology are the key question. This is a great challenge for scientists in influencing the policy makers to shift the emphasis towards directing resources to apply biotechnology to enhance sustainable crop production. In this connection, the prominent role of multinationals in biotechnology cannot be ignored. They have several factors securing their position: preferential access to research results of commercial potential, use of patent law to protect their interests, the ability to take over small competing firms, erosion of public sector capacity by commissioning university research and support from governments in legislation (Dembo *et al.*, 1987). However, at the same time as the values of the public at large are shifting towards environmentally sound agriculture and reduced use of chemical inputs, the private sector will also have to change their priorities in product development. There is already evidence of this in some agrochemical companies.

### *Towards appropriate biotechnology for sustainable agriculture*

Recent discussions relating to plant biotechnology and some of the areas presented above present views that plant biotechnology as it is currently developing can have a negative impact on sustainable crop production. However, as also pointed out earlier, the technology itself will not result in this, but rather it could provide the means for making a significant contribution towards solving problems in low-input agriculture.

In the author's view, national and international programmes should immediately embark on research initiatives which can supplement existing crop improvement programmes in order to develop varieties with satisfactory yield performance with reduced external inputs. It is important to note, though, that as biotechnology requires high-level equipment and personnel, strategic research planning should be carried out in view of the physical, financial and human capacity available. Certain counter arguments are often presented in discussions relating to introduction of biotechnology in developing countries (Dembo *et al.*, 1987), which are equally applicable in the discussion in relation to sustainable agriculture. These are:

- the 'innocent bystander/wait and see' fallacy, which states that research experience for 'softer biotechnology' needs to be accumulated continuously;
- the fallacy of time, which states that there is no need to act now, since the effect will not be felt one or two decades hence.

Pressures for change must be exerted now, before certain policy options are foreclosed. If we are to achieve a strong commitment in applying biotechnology towards the goal of sustainable agriculture, then scientists of different disciplines and policy makers should have greater interaction so that both sides are better informed of the realistic possibilities of the application of biotechnology in sustainable crop production.

# References

Beck, C. and Ulrich, T. (1993) Biotechnology in the food industry. An invisible revolution is taking place. *Bio/Technology* 11, 895–902.

Clark, N. and Juma, C. (1991) Biotechnology for sustainable development. *Nature and Resources* 27, 4–17.

Dembo, D., Dias, C. and Morehouse, W. (1987) Biotechnology and the Third World: caveat emptor. *Development* 4, 11–18.

Mantell, S.H., Matthews, J.A. and McKee, R. (1985) *Principles of Plant Biotechnology.* Blackwell Scientific Publications, Oxford.

Sasson, A. and Costarini, V. (eds) (1991) *Biotechnologies in Perspective: Socioeconomic Implications for Developing Countries.* UNESCO, Rome.

Scowcroft, W.R. (1985) Somaclonal variation: the myth of clonal uniformity. In: *Genetic Flux in Plants.* Springer Verlag, Vienna, New York.

# 12

# DEINTENSIFICATION STRATEGIES OF CEREAL FARMS IN LOWER SAXONY: A Contribution Towards More Sustainable Farming Systems

*Cord Stoyke and Hermann Waibel*

## Introduction

Farming systems research has a long tradition in Germany and dates back to the basic research carried as early as 1842 (Von Thünen, 1921; Brinkman, 1922). There it had been clearly pointed out that farming systems change with location and according to location factors such as distance to markets. For a long period most of the research work done in agriculture in Germany was following a rather reductionist approach. This is explained by the type of structural change which agriculture had undergone.

In Germany from 1965 to 1990 the number of farms decreased by 50% and the number of people gainfully employed in agriculture decreased from 11% to 3% of the total labour force. The average farm size increased from 13.7 to 28.1 ha (Bundesministerium für Ernährung, Landwirtschaft und Forsten, 1971–1993). Land transactions increased mainly by rental arrangements.

Relative prices of agricultural inputs and outputs were strongly in favour of intensification and specialization, resulting in an increase in land and labour productivity. Rapid technological change and the easy access to external inputs facilitated specialization of production activities (de Haen, 1985). Intensive forms of agriculture became concentrated in areas with a comparative advantage. For example, the northwestern part of Germany became a centre for pig and chicken meat production (Becker, 1989), while in large parts of Lower Saxony specialized cereal-based farming systems emerged. Overall, there was a general decline in the existence of integrated crop–livestock farming systems. Growth of specialized livestock farms (Landwirtschaftskammer Hannover, 1991/1992) was facilitated by the absence of regulations as regards the number of animals per unit of farm area, rather liberal animal protection laws and the availability of low-priced imported feedstuff. Similarily, in crop production, the use of external inputs, particularly nitrogen and pesticides, was unrestricted as regards the amount to be used per unit area. Despite existing laws such as the plant protection law with pesticide use regulations promoting integrated pest management, monitoring of implementation and law enforcement remained weak.

In fact, nitrogen and pesticide use has increased considerably during the past 20 years. The amount of nitrogen applied to field crops such as wheat has reached levels of $250-300$ kg ha$^{-1}$.

These developments had two important consequences. First, there was the emergence of an enormous surplus in agricultural production within Germany and the EC, as shown by the degree of self-sufficiency in crop and livestock products. Owing to the previous EC Common Agricultural Policy (CAP), with guaranteed minimum prices for a number of agricultural products, fiscal expenditure soon reached unacceptable levels. Second, there was a continuous use of natural resources and negative environmental impacts attributable to agricultural activities. Indicators are the contamination of groundwater with nitrate and pesticides, resulting in increased costs of water supply (Rat der Sachverständigen für Umweltfragen, 1985; Wissenschaftlicher Beirat beim Bundesministerium für Ernährung, Landwirtschaft und Forsten, 1992).

With the reform of the CAP, output prices are being lowered to near world-market levels. As a consequence, policy makers expect a change in the intensity of land use, resulting in less environmental problems caused by agriculture. However, doubt has been raised as to whether CAP reform is sufficient to solve the environmental problems caused by agriculture, because intensity of land use in areas with a high comparative advantage in agriculture will continue to increase with technological progress. Therefore, additional environmental measures need to be taken into consideration.

Among scientists, agricultural administrators and policy makers there is considerable disagreement as regards the most efficient strategy to solve environmental problems caused by agriculture. Because of the public goods nature of many of the resources affected by pollution caused by agriculture, doubt is raised as to whether market-based solutions will be efficient. Therefore, direct government interventions are proposed as an alternative. Recent research on the problem of nitrate pollution (Scheele *et al.*, 1992) indicates that the search for efficient solutions has to be composed of three specifications:

1. entry point of a measure, i.e. fertilizer use level, nutrient balances or water quality;
2. the target group, i.e. the farmer, the fertilizer industry or the water authority;
3. the target area, i.e. the plot, the farm, a watershed, a region, etc.

Taking regional differences into account, in the state of Lower Saxony a pilot project was started in 1991 which is investigating the impact of a nitrogen quota applicable to the entire farm. The objective of the project is to study the impact of farmers' adjustment strategies with regard to production, income and environment. The research which accompanies this project calls for a systems approach as interdisciplinarity and farmer participation are essential research components.

# Analytical Framework

In measuring the impact of an on-farm intervention such as a quota on nitrogen, a conceptual framework is needed that combines economic theory with quantitative indicators which are meaningful in describing the change. Most importantly, the framework has to capture the agriculture–environment interaction.

One of the major long-term environmental consequences of a continous high amount of external inputs is increasing pollution of groundwater. Only part of the nitrogen (N) applied is taken up by the plant; the rest is deposited in the soil and eventually leaches to the groundwater. Figure 12.1 shows the concept of an N response and a related damage function. With increasing N application the absorption of N by the plant decreases, resulting in an increasing surplus of nitrogen in the soil. Damage is a function of N surplus and increases progressively with a constant increase in N fertilization. Damage is further augmented by the accumulation of N in the soil so that a short-term reduction in N does not result in a corresponding reduction of N leaching.

In addition to the problem of nitrate pollution caused by N surpluses, the fertilizer–pesticide interaction has to be taken into account. Higher levels of mineral fertilizer trigger more intensive pesticide strategies, because the yield potential results in a decrease in the pesticide use threshold. A change in relative prices or technological progress changes the optimal level of fertilizer input and at the same time justifies the adoption of a higher pesticide level. The latter can take place in terms of increasing application numbers, e.g. fungicide treatments in wheat during the panicle initiation phase or higher quality and more expensive pesticides. It is important to realize that a decrease in the ratio of output to fertilizer price will not reduce pesticide use intensity at the same rate as that of fertilizer because pesticide use takes place in discrete steps.

Intensive cropping systems with few crops and a high proportion of wheat in the rotation become increasingly dependent on external inputs. The self-regulating forces of the system weaken, resulting in a deterioration of the natural factors which keep the system on a healthy status. The increased occurrence of diseases, pests and weeds is the ultimate result. The consequence of this is that farmers have to spend more on measures mitigating

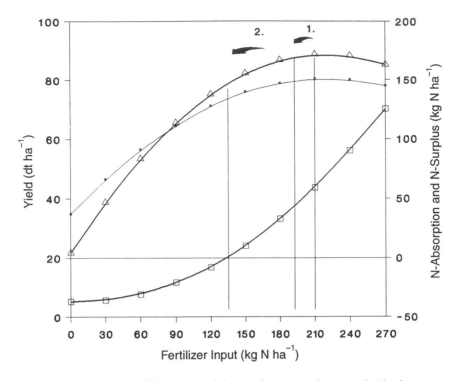

**Fig. 12.1.** Concept of yield function and damage function in the case of N fertilizer use on cereals. **1.** Possible N reduction because of a change in input–output price relationship; **2.** environmentally necessary N reduction. (From de Haen, 1985.)

damage caused by pest organisms (weeds, pathogens and insects), which is reflected in the increasing amount of pesticides. It can be observed that the increase in damage prevention costs is faster than the increase in the costs of attaining the yield potential. An indicator of this is the change in the ratio of fertilizer to pesticide cost in real terms. Whereas in 1960 per 1 DM worth of fertilizer only 0.05 DM worth of pesticides were used, this had changed to 1: 0.35 DM in 1990 (Keller, 1991; Bundesministerium für Ernährung, Landwirtschaft und Forsten, 1971–1993).

With the reform of the CAP, the relative importance of self-regulating factors in theory has increased. Agricultural production can be achieved as the result of a combination of external inputs and inputs produced on-farm. Which combination will turn out to be optimal from an economic point of view depends on the relative costs of both types of inputs. The relationship can be conceptualized as an isoquant which gives all possibilities of obtaining a given level of revenue (see Fig. 12.2). With CAP reform, the relative prices of field crops have changed in favour of those crops whose non-marketable

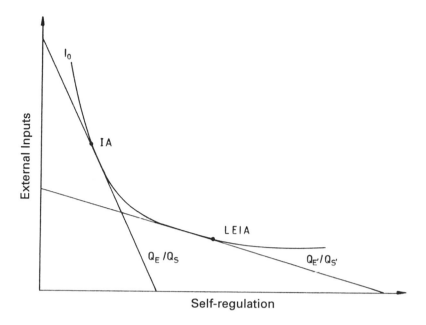

**Fig. 12.2.** Relationship between self-regulation and external inputs. $I_0$ = Iso-revenue curve; $Q_E/Q_S$ = cost ratios; IA = intensive agriculture; LEIA = low external input agriculture.

by-products in terms of positive nutritional and phytosanitary effects within the cropping system are higher. For example, legume crops contribute much to the organic nitrogen content of the soil and oats increases the phytosanitary status of a rotation. However, since markets for these crops are rather limited, even on the world market, their output prices may be too low to justify their planting. On the other hand, their inclusion in the rotation for mere phytosanitary reasons is hardly justified.

# Pilot Project: Nitrogen Quotas in Lower Saxony

## *Project concept*

The rationale of the pilot project is derived from growing concern of policy makers and the public at large about the problem of nitrate pollution. The project was initiated by the State Government of Lower Saxony in 1991.

Implementation of the project is being done by the agricultural administration of Lower Saxony, while the University of Göttingen is entrusted with an accompanying evaluation. Cooperation contracts were negotiated with 18 representative farmers in two regions of Lower Saxony. In addition to the project (quota) farmers, a control group of seven farmers was motivated to participate and supply reference data. The contract between the State Government and the quota farmers defined the level of the N quota in kg N per farm and the amount of compensation payment. The duration of the project has been planned for five years starting in 1992.

Participating farmers were offered two kinds of contracts. One possibilty was that the quota was derived from the fertilizer level as defined by the Chamber of Agriculture as being in accordance with crop-specific, officially recommended levels of nitrogen supply. The amount of N per farm was then derived as a weighted average of the crops grown by the respective farms during a reference period before the start of the project. The so-calculated farm-specific reference level, which ranged from 180 to 220 kg N ha$^{-1}$, was then reduced to 60%, giving the farm-specific maximum level of nitrogen the farmer was allowed to apply. For a farm with livestock production, the maximum level was further reduced, because of the on-farm supply of nitrogen from manure. The amount is based on standard values of nutrients per unit of livestock and a nutrient efficiency of 50%.

The second kind of quota setting differs from the first only with respect to the maximum level. Here the maximum level is set to a fixed value of 90 kg N ha$^{-1}$. For this case the compensation payment was increased by 100 DM ha$^{-1}$. The allowed mineral fertilizer level is then calculated in the same way as described above. The external supply of any other sources of nitrogen such as manure and compost in addition to manufactured mineral N fertilizer was also taken into account. Furthermore, the share of grain legumes as a main crop was restricted to 10% of the arable area of the farm in order to limit additional on-farm supply of nitrogen.

As the N quota refers to the whole farm, the farmer can apply a wide range of adjustment strategies for the reallocation of nitrogen within the farm.

## Description of study area and farms

The project is located in two regions of Lower Saxony with different soil and climatic conditions. One group of farms (nine quota farms, four control farms) is located in the eastern part of Lower Saxony (Lüchow area). Sandy soils with a low nutrient content and occasional drought periods in early summer constitute less favourable production conditions. Use of arable land is dominated by cereals, potatoes, rape-seed and, whenever irrigation is possible, also sugarbeet. The other group of farms (nine quota farms, three control farms) is located in the northwestern part of Lower Saxony in the costal area. The major share of arable land of these farms is located in the costal polder area with nutrient-rich clay soils and sufficient rainfall. The natural production conditions are excellent, especially for wheat.

The difference in location factors leads to differences in the dominating farming systems within the project areas. This is reflected in the farm types found in the two samples of project farms. In the Lüchow area all nine quota farms are in general crop production based, but five farms produce milk, while on three other farms pigs are produced. Only one farm is specialized in crop production. Farm size varies from 40 to 100 ha. In the costal area most of the nine quota farms are cereal based; only on three farms is milk additionally produced and on two farms pigs are raised. Except for one case, the share of income derived from livestock is low in comparison with the mixed farms in the Lüchow area. The acreage varies from 20 to 100 ha.

Although the sample size is small in both areas, the group of control farms is comparable to the group of quota farms with respect to farm type, intensity of N fertilizer use and chemical plant protection.

## Methodology of economic analysis

The point of departure of the economic analysis of a nutrient quota is the change in the supply of a production factor from an unlimited to a restricted one. For a farmer participating in the project, nitrogen becomes a scarce resource. Hence the competition for nitrogen among the different crop enterprises results in a positive shadow price for nitrogen. Based on economic theory, the optimal allocation of scarce nutrients is reached if the marginal value product is equal in all alternative uses.

The consequence of the competition is a substitutional relationship between different products, leading to the fact that the nutrient has to be valued with its shadow price instead of its market price. Under a situation of restricted nitrogen supply, the optimal crop combination is likely to change according to differences in the marginal value product of nitrogen in the different crops. Furthermore, changes in the level of nitrogen use lead to an adjustment in the level of complementary inputs, especially of fungicides. Whenever the shadow price of nitrogen exceeds its market price, techniques which mobilize 'nutrient reserves' become profitable. Examples are the use of intercrops which reduce nitrogen leaching and of grain legumes which accumulate additional nitrogen. Another strategy is the change of timing and the change in the application technique for liquid manure in order to reduce nutrient losses.

Based on economic theory, it can be expected that relative to a situation without a quota, participating farmers will undertake measures which minimize loss of income caused by the imposed scarcity of N, which as a by-product will reduce environmental stress caused by agriculture. In particular it can be expected that farmers will:

- change their cropping pattern;
- modify allocation of nitrogen across crops;
- adjust the use of complementary inputs;

- mobilize nutrient reserves in a way which does not conflict with the quota.

To test these hypotheses, the following quantitative indicators were defined:

- the percentage of less intensive crops such as oats in the rotation;
- N supply and N balance per plot, both in kg N ha$^{-1}$;
- composition and level of pesticide use in monetary units (DM ha$^{-1}$);
- percentage of arable land planted with intercrops and mangement of manure application.

Measurable changes of these indicators help to explain if the restriction of a key input factor such as nitrogen leads to a decrease in the use of external inputs and to a strengthening of the self-regulating forces within the cropping system. An important factor in assessing these changes, especially for the assessment of the sustainability of changes in farming systems, is the accumulation of farmers' knowledge and the changes in the rationale of decision making.

In order to be able to test the hypothesis mentioned, input–output data are collected on a plot level. In addition, farm-specific data such as resource endowment and the extent of livestock production are compiled. Also, frequent discussions with farmers are conducted in order to capture information as regards the learning process induced by the project. The plot-level data are used to calculate gross margins and nutrient balances and to describe adjustment strategies. As of now, data from two years are available, i.e. the year before the start of the project and the first year. Therefore, the results merely provide indications as regards possible ways of analysis and allow conclusions as regards potential changes.

In the analysis, two types of comparisons can be made: 'before and after' and 'with and without.' Their rationale depends on the respective character of the variable to be analysed. In the first comparison, quota farms are compared with control farms in year $t$, whereas in the second comparison quota farms in year $t-1$ are compared with quota farms in year $t$. Variables which are highly farm specific such as the share of contract-based crops can only be compared within the same farm over time, whereas highly year-specific variables, which are influenced by weather conditions such as yield and product quality, must be compared across farms. Ideally, combined comparisons would have to be done, i.e. comparing the changes of the quota farms with those of the control group.

### Results

Preliminary results can be shown as regards changes in the cropping pattern, fertilizer and pesticide use and changes in the N balances.

## Cropping pattern

In both regions, particular adjustments of the cropping pattern can be observed. In Lüchow, quota farmers reduced the share of N-intensive crops such as wheat, barley and rape-seed (Table 12.1). These were replaced by crops with less N requirements such as summer barley and linseed or even with N-supplying crops such as grain legumes. Crops with a comparative advantage such as rye (because of drought resistance), potatoes and sugarbeet (irrigated) were maintained in terms of their cropping share.

In the coastal area, the change in the cropping pattern took place in the same way as in the Lüchow area, but owing to the differences in location factors other crops were concerned. Rape-seed was reduced heavily so that the share of crops such as wheat and grass-seed could be maintained, whereas oats, summer barley, grain legumes and linseed had been increased.

## Fertilizer use

As expected, nitrogen was disproportionately reduced across the different crops. There were also great differences between the two regions.

In Lüchow (Table 12.2), the simple average of N use in the first year after introducing the quota was reduced by 32%. Some crops such as wheat,

**Table 12.1.** Changes in cropping pattern (% of total farm land).

| | Lüchow area | | | | Coastal area | | | |
| --- | --- | --- | --- | --- | --- | --- | --- | --- |
| | Quota farms | | Control farms | | Quota farms | | Control farms | |
| | 1991 | 1992 | 1991 | 1992 | 1991 | 1992 | 1991 | 1992 |
| Winter wheat | 12 | 8 | 17 | 18 | 44 | 42 | 59 | 41 |
| Winter barley | 12 | 9 | 7 | 9 | 7 | 5 | 11 | 10 |
| Winter rye | 10 | 11 | 13 | 9 | – | – | – | – |
| Summer barley | 2 | 4 | 7 | 4 | 0 | 1 | 3 | 1 |
| Oats | – | – | – | – | 4 | 9 | 0 | 5 |
| Rape-seed | 11 | 5 | 16 | 14 | 12 | 2 | 11 | 7 |
| Sugarbeet | 7 | 6 | 7 | 6 | – | – | – | – |
| Potatoes | 13 | 12 | 15 | 16 | – | – | – | – |
| Grass-seed products | – | – | – | – | 11 | 11 | 0 | 0 |
| Grain legumes | 0 | 3 | 0 | 0 | 1 | 6 | 0 | 0 |
| Linseed | 0 | 6 | 0 | 2 | 0 | 2 | 0 | 0 |
| Maize (silage) | 9 | 7 | 3 | 3 | – | – | – | – |
| Pasture | 18 | 20 | 8 | 8 | 11 | 12 | 11 | 19 |
| Other | 6 | 9 | 7 | 11 | 10 | 10 | 5 | 17 |

sugarbeet and pasture were reduced above average and barley, rye and potatoes were reduced below average. The reduction is dependent on the level of fertilization before the quota and the marginal value product of nitrogen. For example, before the quota, sugarbeet was fertilized at inefficiently high levels, so that the potential to save scarce nitrogen was much higher than with barley, rye or potatoes, where the nitrogen input was at its optimal level. On the other hand, wheat has unfavourable conditions in the Lüchow area because of dry stress. The reduction in its cropping share is therefore accompanied by a relatively large decrease in N fertilizer use, because there is a high probability that water might be insufficiently supplied. The fact that the control farms also reduced the nitrogen input in 1992 can be explained by the extraordinarily low rainfall in northern Germany in that year.

In the coastal area (Table 12.2), a comparable pattern of adjustment can be observed. Again, crops with less comparative advantages in that region (barley) or crops which were fertilized at a very high level with a high 'insurance' topping (grass-seed, pasture) were reduced above average. Consequently, wheat with its outstanding regional importance because of its regional advantages had to be reduced below average.

### Allocation and management of N fertilizer use

The fertilizer allocation among crops is the key question if the N requirements of the entire farm can exactly be determined in accordance with the N quota.

**Table 12.2.** Changes in N fertilizer use (kg N ha$^{-1}$ and change in %).

|  | Lüchow area | | | | Coastal area | | | |
|---|---|---|---|---|---|---|---|---|
|  | Quota farms | | Control farms | | Quota farms | | Control farms | |
|  | 1991 | 1992 | 1991 | 1992 | 1991 | 1992 | 1991 | 1992 |
| Total farm land | 160 | −32% | 167 | −9% | 169 | −38% | 225 | −15% |
| Winter wheat | 181 | −42% | 175 | +3% | 191 | −28% | 218 | 0% |
| Winter barley | 165 | −23% | 161 | +13% | 161 | −39% | 226 | −43% |
| Rye | 135 | −16% | 128 | −9% | − | − | − | − |
| Oats | − | − | − | − | 79 | −6% | − | − |
| Sugarbeet | 194 | −40% | 169 | 0% | − | | | |
| Potatoes | 126 | −4% | 166 | −9% | − | | | |
| Grass-seed products | − | − | − | − | 119 | −41% | − | − |
| Maize (silage) | 151 | +4% | 213 | −2% | − | − | − | − |
| Pasture | 183 | −33% | 179 | +27% | 229 | −47% | 253 | −22% |

However, this is only possible for farms without livestock production which use only mineral fertilizer.

An important question in the context of a N quota concerns the adjustment strategies of farmers with livestock production, particularly with regard to organic fertilizer mangement. In this case the mineral N fertilizer quota is derived on the basis of the organic N fertilizer based on standard values. If the farmer succeeds in mobilizing additional nutrients by realizing a higher nutrient efficiency than assumed, his 'effective' quota is higher than the 'computed' quota. Two different approaches could be observed in the pilot project. One possibility is a crop-specific allocation of organic nitrogen which requires a change of timing in liquid manure application.

A decrease of liquid manure application to sugarbeet explains partly why wheat, barley and maize are absolutely and relatively more highly fertilized with organic nitrogen in the first year of the project. A new technique is the top fertilization of wheat and barley in spring. The latter is indicated by an increase in organic nitrogen supply from 8 kg N ha$^{-1}$ to 17 and 21 kg N ha$^{-1}$, respectively.

An increase in organic nitrogen supply by 14% on average per farm area is only explained to a minimal extent by an increase in livestock density. The major share can be explained by the fact that the quota farmers shifted their liquid manure application predominantly from autumn to spring, thus practising top fertilization of cereals. Consequently, nutrient efficiency is higher owing to reduced leaching losses. The comparative advantage of this strategy depends on the scarcity of labour in spring. The marginal value product of these nutrients must be clearly higher than the market price of nitrogen, or else the farmer would have done the same before or without an N quota. In fact, control farmers who did so before even changed their strategy, contrary to the quota farmers.

## Pesticide use

As indicated above, the reduction in pesticide use is closely related to the reduction in N. How far the adjustment of pesticide use can go depends on the crop. Sugarbeet, for example, shows high costs for herbicides which depend on the location and the quality of soil preparation and can therefore hardly be influenced by N fertilization. The same is valid for potatoes in the case of fungicide and insecticide use.

In the case of cereals, herbicide use is also nearly independent of the N fertilizer level, whereas the use of fungicides, insecticides and growth inhibitors can be considered as complementary factors. For the Lüchow area adjustments in the pesticide inputs for wheat and barley can be presented as an example.

In 1991, quota farmers spent about 330 DM ha$^{-1}$ on pesticides for wheat, of which roughly one third was on herbicides. As a result of the lower N fertilizer level and the lower expected yield level, pesticide costs were reduced by 130 DM ha$^{-1}$ in 1992. Fungicide use was reduced to nearly 50% of the previous amount. Control farmers maintained the same absolute levels in both years. In the case of barley, the same situation can be observed, except that the absolute level of pesticide cost is lower, with roughly the same absolute amount spent for herbicides. Consequently, the adjustment potential (fungicides, insecticides, growth inhibitors) in accordance with a reduced N level is lower. Reducing the level of pesticide use is an indicator of greater allocation efficiency and at the same time is an environmental indicator.

### N balances

Figure 12.3 shows the results from 712 plots representing two regions and two farm groups. The crops grown were cereals, rape-seed, sugarbeet, potatoes and grain legumes. N balances are divided into four 'damage classes' defined by the level of N balance surplus (<0, 0–50, 51–100, >100 kg N ha$^{-1}$). All sources of N fertilization and the nitrogen content of the products which are removed from the plot are taken into account. However, the input by grain legumes has not yet been taken into account. For this the relative shares of the class <0 kg N ha$^{-1}$ are slightly overestimated.

In both regions the implementation of the N quota led to a decrease in the relative share of plots with more than 100 kg N ha$^{-1}$ balance surplus. This class can be interpreted as 'highly polluting.' The next lower level (51–100 kg N ha$^{-1}$) maintains its share in Lüchow but it decreases in the coastal region. The last two classes indicate a decrease in potential water contamination. Compared with

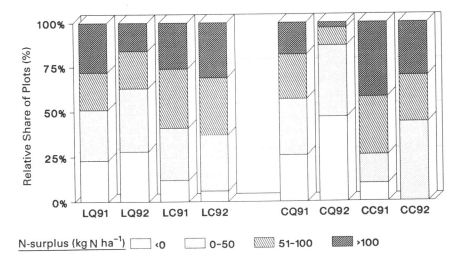

**Fig. 12.3.** Distribution of N balances (arable land only). L— = Lüchow area; C— = coastal area; —Q = quota farms; —C = control farms. 712 plots: cereals, root crops, grain legumes.

the quota farms, there is no remarkable reduction of N surplus in the plots of the control farms in both areas.

## Implications for Sustainability

The purpose of the pilot project is not to show whether N quotas would be a better policy tool than taxes. From an administrative point of view there is no doubt that nitrogen taxes would be a better choice, although the problem of liquid manure and accounting for the tremendous regional differences of the external costs of nitrogen still remains. Taxes on fungicides might also be considered because they would induce lower nitrogen levels regardless of the source. Taxes on inputs would have to be substantial if a measurable effect on production and the level of input use is to be achieved. In any case, to make agricultural systems sustainable means maintaining the function of the ecosystem which interfaces agricultural production. This requires a better balance between external inputs and self-regulating forces. True costing of external inputs such as pesticides and fertilizer through either taxes or direct interventions would change the balance between these inputs and those produced on-farm.

As regards the quantitative results, it must not be forgotten that they are only preliminary. Nevertheless, they are consistent with research which indicates that considerable reductions in external inputs can be undertaken without any effect on production. There seems to be an enormous potential for replacing external inputs by improved crop management (Baumer *et al.*, 1992).

On the other hand, the intention of this chapter is to identify indicators for positive changes of high external input agriculture towards a better recognition of the natural resource base of agriculture. What is most important, though, as a result of the pilot project is the measurement and the description of the adjustment process farmers undertake in response to specific environmental interventions. It can be expected that the innovative capability of farmers will be stimulated and that farmers will come up with solutions which they have developed themselves instead of being bought in from outside. Hence there is a transfer of ownership in technology from the off-farm to the on-farm sector. Environmental restrictions can increase the awareness of the consideration of user costs (off-time costs) of natural resources. In the long run, farmers are expected to ask different questions of the extension service. This will demand a change in the contents of agricultural education. Agricultural education, in addition to skills in managing machines, livestock and accounting procedures, will have to give emphasis to strengthening the understanding of the ecosystem and the environment–production technology interaction. The latter aspect is expected to become the core of a profile for modern farming in Europe.

# References

Baumer, K., Claupein, W. and Wildenhayn, M. (1992) Extensivierung der Pflanzen-produktion: Ziele, Wege und mögliche Folgen. *VDLUFA Schriftenreihe* 35, 1–17.

Becker, H. (1989) The impact of soil productivity regulating measures on supply, demand and technology in German agricultural production systems. In: Dub-gaard, A. and Nielsen, A.H. (eds) *Economic Aspects of Environmental Regulations in Agriculture*. Proceedings of the 18th Symposium of the European Association of Agricultural Economists, Kiel, pp. 187–196.

Brinkman, T. (1922) *Die Oekonomik des landwirtschaftlichen Betriebes*. Grundriß der Sozialoekonomik, Tuebingen.

Bundesministerium für Ernährung, Landwirtschaft und Forsten (1971–1973) *Agrar-bericht der Bundesregierung*. Bundesministerium für Ernährung, Landwirtschaft und Forsten, Bonn.

de Haen, H. (1985) Interdependence of prices, production intensity and environmen-tal damage. *Zeitschrift für Umweltpolitik* 3/85, 199–219.

Keller, H. (1991) Chemischer Pflanzenschutzmitteleinsatz in der Landwirtschaft. *Europäische Hochschulschriften Reihe* V, 1158.

Landwirtschaftskammer Hannover (1991/1992) *Betriebsstatistik der Landwirtschafts-kammer Hannover*. Landwirtschaftskammer Hannover, Hannover.

Rat der Sachverständigen für Umweltfragen (1985) *Umweltprobleme der Land-wirtschaft*. Sondergutachten, Rat der Sachverständigen für Umweltfragen, Stutt-gart.

Scheele, M., Isermeyer, F. and Schmitt, G. (1992) Umweltpolitische Strategien zur Lösung der Stickstoffproblematik in der Landwirtschaft. *Arbeitsberichte des Insti-tuts für Betriebswirtschaft der Bundesforschungsanstalt für Landwirtschaft, Braunsch-weig*, No. 6.

Von Thünen, H. (1921) *Der Isolierte Staat in Beziehung auf Landwirtschaft und Nationalökonomie*, 2nd edn. Jena.

Wissenschaftlicher Beirat beim Bundesministerium für Ernährung, Landwirtschaft und Forsten (1992) *Strategien für eine Umweltverträgliche Landwirtschaft. Reihe A: Angewandte Wissenschaft*, No. 414. Wissenschaftlicher Beirat beim Bundesminis-terium für Ernährung, Landwirtschaft und Forsten, Münster.

# 13

## BIOMASS AS AN ALTERNATIVE LAND USE FOR SOUTHERN EUROPEAN AGRICULTURE

### Spyros Kyritsis and Peter G. Soldatos

## Introduction

The EC agricultural food production surpluses have forced the European Commission (through changes in CAP) to adopt a large number of financial measures aimed at eliminating the disparities between internal supply and demand. The effects of these changes are now being felt by all European farmers.

These measures were of particular importance for Greek agriculture, which still employs almost 30% of the active population, which is significantly above the Community average of 10%. Greek farmers currently operate under very unfavourable terms and, as a result, many young farmers have abandoned agriculture in search of more profitable activities. These social and economic problems are increasing daily and require immediate action and careful assessment of the possible alternative futures for Greek agriculture.

One of the proposals, which is of special interest, is the gradual replacement of several unprofitable crops, such as cereals and corn, with biomass plantations, i.e. short-rotation or fast-growth crops, which may be used as raw materials for energy production. This would not only secure the production of a highly demanded commodity, but would also serve other EC and national targets such as a reduction in energy dependence and balance of payments alleviation. Biomass energy products are not harmful to the environment and, unlike other soft energy sources, can be produced and stored in relatively large quantities.

Given today's low oil prices, energy production from plant biomass (in the form of alcohol, oil, gas, etc.) has generally been found to be uneconomic, at least from the point of view of the producer. This chapter describes and discusses the conditions and levels of profitability of the new technology. The results of a number of carefully selected scenarios are presented, together with the associated sensitivity analyses, which define the critical values of all important parameters.

# Background

The small agribusiness units in southern Europe, usually run by the farmer and his family, are asked by society to perform a rather complex role in rural areas. Specifically, the agricultural family is asked to:

- produce high-quality–low-cost products in order to survive in a competitive market with diminishing economic protection;
- give an all-year-round care to their own land and protect natural resources and the environment;
- save and propagate social and cultural traditions;
- apply both indigenous knowledge and new methods of production and pass the acquired know-how to their successors.

The real cost of what the agricultural family offers is hard to estimate, but it surely is higher than the mere cost of production.

There is GATT pressure for less protectionism of EC products and pricing schemes based on international production cost calculations. However, since the social and environmental contribution of the European farmer is much more important than their produce, someone should pay the difference. In effect, if subsidies were to be withdrawn tomorrow, it would be uncertain how many European farmers would be in business the day after. The result of such an event would have very serious consequences on food sufficiency, land maintenance, indigenous knowledge, etc. On the other hand, EC protectionism has resulted in overproduction and the waste of large amounts of resources.

Under these conditions, land use for non-food agriculture emerges as a unique opportunity for the European agricultural sector to achieve both gradual elimination of food overproduction and, at the same time, to provide increased opportunities for farmers in rural areas.

The key factors to be considered when encouraging alternative land use in southern EC regions are the following:

**1.** *Balance of trade.* All southern European countries are very strongly dependent on imported fossil fuels (coal, crude oil and natural gas) for their energy needs. However, as is well known, biomass in general can successfully replace oil and gas for all energy uses (e.g. ethanol, biodiesel, gasification, charcoal, direct combustion). Besides its contribution to the energy sector, there are other areas of European industry where biomass is a scarce basic raw material, such as paper pulp and chipboard. These raw materials are today being imported in large quantities from third countries and transported over long distances. In fact, in 1989 the European trade deficit of wood and pulp paper was about ECU 17 billion.

**2.** *The environment.* The environmental advantages from using biomass for energy or as building materials are the following:

(a) Alleviation of the greenhouse effect and of the problems of global change. Biomass can replace fossil fuels without increasing the $CO_2$ content of the atmosphere.

(b) Delay of oxygen depletion in the atmosphere.

(c) Less $SO_2$ emissions, contributing to less harmful acid rain effects.

(d) Improvement of the microclimate through water use and recycling mechanisms.

(e) Reduction of soil deterioration and pollution of water ways and groundwater by the production of compost and its use.

(f) Stabilization of certain soils in southern Europe by reducing desertification and erosion.

(g) Reduction of the risk of forest and brushwood fires, a constant threat for the forests in southern Europe.

**3.** *Renewable source.* Biomass is a renewable energy source capable of providing a significant proportion of the southern European energy and other raw material needs.

**4.** *Agricultural policy.* Food production in the EC has to be controlled by measures such as land setaside, reduction of production subsidies and other socioeconomic incentives. The possible abandonment of agricultural land can have, especially in southern Europe, serious socioeconomic and environmental effects. There could, therefore, be a profitable shift in the use of some land from food crops to biomass plantations for the production of raw materials for the energy and industrial markets.

## The Need for a New Farming System for Alternative Land Use

The new CAP mechanism that was adopted by the European Council in May 1992 demands that:

- There should be a progressive narrowing of the gap between the level of prices of the European and international products.
- The European Community will pay a compensatory price per hectare in order to maintain agricultural income at satisfactory levels. In this case the income of the farmer will be the sum of the international prices plus the EC subsidy.
- EC Member States should setaside 15% of their cultivated land (excluding the land of small European farmers). However, the small producers of olive

*Spyros Kyritsis and Peter G. Soldatos*

and other oil seeds, which may be used as raw material for biodiesel, are allowed to choose whether to adopt the status of the large producers, i.e. to setaside 15% of their land. EC subsidies for setaside in southern Europe vary between ECU 67 and 243 ha$^{-1}$ according to the 'agricultural zone.'

At present, it is too early to estimate the effects of the new CAP on farmers' income, the cultivated area and the potential restructuring of European cultivation. However, the new CAP will come as a shock to many farmers who, up to now, were seeking a farming system which gave them the opportunity to modernize their farms and allowed them to increase inputs in order to improve their yields. On the other hand, small land holders are likely to continue aiming at maximizing profits, using all the available resources and land at their disposal.

After a long period of continuous effort aimed at increasing agricultural productivity, European agriculture is today facing the dawn of a new era. There is a need for farming systems which incorporate new uses of land such as biomass cultivation. The main features of the new farming system are that:

- The cultivation techniques, which incorporate less direct energy inputs, are suitable for part-time farming, especially for marginal land exploitation. For example, the short-rotation crops need some initial investment for planting or seeding but cost nothing once established until harvesting.
- Research may be needed on the utilization of waste water or brackish water from nearby municipalities for the irrigation of biomass plantations.
- There will be lower chemical inputs in the form of fertilizers, herbicides, etc.
- Existing soil and water pollution levels cannot be tolerated by the new farming system. On the contrary, there is a need to give up traditional farming systems based on the uncontrolled use of chemicals.
- Low direct and indirect energy inputs will give an energy input/output advantage in the context of the new farming system.
- There is an urgent need for farming systems research in the area of harvesting, transport and especially storage of biomass yields. In some cases biomass harvesting takes place only during a short period of the year (e.g. in autumn), whereas biomass is consumed more evenly throughout the year. This means that in some cases the volume of stored biomass is exceptionally large, whereas in other cases special storage conditions may be necessary to prevent biomass transformation; for example, sugar should quickly be converted into ethanol.

## Economic Analysis

Tables 13.1 and 13.2 illustrate the results of a detailed financial investigation of selected conventional and biomass land-use systems.

**Table 13.1.** Analysis of costs and benefits – conventional cultivations.

| | Unit | Hard wheat | Soft wheat | Hard wheat with 15% setaside | Soft wheat with 15% setaside | Gravity-irrigated corn | Machine-collected cotton | Hand-collected cotton |
|---|---|---|---|---|---|---|---|---|
| Annual yield[a] | t ha$^{-1}$ | 2.8 | 2.8 | 2.4 | 2.4 | 9.0 | 2.4 | 2.4 |
| **Production costs:** | | | | | | | | |
| Cost of: | | | | | | | | |
|   Seeds, saplings, water, etc. | ECU ha$^{-1}$ | 138 | 109 | 117 | 93 | 300 | 281 | 281 |
|   Machinery | ECU ha$^{-1}$ | 181 | 188 | 154 | 159 | 448 | 1164 | 1114 |
|   Labour | ECU ha$^{-1}$ | 38 | 38 | 32 | 32 | 174 | 201 | 809 |
|   Land rent | ECU ha$^{-1}$ | 116 | 81 | 116 | 81 | 328 | 247 | 247 |
|   Working capital | ECU ha$^{-1}$ | 9 | 9 | 8 | 8 | 9 | 9 | 9 |
|   Depreciation, etc. | ECU ha$^{-1}$ | 16 | 16 | 13 | 13 | 16 | 16 | 16 |
| Total production cost | ECU ha$^{-1}$ | 497 | 441 | 440 | 387 | 1275 | 1918 | 2477 |
| | ECU t$^{-1}$ | 177 | 157 | 185 | 162 | 142 | 799 | 1032 |
| Total subsidies | ECU ha$^{-1}$ | 367 | 70 | 374 | 77 | 238 | 0 | 0 |
| | ECU t$^{-1}$ | 131 | 25 | 157 | 32 | 26 | | |
| Selling price | ECU t$^{-1}$ | 141 | 141 | 141 | 141 | 141 | 859 | 969 |
| **Income and expenses:** | | | | | | | | |
| Gross product | ECU ha$^{-1}$ | 394 | 394 | 335 | 335 | 1266 | 2063 | 2325 |
| Minus expenses | ECU ha$^{-1}$ | 319 | 297 | 271 | 252 | 748 | 1446 | 1396 |
| Gross value added | ECU ha$^{-1}$ | 75 | 97 | 64 | 82 | 518 | 617 | 929 |
| Plus subsidies | ECU ha$^{-1}$ | 367 | 70 | 374 | 77 | 238 | 0 | 0 |
| Minus land, working capital, etc. | ECU ha$^{-1}$ | 141 | 106 | 137 | 103 | 353 | 272 | 272 |
| Farm income | ECU ha$^{-1}$ | 301 | 61 | 301 | 57 | 402 | 345 | 658 |
| Minus cost of labour | ECU ha$^{-1}$ | 38 | 38 | 32 | 32 | 174 | 201 | 809 |
| Profit | ECU ha$^{-1}$ | 264 | 23 | 269 | 25 | 228 | 144 | (152) |

[a]Dry matter for all perennial plantations; the cost of working capital is included in the cost of saplings.

**Table 13.2.** Analysis of costs and benefits – biomass cultivations.

| | Unit | Non-irrigated black locust | Irrigated mischanthus | Non-irrigated mischanthus | Non-irrigated eucalyptus | Irrigated sweet sorghum | Non-irrigated sunflower[b] | Irrigated sunflower[b] |
|---|---|---|---|---|---|---|---|---|
| Annual yield[a] | t ha$^{-1}$ | 18.0 | 28.0 | 20.0 | 26.0 | 30.0 | 1.3 | 2.5 |
| Production costs: | | | | | | | | |
| Cost of: | | | | | | | | |
| Seeds, saplings, water, fertilizers, etc. | ECU ha$^{-1}$ | 469 | 350 | 313 | 622 | 194 | 75 | 94 |
| Machinery | ECU ha$^{-1}$ | 69 | 219 | 163 | 150 | 650 | 294 | 809 |
| Labour | ECU ha$^{-1}$ | 13 | 44 | 25 | 19 | 97 | 106 | 203 |
| Land rent | ECU ha$^{-1}$ | 116 | 247 | 172 | 172 | 247 | 116 | 247 |
| Working capital | ECU ha$^{-1}$ | 16 | 16 | 16 | 16 | 9 | 9 | 9 |
| Depreciation, etc. | ECU ha$^{-1}$ | 16 | 16 | 16 | 16 | 16 | 16 | 16 |
| Total production cost | ECU ha$^{-1}$ | 681 | 875 | 688 | 978 | 1213 | 616 | 1378 |
| | ECU t$^{-1}$ | 38 | 31 | 34 | 38 | 40 | 493 | 551 |
| Total subsidies | ECU ha$^{-1}$ | 400 | 0 | 0 | 60 | 0 | 313 | 313 |
| | ECU t$^{-1}$ | 22 | | | 2 | | 250 | 125 |
| Selling price | ECU t$^{-1}$ | 31 | 31 | 31 | 31 | 38 | 156 | 156 |
| Income and expenses: | | | | | | | | |
| Gross product | ECU ha$^{-1}$ | 563 | 875 | 625 | 813 | 1125 | 195 | 391 |
| Minus expenses | ECU ha$^{-1}$ | 538 | 569 | 475 | 772 | 844 | 369 | 903 |
| Gross value added | ECU ha$^{-1}$ | 25 | 306 | 150 | 41 | 281 | (173) | (513) |
| Plus subsidies | ECU ha$^{-1}$ | 400 | 0 | 0 | 60 | 0 | 313 | 313 |
| Minus land, working capital, etc. | ECU ha$^{-1}$ | 131 | 263 | 188 | 188 | 272 | 141 | 272 |
| Farm income | ECU ha$^{-1}$ | 294 | 44 | (38) | (87) | 9 | (2) | (472) |
| Minus cost of labour | ECU ha$^{-1}$ | 13 | 44 | 25 | 19 | 97 | 106 | 203 |
| Profit | ECU ha$^{-1}$ | 281 | 0 | (63) | (106) | (88) | (108) | (675) |

[a] Dry matter for all perennial plantations; the cost of working capital is included in the cost of saplings.
[b] Sunflower seeds.

- The figures reflect the financial details of the most common crops in Greece (conventional crops) and some of the most promising biomass plantation alternatives, suitable for southern European climates.
- 'Yields' are averages for Greece as a whole. The biomass yields are averages for a series of trial plots scattered throughout the country. In our opinion, these yields are pessimistic and could justifiably be increased for long-term budgeting purposes.
- The cost analysis is the result of elaborate calculations, and is based on official data and data from the biomass trial plots.
- The item 'Machinery cost' includes all associated expenses and the cost of the operator(s) who is (are) usually hired by the farmer. 'Land rent' reflects the current average market values.

The first impression gained from the results is that biomass production is not economic. Profit figures (last row of the tables) indicate that conventional land uses are generally more attractive with the possible exception of black locust production. It is obvious that farmers will not decide to engage in biomass production unless they expect to earn sustained profits higher than those which they currently enjoy. On the other hand, most biomass options result in losses for the producer, indicating that under these circumstances, no farmer can be persuaded to change.

However, given the subsidy mechanism of the CAP as it stands today, it is relevant to examine the possibility of biomass cultivation on cereals setaside (15%), or unused land, thereby eliminating the cost of land from the biomass calculations. This results in increased biomass production profitability, and significantly improves the viability of biomass production.

Also of interest is the price used for biomass in the tables. Currently there is no market for biomass, therefore prices cannot be predicted with any degree of certainty. The prices used in Table 13.2 are very pessimistic and are likely to be the lowest that could be expected.

A final point of interest is that mischanthus and sweet sorghum crops are currently unsubsidized, but given a subsidy structure analogous to the other land uses they could also become financially attractive.

## Conclusions

Europe and especially its southern regions currently need to diversify from conventional land uses. European food surpluses are a strong signal towards this kind of reform. From the point of view of the farmer, under current economic conditions, biomass crops are generally uneconomic, but may be profitable under special circumstances, such as where they utilize setaside land, as short-rotation crops on unused pieces of land and where adapted by part-time farmers. Such conditions do exist in many parts of Europe.

The advantages of biomass production for energy and industry (such as in balance of payments, reducing production surpluses, increasing environmental protection and decreasing energy dependence) dictate the need for a strategy of incentives for biomass cultivation, in order to encourage European farmers to disengage from the less profitable conventional land uses. These incentives must take the following forms:

- Research on new farming systems for increased biomass yields which impose less burden on the environment. Build up knowledge (steep learning curve) to improve harvesting, transport and storage of biomass products.
- Restructuring the systems of subsidies in favour of biomass production, thus recognizing its environmental and strategic advantage.
- Imposing environmental pollution penalties on fossil fuels (e.g. carbon dioxide taxes), a measure that will directly push up biomass prices, thus improving the economics of biomass cultivation.
- Biomass subsidization may also be justified in cases of severe foreign exchange and balance of payments pressures or in cases of increased unemployment, as is the case, for example, in eastern European and other less developed countries.

# 14

# ENVIRONMENTAL ISSUES: USE OF FARMING SYSTEMS RESEARCH/EXTENSION TO RESOLVE ENVIRONMENTAL AND SPATIAL PROBLEMS

*Marc Benoit*

## Introduction

Developed countries are currently experiencing food surpluses as a result of their highly efficient agricultural systems. Former limiting factors were related to yield levels only. There has been little work in either agronomic or economic research on the relationships between resource use and techno-logical change (de Wit, 1992). Technical change has sociological, economic and environmental consequences in addition to being a response to socio-logical, economic and environmental change (Benoit *et al.*, 1990). Two problems emerge in research into these relationships: accurate local environ-mental data are not easily found and detailed research on resource use trends and changes in farming practices is very recent. This applies both on a nationwide and on a local scale.

In France, the first eminent 'advocate' in this area was René Dumont (Dumont, 1961, 1974). The presidential vote in 1974 was the first step towards a national ecological movement. Some years later, INRA's President, Jacques Poly, defined a new alternative course for French agriculture (Poly, 1977). However, there remained a long period of inaction in research on environmental issues. In the last four years, the Centre National de la Recherche Scientifique (CNRS) and INRA have been developing new struc-tures to include environmental issues in their scientific programmes. Some hypotheses and methods on which the approach is based are briefly reviewed here.

# Case Studies Providing Information to Determine the Future of Environmental Research

## *Background case studies*

Real-situation case studies are part of the French academic tradition (Vidal de La Blache, 1903; Bloch, 1931). For SAD researchers, this emphasis on case studies results from four requirements:

**1.** a necessary contact with the actors (i.e. the farmers) in attempting to develop tools enabling them to improve their ability to manage their problems;
**2.** building interdisciplinary research to deal with the complexity of our research issues;
**3.** understanding how general influences are adjusted locally (adaptation mechanisms);
**4.** developing scenario models with assessable feedbacks.

A systems approach (Le Moigne, 1977) is used to deal with these issues. The approach to agrarian systems is constructivist, and a representation of such systems is constructed through the research process on the basis of questions posed and the theory and concepts used.

Environmental research is included in studies of agricultural development: environmental issues are specific aspects of development issues. In the case of research on environmental issues, it is the research question that creates the system to be investigated (Hubert, 1992), and this research question is a product of the view of, and work on, a social issue.

Current work in INRA–SAD on environmental issues in agrarian systems results from questions posed by a range of partners: public partners, including river basin agencies for potable water, national parks and the Ministry of the Environment and private partners including the Vittel and Evian mineral water companies and CERPAM for the preservation of Mediterranean forests against fire and the control of soil erosion in Picardie. In total, the research on environmental issues deals with biodiversity maintenance, preservation of water resources, control of soil erosion and conflicting land uses and landscape conservation.

In each case, the first step consists of constructing a system that takes into account the components which are useful in developing the research question and their interrelationships. Since our aim is to provide the actors with new tools and references enabling them to manage their problems by themselves, informal groups involving the researchers and the actors have to be set up (see also Röling, 1992).

This approach can be illustrated with two examples. The first investigates multiple use landscapes in Mediterranean woodland areas (Etienne, 1990), where it is important to construct organizational models for each activity taking place. Then, by superimposing all these activities in the same model, new spatial structures emerge. It is then possible to represent the system of activities and the actors who compete for use and management of the forest area (forestry, hunting, tourism, farming). In a second example, which has the objective of designing a research programme for groundwater conservation (Deffontaines, 1990), there was an attempt to integrate highly efficient local farming activities with the simultaneous control of farm effluents. The researchers used a systems approach in this case to investigate the ecological, economic and social implications of this issue. Links between the various scientific disciplines were established around three focal points of the programme: modelling the way the farms operate, mapping the diversity of spatial structures and developing the structures which stimulated consultation between the actors concerned with this issue and the research scientists.

### *Proposed model for research on environmental issues arising from changes in farming systems*

These general considerations and examples of research practices have resulted in the formulation of a general model of environmental issues seen as a complex system and summarized as follows:

Three aspects are emphasized in this simple model:

**1.** Land is studied as a factor of production or as an outcome of a set of farming practices. For instance, soil type is a factor guiding the farmer's choice of a given activity whereas the fertility level of a particular field is the result of the farmer's activities on that field.
**2.** When environmental factors are to be considered, it must be recognized that farmers are not the only users of the land and therefore it is necessary to take into account all other users or actors and their activities in the particular area being investigated.
**3.** Finally, in order to determine the future of rural areas and their environmental aspects, it is necessary to appraise future activities planned by the existing and future actors.

The model described above can be developed using both a diagnostic approach which describes the state of the system or a prognostic approach which negotiates between the set of 'actors' concerning the future of the system.

# The Diagnostic Approach

The diagnostic approach to the assessment of a farming system requires that initially the environmental problems and processes be identified and that activities and their influence on these processes on the area of land being studied are identified. Second, it involves the development of a model of the system (actors–activities–land) – a set of references on the known responses of the system. This will permit the comparison of the present state of the system with desired states and permit assessment of possible differences.

This approach can be illustrated by reference to a number of case studies which form only part of this approach as adopted by INRA–SAD:

**1.** The first investigates the spatial dimension with respect to land viewed as an outcome of farming practices. The research programme has investigated the role of field boundaries in promoting biodiversity in agricultural landscapes (Baudry, 1984a,b; Burel and Baudry, 1990). Clearance of the land for agricultural purposes has driven out most of the species adapted to forested landscapes. The maintenance of biodiversity (a top-level target in most administration agendas) requires the presence of wooded elements such as hedgerows in agricultural landscapes. Therefore, it is important to understand which type of species live in hedgerows and what the factors are that affect hedgerow species diversity. Studies on forest plants and carabid species demonstrate the importance of hedgerow structure (wide hedgerows with a dense shrub and tree layer contain more forest species than thin, gappy hedgerows) and the hedgerow network structure (many forest dwellers will only move along hedgerows, therefore requiring interconnected corridors of hedgerows). The current trend toward integrated agricultural systems also requires that field boundaries ensure the maintenance of predator species that might control crop pests. These boundaries must be stable but open habitats so that the species inhabiting them can also live in the surrounding crops.

Field boundaries can therefore play an important role in sustaining biodiversity as well as agricultural systems if properly designed at the boundary (woody structure and herbaceous margins) and at the landscape levels (connected boundaries). These structured patterns are more or less correlated with farming systems structure: large farms usually have fewer boundaries per hectare than small ones; management practices also affect boundary structure (e.g. spraying herbicides).

This brief case study illustrates how the integration of both ecological and farming systems research within the framework of landscape ecology provides a better understanding of interactions between activities, landscapes and ecological processes.

**2.** The second case study illustrates the spatial dimension with respect to land as a factor of production. In most cases, farmers take into account the productive capability and layout of their property when deciding on the location of their cropping and grassland systems (Morlon and Benoit, 1990). The case study focuses on the management of farmyard manure (FYM) and groundwater pollution in Lorraine (Teilhard de Chardin, 1990; Kung-Benoit, 1992; Le Houérou, 1993). It is well known that the inappropriate application of FYM, especially in the winter on permeable or well drained soils, can lead to negative effects on groundwater quality. When farmers choose to spread all their organic manure on soils with good trafficability, they make a logical decision with regard to management of their agricultural production. However, such a decision can be disastrous for water quality. For instance, if the soils are trafficable, then they are also permeable, leading to degraded water quality in the underlying aquifers. A vicious circle ensues. Soils permeable to water are also trafficable for heavy machinery (silage, FYM spreading in winter). The only solution at present would be to spread FYM elsewhere, or in another form. In the Lorraine it has been proposed that traditional practices relating to FYM application be changed to allow spreading in the spring and summer. A major element in this change is changing the form of the applied product from wet slurry to a composted material.

**3.** The time dimension also requires consideration alongside the spatial factors which have been discussed above. A major concern of farmers is the time elapsing between the moment they carry out an operation and the effects of this operation on environmental parameters. This is also a major issue for all those responsible for managing environmental resources in association with farmers. For instance, three levels of delayed action can be identified in the groundwater improvement process (Benoit and Muhar, 1994): a hydrological delay between pollutant source and subsoil (under the roots); an agronomic delay between agricultural operations on the soil and nitrate leaching under the roots; and a 'negotiation' delay between problem detection and change in farming practices. This phenomenon emerged clearly in the research described above in the Lorraine. The 'hydrological' lag ranged from a few months to one year in 28 case studies of watersheds. The 'agronomic' lag lasted from a few months to two years in 44 field experiments and the 'negotiation' lag lasted from three to over five years in six case studies of agrarian systems.

## The Prognostic Approach

The prognostic approach to systems research requires a change in the behaviour of researchers towards a more participative systems approach. The basis of the approach is a diagnostic stage, where the problem is defined, which is followed by a prognostic or predictive stage. The prognostic stage involves the following steps:

**1.** negotiation with the 'actors' on the possible desired state of their farming system;
**2.** identification of differences between the actual state of the system and the desired state;
**3.** construction of models of system change to the desired state;
**4.** discussion with the 'actors' about the ways and means to achieve the desired state.

A fundamental question underlies the adoption of this approach: 'Are environmental problems an effect or a consequence of farmer practices?' This question is not merely semantic; it is also involves social considerations. If we take 'effect' as meaning 'the future result of a voluntary action' and 'consequence' as meaning 'a secondary, involuntary result of an action,' then environmental problems are almost always the consequences and not the effects of farmer practice. Therefore, 'actors' must be enlightened about the links between their objectives, their practices and the consequences of their practices (Gras *et al.*, 1989). To be more precise, this means that as partners investigating this type of issue we must not set out with the assumption that a farmer has voluntarily damaged the environmental parameter that is being investigated.

Given this understanding, it is then necessary to develop and test a range of scenarios with the 'actors.' Two broad types of scenario can be developed: those answering 'What ... if ... ', and 'How ... to ... ' questions. This approach is described more fully by Papy (Chapter 18). The discussion here will concentrate on model building.

### The development of models

The model-building process serves as a tool for constructing and discussing scenarios with the actors. Two approaches have been used in INRA–SAD which recognize farmers as either 'research objects' or 'research subjects.' The models developed as an integral part of this approach are usually of two types, either graphical (or drawing) or mathematical approaches involving methods used in landscape ecology and linear programming.

The graphical methods can be viewed as an interactive form of research: the ability of most people to understand a drawing is used as a fundamental tool in describing and discussing research results. One research approach developed by geographers (Brunet, 1986) is to represent spatial problems using a dictionary of graphic symbols or 'choremes.' The use of this form of qualitative modelling ensures that models can be built that incorporate the spatial dimension of farming practice. This approach proved very useful in modelling agrarian systems in Argentina (Albaladejo, 1990; Lardon and Albaladejo, 1990; Lardon *et al.*, 1991).

Models can also be used to help the 'actors' in their negotiation. The objective here is to develop tools that will help 'actors' make decisions and assist negotiations between 'actors.' To facilitate this, it is necessary for researchers to develop their own system of representations and establish negotiation structures in which they themselves participate; this means that researchers are themselves 'actors' in their own case studies.

Since the aim of the research is to help the 'actors' negotiate, simple indicators must be developed to describe the effects their actions have on the environment. These indicators should be suitably structured for use by all 'actors', not only by high-level researchers involved in the mathematical model building. The major task that requires further work is to compare the value of these indicators with real environmental parameters while also making them transferable between environments. The development of such indicators has started with the creation of indicators to describe bad farming practices that impact on groundwater quality (Benoit, 1992). The BASCULE (Balance Azotée Spatialisée des Systèmes de Culture de l'Exploitation) system only requires a thorough knowledge of the production practices used on the farm. The computation of an N input–output balance for each field and for each year provides a weighted measure for each cropping system. Cumulated positive balances for each farm provide an assessment of the extent to which an individual farm is denigrating groundwater resources. In a similar way, the cumulated balances over a whole catchment provide an assessment of the risks to water quality with respect to nitrate levels. The advantage of this system is that calculations can be done easily with pen and paper and all the 'actors' are able to negotiate on the basis of a single indicator, the BASCULE value. A key element in this process is that the time taken in analysis must be minimized to enable the 'actors' (farmers, administrators, etc.) to relate their practices to the resultant environmental outputs and therefore modify their existing practices.

Linear programming is frequently used as a normative method to help in the resolution of conflict between 'actors' (see, for example, Brossier and Chia, 1991). Output from these models is often useful for encouraging discussion about issues related to changes in system dynamics. For instance, discussion on the sensitivity of the results from models can be useful in focusing discussion on the most important issues. This can be achieved by using the results to isolate and rank the most sensitive farming practices.

In seeking to stimulate the negotiation process between 'actors' on the environmental consequences of farming, researchers must also try to predict the consequences of their own acts. Obviously, it is very easy to publish papers on the consequences of farmer practices for the environment but are we, as researchers, able to take into account the possible consequences of our own work? This must be set in a background of changing priorities. For example, 20 years ago the emphasis was on increased production, which led to the introduction of maize silage in many parts of Europe. At that time, there was no emphasis on the environmental impacts of this new farming practice.

Today, researchers must make every effort to predict the possible environmental consequences of their scientific work and accept responsibility for these (Jonas, 1990).

The discussion so far has concentrated on localized case studies, but such studies allow researchers to:

**1.** understand the local consequences of higher level decisions, such as the level of deterioration of water quality resulting from changes in farming systems emanating from the introduction of, say, new CAP structures; although the effects may be localized, researchers have the responsibility to inform national or international decision makers of the consequences of their decisions;

**2.** help local actors define their own direction of change which incorporates the impacts on environmental resources. Here farmers have three possible courses of action: protective, preventive and curative. A protective approach seeks to maintain existing situations by setting up structures and institutions such as natural parks or water conservation areas. Prevention attempts to influence the future state of environmental parameters, which is a far more difficult course but is an integral component in the farming systems approach.

# Conclusions

The systems research approach adopted by researchers within INRA–SAD consists of both diagnostic and prognostic methods. Adopting this approach ensures that a large number of actors are involved and interact in the process of change in rural systems. These actors bring a wide and diverse range of objectives into the discussions of change. The farming systems approach adopted demands that we pinpoint these actors and their objectives and detect conflicting and converging interests. In addition, different actors have different perceptions of space and a variety of functions in the management of environmental issues. The approach outlined in this chapter seeks to understand the general patterns of organization and to identify levels that are pertinent for farming systems studies. A challenge for researchers in farming systems, and farm advisors, is to define the set of new objectives for agricultural production. These new objectives might, for instance, involve a shift in perspective away from agricultural production to seeing a role for agriculture in producing water of drinking quality.

It is proposed that the following three research objectives, which relate directly to the interface between farming systems and environmental issues, be considered in farming systems research studies:

**1.** maintenance of biological diversity (species, ecosystems) and of landscape diversity, and conservation of the physical environment (air, soil, water resources);

**2.** development of sustainable farming practices and processes to improve the quality and diversity of the environment, of landscapes and of agricultural production;
**3.** detection and interpretation of social demands regarding the environment and of conflicts between the actors involved.

Using these objectives as a basis, it is possible to define five steps in a methodology for investigating environmental issues in farming systems:

**1.** understand farmer objectives and motivations for adopting individual farm production practices;
**2.** widen the scope of the analysis to include the analysis of conflict at local and higher levels. Investigation at the field and farm level is necessary but not sufficient and must be widened to encompass a wider set of 'actors' which should include, for example, officials in local and national government and the wider community;
**3.** adopt a new view of rural issues which identifies new significant spaces with natural, technical, economic and sociological dimensions such as landscapes, watersheds and biotopes;
**4.** use typologies and mapping to develop models of 'actor–activity–land' relationships;
**5.** devise approaches and tools for negotiation with which the 'actors' concerned can develop appropriate changes to rural systems. Diagnosis of output from these methods must be understandable and solutions acceptable to all 'actors'.

## Acknowledgements

This chapter benefited from valuable comments by Jacques Baudry, Laurence de Bonneval, Jean-Pierre Deffontaines, Isabelle Duvernoy, Alain Langlet, Sylvie Lardon, Brigitte Le Houérou and François Papy.

## References

Albaladejo, C. (1990) Marginalisation de la paysannerie en Patagonie. *Mappemonde* 90 (4), 34–37.

Baudry, J. (1984a) Utilisation des concepts de Landscape Ecology pour l'analyse de l'espace rural. Utilisation du sol et des bocages. Thèse de Doctorat d'Etat, Université de Rennes, 380 pp. + appendices.

Baudry, J. (1984b) Effects of landscape structure on biological communities: the case of hedgerow network landscapes. In: Brandt, J. and Agger, P. (eds) *Methodology in Landscape Ecological Research and Planning*. Roskilde University Centre, Roskilde, Denmark, pp. 55–65.

Benoit, M. (1992) Un indicateur des risques de pollution azotée nommé BASCULE

(Balance Azotée Spatialisée des Systèmes de Culture de l'Exploitation). *Fourrages*, 129, 95–110.

Benoit, M. and Muhar, M.C. (1994) Farmers, landuse and groundwater quality: an interdisciplinary approach. In: *Future of the Land*, Wageningen, in press.

Benoit, M., Fiorelli, J.L., Morlon, P. and Pons, Y. (1990) Technical management: a central point for agronomy challenge. Paper presented at the First European Congress of Agronomy, Session V-01, European Society of Agronomy, Paris.

Bloch, M. (1931) *Les Caractères Originaux de l'Histoire Rurale Française*, 2nd edn. Armand Colin, Paris.

Brossier, J. and Chia, E. (1991) Pratiques agricoles et qualité de l'eau. Construction d'une recherche-développement dans le cadre d'un périmètre hydrominéral. *Economie Rurale* Sept/Oct, 6–13.

Brunet, R. (1986) La carte-modèle et les chorèmes. *Mappemonde* 4 (1), 2–6.

Burel, F. and Baudry, J. (1990) Hedgerow networks as habitats for colonization of abandoned agricultural land. In: Bunce, R.G.H. and Howard, D.C. (eds) *Species Dispersal in Agricultural Environments*. Belhaven Press, Lymington, pp. 238–255.

Deffontaines, J.P. (1990) Programme agriculture–environnement–Vittel (AGREV). In: Calvet, R. (ed.) *Nitrates–Agriculture–Eau*. INRA, Paris, pp. 121–129.

Dumont, R. (1961) *Voyage d'un Agronome Autour du Monde. Terres Vivantes*. Plon, Paris.

Dumont, R. (1974) *L'Agronome de la Faim*. Robert Laffont, Paris, 394 pp.

Etienne, M. (1990) Superpositions d'usages en forêt méditerranéenne soumise. *Mappemonde* 90 (4), 22–23.

Gaury, F. (1992) Systèmes de culture et teneurs en nitrates des eaux souterraines. Dynamique passée et actuelle en région de polyculture – élevage sur le périmètre d'un gîte hydrominéral. Thèse ENSA de Rennes, INRA–SAD, Mirecourt, 229 pp + appendices.

Gras, R., Benoit, M., Deffontaines J.P., Duru, M., Lafarge, M., Langlet, A. and Osty, P.L. (1989) *Le Fait Technique en Agronomie. Activité Agricole, Concepts et Méthodes d'Étude*. INRA–L'Harmattan, Paris, 160 pp.

Hubert, B. (1992) Programme interdisciplinaire de recherches sur l'environnement, Comité 'Systèmes Ruraux.' *Lettre des Programmes Interdisciplinaires de Recherche du CNRS* 5, 46–49.

Jonas, H. (1990) *Le Principe de Responsabilité. Une Éthique pour la Civilisation Technologique*. Editions du Cerf, Paris, 336 pp.

Kung-Benoit, A. (1992) Reduction de la pollution nitrique: exemple d'un diagnostic en Lorraine. *Fourrages* 131, 235–250.

Lardon, S. and Albaladejo, C. (1990) Modeling an agrarian system on a local scale as a tool for farmer participation in rural development: examples from South America. *Journal of Farming Systems Research–Extension* 1 (2), 81–103.

Lardon, S., Kaan, J. and Antoine, C. (1991) SIG et morphologie mathématique: interface ARCINFO–VISILOG pour l'analyse des systèmes de culture. In: Busche, P., King, D. and Lardon, S. (eds) *Colloque 'Gestion de l'Espace Rural et Système d'Information Géographique.' Florac, 22–24 Octobre 1991*. INRA, Paris, pp. 339–340.

Le Houérou, B. (1993) Les dépôts de fumier au champ: pertes en azote par percolation des jus sous les tas. In: *La Gestion des Effluents d'Élevage*. Dossier LIGET 13, pp. 73–83.

Le Moigne, J.L. (1977) *La Théorie du Système Général: Théorie de la Modélisation*. PUF, Paris.

Morlon, P. and Benoit, M. (1990) Etude méthodologique d'un parcellaire d'exploitation agricole en tant que système. *Agronomie* 6, 499–508.

Papy, F. (1992) Agriculture et environnement: des éléments de réflexion. *Bulletin Technique d'Information* 8, 2–11, Ministère de l'Agriculture, Paris.

Poly, J. (1977) *Pour une Agriculture plus Econome et Plus Autonome*. INRA, Paris.

Roling, N.G. (1992) From strategy to dialogue: the consequences for using information in land use planning. Paper presented at 'The Future of the Land' Conference, Wageningen, 22–25 August 1992.

Teilhard de Chardin, B. (1990) Gestion des déjections de bovins et pollution par les nitrates. Diversité des pratiques dans les élevages laitiers du Plateau Lorrain. *Etudes et Recherches sur les Systèmes Agraires et le Développement*, No. 18. INRA, Paris, 46 pp.

Vidal de la Blache, P. (1903) *Revue de Synthèse Historique*. Paris.

Wit, C.T. de (1992) Resource use efficiency in agriculture. *Agricultural Systems* 40, 125–151.

# IV

# UNDERSTANDING FARM HOUSEHOLDS

# 15

# FARMING SYSTEMS AND THE FARM FAMILY BUSINESS

*Andrew Errington and Ruth Gasson*

## Introduction

The transformation process which characterizes agricultural systems in Europe is greatly influenced by the fact that most production units are family businesses, in the sense that:

- business ownership is combined with managerial control in the hands of business principals;
- these principals are related by kinship or marriage;
- family members (including these business principals) provide capital to the business;
- family members including business principals do farm work;
- business ownership and managerial control are transferred between the generations with the passage of time;
- the family lives on the farm.

The interaction between the farm family on the one hand and the farm business on the other gives rise to characteristic behaviours (and indeed some fundamental problems) that do not face agribusiness enterprises where there is separation of ownership (in the hands of shareholders) from managerial control (in the hands of salaried managers). But if the interaction may bring particular problems to the farm family business it may also give some distinctive advantages. Indeed, the assumption that family farming in Europe is somehow an inefficient and outmoded form that will soon disappear in the face of all-pervasive agribusiness is now increasingly challenged (Winter, 1984; Marsden *et al.*, 1989). To paraphrase Mark Twain, news of the death of the farm family business has been greatly exaggerated. One of its most important advantages over other business forms in agriculture is its flexibility.

In the face of pressures, whether internally or externally generated, it is able to draw on a wider range of survival strategies than its agribusiness counterpart. These include a substantial capacity to reduce or postpone consumption, the ability to internalize capital and labour markets (so minimizing transactions costs) and the capacity to accept a degree of self-exploitation which cannot reasonably be imposed on a hired workforce.

The farm family business may be a more sustainable business form in the agricultural context because it is better able to mutate into forms appropriate to an ever-changing social, economic and political environment. This is not to say that individual farms or indeed subspecies are assured of survival – far from it, for different individuals are not equally adaptable and some mutations prove unsuccessful. However, having reviewed the available evidence, our own conclusion is that the prognosis for the business form whose essentials are outlined at the head of this chapter is good – it will survive, although not necessarily in the form that we know today.

The purpose of this chapter is to illustrate our central thesis that the interaction of the family unit with the farm business gives rise to distinctive behaviours that agricultural researchers, extension workers and policy makers (and also the families themselves) need to understand. While our analysis is based on our own (largely British) research and an extensive review of the literature from other OECD countries, we suspect that the same (or similar) analysis will be relevant to the countries of the south. Research into the farm family business is one facet of farming systems research where there is already likely to be much common ground between researchers who have hitherto concentrated on one or other of these discrete geographic areas. Moreover, the starting point for our recent work of synthesis (Gasson and Errington, 1993) has been a recognition that the study of the farm family business requires an interdisciplinary approach, combining the insights of the economist with those of the sociologist, anthropologist and others. This premise sits very comfortably with the more holistic 'farming systems' approach.

## Family and Business

As suggested above, it is the way the farm business and the farm family relate to one another, the 'chemistry' of the reaction between them, that gives rise to particular features in the farm family business. These features may confer particular benefits or disadvantages on the family enterprise, and some of these will now be discussed.

## The decision process

In any attempt to identify the relevant objective function underlying the decision process, the farm family business presents a number of problems. In the first place, the farm family business tends to be associated with objectives not found among agribusiness companies. Most notable among these is the desire to 'keep the name on the land,' although as a number of commentators have pointed out there is an important distinction to be made between those farmers wanting the family to continue to farm a particular piece of land and those merely seeking a successor who will carry on in the occupation of farming (Harrison, 1981; Laband and Lentz, 1983; Blanc 1987). Where this objective is paramount, the farmer may remain in the business of farming, or on a particular farm, long after agribusiness would have reallocated its resources to another locality or another line of economic activity.

The multiplicity of objectives encountered in most farm businesses (Romero and Rehman, 1984) is compounded by the fact that in some farm family businesses, decisions will be the outcome of a complex process of negotiation or arbitration involving a number of decision makers, each with a different set of objectives. Moreover, both the members of the decision-making group and their individual objectives may change over the family cycle as one generation is born, grows up and eventually succeeds its predecessors. While this complexity undoubtedly presents problems to the researcher or extension worker seeking to understand or influence decisions, it also presents significant problems to the family members themselves.

A further characteristic of the decision process in the farm family business concerns time horizons and discount factors. Even if we were to assume an identical and very simple objective function predicated on profit maximization, the behaviour of the farm family business will often be very different from that of the non-family business because of differences in the time period over which costs and returns are evaluated. The employed manager, motivated by his own personal objectives in addition to the demands of shareholders, may seek to weigh costs and returns over the next 10–15 years when considering a long-term investment. For decision takers in the farm family business, the relevant time-scale may be measured in generations and the expected utility to be derived from such investments by future generations will enter the equation. Such considerations are particularly relevant where the investments involve land purchase or land improvement.

## The division of labour

The unity of business and family implies a single fund of capital to satisfy both investment and consumption needs. Particularly in the early stages of the business cycle, consumption may be deferred in favour of building up the enterprise. When the business is under pressure, the family's level of living is depressed; wives and children are expected to do more manual work as expenditure on regular or seasonal labour is reduced. Unity of business and family also means that fundamental decisions have to be made about the allocation of family members' time between competing activities – production and 'reproduction' in the farm business, off-farm work and leisure (Errington, 1993).

In the farm family business, family members are involved in farm work. The unity of kin group and work group creates multiple roles for each member: father/farm manager/farm worker; mother/domestic worker/child minder/accountant/personnel manager/occasional farm worker; child/farm worker/domestic help (Friedmann, 1986). The combination of family roles and relationships with working roles and relationships can be stressful. At the same time, tasks may be customarily assigned on the basis of gender and age, not according to the skill and knowledge of the workers, with consequences for labour productivity (Buchanan *et al.*, 1982; Siiskonen *et al.*, 1982; Whatmore, 1991). Task allocation is not necessarily rigid or immutable, however. Technology may alter the rationale for the gender and age division of labour. For example, the introduction of new technology such as agrochemicals and on-farm computers may give the younger generation a comparative advantage that the older generation is ready to acknowledge and use (Errington and Tranter, 1991). Within families there is normally some room for negotiation over the allocation of tasks, even if patriarchal authority sets the limits within which this exchange takes place.

### Labour productivity

One corollary of the use of family labour in the farm business is that the labour force will vary in quality and quantity over the course of the family cycle. Where family labour is the principal input, this can create substantial variation in labour productivity over the family cycle. Indeed, Lorenz and Errington (1991) have argued that in some Indonesian settlement schemes the ability to match the cropping pattern with the family labour supply is as critical to the sustainability of farming systems as the use of mulch rotations to preserve the fertility of the soil.

Where markets are better developed, there is a very large range of strategies used by farming families to overcome this problem. The family may move to a larger (or a smaller) farm at a given point in the family cycle; they may buy or sell land; they may move to a farm with better productive potential (Nalson, 1968); and so on. With larger farms, periodic employment of hired labour may provide a solution (Nalson, 1968; Symes, 1990) and it may be a gross over-simplification to classify farms as 'family worked' on the basis of the labour input pattern observed at one particular point in time. Alternatively, the farm may shift between more intensive and more extensive forms of production (Blanc, 1987) with substantial on-farm investment coinciding with the end of the children's formal education. In other cases, a solution may be sought in the introduction of an alternative farm enterprise such as an agricultural contracting business or a farm shop. If either resources or objectives do not permit these solutions, the children may seek (temporary) employment elsewhere and indeed the *détour professionel* is a well established stage in the farm family cycle in many continental European countries. In short, the significant points in the family cycle may be marked by substantial changes in farm size, location or farming practice. If none of these solutions is pursued, the fluctuating labour supply will lead to considerable variation in labour productivity and the occurrence of under-employment over a substantial portion of the family cycle (Errington, 1988).

Finally, in farm family businesses run on strongly patriarchal lines, low labour productivity may be endemic because of a persistent tendency for the primary decision taker to undervalue family labour. In the first place, this may lead to the sub-optimal allocation of labour among both farming and non-farming activities. Second, the low valuation placed on family labour may discourage investment in complementary capital or training inputs that would enhance its productivity.

### Home and workplace

Since the farm is usually a place of residence as well as a workplace, the family's consumption and leisure activities are also likely to revolve around the farm, making it difficult to separate the business from the way of life. Activities usually regarded as sporting or recreational, such as shooting rabbits or simply walking the dog, can also be functional for the business. Operating a business from the family home makes it especially difficult to draw a line between 'productive' and 'reproductive' activities. To a degree all households with productive workers must purchase inputs of food, shelter and so on to maintain themselves in good health so that they can continue to sell their labour services. The need for subsistence in order to maintain the stock of labour is not usually considered a business cost. Instead, tax law normally provides for subsistence inputs by giving individuals a fixed personal allowance against tax (Casson, 1982). When the family business is run from home, the overlap between production and reproduction is considerable. By securing part of the costs of reproducing the labour force by consuming what is produced at home, the family farm is able to compete in selling its products with non-family firms which may have the benefits of larger scale.

These, then, are some of the issues that arise where agricultural production takes place within a farm family business. There are many others, two of which will be considered in more detail in the remainder of this chapter, namely the intergenerational transfer of the farm family business and the distinctive investment patterns to be found in such businesses. As we shall see, these two issues are very closely related.

# Succession, Inheritance and Retirement

French sociologists and economists use a single word – *transmission* – to describe the amalgam of processes in which the farm family business is passed as a 'going concern' from one generation to the next (Perrier-Cornet *et al.*, 1991). However, as Gasson and Errington (1993) have shown, three distinct processes are involved – *inheritance* involves the transfer of business assets and *succession* the transfer of managerial control while *retirement* from farming is usually not a single event but an 'extended series of transitions' as the farmer moves through successive phases of semi-retirement.

A good deal of the professional advice received by farmers wishing to secure the smooth transition of the business concerns the tax efficiency of asset transfer. While this aspect of the process may seem complicated, it is but one small part of a process that is critical to the survival and subsequent success of the business.

## *The inheritance dilemma*

Every business and organization faces the problem of succession, but in the farm family business it is peculiarly complex. It is certainly true that in every business there is a need to identify and prepare a successor to the current chief executive, but in the farm family business succession is inextricably linked to inheritance. As Gasson and Errington (1993) have shown, the combination of changing social norms and inflated land values can present the owner-occupying farmer with a fundamental dilemma. In the interests of fairness, parents might want each child to receive an equal share of the business, but this may lead to fragmentation of the asset base with the resulting loss of economic viability so that the very survival of the business may be placed in jeopardy. Alternatively, the quest for fairness may leave the eventual farming successor not only with the farm but with substantial financial obligations either to other family members or to the bank. These may place such a millstone round their neck that the future survival of the farm is again threatened. As Salamon and Davis-Brown (1986) point out, 'Farm families planning intergenerational farm transfers confront a dilemma: how to treat all members equitably without destroying the farm in the process.'

However, as always, the family business has proved adaptable. In countries dominated by the requirements of the Code Napoléon, a variety of strategies has developed to ensure the survival of both farm and family. In the first place, the successor may be helped to buy the farm from the parents (who use the resulting funds to finance their retirement) or they may 'pay out' sibling shares (*soultes*). Thus it has been common practice in Denmark for one son to buy the farm from his parents, although his father will often make over 10–15% of its value as a gift at the time of purchase and the State will provide a capital grant and low-interest loan to help finance the transaction. One significant by-product of this approach is the high level of indebtedness among young farmers in countries such as Denmark (Perrier-Cornet *et al.*, 1991). The Dutch 'Maatschap' or two-generation partnership seeks to overcome this problem by allowing the successors to build up their own share in the business gradually over a period of years in a way that may mirror the transfer of managerial control. In other cases, the amount paid for the education of non-succeeding children and also the wages foregone (the *salaire différé*) by the child who has worked alongside the father up to the point of transfer may be taken into account when they buy the land.

A second strategy involves the so-called 'family advantage,' an under-valuation of farmland when determining the value of assets to be divided. In some countries such as Germany, Switzerland, The Netherlands and Luxembourg, farmland is valued at its 'economic,' 'farming' or 'capitalized income' value, which may be half or less of the market price. In Spain, the use of a *Valeur de convenance familiale* has a similar effect. A third strategy is to divide the ownership of the farm equally between the various beneficiaries but to allow one *successeur professionel* to lease the farm from the co-inheritors. Thus, in France, from 1980 the successor has been able to take a long-term lease from the siblings who can form themselves into a company, a *Groupement Foncier Agricole* (GFA). Finally, farmers may build up a fund of off-farm investments during their working lifetime, perhaps in the form of a life assurance policy, and this will eventually provide a separate estate from which the non-succeeding children can receive their inheritance. This can 'reduce the costs of asset liquidation and asset splitting and, in some cases, eliminate conflicts of interest that might arise because of co-ownership of property' (Boehlje and Eisgruber, 1972).

### *Provision for retirement*

Although the dilemmas surrounding the issue of inheritance make business succession more complex for the farm family business than it is for the public company, this is not unique to farming. Any family business will face the same problem, particularly where substantial quantities of real estate are involved. However, there is yet more complexity in the case of the farm family business, since the processes of succession and inheritance are inextricably tied to those of retirement because many farmers will look to the farm to provide for their financial and housing needs after they retire.

Figure 15.1, taken from a recent survey of over 800 English farmers (Errington and Tranter, 1991), shows that approximately one third of post-retirement or semi-retirement income is expected to come from the farm, despite the increased investment in private pension schemes by farmers in recent years. Although it might make good economic sense to reinvest in one's own business rather than some external pension fund, problems will arise where the new generation's desire to expand the business coincides with

*Full retirement*

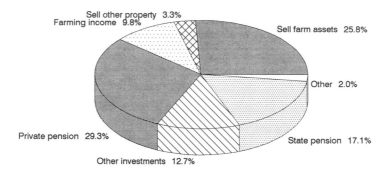

*Semi-retirement*

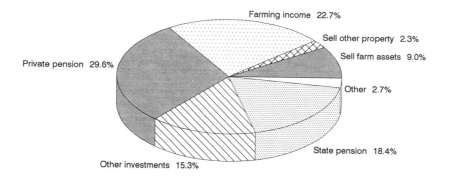

**Fig. 15.1.** Anticipated sources of income after retirement and semi-retirement (*n* = 533) (from Errington and Tranter, 1991, p. 86).

the older generation's need to disinvest.

Figure 15.2, which comes from the same survey, highlights the fact that the farmhouse may also be required to provide accommodation. Over 50% of respondents planned to remain on the farm in retirement or semi-retirement. This can again generate problems and conflicts not encountered in the non-family business. However, once again, various patterns of adaptation are found in different parts of Europe. In The Netherlands, the succeeding child often moves to the local village on marriage and later exchanges the farmhouse with the parents as they retire. In Denmark, only 2% of farms have two generations living together in the same house; in most cases, the older couple moves into a house in the village on their retirement. In Lower Saxony and Finland, the tradition has been to build a separate dower extension on to

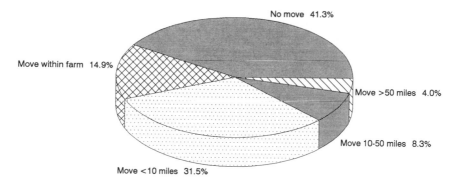

**Fig. 15.2.** Plans to move house after retirement or semi-retirement (*n* = 606) (from Errington and Tranter, 1991, p. 73).

the farmhouse at the time of the successor's marriage, while Arensberg and Kimball (1968) refer to the Irish tradition of making the 'west room' available to the parents as they enter the sunset of their lives.

## Investment Behaviour in the Farm Family Business

As we have seen, the familial character of the farm business may impinge on a whole range of decisions and behaviours. Particularly important is its influence on investment decisions. For the rational profit-maximizing entrepreneur posited by some traditional farm management texts, investment behaviour is seen to be influenced primarily by the expected stream of future income arising from the investment, suitably discounted to take account of inflation, time preference and the opportunity cost of capital. Together with the current cost of capital, as indicated by real interest rates and their anticipated trends, the buoyancy of expectations of future farming profitability will be of paramount importance.

Apart from differences in business objectives and the decision-making time horizon already mentioned, another crucial factor where the farm family business is concerned will be the stage reached in the farm family cycle. In seeking to make most efficient use of the available family labour, families facing few external employment opportunities or whose children are ambitious to remain in farming will time additional investments to provide the extra income required when the child finishes full-time education and gets married. Except where the returning family member is replacing an employed worker, such investment will also be necessary to increase the marginal product of labour which might otherwise fall so low that disguised unemployment would ensue (Errington, 1988). More recent work by Potter and Lobley

(1992) highlights the fact that the investment behaviour of farmers without successors is radically different from those with a successor already identified, while Bryden *et al.* (1992) suggest that the selection of a single baseline year for quota calculations is fundamentally unfair because different farms will be at different stages in their family/investment cycle.

However, the timing and nature of farm investments are also influenced by succession strategies within the farm family business. In their typology of succession patterns in European farming, Gasson and Errington (1993) identify the establishment of a separate enterprise, financially independent of the home farm, as a common means by which the younger generation is brought into the farm family business. Not only does this strategy give the potential successor the opportunity to develop managerial skills without jeopardizing the survival of the home farm, it also allows them to build up a financial base from which to buy into the main business or 'pay out' sibling claims on the inheritance.

In the UK, the prevailing tradition (Hastings, 1984) was to establish the potential successor on a separate (perhaps adjoining) holding, giving some initial support, perhaps in the form of a few youngstock or help with particular tasks through the loan of machinery and/or labour. Once the successor had proved him/herself on the other holding, it might either be amalgamated with the home farm or father and successor might exchange farms (and homes), the smaller farm becoming a post-retirement 'hobby' farm for the parents. The substantial reduction in the number of available tenancies, together with inflated land prices, mean that this strategy is no longer open to most UK farmers. In this case, the adaptation of the farm family business frequently takes the form of establishing a separate enterprise which is either located on the home farm (perhaps a pig unit or sheep flock) or simply based there (perhaps an agricultural contracting business or crop advisory service).

## Conclusions

The latter two examples – of intergenerational transfer and of investment decisions – illustrate the ways in which the interaction between farm family and farm business modifies behaviour and gives rise to a range of issues and problems not found in other farm businesses. If we are to understand farmers, and their likely response to a whole range of interventions, whether they emanate from the agricultural researcher, extension worker or policy maker, we must have a clearer understanding of the nature of the complex interactions between economic and social factors within the farming systems prevalent in Europe.

Although there is certainly a need for further research in this area, there is an even greater need for the synthesis of existing knowledge and for better communication across the disciplinary and geographic divide, for the insights into the farm family business that have already been gained reside in a number of different disciplines and on a number of different continents. At the very least the Farming Systems Research/Extension movement has an important role to play in facilitating communication across these barriers. Also, as this chapter has argued, the investment will be well worthwhile for the farm family business is not a transient or outmoded business form – it is here to stay. Its inherent capacity for adaptation will ensure that it is still around long after other business forms have been assigned to the domain of the economic historian.

# References

Arensberg, C.M. and Kimball, S.T. (1968) *Family and Community in Ireland*, 2nd edn, Harvard University Press, Cambridge, Massachusetts.

Blanc, M. (1987) Family and employment in agriculture; recent changes in France. *Journal of Agricultural Economics* 38, 289–301.

Boehlje, M.D. and Eisgruber, L.M. (1972) Strategies for the creation and transfer of the farm estate. *American Journal of Agricultural Economics* 54, 461–472.

Bryden, J.M., Bell, C., Gilliatt, J., Hawkins, E. and MacKinnon, N. (1992) *Farm Household Adjustment in Western Europe 1987–91, Final Report on the Research Programme on Farm Structures and Pluriactivity*. Arkleton Trust (Research), Nethybridge.

Buchanan, W.I., Errington, A.J. and Giles, A.K. (1982) *The Farmer's Wife: Her Role in the Management of the Business*. Study No. 2, Reading University Farm Management Unit, Reading.

Casson, M. (1982) *The Entrepreneur: An Economic Theory*. Martin Robertson, Oxford.

Errington, A.J. (1988) Disguised unemployment in British agriculture. *Journal of Rural Studies* 4, 1–7.

Errington, A.J. (1993) Labour demand and labour supply in the UK farm family business. Paper presented at the XVth Congress of the European Society for Rural Sociology, Wageningen, 2–6 August 1993, 18 pp.

Errington, A.J. and Tranter, R.B. (1991) *Getting out of Farming? Part Two: The Farmers*. Study No. 27, Reading University Farm Management Unit, Reading.

Friedmann, H. (1986) Family enterprises in agriculture: structural limits and political possibilities. In: Cox, G. Lowe, P. and Winter, M. (eds) *Agriculture: People and Policies*. Allen & Unwin, London, pp. 41–60.

Gasson, R. and Errington, A.J. (1993) *The Farm Family Business*, CAB International, Wallingford, 304 pp.

Harrison, A. (1981) *Factors Influencing Ownership, Tenancy, Mobility and Use of Farmland in the UK*. Information on Agriculture No. 74, Commission of the European Communities, Luxembourg.

Hastings, M. (1984) Succession on farms. Unpublished MSc thesis, Cranfield Institute of Technology.

Laband, D. and Lentz, B. (1983) Occupational inheritance in agriculture. *American Journal of Agricultural Economics* 65, 311–314.

Lorenz, C. and Errington, A.J. (1991) Achieving sustainability in cropping systems: the labour requirements of a mulch rotation system in Kalimantan, Indonesia. *Tropical Agriculture* 68, 249–254.

Marsden, T., Munton, R., Whatmore, S. and Little, J. (1989) Strategies for coping in capitalist agriculture: an examination of the responses of farm families in British agriculture. *Geoforum* 20, 1–14.

Nalson, J.S. (1968) *Mobility of Farm Families*. Manchester University Press, Manchester.

Perrier-Cornet, P., Blanc, M., Cavailhes, J., Dauce, P. and Le Hy, A. (1991) *La Transmission des Exploitations Agricoles et l'Installation des Agriculteurs dans la CEE*. INRA, Dijon.

Potter, C. and Lobley, M. (1992) Ageing and succession on family farms: the impact on decision making and land use. *Sociologia Ruralis* 32, 317–334.

Romero, C, and Rehman, R. (1984) Goal programming and multiple criteria decision-making in farm planning: an expository analysis. *Journal of Agricultural Economics* 35, 177–190.

Salamon, S. and Davis-Brown, K. (1986) Middle-range farmers persisting through the agricultural crisis. *Rural Sociology* 51, 503–512.

Siiskonen, P., Parviainen, A. and Koppa, T. (1982) *Women in Agriculture. A Study of Equality and the Position of Women Engaged in Agriculture in Finland in 1980*. Report No. 27, Pellervo Economic Research Institute, Espoo.

Symes, D.G. (1990) Bridging the generations: succession and inheritance in a changing world. *Sociologia Ruralis* 30, 280–291.

Whatmore, S. (1991) *Farming Women*. Macmillan, Basingstoke.

Winter, M. (1984) Agrarian class structure and family farming. In: Bradley, T. and Lowe, P. (eds) *Locality and Rurality: Economy and Society in Rural Regions*. Geo Books, Norwich, pp. 115–128.

# 16

## Farmers' Objectives and Their Interactions with Business and Life Styles: Evidence from Berkshire, England

*Penny Perkin and Tahir Rehman*

### Introduction

It is generally recognized that central to the management of a farming system is the setting of objectives followed by planning, decision making and controlling (Giles and Stansfield, 1990). Similarly, a greater recognition is now accorded to the fact that the objectives of the operators of farming systems are numerous, diverse and often in conflict with each other. Methodologies for modelling such situations have been in existence for some time and have already been explored and refined for their application to agricultural systems (Rehman and Romero, 1993). It is surprising, then, to observe how limited is the amount of empirical work that has been done to discover and establish the nature of farmers' objectives, particularly in Britain. A pioneering study by Gasson (1973) was followed by Ilbery (1983), Gillmor (1986) and Whatmore *et al.* (1987). Most of the other notable studies have originated from the USA (Harman *et al.*, 1972b; Smith and Capstick, 1976; Brink and McCarl, 1978; Harper and Eastman, 1980; Kliebenstein *et al.*, 1980; Patrick and Blake, 1980; Patrick *et al.*, 1981) and some from Australia (Kerridge, 1978), Canada (Pemberton and Craddock, 1979) and New Zealand (Fairweather and Keating, 1990).

Almost all of these studies have attempted to address the fundamental issues of identifying, classifying and measuring the objectives of farmers. Even though Gasson's work in Cambridgeshire and Suffolk is essentially a descriptive and sociological study undertaken as part of a larger investigation, it does provide a convenient way of examining the goals and values that farmers hold and thus establishes their behavioural orientations and inclinations. It has provided inspiration for Ilbery, Gillmor, Whatmore *et al.* and Pemberton and Craddock. The American literature has moved on to more analytical approaches using techniques developed by psychologists and sociologists for attitude elicitation and measurement. This has enabled researchers to gain valuable insights into the working of agricultural systems and identify relationships between a system's characteristics and the farmer's objectives. Thus a better understanding of farmers' motivations and constraints is provided for extension, policy analysis and research.

The common feature of the above studies is the nearly universal conclusion that personal, family and farm business objectives are not independent of each other and need to be considered together and that the highest ranked objectives reflect a combination of lifestyle and economic goals. In a study in New Zealand (Fairweather and Keating, 1990) this observation has been used to present a unified concept of management style, which in turn was originally defined as

> ... an amalgam of factors such as the rate and number of innovations: economic performance variables, attitudes and practices in relation to uncertainty and risk, particular strategies of balancing prices and costs, sense of the future and its relationship to investment, and other factors ...
>
> (Bennett, 1980, p. 210)

Gasson's value orientations, the idea of management styles, along with the possibility of gaining meaningful insights into how objectives influence behaviour, by using techniques that have been hitherto used only with the American data, provide the backdrop against which the Berkshire study was conducted. The study had the following specific aims:

**1.** to obtain empirical evidence about the importance given to a range of monetary and non-monetary objectives amongst a random sample of farmers;
**2.** to discover the relationship of objectives to a variety of farm and farmer characteristics; and
**3.** to use some standard and new techniques of (i) eliciting objectives; and (ii) subsequent analysis of data collected.

## The Study Area and Characteristics of Sample Farms

The survey was conducted in the county of Berkshire, which lies to the west of London. Reading, Maidenhead and Newbury are the major towns in the area. Farming in these areas is being carried out on the urban fringe. There has been considerable growth in industrial activity. In addition, the villages are domiciles for commuters and thus the urban and rural lifestyles are juxtaposed. To the north of Newbury is an area of great natural beauty where large farms are found along with thriving racehorse enterprises. Geologically

Berkshire is characterized by high downland plateaux, downland slopes and escarpments, downland dry valleys, clay lowland areas in central and eastern Berkshire and river valleys. Because of increased building and expansion around Reading and Newbury, some of the farms have been built upon, notably the smaller holdings. There has also been amalgamation of small farms. Cereal crops predominate but there is a wider range of crops being grown and dairying tends to be the major livestock enterprise.

## The Sampling Frame

The survey was aimed at obtaining a representative sample of farms by taking 100 farmers at random from Berkshire. Three steps were involved: the choice of sampling frame, the sampling procedure and substitution depending on the rate of response of the survey (Errington, 1985).

The sampling frame was that of the British Telecom Business Database, which contained 454 farmers in total. The sample was stratified according to the geographical areas as noted by Jarvis *et al.* (1979), which also indicated the dispersal of large and small farms. A balanced selection of the different farm sizes was achieved by obtaining a sample from each geographical area. Farm numbers were selected according to the proportion in which they occurred in these areas; 125 were initially selected as the basis for the sample, with the view to obtaining 100 final contacts. Twenty-five non-contacts or refusals were anticipated but in fact this number was 76. Although 18 of these were numbers that could not be contacted, the majority of the refusals reflected the changes that have taken place in farming as most of these were people who had switched to alternative land use, usually non-farming or leisure enterprises, and others who had retired. Replacement farms were found by drawing additional names randomly, keeping the proportions in the stratified areas correct.

The initial contact with the respondents was made through a letter informing them of the survey and its aims, followed by a telephone call to make an appointment for the interview. During the meeting with the farmer, the questionnaire was either read out and the answers recorded by the researcher, or the respondent read it and filled in the answers himself. It was the respondent who made that choice. The survey was completed during the 1989–1990 cropping period.

For the sample farms, the largest area of land is run by managers and mixed tenure of owner occupation and renting or tenancy accounted for the second largest area of land farmed. The average acreage farmed for the sample was over 243 ha, which is above average for the country as a whole. Although the median age of farmers interviewed was over 50 and under 60 years of age, the farm businesses were frequently family run, either jointly by a father and a son or some other form of family partnership.

The questionnaire used was specifically designed to suit the purposes of the study, containing three means of eliciting objectives: a numerical rating scale, paired comparisons and magnitude estimation. The nature of these methods is explained further in the next section.

The statements reflecting the 36 objectives that were perceived for the study were an adaptation of the style and approach used by Patrick *et al.* (1981) for similar research in the USA. These adaptations fell within the framework of Gasson's value orientations of British farmers and were therefore considered suitable for use in Berkshire. However, the questionnaire was tested on a pilot survey of ten farmers and the necessary adjustments were made to its final version. The participants in this initial survey were excluded from the later sample of respondents.

## Methods of Data Elicitation and Analysis

The quantitative approaches used to elicit farmers' objectives and the techniques of subsequent analysis are usually interdependent. In this association, the first step is to derive scale values, referred to as 'measurement of objectives', to permit the use of statistical techniques to explore relationships between the subjective data measured by the scale and other variables. The different methods of elicitation and analysis that have been used in this study and their mutual correspondence are shown in Table 16.1.

The questionnaire was divided into four parts: the first three were devoted to the elicitation of objectives and the last enquired into the business background of the respondent. The sequential order in which the 36 statements on farmers' objectives appeared in the questionnaire is given in Table 16.2.

In the first part of the questionnaire, respondents were asked to place each of the statements individually on a scale of importance ranging from 0

**Table 16.1.** The methods of data collection on objectives and subsequent data analysis.

| Methods of data collection | Methods of analysis |
| --- | --- |
| Numerical rating | Ranking<br>Principal components<br>　analysis |
| Paired comparisons | Thurstone scaling<br>Multidimensional scaling |
| Magnitude estimation | Ranking |

**Table 16.2.** The objectives postulated for the Berkshire study.

| No. | Statement reflecting an objective |
| --- | --- |
| 1 | Maintain standard of living |
| 2 | Reduce physical effort in farming |
| 3 | Pay mortgage and other loans on time |
| 4 | Have all-year-round work |
| 5 | Stable product prices |
| 6 | Show a yearly profit |
| 7 | Live in country |
| 8 | Increase family's standard of living |
| 9 | Know minimum gross income for the year |
| 10 | Retain 5% turnover to invest in farm |
| 11 | Reduce long hours of work |
| 12 | Have an enterprise with a high return |
| 13 | Employ more people |
| 14 | Have a day off per week |
| 15 | Buy more land |
| 16 | Rent more land |
| 17 | Involve family in decision making |
| 18 | Have a holiday away from farm at least once a year |
| 19 | Avoid borrowing for farm business |
| 20 | Save for retirement |
| 21 | Save for children's education |
| 22 | Be recognized as a top farmer |
| 23 | Have an investment that pays quickly |
| 24 | Have time away from farm for other activities |
| 25 | Increase net worth |
| 26 | Keep loans below 50% of the net worth |
| 27 | Increase farm income |
| 28 | Stable income |
| 29 | Have an income comparable to another job |
| 30 | Receive recognition for special achievements |
| 31 | Have a job without repetitive tasks |
| 32 | Use insurance where possible |
| 33 | Be own boss |
| 34 | Leave business for next generation |
| 35 | Be part of community and church |
| 36 | Obtain the highest yields in the area |

to 8; the higher the number, the more important is the statement to the respondent, 0 representing 'not important at all'. The second part asked the farmer to rank a set of objectives based on their assessment of the relativities between each individual objective and a selected base objective. One of the schemes used is reproduced in Table 16.3 below to illustrate the method.

The penultimate part of the questionnaire offered statements of objectives in pairs and invited farmers to choose which of the two was more important. The data collected were analysed using the techniques mentioned in Table 16.1, brief descriptions of which now follow.

## *Numerical rating*

This method of eliciting data on objectives assumes that the respondents can equate intervals between responses to stimuli. It is one of the most commonly used approaches to the collection of data on the importance of business and other objectives. The respondent rates statements on a continuum representing an increasing or decreasing level of the property, or attribute, under investigation. The cues to the respondent can be verbal, such as phrases ranging from 'most unpleasant', through to 'mildly', 'indifferent', 'moderately' to 'most' and 'extremely' pleasant, to which numbers are assigned later by the researcher. 'It is probable, however, that if the experimenter wants to

**Table 16.3.** Part of the questionnaire dealing with the elicitation of objectives.

Below are some objectives that many farmers have. How important is each one to **you**? The first objective, A, has a score of 100 points. Compare each objective to this first one. If an objective is **less important** than the first objective, give it **less** than 100 points. If it is **more important** than the first objective, give it **more** than 100 points. You may give any amount of points to objectives B to H (e.g. 525, 70, 1000, 10, etc.) as long as the score given by you reflects the importance of that objective as compared to the first one.

| Objectives | Points |
|---|---|
| A    A farm business that produces a stable income | 100 |
| B    Be able to meet mortgage and loan repayments on time | _____ |
| C    Select a farm enterprise with the highest return | _____ |
| D    Steadily increase my net worth | _____ |
| E    Attain a desirable standard of living for the family | _____ |
| F    Receive recognition for special achievements | _____ |
| G    Have time away from the farm to spend in leisure and other activities | _____ |
| H    Reduce the physical effort of farming | _____ |

achieve greater equality of psychological intervals between categories, he will do well to attach numbers for the Respondent to use' (Guilford, 1954, p. 264). This approach was used for the statements appearing in the first part of the questionnaire used for the current study.

## Paired comparisons

In this case the respondent is presented with pairs of alternative statements on objectives and asked to select the preferred statement. The total number of pairs is $[n(n-1)]/2$, where $n$ is the number of statements. Each objective is compared with every other objective in turn. The frequency with which a specific objective is selected relative to others by the whole group of respondents is calculated. Such frequencies are derived for all objectives and are then used to obtain a hierarchy of preferences. This method has been used frequently in the empirical studies of farmers' objectives (Krenz, 1964; Harman *et al.*, 1972a; Smith and Capstick, 1976; Barnett *et al*, 1982).

## Magnitude estimation

This is a direct method of obtaining ratio judgements. One means of implementing it is to ask the respondent to assign points to a variety of statements on objectives when one, say A, is given a point score of 100. If another one, say B, is preferred by the respondent twice as much as A, then they assign it a value of 200 to reflect its importance relative to A.

## Ranking

The arithematic means of scores given to each of the 36 statements by all the respondents were obtained to rank objectives. The one with the highest mean score is the most preferred objective of the group as a whole, followed by others in descending order of mean score values. The standard deviations about these mean scores reflect the extent to which individual farmers differed about the ranking of a specific statement; the higher the value of a particular standard deviation estimate, the less is the unanimity amongst the respondents on the relative importance of that objective.

## Principal components analysis (PCA)

Previous studies such as that of Gasson (1973) suggest that farmers' objectives fall into two broad categories, life style or monetary. Intuitively, it is feasible to regard such categories as the principal components around which the scores given to various statements are scattered. The first aim of the principal components analysis in the current study was first to see if it was possible to achieve a reduction of the 36 rating scale statements to a small set of uncorrelated objectives or principal components, and second, to link these components to particular characteristics relating to the farmer and farms found in the Berkshire sample. To achieve the first aim, a principal components analysis was done on the 36 variables rated by respondents on the numerical rating scales. To achieve the second aim, multiple regression was used to identify characteristics that were significantly related to the objectives (reduced to their principal components).

## *Thurstone scaling*

This technique has originated from laboratory-based experiments in psychology which investigated the relationship between the ordering of objects on a known physical continuum, such as heaviness, and the ordering of the same stimuli or perceived objects on a psychological continuum. Thurstone's law of comparative judgement (Guilford, 1954) provides the rationale for ordering stimuli along a psychological continuum which do not have a physical continuum counterpart. It assumes that for a given stimulus there is associated a most frequently aroused or modal discriminal process. This represents the reaction of an individual when asked to make a judgement of the attribute assuming that the distribution of all discriminal processes aroused by the stimulus are normal about the mode. The mean or median is taken as the *scale value* of the stimulus. The standard deviation is known as the discriminal dispersal.

The modal discriminal process for a stimulus will depend upon the attribute by which respondents judge the stimulus. A stimulus can be characterized by several attributes; if two stimuli are judged according to the degree each holds of the attribute, the two may differ in that degree, as perceived by the person who is doing the judging. Assuming an attribute of interest is held constant and a large group of people are asked to judge the two stimuli, according to whether $i$ is more important that $j$, if 50% of the subjects say $i$ is more important than $j$ and the next 50% say that $j$ is more important than $i$, it is argued that stimulus $i$ and stimulus $j$ are exactly equal with regard to the attribute. The scale separation between the two is a function of the amount of importance attached to the one stimulus as compared with the other stimulus, in other words, it is a function of the proportion of times $i$ is judged greater than $j$. Therefore, through obtaining comparative judgements of stimuli, an empirical frequency can be obtained corresponding to the number of times one is judged greater, according to the selected attribute such as importance, than another:

$$p_{ij} = f_{ij}/N$$

where $p$ is the proportion of times $i$ is judged greater than $j$.

From this information, the aim is to achieve for each stimulus a single value on a unidimensional linear scale which will have the properties of an interval scale. The values of $p_{ij}$ can be expressed as unit normal deviates $z_{ij}$, or standard scores (Guilford, 1954, p. 154). These scores rate how far an individual deviates from the average using data obtained through pairwise comparisons of objectives.

### Multidimensional scaling (MDS)

In common with a number of authors (Krenz, 1964; Harman *et al.*, 1972; Patrick *et al.*, 1981; Barnett *et al.*, 1982), we have found that using the Thurstone scaling approach can lead to a number of difficulties. The main difficulty being that on applying the chi-squared test on the Thurstone scales, the results obtained do not represent the situation for the group studied as a whole. Similarly, it does not help to divide the sample into distinct subgroups where agreement on a particular ranking of objectives might be possible. This shortcoming of the Thurstone scale analysis can be overcome by resorting to multidimensional scaling which replaces the concept of a single uni-dimensional continuum with that of an underlying multidimensional space. Stimuli are represented by points in space rather than as points along a continuum. Instead of a single scale value being assigned to a stimulus, scale values are assigned to stimuli for each continuum in the multidimensional space. The basic idea upon which the multidimensional models are based is that the distance between two points in the space is a function of the degree of similarity between them.

The data used in multidimensional scaling are the amount of perceived similarity or difference between each object in a pair of a set of stimuli. Objects need to be presented to respondents in pairs, or triads, or in some form where one object is compared with another object. A *proximity* is a number that indicates the amount of similarity or difference between a pair of stimuli.

The multidimensional scaling process initially assumes a set of coordinates for the stimuli. This is termed the starting configuration. Distances, using the Pythagorean and Euclidean concepts of space, are calculated from these coordinates and compared with the data. Comparisons between distances and data continue until the distances fit the data as well as possible (Schiffman *et al.*, 1981).

## Results and Discussion

The methods of data elicitation and the analytical techniques used in this study have been described in the preceding section and attention is now focused on the results of the analyses.

### Hierarchy of objectives and the derivation of principal components

The numerical rating scale data are analysed in two different ways: first, the mean scores were used to rank the objectives in order of importance for the total set of respondents, and second, principal components analysis (PCA) was used to determine the objectives about which there is greatest disagreement amongst the respondents.

Table 16.4 provides the hierarchy of the objectives as achieved by arranging them in their descending level of mean scores. The last column gives the standard deviation associated with each mean score. A comparison of the variability indicated by the standard deviations provides a basis for differentiating objectives into those which receive most or least endorsement by the farmers.

An initial look at Table 16.4 shows that the first four in the ranking by means receive the greatest number of 'very important' ratings, even though the high value of standard deviation for 'keep loans below 50% of the worth' indicates greater disagreement about its importance amongst the respondents. The data on this particular objective are indicative of the desire for independence, as picked up by the results of the principal components analysis discussed below. The main points that emerge from Table 16.4 are that: (i) intrinsic and monetary objectives are equally important; and (ii) there is greater consensus among farmers on some objectives than others – for instance, there is almost complete agreement on the importance of 'country living' as indicated by the very low standard deviation.

The next step in the analysis used PCA to reduce the data to a smaller number of more basic dimensions.

PCA is not dependent on any underlying statistical distribution; therefore, it is not possible to decide how many components to retain by a significance test. Instead, the number of components is assessed by 'proportion of variance' explained. If a few components account for the variability of data, then the dimensionality of the data has been successfully reduced. According to Child (1970), the proportion of variance accounted for by each component gives an idea of the contribution of each component to the total variance. The higher the figure, the more substantial can be the claim that the variables with significant coefficients have some property in common. The amount of variance explained by a 'principal component' or a 'dimension' is the criterion used for deciding how many components to retain for further analysis. The rating scale data on the 36 statements allowed the calculation of a correlation matrix from which the principal components were extracted. The amount of variance attributable to each 'principal component,' according to the order of extraction, is shown in Table 16.5.

The first principal component accounts for a greater proportion of the variance, 17.8%, than any of the others. Seven principal components would be needed to account for a little over half of the variance. However, with each

**Table 16.4.** Farmers' objectives in order of importance according to mean scores.

| No.[a] | Objective | Mean | Standard deviation |
|---|---|---|---|
| 7 | Live in country | 7.72 | 1.50 |
| 33 | Be own boss | 7.71 | 1.63 |
| 6 | Show a yearly profit | 7.68 | 1.74 |
| 26 | Keep loans below 50% of the net worth | 6.94 | 2.40 |
| 1 | Maintain standard of living | 6.88 | 1.79 |
| 34 | Leave business for next generation | 6.39 | 2.57 |
| 28 | Stable income | 6.31 | 2.09 |
| 5 | Stable product prices | 6.23 | 1.96 |
| 10 | Retain 5% turnover to invest in farm | 6.14 | 2.11 |
| 27 | Increase farm income | 6.08 | 2.39 |
| 25 | Increase net worth | 6.08 | 2.00 |
| 32 | Use insurance where possible | 5.91 | 2.14 |
| 18 | Have a holiday away from farm at least once a year | 5.87 | 2.79 |
| 9 | Know minimum gross income for the year | 5.74 | 2.31 |
| 11 | Reduce long hours of work | 5.73 | 2.41 |
| 3 | Pay loans on time | 5.55 | 3.13 |
| 31 | Have a job without repetitive tasks | 5.51 | 2.10 |
| 19 | Avoid borrowing | 5.32 | 2.68 |
| 8 | Increase standard of living | 5.29 | 2.39 |
| 17 | Involve family in decision making | 5.25 | 2.91 |
| 4 | Have all-year-round work | 5.16 | 2.39 |
| 12 | Have an enterprise with a high return | 5.03 | 2.47 |
| 35 | Be part of community and church | 4.96 | 2.63 |
| 23 | Have an investment that pays quickly | 4.84 | 2.57 |
| 36 | Obtain the highest yields | 4.80 | 2.58 |
| 29 | Have an income comparable to another job | 4.69 | 2.57 |
| 2 | Reduce physical effort in farming | 4.65 | 2.46 |
| 20 | Save for retirement | 4.83 | 2.88 |
| 14 | Have a day off per week | 4.25 | 2.99 |
| 22 | Be recognized as a top farmer | 4.16 | 2.78 |
| 24 | Have time away from farm for other activities | 4.16 | 2.69 |
| 30 | Receive recognition for special achievements | 4.06 | 2.58 |
| 16 | Rent land | 3.54 | 2.98 |
| 15 | Buy land | 3.54 | 3.17 |
| 21 | Save for children's education | 2.75 | 3.17 |
| 13 | Employ more people | 3.12 | 2.56 |

[a]Sequential order of a statement in the questionnaire.

**Table 16.5.** Number of principal components extracted and per cent of variance accounted for by each.

| Principal component | Eigenvalue | Variance accounted for by principal component (%) | Cumulative % |
|---|---|---|---|
| 1 | 6.40219 | 17.8 | 17.8 |
| 2 | 2.65367 | 7.4 | 25.2 |
| 3 | 2.45869 | 6.8 | 32.0 |
| 4 | 1.97254 | 5.5 | 37.5 |
| 5 | 1.92669 | 5.4 | 42.8 |
| 6 | 1.77786 | 4.9 | 47.8 |
| 7 | 1.46413 | 4.1 | 51.8 |
| 8 | 1.28229 | 3.6 | 55.4 |
| 9 | 1.22441 | 3.4 | 58.8 |
| 10 | 1.15786 | 3.2 | 62.0 |
| 11 | 1.12544 | 3.1 | 65.1 |
| 12 | 1.02177 | 2.8 | 68.0 |
| 13 | 0.99404 | 2.8 | 70.7 |
| 14 | 0.91579 | 2.5 | 73.3 |
| 15 | 0.85041 | 2.4 | 75.6 |
| 16 | 0.75090 | 2.1 | 77.7 |
| 17 | 0.73151 | 2.0 | 79.8 |
| 18 | 0.68433 | 1.9 | 81.7 |
| 19 | 0.65786 | 1.8 | 83.5 |
| 20 | 0.59694 | 1.7 | 85.1 |
| 21 | 0.56444 | 1.6 | 86.7 |
| 22 | 0.55813 | 1.6 | 88.3 |
| 23 | 0.49964 | 1.4 | 89.6 |
| 24 | 0.47558 | 1.3 | 91.0 |
| 25 | 0.46591 | 1.3 | 92.3 |
| 26 | 0.38801 | 1.1 | 93.3 |
| 27 | 0.37881 | 1.1 | 94.4 |
| 28 | 0.32041 | 0.9 | 95.3 |
| 29 | 0.29650 | 0.8 | 96.1 |
| 30 | 0.29372 | 0.8 | 96.9 |
| 31 | 0.24324 | 0.7 | 97.6 |
| 32 | 0.22893 | 0.6 | 98.2 |
| 33 | 0.19268 | 0.5 | 98.8 |
| 34 | 0.17376 | 0.5 | 99.2 |
| 35 | 0.15774 | 0.4 | 99.7 |
| 36 | 0.11317 | 0.3 | 100.0 |

succeeding component a smaller amount of variance is explained and the less likely are the components to be uncorrelated. On these grounds, only the first three principal components are retained for further analysis.

In Table 16.6 the variables are listed in the rank order of the first principal component, with the equivalent coefficients on the other two components shown alongside [correlations of the variables with the principal components are obtained by multiplying the latent roots from the original correlation matrix for the 36 objectives by the square root of the corresponding latent root (Dunteman, 1989, p. 36)]. The coefficients refer to the correlations of the principal components with 36 objectives. This enables a comparison to be made between coefficients.

The first principal component (*monetary*) has large correlations with 16 of the objectives, taking values over 0.30 as the criterion. These objectives are essentially financial in nature. Further analysis shows that family living standards are of the greatest concern, followed by objectives related to expansion and growth: 'renting more land', 'developing a bigger business'. There are therefore two elements, family living standards and business growth which are closely connected and can be assumed to form one dimension. For the second principal component (*life style*), the variable with the largest loading on it is that of having time away for other activities, followed by having a holiday at least once a year. This dimension can be regarded as a personal rather than a farm business one and can be termed life style rather than leisure, to indicate the use of the word in the sense of

**Table 16.6.** Principal component coefficient for the 36 objectives on the three principal components, monetary (M), life style (L) and independence (I).

|  |  | Principal components | | |
| --- | --- | --- | --- | --- |
| No.[a] | Objective | M | L | I |
| 8 | Increase family's living standard as quickly as possible | 0.647 | 0.275 | 0.044 |
| 12 | Select farm enterprise with highest return | 0.643 | 0.181 | −0.047 |
| 3 | Make mortgage and loan repayments on time | 0.560 | 0.056 | −0.039 |
| 9 | Know the minimum gross income of the farm for the year | 0.552 | 0.143 | −0.178 |
| 16 | Rent more land | 0.550 | 0.144 | 0.165 |
| 13 | Develop a farm business which will grow to employ more people | 0.494 | 0.142 | 0.225 |
| 5 | Have stable prices for my products | 0.478 | 0.019 | −0.078 |
| 27 | Increase family income next year | 0.462 | 0.016 | −0.183 |
| 4 | Have work that occupies me all year round | 0.436 | −0.231 | −0.105 |
| 28 | Have a farm business which produces a stable income | 0.435 | 0.208 | 0.268 |

**Table 16.6.** *Continued*

| No.[a] | Objective | Principal components | | |
|---|---|---|---|---|
| | | M | L | I |
| 1 | Maintain my family's standard of living at its current level | 0.394 | −0.124 | 0.119 |
| 6 | Show a yearly profit from the farm operation | 0.380 | −0.218 | 0.268 |
| 36 | Obtain the highest yields in the area | 0.366 | 0.299 | 0.243 |
| 14 | Have at least 1 day off per week from the farm work | 0.360 | 0.478 | 0.028 |
| 20 | Save 5% or more of my profits for retirement | 0.328 | 0.229 | 0.518 |
| 23 | Have a farm investment that will pay for itself quickly | 0.314 | 0.390 | 0.278 |
| 17 | Involve members of my family in the farm's planning and decision making | 0.272 | 0.202 | 0.520 |
| 2 | Reduce the physical effort involved in farming | 0.263 | 0.382 | 0.003 |
| 26 | Keep my loans and mortgages below 50% of my net worth | 0.261 | −0.083 | 0.627 |
| 11 | Reduce long work hours but only for short periods of the year | 0.277 | 0.150 | 0.290 |
| 15 | Buy more land | 0.189 | −0.041 | 0.111 |
| 10 | Retain at least 5% of my turnover to put back into the farming operation | 0.187 | −0.109 | 0.566 |
| 18 | Have at least one holiday away from the farm each year | 0.176 | 0.635 | 0.063 |
| 29 | Have a family income comparable to another job | 0.148 | 0.601 | 0.113 |
| 32 | Use insurance to protect myself where possible | 0.136 | 0.309 | 0.417 |
| 7 | Live in country | 0.123 | 0.071 | −0.117 |
| 22 | Be recognized as a top farmer | 0.182 | −0.382 | −0.125 |
| 34 | Develop a business for the next generation | 0.112 | 0.165 | 0.666 |
| 30 | Receive recognition for special achievement | 0.001 | 0.634 | −0.029 |
| 35 | Be a part of church and/or community organizations | 0.074 | 0.279 | 0.359 |
| 21 | Save 5% or more of my profits for children's education | 0.028 | 0.557 | 0.236 |
| 19 | Avoid using borrowed funds for the farm business | −0.061 | 0.071 | 0.618 |
| 25 | Steadily increase my net worth | −0.091 | 0.257 | 0.406 |
| 33 | Be my own boss | −0.160 | −0.216 | 0.518 |
| 24 | Have more time away from the farm to spend in other activities | −0.243 | 0.674 | 0.134 |
| 31 | Have a job without a lot of daily repetitive tasks | −0.237 | 0.360 | 0.035 |

[a]Sequential order of a statement in the questionnaire.

pursuing activities for relaxation or enjoyment. The most important variables found for the third principal component (*independence*) are: (i) to have a business for the next generation; (ii) to avoid borrowing and keep loans below 50% of net worth and to invest at least 5% of income in the farm; (iii) to involve the family in decision making; and (iv) to be 'your own boss'. Of less importance, but still significant, is to be part of the community and church. The rankings shown for these factors reflect a long-term objective of maintaining the continuity of the farm business in the hands of the family and of retaining independence.

This analysis enables the following association to be established between the principal components and farmers' objectives:

| **Monetary** | **Life style** | **Independence** |
|---|---|---|
| Family/farm income | Time away for other activities | Own boss |
| Growth versus stability | | Long-term objectives |

At this stage, multiple regression was used to establish the relationship of different types of personal or farm characteristics such as consumption expenditure, debt levels and gross value of agricultural production, hours worked and time taken off work, and finally the tenurial status of an operator, to the three principal components. The information on these farm and farmer characteristics was obtained through the fourth part of the questionnaire. The results of this analysis are summarized in Table 16.7.

Table 16.7 shows those characteristics which have a statistically significant relationship with any of the three components; therefore, the presence of a figure in the table itself has two meanings: first, if there is no figure reported it means there is no such relationship, and second, the figures reported imply the existence of a relationship in addition to the level of significance.

The main findings are the relationships between a variety of business and personal variables related to farm and farmer characteristics and the 'monetary', 'life style' and 'independence' principal components:

- Long-term debt was related to 'independence', particularly the purchase of land that is the 'ownership of property.' The life-style component exerts an influence over the level of intermediate debt.
- Age and education were also related to 'life style'. Older persons are more likely to want to remain on the farm and less likely to want time away to do other things. The converse is true for those respondents who have received formal higher education at a college of agriculture or a university.
- There is a relationship between age and education in that an older person is less likely to have undertaken further education owing to the smaller range of opportunities for such a pursuit at an earlier stage in his life.
- Having tertiary education is related to wanting time away from the farm for other activities. Those without tertiary levels of education tend to take

no holidays or short breaks of a few days rather than holidays of a week or longer. A further finding was the longer peak-season hours worked by those with higher education, which might be related to the type of farming.

These results indicate that there are certain characteristics which are associated with the principal components identified above and this association

**Table 16.7.** Farm/farmer characteristics which have significant association with the monetary (M), life style (L) and independence (I) components.

| Characteristics | Principal components M L I (significance level)[a] | | |
|---|---|---|---|
| 1. Debt: | | | |
| Short-term[b] | | | |
| Intermediate[c] | | 0.0073 | |
| Long-term[d] | | | 0.0112 |
| Education | | | |
| Total assets | | | |
| Consumption spending: | | | |
| 1987 | | | 0.0818 |
| 1988 | | | |
| 1989 | | | |
| 2. Gross value of production (1989) | | | |
| Acreage | | | |
| Education | | 0.0928 | |
| 3. Holidays taken | | 0.0046 | |
| Holidays wanted | | | |
| Working hours wanted | | | |
| Normal hours worked | | | |
| Peak hours worked | | 0.0041 | |
| Intermediate debt | | | |
| 4. Manager versus owner | 0.0747 | | |
| Owner versus tenant | | | |
| Age | | | |
| Education | | 0.0001 | |
| Acreage | | | |
| Gross value of production | | | |

[a]Significance levels at 10% are given in addition to those at 5%, as for survey data this can be considered as an indication of a relationship between variables.
[b]Mortgages or loans for land purchase.
[c]Leases and/or loans for machinery costs.
[d]Bank overdraft to cover variable costs.

can, in turn, be related to other aspects of business behaviour of farmers, such as levels of outstanding debt. Ilbery (1983, p. 336), commenting on his follow-up to the research by Gasson (1973), notes that establishing a pattern of values that differentiates one group of farmers from another is more complex than initially thought. Some relationships are cross-cut by a multiplicity of factors; for example, age interacts with experience of farming, whereas farm size, as a proxy for a social class of the respondent, may cut across age effects. He continued further to state that it was the relative emphasis that was put on the different value orientations that was important. From the results of the Berkshire survey it is apparent that a similar observation can be made for objectives.

### Delineation of the sample into subgroups and their hierarchies

The unidimensional method of Thurstone scaling was applied to the paired comparisons data to obtain a ranking of objectives and to test if this ranking would permit the treatment of the whole sample as one group and, if the sample were divided into subgroups on the basis of some farm or farmer characteristic, what different rankings would exist. The results showed that the ranking obtained did not describe the whole group. This was a result similar to that of Harman *et al.* (1972). However, for the Berkshire sample, a quarter of the respondents were unwilling to rate one objective as more important than another for several of the objectives. To be able to state which characteristics affect the ranking of objectives it was necessary, therefore, to devise an alternative system of analysis.

*Multidimensional scaling* was applied to the same paired comparison data in order to obtain the number of dimensions that would represent, or describe, the data more accurately and to discover which groups of farmers differed from other groups. This was achieved by segmenting the Berkshire sample into four subgroups according to the level of assets (market value of land, if owned, buildings, machinery and stock), as shown in Table 16.8.

**Table 16.8.** The Berkshire sample divided into four subgroups according to total value of assets.

| Group number | Assets (£) | No. of farmers |
|---|---|---|
| 1 | 10,000–2,000,000 | 22 |
| 2 | 2,000,001–4,000,000 | 25 |
| 3 | 4,000,001–6,000,000 | 23 |
| 4 | 6,000,001–8,000,000 | 23 |
| Total: | | 93 |

As an 'objective' is the direction in which an individual strives to achieve better results, there are clearly identifiable differences between the various groups. In that sense, the differences in the importance attached to various objectives by the subgroups indicate that Group 4, the one with the highest asset values, favours the objective of net worth over the other objectives. The explanation of this, not unexpected finding, is that the satisfactory standard of living having been met already makes another objective salient. It should be pointed out, however, that this group contains mainly managers, thus net worth improvement may reflect the objective of an owner rather than of a manager.

Group 3 attaches highest importance to the monetary dimension of standard of living, indicating that there may be perceived scope for improvement in their incomes. The next two groups have importance spread more evenly over the objectives; there is possibly less emphasis on a solely monetary dimension or limited scope for improvement in the other objectives as well.

As regards the relative importance of one objective in relation to another, a direct ratio scale is obtained by using the *magnitude estimation* technique, which allows it to be said that one objective is twice as important as another. For the sample as a whole, the objective 'attaining a reasonable standard of living' was almost twice as important as the 'stable income' objective and 2.5 times more important than 'obtaining recognition for special achievements.'

## Conclusions

The research work reported here permits a number of observations to be made about the nature of farmers' objectives and the applicability of empirical studies:

**1.** The 'paired comparison' technique showed that there is no clear hierarchy of objectives when all the farmers are treated as one group.
**2.** Decision makers seem to find it difficult to rank any one objective as being more important than another – a situation that applies to 23% of the respondents included in the Berkshire sample.
**3.** Multidimensional scaling methods produced better results for highlighting the multidimensional nature of farmers' objectives than any other analytical technique used in the study.
**4.** As regards the importance of various objectives, it would appear that an intrinsic value, that is 'pursuing an activity in its own right,' is most important. 'Standard of living' as an objective is becoming an intrinsic one as it is now perceived to include an increasing number of non-monetary influences and variables.
**5.** The 36 objectives postulated for this investigation can be reduced to three composite dimensions – monetary, life style and independence – as a result of using principal components analysis. These results seem to endorse the

findings of similar research in New Zealand by Fairweather and Keating (1990).

**6.** Of the various techniques that have been used in the studies on the elicitation of objectives, the paired comparisons method has been used most frequently; its popularity is derived from its theoretical validity (in that one stimulus is compared directly with another), its ease of application and the absence of restrictive assumptions that need to be made about the discriminatory ability of respondents since they are asked simply which of two alternatives they prefer.

**7.** The present study shows that results on farmers' ranking of objectives differ somewhat depending on the method of elicitation and analysis used. The variation tends to be greater when a wider range of expression is allowed to be recorded, as in magnitude estimation.

**8.** Finally, the variety of methods of research and analysis used in this study has shown aspects of methodological interest, particularly with regard to the elicitation of objectives. A good proportion of responses seem to violate the transitivity assumption of utility theory. In common with some other recent studies, this would suggest that the issue of 'standard of living' and its relationship with objectives need to be explored further within a multi-dimensional framework, in addition to the link between farmers' objectives with economic behaviour and life styles.

# References

Barnett, D.A., Blake, B. and McCarl, B.A. (1982) Programming via multidimensional scaling applied to Senegalese subsistence farms. *American Journal of Agricultural Economics* 64, 720–727.

Bennett, J.W. (1980) Management style: a concept and a method for the analysis of family-operated agricultural enterprise. In: Bartlett, P. (ed.) *Agricultural Decision Making. Anthropological Contributions to Rural Development.* Academic Press, New York, pp. 203–237.

Brink, L. and McCarl, B. (1978) The trade-off between expected return and risk among corn belt farmers. *American Journal of Agricultural Economics* 60, 159–163.

Child, D. (1970) *The Essentials of Factor Analysis.* Brown, Knight and Truscott, New York.

Dunteman, G.H. (1989) *Principal Components Analysis.* Sage Publications, London.

Errington, A. (1985) Sampling frames for farm surveys in the UK: some alternatives. *Journal of Agricultural Economics* 36, 251–258.

Fairweather, J. and Keating, N.C. (1990) *Management Styles of Canterbury Farmers.* Research Report No. 25, Agribusiness and Economics Research Unit, Lincoln University.

Gasson, R. (1973) Goals and values of farmers. *Journal of Agricultural Economics* 24, 521–537.

Giles, A.K. and Stansfield, J.M. (1990) *The Farmer as Manager*, 2nd edn. CAB International, Wallingford.

Gillmor, D.A. (1986) Behaviourial studies in agriculture: goals, values and enterprise choice. *Irish Journal of Agricultural Economics and Rural Sociology* 11, 19–33.

Guilford, J.P. (1954) *Psychometric Methods.* McGraw-Hill, New York.

Harman, W.L., Eidman, V.R. and Hatch, R.E. (1972a) Relating farm and operator characteristics to multiple goals. *Southern Journal of Agricultural Economics* 4, 215–220.

Harman, W.L., Hatch, R.E., Eldman, V.R. and Claypool, P.L. (1972b) *An Evaluation of Factors Affecting the Hierarchy of Multiple Goals.* Technical Bulletin T - 134, Oklahoma State University Agricultural Experiment Station, Oklahoma.

Harper, W.M. and Eastman, C. (1980) An evaluation of goal hierarchies for small farm operators. *American Journal of Agricultural Economics* 62, 742–747.

Ilbery, B.W. (1983) Goals and values of hop farmers. *Transactions of the Institute of British Geographers* 8, 329–341.

Jarvis, M.G., Hazeldon, J. and Mackney, D. (1979) *Soils of Berkshire.* Rothamsted Experimental Station, Harpenden.

Kerridge, K.W. (1978) Value orientation of farmer behaviour – an exploratory study. *Quarterly Review of Agricultural Economics* 31, 61–72.

Kliebenstein, J.B., Barrett, D.A., Hefferman, W.D. and Kirtley, C.I. (1980) An analysis of farmers' perceptions of benefits received from farming. *Northern Central Journal of Agricultural Economics* 2, 131–136.

Krenz, R.D. (1964) Pair-wise comparison as applied to seeding crop land to grass. *Journal of Farm Economics* 46, 1219–1226.

Patrick, G.F. and Blake, B.F. (1980) Measurement and modelling of farmers' goals: an evaluation and suggestions. *Southern Journal of Agricultural Economics* 12, 199–204.

Patrick, G.F., Blake, B.F. and Whitaker, S.H. (1981) Magnitude estimation: an application to farmers' risk-income preferences. *Western Journal of Agricultural Economics* 6, 239–248.

Pemberton, C.A. and Craddock, W.J. (1979) Goals and aspirations: effects on income levels of farmers in the Carman region of Manitoba. *Canadian Journal of Agricultural Economics* 27, 23–34.

Rehman, T. and Romero, C. (1993) The application of the MCDM paradigm to the management of agricultural systems: some basic considerations. *Agricultural Systems* 41, 239–256.

Schiffman, S., Reynolds, M.L. and Young, W.F. (1981) *Introduction to Multidimensional Scaling.* Academic Press, New York.

Smith, D. and Capstick, D.F. (1976) Establishing priorities among multiple management goals. *Southern Journal of Agricultural Economics* 6, 37–43

Whatmore, S., Munton, R., Marsden, T. and Little, J. (1987) Towards a typology of farm businesses in contemporary British agriculture. *Sociologia Ruralis* 27, 21–37.

# =17=

## AN INTRODUCTION TO FAMILY AND BUSINESS STRESS IN FARM FAMILIES

### Ian Deary

## Introduction

Stress is usually defined as a perturbation that threatens to upset the equilibrium of an organism. Sources of stress are sought in the organism's environment, and the resulting effect on the organism, borrowing from engineering parlance, is referred to as strain. Because of the threat to equilibrium associated with stressors, there is a need for the organism to respond to stress in order to return to equilibrium. Much recent research in psychology has been orientated toward understanding the psychological, social and physiological aspects of the stress process, in particular the nature of environmental stressors and the predisposing features of people that make some more prone to experience the negative effects of stress than others (Gray, 1987).

Stress related to the workplace has featured prominently in stress research, and it is accepted that there is both practical and theoretical interest in characterizing the stresses involved in different occupations (Schaufeli *et al.*, 1993). An understanding of the prominent facets of stress involved in different occupations can help to orient strategies for stress alleviation and can help to predict those members of a profession most likely to experience burnout. In addition, the degree to which aspects of the working situation are seen as stressful will influence the decisions made by the person.

The purpose of this chapter is to provide an introduction to some aspects of the study of farm stress. Some examples of research that have attempted to characterize the nature and facets of social and business stress in farmers and their families are presented. Those studies which have sought predictors of farm stress are mentioned. In general, there is an emphasis on research that

has focused on farm families, including farmers' spouses and intergenerational issues.

# The Domains of Farm Stress

Farming is a stressful occupation – the Institute of Occupational Safety and
Health ranked farming as the 12th most stress-related occupation among 130
high-stress jobs – yet the stress of farmers has received relatively little
empirical study (Olson and Schellenberg, 1986). An important first step in
farming stress research has been to discover the particular areas of the job
that are stressful for farmers. This search for the domains of stress within an
occupation has been performed for other professions; for instance, there is
much research aimed at investigating the domains of stress within medicine
and the paramedical professions (Wolfgang, 1988). What follows in this
section is an account of three attempts to map the domains of farm stress. The
first is a large review article, the second is an 'informal' empirical study and
the third is a large study using multivariate statistical techniques.

After acknowledging the lack of research on stress and farming, Olson
and Schellenberg (1986) reviewed various studies of stress among farmers.
One of the studies reviewed included almost 1400 US farmers, and over 50%
of the respondents mentioned the following as stressors: machinery breakdown, harvest, price uncertainties for products sold, machinery costs, interest
rates, when to market, planting and weather conditions. The authors noted
that machinery breakdown was mentioned prominently in two large surveys
and that, in one of them, it ranked as more stressful than divorce or major
personal illness. The review includes a summary of a study by Schellenberg
and colleagues in which 'burnout' among farmers was closely associated with
financial stressors, such as price uncertainties, production costs and not
having enough money or credit.

Olson and Schellenberg's (1986) review also notes that familial aspects
of farming are a source of reported stress. The mutual dependency in farm
families can induce stress, and the close proximity of more than one
generation of a family on a farm can be stressful. Issues related to succession
appear in studies of stress; the decisions related to when or whom to hand the
farm over to can be stressful, as can the situation in which there is no
successor to a family farm. The conflict between farm and family roles,
especially for women, has also been noted as a source of stress.

Within the farming profession, Walker *et al.* (1986) attempted to develop
a pool of self-report questionnaire items relevant to stress in farming. They
collected information from 140 Manitoba farmers and their wives. The
subjects of the investigation were mostly grain farmers, but there were some
mixed and dairy farmers also. Farmers were asked to nominate their top five
stressors.

Financial stressors were noted by 83% of the farmers. Regularly mentioned stressors included commodity prices, increasing expenses, high debt load and irregular cash flow. Unpredictable or unfavourable weather was noted as among the top five stressors by 75% of the farmers. Of the male farmers, 75% found government agricultural policies and regulations to be among their top stressors. Free trade proposals, unrealistic quotas and farm subsidies were additional sources of stress. The investigators noted that: 'Discussions of the role of government as a source of farm stress often reflected signs of heated emotional involvement.'

Also among the stressors indexed by Walker *et al.* (1986) were several daily 'hassles'. The term hassles is being used with increased frequency within psychological studies of stress to indicate recurrent, sometimes unpredictable and relatively minor stressors; minor, that is, when compared with single catastrophic life events, such as a death in the family or redundancy. Hassles noted commonly by the farmers were machinery breakdowns, deciding when to sell produce, heavy work loads, time pressure and unplanned interruptions. On a more general psychological level the farmers indicated that their lack of control over some important factors that impacted upon their work and livelihood was a major source of stress. Such factors included government policy, weather and market conditions; these particular factors were a commonly found triad of stressors. The investigators formed an impression that stress was often associated with hostility to the government (for their policies) and to bankers and the media (for distorting farm problems).

Eberhardt and Poonyan (1990) attempted to improve upon the largely anecdotal and qualitative approaches that had characterized farm stress research by using a more psychometrically sophisticated method of analysis. After a relatively small pilot series, they developed a 28-item measure of farm stress. This measure – the farm stress survey – had five stress-related domains. The first domain was 'economics', and asked questions about loan payment, market prices, federal export policies and the government budget deficit. The second domain was 'geographical isolation', and recorded the farmer's distance from services. The third domain was 'time pressure', indexing the experience of having too much to do in too little time. The fourth domain was 'climatic conditions', adducing information about rainfall, frost and wind erosion. The fifth domain was 'hazardous working conditions', which enquired about chemicals, machinery and crop handling.

Their farm stress survey was sent to 1300 owner-operated farmers in a north-central state in the USA; 362 replies were received, a response rate of 28%, which raises some concern about possible response bias among those who did respond. Nevertheless, multivariate latent trait analysis validated the five-factor structure statistically. However, the 'economic' factor divided into two factors: farmers' concerns about their personal financial situation were statistically separable from their concerns over more general economic matters and national- and government-level matters.

What might at first appear to be an abstruse statistical detail in the Eberhardt and Poonyan (1990) report should not be passed over. They validated a multi-factor stress model among farmers, and it has many areas of concordance with the review of Olson and Schellenberg (1986) and the study by Walker *et al.* (1986) in terms of the stressors that farmers find most pressing. However, farmers' scores on the Eberhardt and Poonyan (1990) six stress factor scales (if one counts the two economic factors separately) were all positively correlated. The average intercorrelation among the six scales was 0.29, with a range between 0.04 and 0.52. In statistical parlance this means that the authors should not underestimate the statistical power of the first unrotated principal component. In common parlance it means that a farmer who tends to report stressors in one domain will be more likely to report stressors in all of the other domains.

Therefore, in addition to a proper discussion about the important separable areas of farm stress, it is important also to note the presence of a general stress factor, common to all domains. This interesting finding has a parallel in medical research where it is widely recognized that individuals who report stress in one area of their lives will tend to report more stress in many other areas also. The origins of this tendency to see many things negatively have been partly traced to enduring temperamental differences captured under the rubric of the 'distress-prone personality' (Stone and Costa, 1990). In fact, in the Eberhardt and Poonyan (1990) study they reported that scores on their 'economic' and 'time pressure' factors were significant predictors of low life satisfaction, emotional strain and illness frequency. Because their study was cross-sectional rather than longitudinal in design, it is not possible to state whether the higher stress led to these outcomes or whether some subjects were responding negatively in a wide range of domains because of a general negative outlook.

## Causes and Consequences of Farm Stress

An obvious variable to examine with respect to its effect on stress is the sex of the respondent, and some studies have sought to discover whether men and women have different experiences of stress. Heppner *et al.* (1991) tested 44 male and 35 female farmers at a workshop for those who were thinking of changing their careers. They noted that men were making greater progress toward handling stressful situations, were more confident with respect to problem-solving appraisal and were less confused about their vocational identity. Levels of stress and depression were measured in the total sample and the significant predictors of these were problem-solving confidence, emotion-focused coping, having barriers to career transition and level of social support. For men, problem-solving confidence was the main predictor of stress, whereas for women vocational identity played a larger role. In general, the study appeared to discover very different predictors for the criterion variables in men and women. However, whereas this might be due to sex, it might equally be due to the small sample sizes, because multiple regression-type models are unstable in samples of the size that were used. Therefore, these findings, although of interest, must await replication in larger samples.

In the previous section, various attempts to map the main domains of stress in farmers were described. A related approach that attempted to identify the stressors responsible for distress in farmers was adopted by Walker and Walker (1987). They assessed 808 Manitoba farmers (470 men and 338 women) on the Farming Stress Inventory in order to index stressors. They used a mixture of questions from the Hopkins Symptom Checklist and the Health Problems Checklist to assess the negative health outcomes of the stress process. To give a flavour of what sorts of health outcomes are important in these scales, the authors state that, for the whole sample, 81% of the symptom variance was accounted for by trouble concentrating, sleep disturbance, change in health and increased arguments with spouse and children. Therefore, it may be seen that the symptoms were indexing the general area of psychological distress rather than physical illness.

Stepwise multiple regression analyses were conducted to examine the contribution made by stressors to the stress-related symptoms. Separate analyses were conducted for men and women. In fact, the main contributor to stress-related symptoms in both sexes was problems related to balancing work and family responsibility, which accounted for 23% of the stress-symptom variance in men and 22% in women. Thereafter there were some male and female differences. In what follows, the factors contributing to male and female stress-symptom incidence (with percentage variance explained in parentheses) are given and, as a comparator, all factors are included which explain as much as or more variance than the 'death of a friend'. For males, contributors were as follows: personal illness during planting or harvesting (14%); conflict with spouse over spending priorities (9%); no farm help or loss of help when needed (4%); worrying about keeping farm in family (3%); death of a friend (2%). For females, contributors were as follows: conflict with spouse over spending priorities (10%); pressures in having too much work to do in too little time (5%); government cheap food policies (3%); major decisions made without her knowledge or input (3%); worrying about owing money (2%); feeling isolated on the farm (2%); death of a friend (2%).

Therefore, the study by Walker and Walker (1987) finds interesting similarities and differences between men and women with respect to the farm stress factors that produce negative health consequences. Moreover, although there are certain congruences with the domains of farm stress outlined in the previous section, we see here the importance of events in the family with regard to stress outcomes for both men and women. The importance of succession worries for men's stress outcomes, and of lack of involvement in decision making for women's stress outcomes, suggests that traditional family roles are a source of tension in farm families.

In the above study by Walker and Walker (1987) and in the study by Heppner *et al*. (1991), it emerged that role identity was a potential source of stress for women in farming. The part played by role conflict in farming women's stress levels was also examined by Berkowitz and Perkins (1984). They studied 126 farming wives in New York State and assessed psychological and physiological stress levels. Role conflict reflected the degree of tension between roles in the family and in farm work. The farm and the home task load were also assessed. Additionally, the level of support offered by the husband was measured by responses to the following factors: how spouses help them cope with tensions; satisfaction with spouse's level of household help; satisfaction with respect to support and help with farm duties; and satisfaction with the amount of time contributed to home and family responsibilities. Among the predictor variables, the level of reported overall husband support correlated negatively (at about $-0.3$) with reported home task load and reported role conflict. More importantly, husband support was negatively associated with stress levels ($-0.36$, $P < 0.01$) and role conflict was positively associated with stress levels ($0.19$, $P < 0.05$).

Berkowitz and Perkins (1984) concluded that 'husbands play an important role in mediating the stress experienced by their wives.' This might be the case but, in a cross-sectional study, it is not the only tenable conclusion from these results. Given what was said above about the 'distress-prone personality,' one must be cautious in making such causal inferences from cross-sectional data. Those under stress are likely to appraise much that takes place around them in a negative way and, therefore, there is no guarantee that the level of role conflict and husband support that was reported was not being caused by the level of stress a woman was under. Therefore, it is tenable that stress was causing subjects to appraise their roles and their husbands more negatively. Only longitudinal studies can decide this important causal issue.

Economic aspects of farm stress can have effects on family farm relationships, especially those of farming husbands and wives. Research on this topic by Rosenblatt and Keller (1983) emphasized the interconnectedness of the different aspects of the stress process. They found that economic vulnerability was associated with economic distress which was, in turn, significantly associated with blaming in the marriage.

Another potential cause of stress for farmers that is related to the family is the presence of members from more than one generation on the farm. However, one relationship that has been perceived as stressful in itself, that between mothers and their daughters-in-law who form a part of the same farm family, has been found to be less associated with stress than expected (Marotz-Baden and Cowan, 1987).

Weigel *et al*. (1987) studied the stresses reported by members of two-generation farms. Younger family members scored higher than the older generation on the farm family stress scale, and scored lower on scales assessing family support and family satisfaction. The authors concluded that 'The younger generation seems to have more stress, perceive less family support, and feel less satisfied in the two-generation farm family than does the older generation.' However, an inspection of the summary data provided in the report reveals that the differences between the generations on all of the scales were small in absolute terms; the differences in scales were highly significantly different because the sample sizes were relatively large. In a more recent report, the same research team studied the predictors of farm stress for the younger and older generations in two-generation farm families (Weigel and Weigel, 1990). The older members of the farm family tended to emphasize unity of the family, whereas the younger members wanted more freedom and independence.

Replication of the finding that the younger generations of two-generation farm families have greater stress levels than the older generations was offered by Wilson *et al.* (1991). They found that, in order of increasing farm-related stress, came fathers, mothers, sons and daughters-in-law. Moreover, these researchers showed also that there were different predictors of stress for the two generations: income satisfaction was significantly negatively related to stress for members of the older generation [as they had indicated previously (Marotz-Baden, 1988)], but not the younger. As the authors state themselves, it is hard to explain the lack of correlation between income satisfaction and stress in the younger generation. Schulman and Armstrong (1989) demonstrated also that younger farmers experience more stress than older farmers, even when they are not a part of a two-generation farm, and have indicated that the relationship between family income and stress might be curvilinear rather than monotonic.

## Conclusions

The study of farm stress, like the study of stress in other professions, is emerging from a period of research that has been characterized by anecdote, general survey and other qualitative methods. There is now more quantitative research, with an increasing emphasis on achieving scales with acceptable psychometric characteristics. That is not to say that qualitative concepts and approaches have no place in the future study of farming stress research. Such concepts and approaches have heuristic value and serve to structure thinking on the topic that can help to formulate testable hypotheses. Two such notions that appear useful, though at present they lack thorough validation, are the 'yeoman–entrepreneur' dimension in farming and the 'ABCX' approach to understanding stress (Davis-Brown and Salamon, 1987; Van Hook, 1987). The former concept has usefully structured ideas about the different motivations and objectives held by different farmers, and the latter usefully attempts to dissect various aspects of the complex process of perceiving and reacting to stress.

The agenda for farming stress research has been briefly outlined above. First, it will be necessary to continue to develop scales to assess stress domains in farming. In order for such scales to be valid, due attention must be paid to the applicability of any scales to the particular country and farm type that is being studied. Whereas we have seen that some farming stressors might well be generally agreed upon – economic worries and uncertainties, government policies, the weather, etc. – other sources of stress will be unique to particular countries, cultures, localities and farming types.

Having developed usable scales of farm stress, it will be important to continue research that has sought the causes and consequences of stress. Individuals report experiencing different levels of stress associated with their work, in farming and elsewhere. The discovery of the personological and environmental factors associated with these individual differences will be important in order to understand the sources of high stress levels. The consequences of stress – in terms of mental and physical ill health, suboptimal decision making, family strife, etc. – must also be studied in order to implement rational stress-alleviation strategies (Keating, 1987; Cecil, 1988).

## Acknowledgement

The author thanks Mrs Joyce Willock for assisting with the compilation of the literature.

## References

Berkowitz, A.L. and Perkins, H.W. (1984) Stress among farm women: work and family as interacting systems. *Journal of Marriage and the Family* 46, 161–165.

Cecil, H.F. (1988) Stress: country style – Illinois response to farm stress. *Journal of Rural Community Psychology* 9, 51–60.

Davis-Brown, K. and Salamon, S. (1987) Farm families in crisis: an application of stress theory to farm family research. *Family Relations* 36, 368–373.

Eberhardt, B.J. and Poonyan, A. (1990) Development of the farm stress survey: factorial structure, reliability and validity. *Educational and Psychological Measurement* 50, 393–402.

Gray, J.A. (1987) *The Psychology of Fear and Stress.* Cambridge University Press, Cambridge.

Heppner, P.P., Cook, S.W., Strozier, A.L. and Heppner, M.J. (1991) An investigation of coping styles and gender differences with farmers in career transition. *Journal of Counseling Psychology* 38, 167–174.

Keating, N.C. (1987) Reducing stress of farm men and women. *Family Relations* 36, 358–363.

Marotz-Baden, R. (1988) Income, economic satisfaction and stress in two-generational farm families. *Lifestyles: Family and Economic Issues* 9, 331–356.

Marotz-Baden, R. & Cowan, D. (1987) Mothers-in-law and daughters-in-law: the effects of proximity on conflict and stress. *Family Relations* 36, 385–390.

Olson, K.R. and Schellenberg, R.P. (1986) Farm stressors. *American Journal of Community Psychology* 14, 555–569.

Rosenblatt, P.C. and Keller, L.O. (1983) Economic vulnerability and economic stress in farm couples. *Family Relations* 32, 567–573.

Schaufeli, W.B., Maslach, C. and Marek, T. (1993) *Professional Burnout: Recent Developments in Theory and Research.* Taylor and Francis, London.

Schulman, M.D. and Armstrong, P.S. (1989) The farm crisis: an analysis of social psychological distress among North Carolina farm operators. *American Journal of Community Psychology* 17, 423–441.

Stone, S.V. & Costa, P.T. (1990) Disease-prone personality or distress-prone personality? The role of neuroticism in coronary heart disease. In: Friedman, H.S. (ed.) *Personality and Disease.* Wiley, New York, pp. 178–200.

Van Hook, M.P. (1987) Harvest of despair: using the ABCX model for farm families in crisis. *Social Casework: The Journal of Contemporary Social Work* May, 273–278.

Walker, J.L. Walker, L.S. & MacLennan, P.M. (1986) An informal look at farm stress. *Psychological Reports* 59, 427–430.

Walker, L.S. and Walker, J.L. (1987) Stressors and symptoms predictive of distress in farmers. *Family Relations* 36, 374–378.

Weigel, R.R. and Weigel, D.J. (1990) Family satisfaction in two-generation farm families: the role of stress and resources. *Family Relations* 39, 449–455.

Weigel, R.R., Weigel, D.J. and Blundall, J. (1987) Stress, coping and satisfaction: generational differences in farm families. *Family Relations* 36, 45–48.

Wilson, S.M., Marotz-Baden, R. and Holloway, D.P. (1991) Stress in two-generation farm and ranch families. *Lifestyles: Family and Economic Issues* 12, 199–216.

Wolfgang, A.P. (1988) Job stress in the health professions: a study of physicians, nurses and pharmacists. *Behavioural Medicine* 14, 43–47.

# ═══ 18 ═══

## WORKING KNOWLEDGE CONCERNING TECHNICAL SYSTEMS AND DECISION SUPPORT

### François Papy

## The Farm Enterprise is a Complex System

Men try to master complex things by simplifying them: either to explain how they work (the theory in this case concerns the technical systems and farming systems researcher), or to organize them (the practice in this case concerns the farmer). Each objective needs to be analysed in a specific way. Differences in points of view need to be considered if communication between theoretical knowledge (gained from scientific research) and working knowledge (gained by experience) is to be achieved.

This is the essential point developed in this chapter, prepared on the basis of work carried out in France over the past 20 years, even before the creation in 1979 of the Agrarian Systems Department (SAD) within the National Institute of Agronomic Research (INRA). This chapter concerns mainly the management of technical systems and aspects concerning family–farm relationships will be simply mentioned in passing.

## Scientific Approach

### *Analysis of practices*

Criticism of the top-down linear model for extending innovation (from its theoretical creation to its implementation) has been sufficiently expressed in the past for further discussion here to be unnecessary. At the beginning of the 1970s in France, agronomists and economists realized how unsuitable existing development models were, created with consideration neither for farmers' goals nor for the concrete conditions for introducing technical innovation into production systems (see Bonnemaire, Chapter 2; Deffontaines, 1973; Osty, 1974, 1978; Sebillotte, 1974, 1987; Petit, 1975). It was gradually being recognized that farmers must have 'reasons for doing what they do' and these needed to be understood. The concepts of 'technique' and 'practice' are now distinct. The former can be formulated independent of farmers and relates to theory. The latter concerns the ways in which farmers work and is heavily influenced by the actual conditions in which technical operations are carried out (Cristofini *et al.*, 1978; Teissier, 1979). Practices are assumed to be the result of a direct intention, which in turn depends on objectives set by the farmer in a context of constraints and effectiveness. Hence, they have become a subject for research: through the analysis of practices, the reasons why a farmer acts as he does can be understood. The following three questions need to be answered: what does he do and how does he do it?; what are the results of his action?; and why does he do this? (Landais and Deffontaines, 1989a). Simple observation of actions is not sufficient. Detailed studies have been carried out on crop management and on maintenance of soil suitability (Milleville, 1985; Capillon and Caneill, 1987; Sebillotte, 1987; Aubry *et al.*, 1992), on livestock management (Lhoste and Milleville, 1986; Gibon and Duru, 1987; Landais and Deffontaines, 1989a; Mathieu and Fiorelli, 1990), cash-flow management (Chia, 1992) and land management (Groupe de Recherche INRA–ENSSAA, 1977).

## Modelling the decision-making process

During the course of these studies, researchers soon felt themselves to be inadequate: was a simple analysis of practices sufficient to provide full understanding? For example, climate variations, operational variations from one year to the next are such that it is sometimes difficult to detect a guiding principle, even after research carried out as described above. This is not only the case for arable crops (Aubry, research in progress) but also for livestock systems (Mathieu and Fiorelli, 1990). Obviously, explanations can often be given by the farmer, but obtaining them retrospectively is not easy. Would it not be better to pinpoint all the solutions that were open to him at a given time *t*, and the reasons why he chose certain solutions rather than others? If this is indeed the case, then the decision-making process needs to be studied in the sense of the term given by Sebillotte and Soler (1990), i.e. the process leading to a choice for which the underlying cognitive procedures are not studied, but which researchers try to express in the form of rules. This process, recognized as a sort of driving force for the practices, has become in its turn a subject of research. Preliminary work in this respect, carried out on cash crop systems (Cerf and Sebillotte, 1988; Duru *et al.*, 1988; Sebillotte and Servettaz, 1989), is being extended to more complex systems: livestock farms or mixed crop–livestock farming (Duru *et al.*, 1988; Chatelin and Havet, 1992; Hubert *et al.*, 1993).

Moving from the study of practices to the study of decision making proved a major step forward: the scientist investigates decision-making situations involving the actor (the term 'actor' is used in social sciences to designate the person acting in given situations, i.e. in our case the farmer) and attempts to reconstruct them. The ideas that Simon developed more than 30 years ago, and recognized by his Nobel Prize for Economics, concerning the organization and management of public services are now being used in the agriculture domain (Simon, 1957). Apparently less well known in American 'farming systems' research circles, his work is familiar to economists and supporters of systems analysis in France. However, INRA–SAD research is original in that the decision-making process is not only studied by economists (or by cognitive science specialists) but also by technical systems specialists working on crop and livestock farming systems.

Preliminary work on the decision-making process concerned beet crop management (Sebillotte and Servettaz, 1989); this relatively simple situation was chosen since, owing to its economic importance, it takes precedence if there is a 'conflict' with other crops. The authors began monitoring a few farmers over a full crop year, not only when they were actually working but also when they were 'surveying their fields' and planning for future action. They were observed and questioned about what they were doing, what they could see and what they intended to do; finally, discussions about the results took place: 'did they reach their objectives?; did they have to make changes?; did they modify their objectives?; etc.' A similar approach was used to study work planning (Papy *et al.*, 1988, 1990; Dedieu *et al.*, 1992; Navarrete, 1993), management on the farm area under wheat (Aubry, research in progress), irrigation management when the water resource is a constraint (Leroy *et al.*, 1992) and food management of herds on pastureland (Duru *et al.*, 1988; Mathieu and Fiorelli, 1990; Osty and Landais, 1991; Chatelin and Havet, 1992; Hubert *et al.*, 1993).

Similar procedures were used to determine decision-making rules: studies have been made by economists concerning overall farm management (Brossier *et al.*, 1990) and strategy management concerning medium- or long-term choices influenced by farmer/family projects (Maxime *et al.*, 1993). However, the results presented here only concern the management of productive technical systems which, owing to its recurrent nature, enables the farmer to acquire experience over the years.

# Concepts

## *Action model*

Decisions concerning the management of technical systems are not taken at the last minute: they are organized ahead of time according to objectives

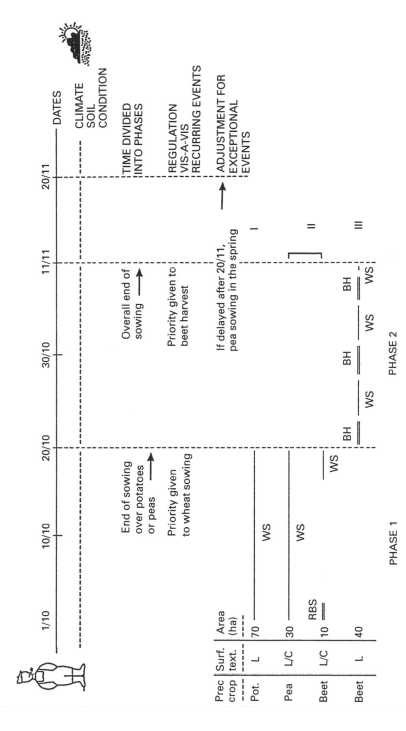

**Fig. 1B.1.** Action model for autumn work on a North Paris Basin farm. Prec. crop = preceding crop; Surf. text. = surface texture; L = loam; C = clay; Pot. = potato; BH = beet harvest; WS = wheat sowing. (According to research in progress by Christine Aubrey; figure from Hubert *et al.,* 1993.)

which the farmer is more or less able to express. The following example will illustrate this point.

Mr A has a cash-crop farm in the Parisian basin and cultivates 150 ha of wheat on 20 fields following a variety of preceding crops, potatoes, beet and peas, as shown in Fig. 18.1 (Aubry, research in progress). His entire wheat cropping section is to be managed intensively (target at least 8000 kg ha$^{-1}$) with subobjectives for the autumn, i.e. finish wheat sowing before 20 October on fields having carried potatoes and peas and which are therefore immediately free for sowing, and complete sowing by 10 November. Since for crop health reasons he cannot start sowing before 5 October, he divides his autumn operations into two phases (Fig. 18.1). However, throughout this autumn period he has to engage in beet harvesting regularly as required by the sugar factory; hence the organization of decisions can be outlined as follows.

*Phase 1:* from the end of the potato harvest to the end of wheat sowing after early harvest of the preceding crops (ideally 20 October):

•   fields affected: 70 ha following potatoes, 30 ha following peas and the beet fields with the highest clay content that need to be harvested first;
•   rules: immediately after the potato harvest, undertake the beet harvest on high-clay soils, then, as of 5 October, give priority to wheat sowing after potatoes and peas; only if climatic conditions are good can beet harvesting be continued during this phase.

*Phase 2:* from the end of the first phase to the end of wheat sowing (ideally accomplished by 10 November and in any case before the end of November):

•   fields affected: beet plots that are to be sown to wheat;
•   rules: priority given to beet harvesting during this phase, i.e. this is carried out according to the requirements of the sugar producer.

In the case of exceptional delays, adjustment rules will be introduced between successive phases. If, during the first phase, the delay is such that these rules are not sufficient to accommodate the adjustments, beyond a certain time Mr A will choose to get the second phase under way, where priority is given to the beet harvest over wheat sowing. This means that he may be unable to sow early enough all his wheat on fields that carried potato and pea crops, with a resulting drop in targeted yield. If, in the rare case where the delay is such that, at the end of the second phase, sowing is not finished by 20 November, then he will not proceed but will sow peas instead in the spring.

Work carried out by several research teams of the SAD on cash-crop farms and on livestock or mixed crop–livestock farms show that plans for action are organized as follows. The crop or livestock farmer knows from the start that his objectives are not certain to be reached. Since predicting future events concerning the climate, the economic situation or incidents of all kinds is impossible, the farmer tries to allow for this by setting himself *ex ante* certain rules that provide him with a degree of flexibility. However, it is impossible for him to imagine at any time an overall adjustment of his farm; for this, he needs to break the problem down. This is essential since eventualities do not all have the same probability or the same consequences and the unknown factors vary in importance according to the stage reached in the production process. The farmer breaks down his end production objective into sub-objectives that he has a better chance of achieving at certain points in time. The entire production cycle (or season) is hence divided into succeeding phases. Each phase is linked to a subobjective and, in order to reach it, to rules applying on specific parts of the farmer's land enabling him to adjust to frequently recurring events. The farmer can counteract exceptional events during a given phase by modifying the rules of the following phase or by taking the necessary resources from other parts of the farming system. Lastly, he makes provisions for cutting back on his objectives if a very rare event occurs.

Therefore, the farmer organizes his decisions by dividing up time and space so as to cope with uncertainties by order of importance. These procedures simplify the management of his farming system because by fixing subobjectives that are reached by following a set of rules during a particular phase on a certain part of his land he avoids constant worry about adjustments that need to be made to reach the end objective. However, this method of breaking down management problems does not mean that he loses sight of the overall management of the farm system. This is a general principle identified by Simon (1957). The term 'action model' has been coined to denote this advance organization of decisions (Cerf and Sebillotte, 1988; Duru *et al.*, 1988; Sebillotte, 1990b; Sebillotte and Soler, 1990). Numerous examples of the action model concept can be found in studies on cash crops (Papy *et al.*, 1988, 1990; Sebillotte and Servettaz, 1989; Cerf *et al.*, 1990; Aubry *et al.*, 1992; Le Gal, 1993) and in work on livestock systems (Landais and Deffontaines, 1989b; Duru *et al.*, 1990; Mathieu and Fiorelli, 1990; Osty and Landais, 1991; Chatelin and Havet, 1992; Hubert, 1993; Hubert *et al.*, 1993).

These action models have a dual logic: synchronic (the farmer makes arbitrary choices during a given phase between activities that cannot be carried out simultaneously) and diachronic (the farmer makes a coherent series of decisions concerning portions of land or batches of animals). Hence, on the 20 fields that make up Mr A's farm, three ways of cultivating wheat can be distinguished:

1. wheat following potatoes;
2. wheat following peas and the first beet harvest;

**3.** wheat following the last beet harvest.

They can be seen as three specific technical systems or three crop management sequences. Each one refers to a number of fields having undergone the same cultivation operations at the same time and which consequently received the same combination of inputs coherent with the likely yield depending on the periods of operation (Aubry, research in progress).

Hence, whereas for the agronomist technical systems, i.e. crop management sequences, or cropping systems (Sebillotte, 1990b) are concepts developed as subjects for study in themselves (analysis of how they work and search for new concepts), for the farmer they result from a complex decision process concerning location of crops on the land and a management system involving all farm activities throughout the year. The same thing applies to livestock farming systems.

### Knowledge model

The action models developed by the farmer to manage his technical systems are interactive with the knowledge models concerning the biotechnical systems that he operates, i.e. that management is not only a result of these models but also produces them (Fig. 18.2). Some of his working concepts are his own, but most are evolved from sharing experience with other farmers together with assimilation of technical knowledge imparted by consultants (Darré, 1989). Hence within a given geographic area, farmers share the same representations concerning the role of maize in animal feeding or the conditions required for working the land after rain. This knowledge is simple to explain since it is linked to the work itself; for example, early wheat sowing is linked to high expected yields, which justifies the plan to apply large quantities of nitrogen, fungicides, etc., to the fields concerned; or, at the end of April there is a high probability of the return of rain, which justifies making the most of each available day before this period to work in the fields.

These operational representations include condition indicators that farmers use to make their decisions to begin work or to wait: leaf colour, disease symptoms, changing colour of soil during desiccation, grass length, animal conformation, etc. Generally, only certain fields are monitored, these acting as indicators for the whole farm.

The concepts described above are guided by the requirement for decision support; let us now examine how the concepts of action models and knowledge models can be used to achieve these goals.

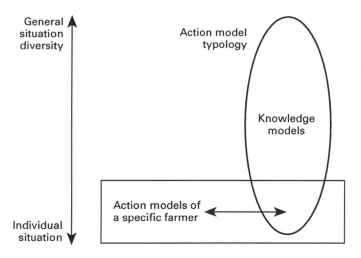

**Fig. 18.2.** Links between action models and knowledge models (figure produced with the help of L.G. Soler).

# Concept Utilization

### *Principles for building action models*

Action models need to be formulated in close collaboration with the farmer. Together with consultants, SAD researchers have, in a limited number of cases, begun to define operational procedures enabling action models to be built. A number of methodological principles can be proposed:

- To begin with, a tentative partitioning of time into phases is made, and subobjectives to be reached at the end of each phase are identified.
- The farmer is placed before different decision situations, using simulation tools, so that he can formulate adjustment rules for reaching these objectives and others to use in situations where they are not reached.
- The model created by these means is then compared with available information which demonstrates the actual practices of the farmer over several successive years; if they do not match, the action model can be refined.

The above procedure is a first type of decision support, since the farmer can analyse his own work with the help of an outside consultant. However, this can be taken further: the outside consultant has henceforward all the information needed to assess in several different ways the technical systems used, which is a step towards more refined decision support (Sebillotte, 1990a; Hubert *et al.*, 1993).

## *Diagnostic assessment*

Returning to the earlier example, the farm advisor points out that wheat following peas, which is generally grown on high-clay fields (Fig. 18.1 above), is infested with weeds every year; this leads to yield losses compared with expected results from early-sown fields. This first diagnostic assessment leads to weeding being proposed in the autumn rather than at the end of February, which is Mr A's usual procedure. The latter agrees with this first diagnostic assessment. However, taking into account room for manoeuvre in the farmer's specific situation, it emerges that weeding the wheat following peas in autumn is impossible, because the work load is already heavy at that time. Therefore, another solution has to be found. The advisor and the farmer consider working these fields by ploughing in the stubble during summer, a method known to be efficient in bringing out and destroying weeds. If Mr A had not yet used this method, it is because in the summer also he does not have enough time between the cereal and potato harvests. But he then has the idea of asking a farmwork company to plough in the stubble during the summer.

The advisor began by making an external assessment of the degree of efficiency of the crop management sequence used on wheat following peas independent of the farmer's way of operating. For this he referred to biotechnical models concerning the process of crop yield build-up, resulting from theoretical knowledge, experimentation networks and his own personal experience. When he noted that the farmer agreed with his assessment he made sure that the latter had the same knowledge model for pea weeding and that no further information was needed by the farmer. This is not always the case, of course. Then he made note of the farmer's constraints, so producing a personalized diagnostic assessment (similar to what Herbert Simon calls effectiveness), enabling Mr A and the advisor to devise an alternative action model for better control of weeds in wheat following a pea crop. Sometimes the advisor realizes that technical knowledge is lacking to help the farmer make his choices. This may provide the starting point for research on new technical references.

Decision support concerns the conception of action models in addition to the development of knowledge models which need to be shared by advisors and farmers. Crop and livestock specialists need to investigate the validity of the knowledge models of farmers, and also the degree of pertinence of those they themselves propagate in technical publications. In this connection, research should be carried out on the condition indicators of technical systems: how valid are the indicators used by farmers such as the changing colour of soil during desiccation or grass length and, on the other hand, which new indicators can be proposed, both simple to use by farmers and efficient? The use in France of the nitrogen balance method for managing nitrogen application has had a series of setbacks, as these principles have been misunderstood (Cerf and Meynard, 1988).

## Assistance in choosing a farm structure

The action model concept for managing technical systems can prove useful in other types of decision situations: those concerning substantial medium- or long-term changes in the farm structure itself, such as cessation or adoption of a given activity, expansion or changes in equipment or staff (Chatelin *et al.*, 1993). Under the new Common Agricultural Policy these issues are becoming particularly relevant. The approach in reasoning out the interconnections between these strategy choices and ways of managing technical systems is as follows:

- action models are constructed jointly with the farmers;
- a simulation of the action model is run, incorporating planned farm changes: expansion, new crops, changes in equipment or staff, etc. Hence an experiment is made: the farmer's mental process is reformulated in the form of a model.

This can be taken further, however, if these mental processes can be transformed into calculation processes: an extremely important step in estimating the risk due to climatic uncertainty. In several cases, thanks to collaboration with economists specialized in computer science tools, and to artificial intelligence researchers, our work has led to the creation of computer programs. These programs connect action models with knowledge models of biophysical systems, specifically created to interrelate the stages in the evolution of crop yield development or of soil conditions with technical operations. Three different stages can be identified in the fine tuning of these advisory tools which interconnect strategy choices and technical system management:

1. formulation of the type of tool;
2. implementation of computer processing;
3. tool testing in the context of actual advisory operations (Chatelin *et al.*, 1993).

The area in which most headway has been made is in modelling work organization: the OTELO program (Attonaty *et al.*, 1990) is used in France by advisory teams in cash-crop areas (Papy and Mousset, 1992) and experimentally in Senegal (Le Gal, 1993). A study with similar objectives enables climatic risk to be calculated relative to hay harvesting equipment and the strategy applied to offset this risk (Gibon *et al.*, 1989; Duru and Colombani, 1992); also, the DECIBLE program provides simulation, using different climatic scenarios, of the consequences of several methods of wheat management on yield and remaining nitrogen at the time of harvest (Aubry *et al.*, 1992). Lastly, other projects, concerning forage systems or irrigation management in a water resource constraint situation, have now reached the stage of computer program creation.

## *Organization of advice*

Technical advice traditionally consists of enriching the pool of knowledge with new technical references which require specification as to their field of application. Two major types of information are combined together: soil and climate characteristics and type of farm. Operating procedures for producing typologies of farm functions have been proposed in this respect (Capillon, 1986; Perrot and Landais, 1993); they are being used in the most efficient technical extension services.

However, in the opinion of the farmers, the advice given is often too limited and partial, as shown by a recent study undertaken by the French National Association for Agricultural Development (ANDA); the farmers would like the advice to be more personalized and to incorporate better the different decision levels (technical systems management and long-term farm prospects). The concepts presented here can help development advisors to satisfy this need, on the condition nevertheless that they create a more interactive advisory relationship with the farmers.

This, then, is the domain of genuine action-research to be undertaken in close partnership with the advisors (see Vallerand, Chapter 26). The research referred to above, which is more often than not the work of researchers in direct contact with farmers, has sometimes left these advisors out; it is hoped that this will not happen in future. In the case of individual advice, studies should be made as to how an advisor can help the farmer to build his action models, can pinpoint the knowledge necessary for their implementation and can undertake simulations which allow the risks inherent to reorientation of the farm production system to be evaluated. However, collective knowledge on the regional level must also be built up, shared by both farmers and farm advisors. This collective knowledge can probably be organized around action model typologies, as a result of a generalization effort (numerous case studies) which highlights the diversity of farmer management problems (Fig. 18.2).

# References

Attonaty, J.M., Chatelin, M.H., Poussin, J.C. and Soler, L.G. (1990) Un simulateur à base de connaissance pour raisonner équipement et organisation du travail en agriculture. In: Bourgine, P. and Walliser, B. (eds) *Economics and Artificial Intelligence.* 2nd Congress of CECOIA, 3–5 July, Paris, pp. 291–297.

Aubry, C., Chatelin, M.H., Poussin, J.C., Attonaty, J.M., Masse, J., Meynard, J.M., Gerard, C. and Robert, D. (1992) DECIBLE: a decision support system for wheat management. Paper presented at the 4th International Congress for Computer Technology in Agriculture, Versailles 1–3 June.

Brossier, J., Vissac, B. and Le Moigne, J.L. (eds) (1990) *Modélisation Systémique et Systèmes Agraires.* INRA, Paris, 365 pp.

Brossier, J., Chia, E., Marshall, E. & Petit M. (1991) Gestion de l'exploitation agricole familiale et pratiques des agriculteurs. Réflexions théoriques à partir de l'expérience française. *Canadian Journal of Agricultural Economics* 39, 119–135.

Capillon, A. (1986) A classification of farming systems, preliminary to an extension program. In: Butler Flora, C. and Tomecek, M. (eds) *Farming Systems Research and Extension: Management and Methodology*. Kansas State University, Manhattan, Kansas, pp. 219–235.

Capillon, A. (1989) *Grassland Systems Approaches, Some French Research Proposals. Etudes et Recherches, INRA, Départment Systèmes agraires Développement* 16, 218 pp.

Capillon, A. and Caneill, J. (1987) Du champ cultivé aux unités de production: un itinéraire obligé pour l'agronome. *Cahiers ORSTOM, Série Sciences Humaines* 23(3/4), 409–420.

Cerf, M. and Meynard, J.M. (1988) Enquête sur la mise en oeuvre des méthodes de fertilisation raisonnée. Paper presented at the 3ème Forum de la Fertilisation Raisonnée, Nancy.

Cerf, M. and Sebillotte, M. (1988) Le concept de modèle général et l'analyse de la prise de décision technique. *Comptes Rendus de l'Académie d'Agriculture de France* 74(4), 71–80.

Cerf, M., Papy, F., Aubrey, C. and Meynard, J.M. (1990) Théorie agronomique et aide à la décision. In: Brossier, J., Vissac, B. and Le Moigne, J.L. (eds) *Modélisation Systémique et Systèmes Agraires*. INRA, Paris, pp. 181–202.

Chatelin, M.H. and Havet, A. (1992) Understanding forage system management to improve it. In: Gibon, A. and Matheron, G. (eds) *Global Appraisal of Livestock Farming Systems and Study of their Organizational Level: Concepts, Methodology and Results*. European Commission, Brussels, pp. 347–354.

Chatelin, M.H., Aubry, C., Leroy, P., Papy, F. and Poussin, J.C. (1993) Le pilotage de production: quelle prise en compte pour l'aide à la décision stratégique? In: Soler, L.G. (ed.) *Instrumentation de Gestion et Conduite de l'Entreprise*. Cahiers d'Economie Sociologie Rurale No. 28. INRA, Paris, pp. 120–138.

Chia, E. (1992) Une 'recherche clinique': proposition méthodologique pour l'analyse des pratiques de trésorerie des agriculteurs. *Etudes et Recherches, INRA, Départment Systèmes agraires Développement* 26, 1–39.

Cristofini, B., Deffontaines, J.P., Raichon, C. and de Verneuil, B. (1978) Pratiques d'élevage en Castagniccia. Exploration d'un milieu naturel et social en Corse. *Etudes Rurales* 71–72, 89–109.

Darré, J.P. (1989) Introducing livestock farmers' way of thinking in the study of grazing systems. In: Capillon, A. (ed.) *Etudes et Recherches, INRA, Départment Systèmes agraires Développement* 16, 173–179.

Dedieu, B., Serviere, G. and Justin, C. (1992) L'étude du travail en exploitation d'élevage: proposition de méthode et premier résultats. *Productions Animales* 5(3), 193–204.

Deffontaines, J.P. (1973) Analyse de situations dans différentes régions de France. Freins à l'adoption d'innovations techniques. *Etudes Rurales* 52, 80–90.

Duru, M. and Colombani, H. (1992) Haymaking: risks and uncertainties in central Pyrenees grasslands. *Agricultural Systems* 38, 185–207.

Duru, M., Papy, F. and Soler, L.G. (1988) Le concept de modèle général et l'analyse du fonctionnement de l'exploitation agricole. *Comptes Rendus de l'Académie d'Agriculture de France* 74(4), 81–93.

Duru, M., Gibon, A. and Osty, P.L. (1990) De l'étude des pratiques à l'aide à la décision. L'exemple du système fourrager. In: Brossier, J., Vissac, B. and Le Moigne, J.L. (eds) *Modélisation Systémique et Systèmes Agraires*. INRA, Paris, pp. 159–180.

Gibon, A. and Duru, M. (1987) Fondements des systèmes d'élevage ovin pyrénéens et sensibilité au climat. In: *INRA, Séminaire Agrométéorologie, Toulouse*, 16–17 April 1986. INRA, Paris, pp. 303–316.

Gibon, A., Lardon, S. and Rellier, J.P. (1989) The heterogeneity of grassland fields as a limiting factor in the organization of forage systems. Development of a simulation tool of harvest management in the Central Pyrenees. In: Capillon, A. (ed.) *Etudes et Recherches, INRA, Départment Systèmes Ágraires Développement* 16, 105–117.

Groupe de Recherche INRA–ENSSAA (1977) *Pays, Paysans, Paysages dans les Vosges du Sud. Les Pratiques Agricoles et la Transformation de l'Espace*. INRA Paris, 200 pp.

Hubert, B. (1993) Comment raisonner de façon systémique l'utilisation du territoire pastoral? Paper presented at the IVème Congrès International des Terres de Parcours, Montpellier (to be published in *Agricultures*).

Hubert, B., Girard, N., Lasseur, J. and Bellon, S. (1993) Les systèmes d'élevage ovins préalpins: derrière les pratiques, des conceptions modélisables. In: Landais, E. (ed.) *Pratiques d'Élevage Extensif*. INRA, Paris, pp. 351–385.

Landais, E. and Deffontaines, J.P. (1989a) Les pratiques des agriculteurs. Point de vue sur un courant nouveau de la recherche agronomique. *Etudes Rurales* 109, 125-158.

Landais, E. and Deffontaines, J.P. (1989b) Analysing the management of a pastoral territory. The study of the practices of a shepherd in the Southern French Alps. In: Capillon, A. (ed.) *Etudes et Recherches, INRA, Départment Systèmes agraires Développement* 16, 199-207.

Le Gal, P.Y. (1993) Processus de décision et innovation: l'exemple de la double riziculture dans le delta du fleuve Sénégal. Paper presented at Séminaire Innovations et Sociétés, Montpellier.

Leroy, P., Bonnefoy, M., Bouthier, A., Deumier, J.M. and Jacquin, C. (1992) *Etude de la Faisabilité pour la Mise au Point d'une Méthode de Conduite des Irrigations*. Rapport INRA/ITCF au Ministère de l'Agriculture, INRA, Paris, 100 pp.

Lhoste, P. and Milleville, P. (1986) La conduite des animaux: techniques et pratiques d'éleveurs. In: Landais, E. (ed.) *Méthodes pour la Recherche sur les Systèmes d'Élevage en Pays Tropicaux*. pp. 247–268.

Mathieu, A. and Fiorelli, J.L. (1990) Modélisation des pratiques de pâturage d'éleveurs laitiers dans le nord-est; les régulations face à l'aléa climatique. In: Brossier, J., Vissac, B. and Le Moigne, J.L. (eds) *Modélisation Systémique et Systèmes Agraires*. INRA, Paris, pp. 135–157.

Maxime, F., Soler, L.G. and Hemidy, L. (1993) Instrumentation du contrôle de gestion stratégique dans la petite entreprise: le cas de l'entreprise agricole. In: Soler, L.G. (ed.) *Instrumentation de Gestion et Conduite de l'Entreprise*. Cahiers d'Economie et de Sociologie Rurale No. 28. INRA, Paris, pp. 91–118.

Milleville, P. (1985) L'Agronome face aux pratiques paysannes. In: Blanc-Pamard, C. and Lericollais A. (eds) *A Travers Champs*. ORSTOM, Paris, pp. 121–138.

Navarrete, M. (1993) L'organisation du travail, déterminant de la conduite technique d'une culture de tomate sous serre. *Comptes Rendus de l'Academie d'Agriculture de France* 79, 107–117.

Osty, P.L. (1974) Comment s'effectue le choix des techniques et des sytèmes de production? Cas d'une région herbagère des Vosges. *Fourrages* 59, 53–69.

Osty, P.L. (1978) L'exploitation agricole vue comme un système. Diffusion de l'innovation et contribution au développement. *Bulletin Technique d'Information* 326, 43–49.

Osty, P.L. and Landais, E. (1991) *Fouctionnement des Systèmes d'Exploitation Pastorale.* IV. Congrès International des Trends de Parcours, Montpellier.

Papy, F. and Mousset, J. (1992) Towards communication between theorical and applied knowledge (the usefulness of simulation software in farm computer technology in search of users?). In: *Farm Computer Technology in Search of Uses? 4th International Congress for Computer Technology in Agriculture,* Versailles, 3–6 June, pp. 173–176.

Papy, F., Attonaty, J.M., Laporte, C. and Soler L.G. (1988) Work organisation simulation as a basis for farm management advice. *Agricultural Systems* 27, 295–314.

Papy, F., Aubry, C. and Mousset, J. (1990) Eléments pour le choix des équipements et chantiers d'implantation des cultures en liaison avec l'organisation du travail. In: Boiffin, J. and Marin-Laflèche, A. (eds) *La Structure du Sol et Son Évolution'. Les Colloques de l'INRA* 53, 157–185.

Perrot, C. and Landais, E. (1993) Exploitations agricoles: pourquoi poursuivre la recherche sur les méthodes typologiques? *Les Cahiers de la Recherche-Développement* 33, 13–23.

Petit, M. (1975) L'adoption des innovations techniques par les agriculteurs. Plaidoyer pour un renouvellement de la théorie économique de la décision. *Pour* 40, 79–91.

Sebillotte, M. (1974) Agronomie et agriculture. Essai d'analyse des tâches de l'agronome. *Cahiers ORSTOM, Série Biologique* 24, 3–25.

Sebillotte, M. (1987) Du champ cultivé aux pratiques des agriculteurs. Réflexion sur l'agronomie contemporaine. *Comptes Rendus de l'Academic d'Agriculture de France* 73(8), 69–81.

Sebillotte, M. (1990a) Les processus de décision des agriculteurs. Deuxième partie: conséquences pour les démarches d'aide à la décision. In: Brossier, J., Vissac, B. and Le Moigne, J.L. (eds) *Modélisation Systémique et Systèmes Agraires.* INRA, Paris, pp. 103–117.

Sebillotte, M. (1990b) Some concepts for analysing farming and cropping systems and for understanding their different effects. Paper presented at the Inaugural Congress, European Society of Agronomy, Session 1–16.

Sebillotte, M. and Servettaz, L. (1989) Localisation et conduite de la betterave sucrière. L'analyse des décisions techniques. In: Sebillotte, M. (ed.) *Fertilité et Systèmes de Production.* INRA, Paris, pp. 308–344.

Sebillotte, M. and Soler, L.G. (1990) Les processus de décision des agriculteurs. Première partie: acquis et questions vives. In: Brossier, J., Vissac, B. and Le Moigne, J.L. (eds) *Modélisation Systémique et Systèmes Agraires.* INRA, Paris, pp. 93-101.

Simon, H.A. (1957) *Administration Behaviour: a Study of Decision-making Processes in Administrative Organisation.* French translation 1983, Economica, Paris, 322 pp.

Teissier, J.M. (1979) Relations entre techniques et pratiques. *Bullétin INRAP* 38.

# 19

# GENDER ISSUES IN EUROPEAN AGRICULTURAL SYSTEMS

## Ruth Gasson

## Introduction

Gender is socially rather than biologically constructed. For example, on farms in South Wales at the turn of the century, women used to do all the milking in addition to calf rearing and dairy work. It was considered degrading for a man to milk, the explanation being that a woman's smaller hands made it 'natural' for her to be better at the job. With the establishment of the Milk Marketing Board in 1933, which guaranteed a market for milk, the production of milk became important for the economic success of Welsh farm businesses. After this, milking was taken over by the men (Jenkins, 1971). Nowadays, milking large numbers of cows through a modern parlour is typically man's work, whereas with small herds milking is more likely to be done by women. Comparing the division of farm tasks between husbands and wives in Wisconsin, USA, and Finland in the early 1980s, for example, milking was carried out mainly or entirely by the wife on 48% of Finnish farms but on only 9% of Wisconsin farms (Wilkening, 1981; Siiskonen *et al.*, 1982).

Most women are involved in European agriculture by virtue of marriage to a farmer. The role that they play is circumscribed by both gender and marriage. In the UK, for instance, the greater part of the female labour input to agriculture comes from farmers' wives (Gasson, 1992). In other European countries where less hired labour is employed, female members of the farm family are still more important in the total labour force. This chapter therefore concentrates on farm wives rather than women farmers or female employees.

The gendered division of labour and management in agriculture and gender inequalities in the distribution of resources, have consequences for farming efficiency and also raise questions about equity. In turn, these issues have implications for possible future trends in female and male involvement in European agricultural systems.

# An Outline of Gender Issues

## *Control of resources*

Typically, most farm property of land and fixed capital is transmitted from father to son(s) (Whatmore, 1991). If a woman inherits a farm, through the untimely death of her husband or because there are no male heirs present or willing, she is usually expected to hold the farm only until some suitable male candidate appears. One consequence is that farms run by women tend to be small – those not considered economically viable by male siblings, holdings they have managed to buy or rent by their own efforts or farms run as a sideline by women whose husbands have other jobs.

As the minimum size of a viable farm enterprise rises, it becomes harder for farmers to launch more than one of their children on a farming career. There can be a direct conflict between efficiency and equity here (Peters and Maunder, 1983). If the family business passes intact to one child (typically a son), how are the other children to be treated? If children are treated equally, how can any one take over the home farm?

In Norway, recent legislation has changed the entitlement to succession to the family farm from the firstborn *son* to the firstborn *child*. The Norwegian Government has tried to encourage farm daughters to take up their rights, as part of the campaign to keep people living in rural Norway. Some recent research suggests that young men tend to base the decision to take over the family farm on purely commercial criteria whereas young women are more exercised by family obligations (Haugen and Brandth, 1994).

## *Division of labour*

Numerous studies have illustrated the gendered division of manual labour in European agriculture. Women tend to be allocated routine tasks which are not mechanized. They work with animals rather than crops, in horticulture more than in agriculture, in the farm buildings rather than out in the fields. Women are much less likely than men to drive tractors and do other mechanical work and very rarely do they repair and maintain machinery. Jobs involving high technology such as milking in a parlour are regarded as men's work, although one Irish study reported that 70% of farm wives regularly cleaned the milking equipment and 52% cleaned cowsheds (Sheridan, 1982). According to Bauwens and Loeffen (1983), the kinds of jobs which Dutch farm wives performed most regularly were, in descending order:

- cleaning the dairy and milking equipment;
- feeding and looking after calves;
- collecting eggs;
- feeding and looking after pigs;
- cleaning sheds;
- feeding and looking after chickens;
- milking cows;
- weeding by hand.

Among the reasons put forward to account for the gendered division of labour on family farms in Europe and the US are:

- women's lack of strength and physique;
- women's superior manual dexterity and patience;
- the maternal instinct;
- a mental blockage about mechanical matters;
- family and domestic ties;
- lack of training;
- inadequate instruction on the job;
- male prejudice.

Biological explanations (strength, dexterity, etc.) are of doubtful validity. On most physical traits, men and women are on overlapping distributions. That is, although the *average* man is stronger and taller than the *average* woman, some women are taller and stronger than the average man, and so on. On small farms with only the farmer and spouse available to do farm work, women may have to do heavy lifting and tractor work which on a larger farm would be considered 'unsuitable for a woman'. It seems more likely that the division of labour is socially or culturally determined.

Should farm tasks be allocated along conventional gender lines or according to the skills, preferences and comparative advantage of the individual woman or man concerned? Should training seek to overcome traditional attitudes towards men's and women's work or should it follow the established boundaries? There are implications here for efficiency and for equity between men and women.

### *Farm management and control*

With increasing mechanization on farms, the gender division of manual labour becomes less relevant. A greater loss in efficiency is thought to stem from the exclusion of women from management roles.

Typically, day-to-day tactical decisions about the running of the farm business are made by men whereas female family members (wife, mother, sister) are more involved in longer term strategic decisions about farm policy – investment, succession, whether to diversify, and so on. No less than 95%

of Dutch farm wives were found to be involved in such discussions (Bauwens and Loeffen, 1983). The actual extent of wives' involvement in farm decision making is difficult to measure, however, being part of the subtle balance of power in the marital relationship. In a recent survey, for instance, farm wives from southern England drew a distinction between 'being there' to help and support their husbands' decision making when necessary and 'interfering' in the farm business (Buchanan *et al.*, 1982).

Women often undertake the greater part of the paperwork for the farm business. Surveys have shown that in France, The Netherlands, Ireland and the UK between one and two thirds of farmers' wives are responsible for the farm accounts (Berlan *et al.*, 1980; Gasson, 1980; Sheridan, 1982; Bauwens and Loeffen, 1983). As a result, women are often in closer contact with the financial side of the farm business and more concerned about the bank balance and cash flow than the men. It is doubtful whether this knowledge is always reflected in the sharing of responsibility for financial decision making. If it is not, there may well be some loss of efficiency in the farm business.

### Legal status

Being made a partner or director in the family business is a sign of involvement. In the UK there is evidence that roughly half of farm wives are partners or directors (Whatmore, 1991; Gasson, 1992). A partnership is a tax-efficient arrangement for the medium-sized farm business, which raises the question of whether women are made partners for tax reasons only. There would be a loss of equity if women were made nominal partners but denied decision-making powers.

Perhaps more pressing nowadays is the issue of divorce. In the UK, women who can demonstrate that they have made a significant contribution to the family business through work, savings, and so on, are entitled to a share of the assets in the event of marital breakdown. This is certainly an improvement on the former situation in which a wife could lose all that she had put into the business if it was in the husband's name. An unlooked-for result of the legislation, however, has been to deter farm families from taking daughters-in-law into partnership until the son's marriage has stood the test of time. This becomes a source of conflict where a young wife feels excluded from the family enterprise and her husband's parents question her motives for wanting to be included – another example of efficiency versus equity.

### Farm household reproduction

Greatest inequality in the gender division of labour in farming systems is seen in the allocation of 'reproductive' tasks, that is, the work of maintaining the members of the farm household in a state such that they can continue with the 'productive' work of farming. Reproductive work includes providing meals, clean clothes and a clean house, caring for the sick and elderly members of the family and literally 'reproducing' the labour force by bearing and rearing children and socializing one or more to become farmers in the future. Among their other activities, women typically cultivate kinship and community links which may be functional for the reproduction of the farm household, for instance by obtaining loans, joining cooperatives or sharing machinery (Symes and Marsden, 1983). Women may be more active than men in public relations and improving the public image of farming.

Farm household reproduction is almost exclusively the province of women and the inequalities are more apparent in farming than in urban families. Research in Switzerland, for instance, has shown that whereas 66% of farm women often help their partners on the farm, only 2% of men often help their spouses with work in the farm household. Whereas 75% of men rarely help their wives, only 4% of women rarely help their husbands in their respective spheres of work (Rossier, 1993). Clearly this is an equity issue, and one with implications for the future of farming systems.

### Farm diversification and off-farm work

The Arkleton Trust's cross-national study on farm structures and rural pluriactivity found that 58% of farm households in 24 study areas scattered across western Europe had other sources of income besides farming [Arkleton Trust (Research), 1990]. Some farm households run alternative enterprises on the farm, adding value to farm products or providing services. This can be a means of reintroducing women to agriculture. Intensification of farming systems is believed to be a major force excluding women, who may feel themselves opposed to the use of ever-larger machines, increasing use of chemicals and 'factory farming' of livestock. Diversification, on the other hand, often builds on women's skills and traditional activities (such as catering or providing tourist accommodation).

Whereas some farm husbands and wives have established alternative farm-based enterprises, many more have employment off the farm. Declining farming incomes can only hasten this trend. Often farm women have been educated to a higher level and have more qualifications and non-farm work experience than men. Depending on the work available, it may be more efficient for men to farm single-handed while women seek off-farm jobs. There is little evidence of farm women who work off the farm being relieved of any of the burden of farm and domestic chores (Gasson and Winter, 1992). Urban women who work outside the home are 'double shifting', but farm women may be 'triple shifting'.

### *Remuneration*

Women who work in family farms are not usually paid the going wage. In one British study (Gasson, 1992), only 15% of farm wives were paid a wage for their contribution to the family business, 14% received payments in kind, 39% were credited with a share of the profits and 32% were paid nothing at all. There were large regional variations, nearly half the wives in Wales and over three quarters in southern Ireland being paid nothing. It must be said that farmers, too, do not normally receive a regular wage but share the profits at the end of the year. If the farm is not in profit, there is nothing to share out. Even if the business shows a profit, it is likely to be reinvested rather than paid out in cash.

It is the ability of family farms to pay family labour less than the market wage which enables them to continue and compete with larger labour-employing businesses. The downside is that in economic terms, not paying resources the proper rate leads to misallocation. Family labour, and notably female labour, is treated as a 'free' input and is therefore used liberally where it might make better business sense to deploy it elsewhere.

## Conclusions

These, then, are some of the features of the gender division of labour in European farming systems. Although there are signs of change, cultural norms still dictate an uneven distribution of manual farm tasks and an unequal division of management responsibility and decision taking. Farm business resources are typically held and transferred within the male line while women are allocated the tasks of reproducing the family labour force. If cultural attitudes which construct gender differences hinder the mobility of resources, there will be a loss of efficiency (however efficiency is defined). The more rigid the cultural taboos which surround the gender division of labour and the more rapid the technological changes occurring within the agricultural sector, the greater will be the loss of efficiency due to friction and time lags in adjusting gender roles.

It also needs to be asked whether the gendered division of labour, decision making, resource ownership and control in the farm business and responsibility for farm household reproduction is equitable. Economists, farm management advisers and other specialists need to be persuaded to employ more realistic models of how farm families operate. They should not ignore the need for women to earn a return on their personal investment in the farm business, including the time they devote to administrative, secretarial and domestic tasks.

If, as this chapter suggests, there are marked inequalities in the distribution of tasks and rewards in European agricultural systems, we need to consider what effect this will be likely to have on the quality of life and life chances of women and men on European farms. If women see little prospect of gaining status, power and economic rewards commensurate with their many-sided contribution as spouses of farmers, will they be prepared in future to enter lifelong partnerships with them? Will they be likely to encourage their daughters to follow in their footsteps? What are the implications for the survival of the farm business and survival of the farm household?

We may well see a selective withdrawal of women's labour as more wives take paid employment off the farm. To achieve a new equilibrium in farm families may require a redistribution of tasks on the farm and in the farmhouse, relieving the woman of part of her 'triple load.'

# References

Arkleton Trust (Research) (1990) *Rural Change in Europe: Research Programme on Farm Structures and Pluriactivity. Second Report to the EC.* Arkleton Trust, Nethy Bridge.
Bauwens, A.L.G. and Loeffen, G.J.M. (1983) The changing economic and social position of the farmer's wife in The Netherlands. Paper presented at the 12th European Congress for Rural Sociology, Budapest.
Berlan, M., Painvin, R.M. and Dentzer, M.-T. (1980) *Life and Work Conditions of Women in French farms.* Regional Centre of Research in Rural Sociology and Economy, Rennes.
Buchanan, W.I., Errington, A.J. and Giles, A.K. (1982) *The Farmer's Wife: Her Role in the Management of the Business.* Farm Management Unit, Study No. 2, University of Reading, Reading.
Gasson, R. (1980) Women on the farm. *Farmers Weekly*, September.
Gasson, R. (1992) Farmers' wives: their contribution to the farm business. *Journal of Agricultural Economics* 43, 74–87.
Gasson, R. and Winter, M. (1992) Gender relations and farm household pluriactivity. *Journal of Rural Studies* 8, 573–84.
Haugner, M. and Brandth, B. (1994) Gender differences in modern agriculture. *Gender and Society* 8.
Jenkins, D. (1971) *The Agricultural Community in South-west Wales at the Turn of the Twentieth Century.* University of Wales Press, Cardiff.
Peters, G.H. and Maunder, A.H. (1983) Equity and agricultural change with special reference to land tenure in Western Europe. In: Maunder, A.H. and Ohkawa, K. (eds) *Growth and Equity in Agricultural Development.* Gower, Aldershot.
Rossier, R. (1993) The farm woman's work today. Paper presented at the 15th European Congress for Rural Sociology, Wageningen.
Sheridan, R. (1982) Women's contribution to farming. *Farm and Food Research* 13, 46–48.
Siiskonen, P., Parviainen, A. and Koppa, T. (1982) *Women in Agriculture. A Study of Equality and the Position of Women Engaged in Agriculture in Finland in 1980.* Report No. 27, Pellervo Economic Research Institute, Espoo.
Symes, D.G. and Marsden, T.K. (1983) Complementary roles and asymmetrical lives: farmers' wives in a large farm environment. *Sociologica Ruralis* 23, 229–241.
Whatmore, S. (1991) *Farming Women.* Macmillan, Basingstoke.
Wilkening, E.G. (1981) Farm husbands and wives in Wisconsin. University of Wisconsin–Madison, College of Agricultural and Life Sciences, Madison.

# =20=

## INTERACTIONS BETWEEN FARM HOUSEHOLDS AND THE RURAL COMMUNITY: Effects of Non-agricultural Elements in Farm Household Decision Making on Farming Systems

*John Bryden*

### Introduction

The basic argument of this chapter is very simple – it is that farm family behaviour in relation to farming cannot be based on an analysis of the farm and the farmer alone. In particular, an understanding of farm household adjustment over time requires analysis of the interrelationships between the farm, the farmer, the family and its context.

This is illustrated with some new results from a recent research programme (see Acknowledgements) which has looked specifically at farm household adjustments in Europe between 1981 and 1991. It offers some information on how farm households adjusted over this period, in terms of their agricultural and non-agricultural investments and work. It then shows how 'internal' and 'external' features influence the different patterns of adjustment observed.

### The Research Programme on Farm Structures and Household Pluriactivity

The final report of this research programme (Bryden *et al.*, 1992) addresses three main questions relating to changes in western European agricultural households in the period 1987–1991, namely, what kinds of changes are occurring, what reasons can be advanced for these changes and what key policy issues emerge from the research programme. The analysis makes use of the longitudinal dataset gathered for the research programme on farm structures and household pluriactivity in Europe. The data used relate to 24 western European study areas, four of which were in three non-EC countries

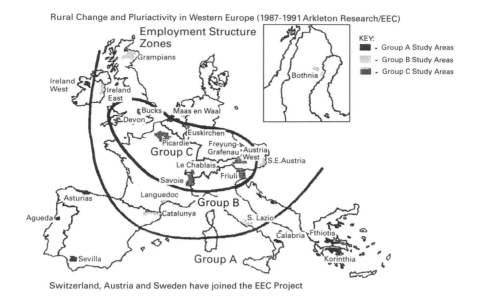

Rural Change and Pluriactivity in Western Europe (1987-1991 Arkleton Research/EEC)

**Fig. 20.1.** Map of study areas showing main context groups.

and 20 were in nine Member States (Fig. 20.1).

The main data sources are the following:

**1.** Baseline and final survey data for some 7000 farm households, about 300 per study area. The baseline survey was undertaken in 1987 and the sample re-interviewed for the final survey in 1991. Data were collected by personal interview covering such things as the agricultural and non-agricultural activities and incomes of household members, farm and non-farm investment and debt, farm size, tenure and production of all commodities, personal data on household members, the farm workforce, contract work, farm management, buildings and equipment, use of a range of agricultural and non-agricultural policies, attitudes and expectations.

**2.** Panel surveys involving in-depth qualitative interviews with a subsample of some 60 households in each study area in 1989, 1990 and 1991.

**3.** Context studies relating to each study area and concerning such things as the development of the local economy and labour markets, the implementation of agrostructural and other key policies and demographic changes.

The kind of data gathered give some clues both to the methodology and the overarching hypotheses. Four key points are:

**1.** The resources, opportunities and constraints facing farm households will affect both their perception of what is possible in future and their ability to make the necessary adjustments to realize these possibilities.

**2.** Resources, opportunities and constraints can be *internal*, i.e. within the farm household itself, or *external*, i.e. beyond the household. For example, the nature of the farm itself – its size, the quality of its land, its location, its buildings, access to irrigation – and the characteristics of the farm household – its size, age structure, education, background – define some part of the internal resources, opportunities and constraints. On the other hand, the surrounding labour market and the nature of policy measures available to, or affecting, farm households are two examples of external resources, opportunities and constraints.

**3.** The farm and 'the farmer' are only one part, and often a minor part, of the bundle of resources, opportunities and constraints influencing decisions and actions over time.

**4.** Economic goals and objectives are important for farm households, but they are not the only ones relevant for long-term adjustment.

Figure 20.2 summarizes the key hypotheses regarding the interrelationship between internal and external resources, opportunities and constraints

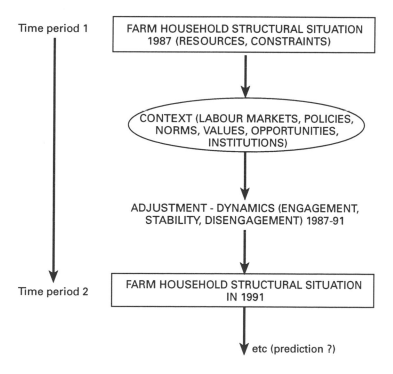

**Fig. 20.2.** Conceptual outline – relationship between structural situation, context and farm household dynamics.

and the patterns of adjustment which farm households adopted between 1987 and 1991.

In the following analysis, the 24 study areas are simply grouped into five 'context types' using a measure of the diversification of the labour market (dependence on agricultural employment in the study area) and a measure of the scale of farm structures. The five types are: A (the most dependent on agricultural employment, all of which have predominately small-scale farming), B1 (intermediate agricultural employment, large farms), B2 (intermediate agricultural employment, small farms), C1 (low agricultural employment, large farms) and C2 (low agricultural employment, small farms). All EC study areas in Group A are 'Objective 1'.

## In What Ways Have Farm Families in Western Europe Adjusted to Changing Conditions and Expectations Between 1981 and 1991?

The results show that farm families in Europe are making very different kinds of adjustments to changing conditions and expectations. In particular, we identified three broad groups – engagers, disengagers and stable – in relation to their farming activities. The starting point in this classification is adjustments made in relation to farming, 'engagement,' involving an increased commitment of resources to farming, 'disengagement,' a withdrawal of resources from farming with exit from farming as the extreme case, and 'stability,' being neither. Households were grouped using changes in the following variables between 1987 and 1991:

- area of land held;
- amount of hired labour;
- output per hectare;
- input per hectare;
- level of technology;
- scale and/or number of farm enterprises;
- use of modernization policy.

A simple scoring system was used to allocate cases. However, since the criteria were strict, stables include some minor changes. Between 1987 and 1991, engagers comprised about one fifth of sample farm households, and disengagers comprised between one fifth and one quarter of farm households in 1987, of which about 40%, or 10% of the whole sample, left farming between 1987 and 1991. The balance of about 50% were stable over this period. Table 20.1 gives a few indications of the effects of these different patterns of adjustment on production, land occupancy and the use of modernization measures.

The simple classification in Table 20.1 shows clearly a few of the

**Table 20.1.** Changes in production and land occupancy and use of modernization policy by engaging, stable and disengaging farm households, 1987–1991, EC sample. (Source: Arkleton Trust (Research) dataset for the baseline and final surveys of the Research Programme on Farm Structures and Pluriactivity in Europe.)

|  | Change in production (esu[a] %) | Change in land occupancy (ha %) | Use of modernization policies, 1987–1991 (% of households in group) |
|---|---|---|---|
| Engagers (20%) | +18.5 | +13 | 45 |
| Stable (57%) | –0.1 | +2 | 9.4 |
| Disengagers (23%) | –52 | –47 | 4.5 |

[a]esu = economic size unit; 1 esu = 1200 ECU of standard gross margin.

agricultural outcomes of different adjustment patterns, and makes the point that farm households are adjusting to changing conditions in very different ways.

Thanks to retrospective questions in the baseline survey, we are able to reconstruct the changes made in relation to both agricultural and non-agricultural investment and work activities over the whole decade from 1981 to 1991. This permits exploration of the articulation of farming and non-farming activities of farm households, especially the function and consequences of non-farming activities both for farm households and for their agricultural activities. A complex combination of adjustments emerged which it is convenient to discuss in three main groups:

**1.** Those farm households who made significant investments on the farm over the decade, i.e. those who apparently committed more resources to agriculture, even where they did other things as well. This group accounted for 23.9% of the sample.
**2.** Those farm households who made no or minimal investments on the farm, and whose main adjustment consisted in either the operator, the operator's spouse or the potential successor taking up off-farm work or making a non-farming investment during the decade, i.e. those whose main form of adjustment was in non-agricultural enterprises or work. This group accounted for 19.2% of the sample.
**3.** Those who made no new major investments or work commitments of any kind, who reached retiring age, or who left farming between 1987 and 1991. This group accounted for 56.9% of the sample.

Table 20.2 shows the relationship of these three groups to the work situation of farm households in 1981. It can be noted from this that agriculturally monoactive farm households in 1981 were more likely to invest

**Table 20.2.** Main adjustment groups, 1981–1991, by the farm household work situation in 1981 (source as in Table 20.1).

| Work situation in 1981 | Main form of adjustment, 1981–1991 | | |
|---|---|---|---|
| | Agricultural investment | Take-up of other gainful activity or non-agricultural investment | Exit, retirement or no significant adjustments |
| Agriculture only | **25.9%** | 16.0% | 58.1% |
| On-farm non-agricultural work present | 23.5% | **26.6%** | 49.9% |
| Operator had regular off-farm work | 20.6% | **21.7%** | 57.7% |
| Spouse had regular off-farm work | 23.3% | **25.9%** | 50.8% |
| Successor had regular off-farm work | 13.8% | 18.1% | **68.1%** |

[a]Figures add up to 100% in rows, i.e. reading across the table.

in agriculture than to take up non-agricultural work or investments, whereas those who were already involved in other gainful activities in 1981 were more likely to continue to take up such activities. However, significant movement between groups over this time period can be seen.

Tables 20.3, 20.4 and 20.5 explore some of the main characteristics of farm households who adopted each of these three main forms of adjustment during the decade. In particular, the relationship with farm size, operator's age, contribution of agriculture to household income and study area or context type is examined.

From Table 20.3, we can see that whilst those making agricultural investments only predominated, there were small groups who did so at the same time as taking up off-farm work or investing in non-agricultural ventures. In other words, farm households engaging in agriculture may also undertake non-agricultural ventures. However, those investing in agriculture alone or in agricultural and non-agricultural ventures tended to be on the largest farms, whereas those where the operator or successor also took up off-farm work were on significantly smaller farms.

We also see that these forms of adjustment predominated in the large-scale farming areas (B1 and C1), although above-average proportions of farm households in the small farm households in the small farming areas of richer countries (C2) had operators or successors who took up off-farm work or also

**Table 20.3.** Main characteristics of farm households making investments in agriculture 1981–1991 (source as in Table 20.1).

| Type of adjustment[a] | % of sample | Above average in study area groups | Mean farm business size in 1987 (esu[b]) | Mean age of operator in 1987 (years) | Mean contribution of agriculture to household income in 1987 (%) |
|---|---|---|---|---|---|
| Ag I only | 15.5 | B1, C1 | 34.3 | 48 | 65.2 |
| Ag I + non-Ag I | 3.1 | C2, B1, C1 | 37.0 | 46 | 60.2 |
| Ag I + operator takes up off-farm work | 1.8 | C2, C1 | 21.2 | 46 | 47.2 |
| Ag I + spouse takes up off-farm work | 2.0 | C1, B1 | 30.8 | 44 | 52.7 |
| Ag I + successor takes up off-farm work | 1.5 | C2 | 17.3 | 51 | 40.5 |

[a]Ag I = agricultural investment.
[b]esu = economic size unit.

invested in non-agricultural ventures. The combination of farm size and the nature of non-farming opportunities for investment or work is thus very important for any explanation of the differences observed.

Table 20.4 indicates that those undertaking no significant agricultural investment and taking up off-farm work or non-agricultural investment are all on significantly smaller farms, and have significantly lower proportions of income from agriculture. However, those whose main form of adjustment is in non-agricultural investment or in the spouse taking up off-farm work are on larger farms within the group, whereas those where the successor or operator takes off-farm work are on the smaller farms within the group.

It is therefore not surprising that these forms of adjustment tend to predominate in the study areas characterized by small-scale farming, i.e. A, B2 and C2, although above-average proportions of farm households where the spouse, or the spouse and the operator, went out to work or where non-agricultural investments were made are also to be found in the large-scale farming areas of C1.

Farm households adopting this form of adjustment were older than those making investments in agriculture. Once again, we can find meaning from the combination of contextual circumstances, farm size and farmer's age as key influences on the precise nature of adjustments.

**Table 20.4.** Main characteristics of farm households who took up off-farm work or invested in non-agricultural ventures, 1981–1991 (source as in Table 20.1).

| Type of adjustment | % of sample | Above average in study area groups | Mean farm business size in 1987 (esu[a]) | Mean age of operator in 1987 (years) | Mean contribution of agriculture to household income in 1987 (%) |
|---|---|---|---|---|---|
| Non-agricultural investment only | 3.9 | B2, C1 | 18.3 | 52 | 40.3 |
| Operator takes up off-farm work | 4.7 | A | 8.3 | 53 | 28.9 |
| Operator and spouse take up off-farm work | 1.3 | A, C1, B2 | 9.3 | 53 | 34.2 |
| Spouse takes up off-farm work | 4.3 | C1, B2 | 19.7 | 49 | 39.7 |
| Successor takes up off-farm work | 5.0 | B2, C2, A | 6.9 | 58 | 35.1 |

[a]esu = economic size unit.

From Table 20.5 we can observe that those with no evident adjustment comprised nearly one third of the sample. They were on relatively large farms, even though they were particularly prevalent in small farming areas of Groups A and B2. They were not particularly old. Those who reached retirement age were also over-represented in the small farming areas of Groups A and B2, where farms are small and off-farm and non-agricultural work opportunities limited. They were on small farms, and only one quarter of them were sure of a successor (compared with 39% of the non-adjusters and 34% for the whole sample). They had low levels of educational attainment, over 78% having no full-time or only primary education. Obviously a relatively high proportion of household income came from social transfers, mainly pensions (36.3%).

Those who exited were also on relatively small farms, but were mainly found in different contexts from the retirers, Groups C2 and B1. They were also generally older than those who adopted other forms of adjustment, except those who retired. Two thirds of those exiting were sure of having no successor in 1987, whilst 63% were over the age of 55 in the same year. They also had relatively low educational attainment – 76% had no full-time or only primary education. About 31% of household income came from off-farm work and a further 30% from social transfers.

**Table 20.5.** Main characteristics of farm households who made no significant agricultural or non-agricultural investments, did not take up off-farm work, reached retirement age or exited (source as in Table 20.1).

| Type of adjustment | % of sample | Above average in study area groups | Mean farm business size in 1987 (esu[a]) | Mean age of operator in 1987 (years) | Mean contribution of agriculture to household income in 1987 (%) |
|---|---|---|---|---|---|
| No adjustment | 34.4 | A, B2 | 18.2 | 50 | 50.1 |
| Reached the age of 65 | 13.8 | A, B2 | 8.2 | 67 | 39.2 |
| Exited from farming after 1987 | 8.7 | C2, B1 | 8.9 | 56 | 32.4 |

[a]esu = economic size unit.

# Key Reasons for Different Patterns of Adjustment

More detailed analysis of the nature of the adjustments made between 1987 and 1991 confirms the influence of three main factors: first, the 'internal' resources opportunities and constraints arising from the nature of the farm and household prior to adjustment; second, the 'external' resources opportunities and constraints which arise from the context in which farm households are living and working; and third, the stage in the life cycle of the farm family.

'Internal' resources, opportunities and constraints tend to be defined by a combination of farm and household characteristics immediately prior to any period of change or adjustment. The main influences came from:

**1.** The proportion of income from different sources (farming, off-farm work, on-farm non-agricultural ventures, and social transfer payments such as pensions and welfare payments). This reflects the existing level of diversification of work and income, and hence the scope for further changes in this respect.

**2.** The size of the farm business. This is a measure of the capacity of the farm business to absorb labour and provide income. In some cases – as for non-EC study areas which lack comparable coefficients for conversion of livestock numbers and crop areas to economic size units – farm size may be used as a somewhat imperfect surrogate.

**3.** The number of economically active persons in the household. Family members resident in the household obviously represent a major labour resource for household enterprises.

**4.** The age of the farmer. As previous studies have shown, the propensity to invest is markedly higher where the operator is younger, although interestingly enough we found this to be true only for agricultural investors. The age of farmer is also a surrogate measure for the 'stage in the life cycle' which the farm household has reached, and which influences other things such as availability of other family members for work, access to pensions and some policy measures.

**5.** The labour input into farming by the farmer and by other household members. Thus, if the farmer works regularly off-farm, then there is less likely to be investment in agriculture.

**6.** The amount of off-farm work by the female member of the farm couple (normally the farmer's wife) and by other family members. Although less influential than the off-farm activities of the farmer, this obviously affects the labour resources available on the farm.

**7.** The background of the farmer and spouse. Outcomes are to some extent linked to whether the farmer and/or spouse had a farming, farm worker or non-farming background, probably because of the attitudes, skills and expectations which are associated with these.

**8.** The education levels of the farmer and spouse. Educational attainment is related to farm size and context, as well as age (since in some countries compulsory universal schooling is a relatively recent phenomenon). Nevertheless, there are significant within-group differences in adjustment (or lack of it) which appear to relate to levels of formal educational attainment.

The main 'external' influences on adjustments were found to be:

**1.** The nature of the labour market, particularly the extent of non-agricultural work available locally, the nature of that work (industry, services, etc.), and indications of dynamism in the labour market.

**2.** The nature and extent of non-agricultural opportunities on the farm. For example, relatively high occurrences of on-farm non-agricultural investments were found in Buckinghamshire, UK, where opportunities for farm-based recreational ventures and use of farm buildings for non-agricultural purposes are extensive, and in Devon, UK, and western Austria, where there are significant opportunities for farm-based tourism.

**3.** The nature of agricultural structures – whether these were small or large scale. Where farms are generally small, there are strong 'push' factors on farm households to seek non-agricultural sources of income and/or exits. Norms and values at local level (for example, relating to farmers who work off the farm) also tend to relate to such structural characteristics.

**4.** The implementation of agricultural and rural policy at national and local levels. Significant variations in the implementation of structural and rural development policies were found, in addition to those relating to taxation, social welfare, land leasing, building and planning, and inheritance, all of which affect farm household behaviour.

# Conclusions

The nature of farm household adjustments reflects a prior process of decision making. The chapter has attempted to illustrate what now appears to be almost self-evidently the case, namely that the process of decision making, and hence the subsequent adjustments or lack of them, depend not only on the farming system itself, but also on the internal features of the farm household and the external or contextual circumstances which they face.

These internal and external factors combine to provide a framework of resources, opportunities and constraints for farmers and farm households, and they also affect values, attitudes, goals and expectations. The more that it is recognized that most farm households not only have relationships with agricultural markets and policies but also, through non-farming activities and work, with the surrounding rural community, the more it is obvious that such interactions matter.

# Acknowledgements

Rural Change in Europe: Research Programme on Farm Structures and Household Pluriactivity, 1987–1991. This research programme was part-funded by the European Communities under Article 22 of Regulation 797/85 and by institutions in nine Member States. The comparative analysis was undertaken with support from the Economic and Social Research Council and under the JAEP programme of the ESRC (Award No. L103251004), the NERC and the AFRC in the UK. Three non-member states, Austria, Switzerland and Sweden, also participated in the programme at their own expense.

The author is grateful to Dr Jo Gilliat of the Arkleton Trust for help with the analysis in this chapter, particularly with the development and analysis of the categories of change over the period 1981–1991. For more detail on the research programme, methodology and results, the reader is referred to Arkleton Trust (Research) (1990); Bryden *et al.* (1992, 1993); Hawkins *et al.* (1993); MacKinnon *et al.* (1993).

# References

Arkleton Trust (Research) (1990) *Rural Change in Europe: Research Programme on Farm Structures and Pluriactivity – Second Research Report to the EC.* Arkleton Trust, Nethy Bridge.
Bryden, J.M., Bell, C., Gilliat, J., Hawkins, E. and MacKinnon, N. (1992) *Farm Household Adjustment in Western Europe, 1987–91.* Rural Change in Europe: Research Programme on Farm Structures and Pluriactivity. Final Research Report to the EC. Arkleton Trust, Nethybridge. (Also published by the Commission of the European Communities, 1993.)

Bryden, J.M., Gilliatt, J., Hawkins, E. and MacKinnon, N. (1993) Farm household adjustment in western Europe, 1987–91: some results of the research programme on farm structures and household pluriactivity, 1986–91. Paper presented at the VIIth European Congress of Agricultural Economists, Stresa, Italy, September 1993.

Hawkins, E., Bryden, J., Gilliatt, J. and MacKinnon, N. (1993) Engagement in agriculture 1987–1991: a West European perspective. In: Marsden, T. and Flynn, A. (eds) *Servicing the City. Journal of Rural Studies* Special Issue Vol. 9, No. 3. Pergamon Press, Oxford, pp. 277–290.

MacKinnon, N., Bryden, J., Hawkins, E. and Gilliatt, J. (1993) Relationships between changes in the farm and non-farm activity of farm households in western Europe, 1987–91. Paper presented at the XVth Congress of the European Society for Rural Sociology, Wageningen, The Netherlands, August 1993.

# 21

# EDUCATION AND EXTENSION: A PERPETUATING PARADIGM FOR SUCCESS

## Kate Corcoran and Barry Dent

## Introduction

The national agricultural extension system in Britain has experienced major modifications in recent years: it has been directed to government agency status and consequently many services previously free to farmers now bear a charge. Discrete market segments are targeted by advisory services in the search for 'profitability'. In a period of six years, the idea of government extension services fostering a competitive agricultural industry has been replaced by the goal of becoming the premier consultancy to these farmers and agribusinesses that can afford to pay for service. One assessment of this (Harter and Hass, 1992) is that government agricultural extension in Britain is now essentially a cost-recovery enterprise with a 'big farm' bias and is contributing to the perpetuation of socioeconomic inequality within the farming sector. Without special provision being made available, commercial extension services, of which the government sector is only one, are unable to support the activities of other than profitable farms. Such special arrangements have emerged in the UK where government has financially supported relatively minor advisory services in support of on-farm diversification, environmental and conservation improvements and rural development.

Obviously, if an agency wishes to achieve substantial self-supporting income, its efforts will be oriented towards those farmers who are likely to succeed and who are generally found on intensive farming systems. It can be postulated (Harter and Hass, 1992) that these farmers are likely to be those who (i) are better educated; (ii) have unencumbered assets and resources; (iii) are already established in other business activities.

It has become evident that many farm families in the UK are extending their activities beyond traditional production farming. Between 50 and 60%

255

of farm families have gainful income from sources other than farming (JAEP, 1993). The motives behind such activities are varied, including simply the need to supplement family income, the desire for higher profits and wishing to follow alternative careers while still resident on the farm. In spite of some government encouragement towards on-farm diversification in the UK, a relatively small proportion of farm families have become involved; this may be related to adverse location or to lack of capital or enthusiasm. Partly because of this, and partly because the small scale of such additional enterprises (such as provision of tourist accommodation – by far the most common form of diversification for UK farm families), the average contribution to farm-family income is minor. Some farms however, have been able to take advantage of a sound business condition, entrepreneurial skills and extension services to establish substantial non-farming operations on the farm.

By contrast and for many farm families, significant non-farming income flows from one or more members working off the farm. Remoteness of location appears to have little impact on this activity provided that good communications to towns and villages exist (Edmond *et al.*, 1993).

It may be hypothesized that the ability to thrive in today's conditions, maintaining a sound farming business while at the same time fostering important additional activity on or off the farm, is related to the educational background of the farm family. In addition, the drive to use more commercial extension services is related to entrepreneurial character, which in turn is partly correlated with exposure to conditions off the farm and strengthened by gaining a post-school education.

An associated hypothesis might be that those farm families that have most benefited from post-school education or training are those who had been associated with larger business units, run in an entrepreneurial fashion, but certainly related to a measure of financial stability (high net worth or low debt to earnings ratio).

These hypotheses will be explored in this chapter by way of new data generated from a recent large-scale survey (approximately 7% of Scottish farms), investigating multiple job holding (MJH) in three Scottish regions in 1991 (JAEP, 1993). Three distinct Scottish regions were identified as potentially providing different farm-family profiles on the basis of their diverse locations and farming systems. The first was Dumfries and Galloway (156 survey farms), a region with a low population density with dairying being the predominant farm type. Second, Fife was chosen (55 survey farms) as a region noted for tourism, with a high proportion of cropping farms, but also locationally well placed for off-farm employment. The third region was the Grampian region (295 survey farms), which had areas with good locational opportunities for on-farm enterprises and off-farm employment. Grampian farms encompassed a wide range of farm types.

# Education and Rural Farm Families

## *Post-school education*

Taken across the three regions, about 30% of farmers had the benefit of post-school education of some type. Normally this included an agricultural qualification with only 11% having a post-school qualification not related to agriculture (see Table 21.1). Important regional differences were observed: in particular, more farmers in the Fife region had an agricultural qualification (42%). Few spouses (94% female) had post-school agricultural qualifications but were found to be better qualified overall than farmers. Little regional variation was observed between the level of education received by spouses.

Cropping farms are the most numerous of the official farm types in Scotland and made up 22.5% of the overall MJH survey sample. Farmers in

**Table 21.1.** Post-school educational qualifications of farmers by survey region (% of members).[a]

| Educational status | Dumfries and Galloway | | Fife | | Grampian | | Total | |
|---|---|---|---|---|---|---|---|---|
| | Farmer | Spouse | Farmer | Spouse | Farmer | Spouse | Farmer | Spouse |
| Agricultural | 17 | 2 | 42 | 4 | 21 | 3 | 22 | 3 |
| Non-agricultural | 7 | 38 | 9 | 42 | 14 | 40 | 11 | 40 |
| No qualification | 76 | 59 | 49 | 54 | 65 | 57 | 70 | 57 |

[a]Tables are derived from data derived from the survey of multiple job holding (MJH) in the agricultural sector in Scotland during 1991.

**Table 21.2.** Post-school qualifications of cropping farmers and first sons (% of members).[a]

| | Farmers on larger[b] cropping farms | Farmers on small/medium farms | 1st sons on large cropping farms | 1st sons on small/medium farms |
|---|---|---|---|---|
| Non-agricultural qualification | 0 | 13 | 18 | 17 |
| Agricultural qualification | 50 | 30 | 45 | 43 |

[a]See footnote to Table 20.1.
[b]Defined as being farms in excess of 45 British size units (BSU).

Fife were found to be relatively more prosperous and operate farms which generate much of the income from arable crops. The educational status of current farmers and of their first sons on larger and small/medium cropping farms is given in Table 21.2.

Sons, particularly first sons, were more likely than their fathers to have a qualification of some sort and this was, in the majority of cases, an agricultural diploma or degree. The presence of many entrepreneurial farmers on arable holdings (Bryden *et al.*, 1990), not yet ready to hand over 'profitable' farms to succeedants, could see encouragement being given to their sons to improve their agricultural management capability through a post-school agricultural education.

The existence of a higher number of agriculturally qualified farmers and first sons on cropping farms suggests that post-school education was not sought principally as a means of accessing off-farm employment, but might have been acquired for a variety of reasons ranging from a desirable means of benefiting the pool of on-farm expertise to a sort of agrarian finishing school. Daughters in general were found to have almost twice the rate of degree-level education than sons and these qualifications were almost entirely non-agricultural in nature.

# Employment Off-farm

Diversification strategies and off-farm employment are no longer simply means of risk avoidance but are an integral part of farm business strategies (Marsden and Symes, 1987). Although off-farm employment has always been recognized as an important element in reconciling the farm family income/ labour equation, for many small and part-time farmers it now represents the more stable part of farm family income (JAEP, 1993). The importance of off-farm employment was evident from the MJH data with almost 50% of farm families in Scotland having one or more members working off-farm. For comparison a survey of less favoured areas (LFA) areas in Wales in 1991 returned a slightly lower proportion of families with off-farm work at 44%; (Bateman *et al.*, 1993). This difference might be attributable to the degree of 'rurality' and the different potential for work found in both surveys. Phillips and Williams (1984) reported on work carried out by Dench on the aspirations of school leavers in rural mid-Devon, concluding that their aspirations were greater than their achievements in employment, prospects being frustrated by unavailability of work, lack of education and remote location.

## The extent of off-farm employment

In the MJH survey, 41% of survey households in Dumfries and Galloway had one or more members employed off-farm. Fife had the lowest level of off-farm employment in the three regions at 38% of survey households, despite good access to large centres of employment. Grampian had the greatest percentage of farms with a member working off-farm (56%), with 9% of farms with members having both off-farm employment and non-agricultural, but on-farm, enterprises. About 23% of household members in the Grampian survey gained their income solely from outside sources.

The levels of off-farm work were found to vary with farm type. The lowest levels were recorded on dairy farms (18%) and LFA sheep farms (12%). On dairy farms, the nature of the on-going intensity of the farming system and unsociable work patterns ensures that those household members involved in production have little residual labour for other activities. In addition, good milk prices at the start of the 1990s will have reduced the low income 'push' factor on this farm type for off-farm work.

For LFA sheep farms with the lowest level of off-farm work, farm location might be a limiting factor to uptake of work off-farm, particularly for employment in sizeable centres of population. No evidence was found to suggest that off-farm employment increases as distance to labour markets improves at subregional levels, with acceptable travel times appearing to overcome the disadvantage of remoteness (Edmond *et al.*, 1993). With LFA sheep farms frequently found at higher altitudes in Scotland, periods of bad weather and isolation in winter might make routine access to centres of employment a less reliable or attractive option. Shucksmith and Smith (1990) found that attitudes to education were frequently negative among traditional, productivist farmers and established that members of this group tended to have few marketable skills, resulting in blocked labour mobility.

## The reasons for off-farm employment

From the MJH data, reasons for engaging in off-farm work can be linked to individual family members (see Table 21.3). For the farmer and spouse, maintenance of family income was important, although for the spouse an intent to follow a separate career was paramount. For both sons and daughters, the requirement to have a separate source of income was the main inducement for working off the farm, with almost all daughters citing this as their principle reason.

The income of those members who work off-farm cannot be presumed to be contributing equally to the 'farm household' *per se*, with 97% of daughters, 70% of sons and 55% of spouses working for their own interest and income. For spouses, however, 'own income' might be contributing indirectly to the farm income as a substitution for personal income normally drawn from the

**Table 21.3.** Principal reasons given by family members for working off-farm (% of members giving reason).[a]

|                              | Farmer | Spouse | Son | Daughter |
|------------------------------|--------|--------|-----|----------|
| To help family income        | 56     | 42     | 16  | —        |
| Personal income/career       | 33     | 55     | 70  | 97       |
| Farm-family opportunity      | 8      | —      | 12  | 3        |
| Tradition/family expectation | 3      | 1      | 2   | —        |

[a]See footnote to Table 21.1.

farm purse. The differences in motivation for off-farm work between sons and daughters might reflect the perceived and anticipated long-term commitment to the farm business from both members.

### The nature of off-farm employment

Males working off the farm were found generally in non-agricultural occupations, although frequently in the agricultural sector. By comparison, females overwhelmingly had non-agricultural jobs in non-agricultural sectors, with just 2% having agricultural jobs. Many factors such as travel time and farm and family responsibilities influence the location of work and full- or part-time status (JAEP, 1993). For those travelling to work, 83% made their way by car but only 3% travelled as passengers. Public transport appears to fail the majority of rural commuters. Sons and daughters, in 1991, preferred to work in larger population centres, being more mobile and of a generation with high personal expectations. Farmers and spouses with heavier farm and family commitments tended to work in smaller population centres and have shorter travel times to work.

Sons, being better educated than their fathers, fitter, younger, more adaptable and in some cases superfluous to farm labour needs, were found in paid employment as distinct from being self-employed off the farm. Paid employment offered the prospect at least of farm household members achieving the national minimum wage in whatever relevant employment sector they adopted. In 1993, the average national agricultural wage in Britain was gauged to be 76% of the average national industrial wage (Agricultural Wages Board, personal communication, 1993; original source, Transport and General Workers Union).

**Table 21.4.** Presence/absence of off-farm job for people with/without experience, qualifications or both (% of members).[a]

|  | No qualification, no experience | Qualification or experience | Both qualification and experience |
|---|---|---|---|
| Have off-farm job | 17 | 31 | 35 |
| No off-farm job | 83 | 69 | 65 |

[a]See footnote to Table 21.1.

### Post-school education and off-farm employment

Off-farm employment of farmers' sons was more likely when they held a post-school qualification, but for daughters this was found to be independent of post-school training or education (Davies and Dalton, 1992). In the MJH survey, a positive link was found between education and work experience on the one hand and employment on the other (see Table 21.4). In general, an education with or without experience can predispose towards employment. Just over a third (male and female) of farm-family members with both experience and qualifications had an off-farm job, while conversely, more than four fifths of those without either, did not (see Table 21.4).

## Education and Use of Extension Services

Bryden *et al.* (1990) have classified farmers into three groups: professional (engagers), stable and disengagers. 'Professional' farmers, according to Shucksmith and Smith (1990), are characterized by working to well thought-out business plans and appear to have ready confidence to expand into unfamiliar enterprises or adapt to changing circumstances. Many cropping farmers in the Fife region in the MJH survey conform to this, with characteristics of the 'type' illustrated in relation to their land holdings. Half the cropping farms surveyed were made up of single holdings, but the balance were found to average three holdings per farm. This would allow farmers the flexibility to build up farm size with resulting economies of scale or, conversely, to dismantle farms piecemeal in response to opportunity or stagnation, particularly when the 'additional' holdings are leased. In Fife, substantially more farmers had mixed ownership–tenancy arrangements than the average for the MJH survey (see Table 21.7) and for cropping farms overall. The number of holdings per farm among cropping farms was greater than for any other farm type in the survey.

In general, Fife cropping farmers would appear to correspond well to the 'professional' typology. In their work, the 'professional' farmer was found to

**Table 21.5.** Use of extension services (% of farmers using the extension services).[a]

|  | Larger cropping farms | Small/medium cropping farms | Overall survey |
|---|---|---|---|
| Farms using extension services | 68 | 53 | 39 |
| Farms using specialist advisory services | 64 | 51 | 32 |
| Farms using general advisory services | 29 | 15 | 21 |
| Farms using diversification advisory services | 18 | 8 | 17 |

[a]See footnote to Table 21.1.

be more aware of policies, the broad policy context in which he operated and the relevance of policy schemes to his operation (Shucksmith and Smith 1990). It is not surprising, therefore, that such a farmer is well placed to exploit such schemes and respond to new policy initiatives in accordance with economic rationality and with the advantage of specific and tailored advice.

In the MJH survey, the use of extension services was the highest among cropping farms (see Table 21.5): an average of 57% used outside advice at least once in a 12-month period. This figure dropped to 51% on dairy farms, 26% on LFA sheep and cattle farms and 22% on small farms. Specialist advice was required by cropping farmers to a much greater degree than for other farms and larger cropping farms had a higher demand than small/medium farms (see Table 21.5). Some of this advice was sought through the national extension service, but some was provided by independent advisors; both groups charged for their services. Clearly, national agencies with indirect public funds supporting extension are in a privileged position in relation to competing consultancies. Use of general advice was also at a high level by larger cropping farms, again on a commercial basis. Interestingly, the uptake of the state-supported free diversification advisory services both by the large cropping farms and the MJH survey farms overall were at similar levels, with farmers looking to exploit grants and farm resources for improved profit or alternative sources of income. Dalton and Wilson (1989) have commented that this type of activity is generally focused on larger business units.

The MJH survey results were analysed to uncover differences in the levels of extension usage related to the presence or absence of post-school education. Farmers who had gained a post-school education qualification used extension services more frequently than other farmers. This was particularly noticeable on larger cropping farms. For such farms, Table 21.6 indicates that 86% of farmers with educational qualifications used advisory services compared with only 50% of farmers without a post-school qualification.

**Table 21.6.** Use of extension services by cropping farmers with/without post-school educational qualifications (% of farmers).[a]

|  | Larger cropping farms | Small/medium cropping farms |
| --- | --- | --- |
| Use of extension services by farmers with educational qualifications | 86 | 44 |
| Use of extension services by farmers without educational qualifications | 50 | 26 |

[a]See footnote to Table 21.1.

A similar trend is seem for small/medium cropping farms. Both cropping farm types (larger and small/medium) show a greater general use of advisory services when compared with the survey average for all farms. It appears a relatively safe assumption, then, that level of education is positively correlated with the use of advisory services, whether free or commercial. The relationship is complicated by the fact that the same characteristics which might predispose farm families to ensure a good education for their children also predispose the same families to seize and exploit opportunities (i.e. sound tenure status, good financial basis).

## Farm Background and Education

The salient characteristics of 'professionalizers' identified by Bryden *et al.* (1990) include the presence of larger farms, smaller household size and younger farmers. Younger farmers on larger farms were found to be most likely to make use of the grants available [Arkleton Trust (Research), 1989]. Again, the average Fife cropping farmer of the 1991 MJH survey shows a 'good fit' for this classification when farm business size, age of farmer, household size and number of dependants are considered (Table 21.7). Although Shucksmith and Smith (1990) did not find the level of post-school education to be highest among the 'professional' farmers, they determined that these farmers saw education and formal qualifications as very important for their children and therefore laid some emphasis upon their children acquiring skills. Fife farmers were found to have the highest level of post-school agricultural qualifications and this could further enhance the professionalism and operating skills of this group (JAEP, 1993). Reasons for the higher educational status of Fife farmers might be explained by a number of factors: first, the presence of a good road and rail communication network allows greater urban contact between this relatively more prosperous farming

*Kate Corcoran and Barry Dent*

**Table 21.7.** Professionalizing characteristics of Fife farmers (% of each characteristic).[a]

|  | In Fife | In total survey |
|---|---|---|
| Percentage of cropping farms | 58 | 23 |
| Percentage of holdings $\geqslant$ 40 BSU[b] | 42 | 24 |
| Percentage of farms with no dependants over 16 | 16 | 36 |
| Average number of family living on the farm | 3.2 | 3.9 |
| Tenure arrangement: |  |  |
| % Owner | 62 | 63 |
| % Tenant | 15 | 21 |
| % Mixed | 24 | 16 |
| Means of acquiring farm: |  |  |
| % Purchased | 39 | 46 |
| % Inherited | 26 | 18 |
| Farmers aged between 25 and 64 | 95 | 88 |

[a]See footnote to Table 21.1.
[b]BSU = British size units.

community and accessible education centres, thereby facilitating schooling. Second, based on the characteristics of the farm and family (generally larger business scale, the farm type, reduced level of dependants and the greater number of farmers in the 25–64 year age group, see Table 21.7), it might have been both financially and operationally possible, indeed desirable in the past, for Fife farmers to have pursued further education. The influence of social class was not assessed here but it must be a relevant factor in the high level of education found in Fife.

# Conclusions

There is a strong positive relationship between the level of educational experience in a group of farm families and the the uptake of off-farm employment. Where a combination of a high level of education, strong business resources and good locational characteristics of the farm exists, there is a tendency for entrepreneurial activity to be expressed by on-farm diversification. In general, the higher the educational status of farmers the more likely it is for them to develop additional income streams.

In spite of efforts of national extension agencies in the UK to commercialize services, it is clear that better educated farmers on more intensive farms exploit both specialist technical advice and general management extension.

Such farmers appear to have a greater awareness of changes in relevant policies and have a clearer understanding of how such policies might impact on their business. It follows that they are likely to respond to policy in order to exploit opportunities.

Younger farmers with smaller families, sound businesses and ready access to urban centres appear to assume that their children will go on to further education. The sense of tautological intergenerational progression seems inescapable: higher education is associated with a diversified business, involving farm and non-farm components and using consultancy services to improve efficiency; such a business is predisposed to ensure that the next generation gains an appropriate level of training.

As CAP is modified away from production emphasis, governments wishing to encourage enduring rural populations should consider two broad planks of policy:

**1.** to invest for high standards and viability in rural education to provide a gateway to further education; and
**2.** ensure investment in rural infrastructure to reduce travel times, thereby encouraging members of farm families in schooling, advanced training or working off the farm.

# References

Arkleton Trust (Research) (1989) *Rural Change in Europe: Research Programme on Farm Structures and Pluriactivity. First Report for the Commission of the European Communities on Structural Change and the Use Made of Structures Policy by Farm Households in the European Community*, Arkleton Trust, Nethybridge.

Bateman, D., Hughes, G., Midmore, P., Lampkin, N. and Ray, C. (1993) *Pluriactivity and the Rural Economy in the less Favoured Areas of Wales*. Report on the JAEP Pluriactivity Study in Wales.

Bryden, J.M., Bell, C., Fuller, A.M., MacKinnon, N., Salent, P. and Spearman, M. (1990) Emerging responses of farm households to structural change in European agriculture. Paper presented at the 6th EAAE Congress, The Hague, 1990.

Dalton, G.E. and Wilson, C.J. (1989) *Farm Diversification in Scotland*. SAC Economic Report No. 12, Scottish Agricultural College, Aberdeen.

Davies, A.S. and Dalton, G.E. (1992) *Farm Household and Business: Their Interrelationship and Off-farm Pluriactivity*. JAEP Working Paper No. 1, Scottish Agricultural College, Aberdeen, 9 pp.

Edmond, H., Corcoran, K. and Crabtree, R. (1993) Modelling locational access to markets for pluriactivity: a study in the Grampian Region of Scotland. *Journal of Rural Studies* 9 (4), 339–349.

Harter, D. and Hass, G. (1992) Commercialization of the British extension system: promise or primrose, *Journal of Extension Systems* 8, 37 41.

JAEP (1993) *Pluriactivity in the Agricultural Sector in Scotland*, Final Report to the ESRC, University of Edinburgh, Edinburgh.

Marsden, T. and Symes, D. (1987) *Survival Strategies in Post-productionist Agriculture.* UK Analytical Paper No. 2, Vienna Centre: Socio-economic Consequences of Agricultural Development in Europe.

Phillips, D. and Williams, A. (1984) *Rural Britain – A Social Geography.* Blackwell, London.

Shucksmith, D.M. and Smith, R. (1990) Farm household strategies and pluriactivity in upland Scotland, *Journal of Agricultural Economics* 42 (3), 340–353.

# V

# SYSTEMS METHODOLOGIES

# 22

## AGRICULTURE: IS THE *ART DE LA LOCALITÉ* BACK? The Role and Function of Indigenous Knowledge in Rural Communities

### *José Portela*

### Introduction

This chapter aims simply at contributing to a discussion on the role of indigenous knowledge in agriculture. To achieve this, it starts by attempting to define the main concepts (agriculture, knowledge and indigenous or local knowledge) and touches on the relationship between scientific and local knowledge, that is, on the invisibility of local knowledge for most research agencies and agents. Next, some of the fundamental roles that local knowledge has played and might play, as far as farming is concerned, are identified. Finally, the question in the chapter title is considered and the optimistic view is put forward that interaction between the systems of scientific and technological knowledge and local knowledge may benefit agricultural producers. Both the context and the examples given in this chapter draw on the author's fieldwork in Trás-os-Montes, particularly participant observation. This region in northeastern Portugal has received a good list of names: backward, marginal, peripheral, underdeveloped, etc. Literally, Trás-os-Montes means behind and beyond the mountains.

### The Main Concepts

#### *Agriculture: a societal issue*

As far as the definition of agriculture is concerned, I take a very wide view. Farming is much more than an economic sector, cheap food and landscapes, regardless of these being the green landscapes of northern Europe or the yellow ones of southern Europe. It is, at least, population, space, patrimony, history, culture and national defence. Of course, physical and biological resource management is essential to production, but this is not an automatic, man-free process. Men and women, young and old, are the artisans of this venture, so often an adventure. However, not only production is at stake, reproduction is also. Normally, farming is not a single activity and the only earning source, so, the labour process has to be fine tuned with respect to differentiated time (past, present, future; short, intermediate, long term), space and people, from both within and without the farm unit. As van der Ploeg (1992) very nicely put it, the necessary coordination, although dealing largely with the technicalities of the process of production, is a conscious and goal-oriented process. So, in his own words, 'farming emerges as a *social construction*: as a coherent, multi-dimensional constellation, in which the unity and synergy of practices, internal and external relations, knowledge, norms, opinions, experiences, interests and perspectives are more striking than the tensions and contradictions. . . . Culture is encountered in the *specific coordination* between internal and external relations, between experience and perspective, between past, present and future. Culture is not a phenomenon 'outside' the so-called 'hard realities of market and technology' . . . culture is not to be eliminated from the analysis, or from the (theoretical) representation of agriculture. Culture is at the heart of it.' (Stress as original.)

In brief, what is agriculture? Essentially, it is neither an environmental matter nor a production question. It is primordially a societal issue [this point is further elaborated elsewhere (Portella, 1993)].

### Knowledge: between wisdom and information

Definitions are always troublesome, but indispensable. So, let us proceed, looking at the concept of knowledge and its closest relatives. Here, again, I take a broad view, accepting Havelock's (1986) notion that 'knowledge is the collective achievement of the human race, nothing less,' in other words, an accumulated and shared stock, which is 'passed' and reshaped from one generation to another. Hence it can stand independently of specific holders. In brief, knowledge is culture bound, conceptually placed between wisdom and information. The former is clearly both the elaboration and the possession of individuals rather than a group or society. The second, a broader and purer term, includes all knowledge, but has no cultural status. According to classical information theory, all forms of life, including plant life, has information. So, loosely speaking one could say that knowledge is social groups' wisdom or culture-bound information.

To clarify further the notion of knowledge, three brief points should be added. First, I share the view that all knowledge is inevitably linked to a given cultural context, this being only partly specific. That is, knowledge is always generated in a particular sociocultural setting, but it can 'travel' (and it does) from one culture to another. However, in addition to generation and transfer, one has to acknowledge that there are other very important, complex and analytically distinct processes: reception, verification, transformation and utilization. Second, placing knowledge in its sociocultural context implies that one does recognize that it is a relational notion, not simply a material, tangible good. As Long (1989) put it, 'the generation and utilization of knowledge is not merely a matter of instrumentalities, technical efficiencies, or hermeneutics ... but involves aspects of control, authority and power that are embedded in social relationships.' Third, it is worth drawing a distinction between empirically verifiable and unverifiable knowledge.

### Local knowledge: a very rich concept

One may say that indigenous knowledge is a very rich concept. Indeed, it is culture and locality bound, heterogeneous, fragmentary, multidimensional, detailed, embedded in practice and experimentation *in situ*, and dynamic knowledge. Let us consider all these traits in more detail.

Indigenous knowledge is, of course, knowledge. So, as we have just said, it is culture bound. This means essentially two things. First, indigenous knowledge is partly unique to a given society or to a particular group within that society. Second, it is passed down from one generation to another, often through a very rich oral tradition. Usually, the ammunition of the discourse is impressive: to start with, a large and peculiar vocabulary, which is also full of ambivalence, nuances and equivocations. Strategic overlapping of interconnected concepts can occur, originating a 'network of meaning', as Hesse would express it [quoted from van der Ploeg (1989)]. Numerous dichotomies and particular taxonomies are also common. Similarly, rich metaphors are also current, many of them divining and humanizing the so-called natural elements. In Trás-os-Montes, a farmer may refer to the irrigation water as 'the land's blood', implying both that land without water is 'anaemic' and that water crosses the soil profile like the blood does in the human body. At this point, it is worth noting that oral tradition develops two very important skills in people: listening and memory. An FAO publication (FAO, 1987) reminds us that

> listening is taken so much for granted that it is rarely considered a skill. Yet, it is a perceptual and conceptual ability or capacity to 'read' reality through the ear. People develop listening skills acutely when they rely exclusively on oral communication. This capacity extends beyond reading the sounds of the natural environment and into the skills of social intelligence, the ability to perceive and interpret social situations. In daily life, it means applying the spoken word deftly to participate and survive in the community. ... When people have no other means of storing information and knowledge, they develop an excellent memory.

As a skill, this is glibly overlooked. The folklore of puns, euphemisms, colloquialisms, proverbs, songs and stories is more than folksy fun. These various and entertaining forms have special functions in an oral culture. Eloquence and subtlety are valued, a well-phrased statement is remembered. People listen for hours to a good storyteller. Particularly older people use proverbs to enlighten or comment on the happenings of the day. Proverbs are ingenious mnemonic devices for communicating the insights and experiences won in the past.

Of course, social and group life are of paramount importance in the development of these skills, as well as in the knowledge processes. Consequently, differences in the skills of listening and memory as well as differences in local knowledge between men and women are expected. Similarly, there is variation of knowledge between individuals positioned differently in the local hierarchical structures and communication networks. For instance, in Trás-os-Montes villages, knowledge on horticultural production, particularly identification and care of bean seeds is the women's domain. There, one may also observe that farmers having off-farm work tend to be much more knowledgeable about state institutions, interventions and opportunities than the other farmers. In brief, local knowledge is heterogeneous and fragmentary rather than homogenous and unitary.

Indigenous knowledge is not de-linked either from society and individuals or from geography. It is prominently locality bound. That is, it emerges within the context of a local ecosystem, and external observers may need a great span of time to order and comprehend the moving, complex local agricultural kaleidoscopes. As Warren (1991) notes, 'western visitors to farms and gardens in many parts of the tropical zone find them messy and chaotic.' The same sense of anarchy impinges on any researcher as he observes the Trás-os-Montes traditional irrigation systems for the first time. The linkages of the indigenous knowledge to the local ecosystem are also reflected in the farm practices. For example, as a farmer is broadcasting fertilizer, he will 'open' his hand in the less fertile spots of the land. Similarly, less or more seed can be distributed according to the variable drainage conditions of the plot. Exposure to the sun and to the winds may justify that the same tree is grafted with two different plants. This is not to say that there are closed frontiers and external knowledge is non-existent or ignored. As we all know, facts and artefacts, ideas and theories have travelled for a long time and pass around very easily nowadays. To state that indigenous knowledge is prominently locality bound simply means that local and specific responses are at stake whenever an outside element makes itself present. In other words, external ideas, modes of rationality, technologies, values, etc., are not simply and passively incorporated. There is an active appropriation and internalization process, which may result in rejection of the external input. For instance, we have observed in Trás-os-Montes that researchers presented a particular triticale seed to farmers on the grounds of being highly productive, as far as grain was concerned. Yet, farmers did not care about that particular criterion and associated information, but, in the framework of the local farming system, they tested the new seed more globally. Trying to maximize resource utilization, they evaluated its particular traits (field loss, lodging, grain density, grain/straw yields, cattle reaction towards the grain and flour as a feed) and searched for a variety of ways and combinations of incorporating that resource in the system. They not only viewed triticale as a grain to be sold at the market, but also as an eventual source of forage, straw and grain feed for cattle and flour for human consumption.

Indigenous knowledge represents a highly multidimensional and detailed knowledge system. One can properly speak of close or intimate knowledge. It concerns all sectors of individual and community life. Education, social organization, health care, food preparation, natural resources management and farming are some of the more prominent ones. Through one's continuous socialization the concepts of work, time, space, social and kinship relationships, religion, moral behaviour, nutrition, body and sexual relationships, view of the world and so on are learned [Moreira (1991) presents an interesting, vivid chapter on the local knowledge in Cotas, a village in the Douro region]. This kind of knowledge is embedded in past and current practice, and it serves particularly the aim of ensuring personal and family survival or livelihood; a crucial purpose, indeed. From this viewpoint, farming is of paramount importance and it can be perceived as the *art de la localité*. Farming is deeply interconnected to the local ecosystem, and the management of the labour process aims at a continuous valorization of their elements. This presupposes an endless interaction between 'mental' and 'manual' labour, in addition to an ongoing observation and analysis of the production process and both intermediate and final results. Unplanned, timely, adaptive interventions (either incremental or remedial, according to unexpected, emergent possibilities or limitations) might take place, thus partly conditioning the yield and the quality of the agricultural good. For instance, a Trás-os-Montes farmer, after a 'considerable' field loss (caused by windy days) and a low harvest, may plough the rye field, sow it lightly and use it subsequently as a pasture, or even a grain field. In doing so he may go against a vaguely scheduled rotation, but very likely the resource utilization will turn out to be higher. Whenever unprecedented decisions are assessed, new knowledge emerges or the old one is confirmed and/or expanded.

Hence indigenous knowledge has a dynamic character, the criteria of evaluation of the production process and results also being permanently under change. Thus, due to a specific reason (known or simply hypothesized), a good farming practice today can turn out to be a bad one tomorrow. For instance, the quantity of seed applied to a particular field may increase significantly from one year to the next, because in this year 'winter time arrived earlier'. As Berger (1992) nicely put it:

the peasant's experience of change is more intense than any list, however long and comprehensive, could ever suggest. For two reasons. First, his capacity of observation. Scarcely anything changes in a peasant's entourage, from the clouds to the tail feathers of a cock, without his noticing and interpreting it in terms of the future. His active observation never ceases and so he is continuously recording and reflecting upon changes. Secondly, his economic situation. This is usually such that even a slight change for the worse – a harvest which yields twenty five percent less than the previous year, a fall in the market price of the harvest produce, an unexpected expense – can have disastrous consequences. His observation does not allow the slightest sign of change to pass unnoticed, and his debt magnifies the real or imagined threat of a great part of what he observes.

Indigenous knowledge does not come out only from current, strict practice *in loco*. It is also the result of experimentation *in situ*. Local actors do not rely blindly on their own knowledge. At a specific point in time, they know its strength, but they do not ignore the weaknesses. As Berger (1992) rightly notes:

> closely connected with the peasant's recognition, as a survivor, of scarcity is his recognition of man's relative ignorance. He may admire knowledge and the fruits of knowledge but he never supposes that the advance of knowledge reduces the extent of the unknown. This non-antagonistic relation between the unknown and knowing explains why some of his knowledge is accommodated in what, from the outside, is defined as superstition and magic. Nothing in his experience encourages him to believe in final causes, precisely because his experience is so wide. The unknown can only be eliminated within the limits of a laboratory experiment. Those limits seem to him to be naive.

This is not to say that farmers disregard scientific knowledge as an eventual import. On the contrary, part of the local knowledge will be the result of a specific process of assimilation, recreation and integration of such an element. This is not to say that farmers do not experiment either. They do, and may question proper researchers, in an intellectually humble way though. As Warren (1991) notes, quoting Rhoades and Bebbington, farmers' experiments may be differentiated on three criteria: pure curiosity, problem solving and adaptation. As an example of the first type of a Trás-os-Montes farmer's experiment I may mention the grafting of *Castanea sativa* (chestnut) on a *Quercus* (oak) tree.

## *In general, and paradoxically, science has ignored 'traditional' farming and local knowledge*

Paradoxically, scientists have lacked both sufficient intellectual humility and the right dose of curiosity, two important prerequisites for having the proper status. Traditional medicine and farming, for instance, have been bluntly ignored, or hastily perceived as obstacles to change. Scholars and researchers and also their disciples have assumed that traditional farmers must change their attitudes and behaviour before they can take the first step out of a bare livelihood. The question then is what farmers are doing to themselves, rather than on what researchers are doing to alleviate constraints and grasping possibilities, given the conditions of both the existing agriculture and wider sociopolitical and economic system. As van der Ploeg (1989) remarked, 'right from the beginning the scientific design of "improved varieties" is inspired and structured by a claim of "superiority", a claim omnipresent in all science as far as its relation with local knowledge is concerned (Hesse, 1978). Outside the immediate scope of scientific circles and especially in the fields, improved varieties appear as something quite magical: they seem to hold promises outside the scope of reality'.

If one accepts that claim of 'superiority,' it is no surprise that indigenous knowledge has been invisible for most scientists, and consequently it has been marginalized. As Warren (1991) notes 'very little effort has been made to record these [indigenous knowledge] systems, to understand the variability in the systems according to gender, age, class or caste, and occupational role, and to explain how they form the basis for local reactions to new problems they face as a result of rapid population growth, intensified farming, environmental degradation, and other changes.'

It is worth noting that in Trás-os-Montes, in spite of their remarkable ecological adaptation in the *Terra Fria* and their very high economic relevance, the local resources and farming practices (such as manuring, *rega de lima*, that is, winter irrigation of meadowland, and the use of *baldios*, that is, the village commons) have generally received little attention from the state agencies concerned, strictly the research organizations (Portela, 1991a,b). Indeed, the general, final conclusion of state-of-the-art papers in several domains (development of chestnut trees, *lameiros*, cattle raising, sheep and goat farming) is that the available data are still scarce and insufficient for a thorough characterization of the evolution and current conditions of Trás-os-Montes farming systems. Contrasting this situation of uninterested and inoperative state services, one should juxtapose the farming community's behaviour. Then, we conclude that farmers' interests in the resources and practices mentioned above are exemplary.

# The Roles of Local Knowledge in Agriculture

It is now time to present the main, interrelated actual and potential roles that indigenous knowledge can play, as far as farming is concerned.

## *Local knowledge has ensured both persistence and development of farming and also maintenance of diversity*

If one looks at the prominent, historical Trás-os-Montes farming systems, it is obvious that they have been sustained and developed through indigenous knowledge, not by 'modern' science and technology. These agricultural systems are founded on a long-lasting, intimate knowledge of soils, topography, climate, water resources, vegetation, pests, etc. Similarly, the local social atmosphere is not disregarded and the individuals are effectively socialized in domains such as communication, decision making, mobilization of resources and conflict management. Such a base allows for flexibility, ingenuity, adaptive behaviour and grasping of guaranteed opportunities, even if they are minor ones. Also part and parcel of that body of knowledge are the sets of strategies designed to cope with perceived risks or uncertainties. These traps concern input, output, market and state, the last two constituting a particularly hostile environment. As is now well known, the ability of laggards and the like to survive is tenacious and has puzzled scholars and bureaucrats. The explanation surely lies in the dynamic character of local knowledge, which continuously balances change and continuity through a self-correcting practice. Failure and success are continuously experienced. As long as farmers survive, the totality or part of the components of farming systems (crops, rotations, animals, herds) and regional landscapes are also maintained. Otherwise, inevitably, the biological capital, sources of genetic resources and landscapes become threatened.

## *Local knowledge is worthy. It challenges and helps science*

Whenever scientists predispose themselves to study 'traditional' farming systems and the embedded knowledge, a frequent outcome appears to occur. The record and analyses of indigenous knowledge feeds back, and researchers start to re-appreciate their views and assumptions concerning knowledge and technology generation and transfer. Obviously, this is a very valuable contribution for the advance of science, particularly agricultural sciences. It is up to researchers to grasp it.

Besides that worthy outcome local knowledge can provide other valuable gifts. It can help to fine tune and prioritize research questions and related issues. Similarly, it can contribute to the conception, testing and adaptation of agricultural technologies. Last but not least, local knowledge favours enormously the diffusion of technologies, particularly via farmer to farmer.

### *Potentially, local knowledge is the bedrock of development. However, it has been threatened with extinction*

For those familiar with the richness of indigenous knowledge, surely there is no controversy in presuming that it may be the bedrock of development. Indeed, on the one hand, local people know a great deal more about their own conditions of livelihood and needs than does anyone else. On the other hand, local resources and skills are not non-existent and, ultimately, a socially sustainable development can be started and consolidated only from those assets that people already have or master. Of course, training in new skills cannot be ruled out, but it is part of the development process itself.

However, as van der Ploeg (1992) convincingly argued, locality and heterogeneity, to an increasing degree, have been abolished. Farming has been increasingly subjected to processes of scientification, technology-led changes, externalization and incorporation into markets. No doubt science and technology have promoted 'modern' farming. For a long time, many actors (politicians, planners, scholars, scientists, technicians and progressive farmers) have perceived farming narrowly. The production of specific farm commodities has been their focus of attention, and productivity growth became their permanent obsession. Thus, farmers and their families, in addition to rural communities, were made invisible for decision makers and researchers. Once a farmer enters into the process of 'modernization,' he becomes highly dependent on external, commercial and financial interests. He replaces nature and locally produced resources and begins to worry himself a lot. The capital outlay and institutional relations for intensive agriculture, the large size of the farm exclusively producing for the market, the specialization of output, etc., feed daily stress. The lost of autonomy is accompanied by an increase in rigidity of management and standardization and homogenization of produce. In brief, local knowledge as well as colourful kaleidoscopes composed of agricultural plants, animals and landscapes are threatened with extinction or have already vanished.

## Is the *Art de la Localité* Back?

No doubt the current processes of technological development and economic globalization are very powerful. However, it is also clear that some countervailing forces are emerging. The concern for the environmental impact of farming has been slow to emerge, but it is now visible and it will very likely grow. No longer can the degradation of rural environments, both biophysical and sociocultural, be ignored. Environmental concerns associated with the social atmosphere of an increasingly demanding, anxious and risk-sensitive society (particularly as to health risks related to food) are leading to an increased acceptance of 'alternative' farming, and probably to a strict regulation and taxation of 'modern' inputs. Thus, local agroecological specificity appears as a basis for providing low- and no-chemical input farming, in addition to high-quality, tasty and rare products, which might be well paid. That is, agriculture as the *art de la localité* is in demand. But is it really back?

The answer is no, but one could also think of an alternative answer: not yet. Indeed, the calls for sustainable and equitable, as well as stable and productive, farming systems appear to be on the increase everywhere. Hence it seems legitimate to conclude that 'the reconstitution of locality' is becoming to be rooted as a contemporary trend. Anyway, under current societal life and farmers' socioeconomic expectations, the *art de la localité* of the old days would be a failure. Success requires that local art and universal science interact both extensively and intensively. This, in turn, presupposes that scientists fully recognize the multiple roles that local knowledge and people *in loco* can play in developing alternative development.

## Acknowledgements

Special thanks are due to Timothy Koehnen and Adri van den Dries for their constructive comments. However, I remain entirely responsible for the contents of this chapter.

## References

Berger, J. (1992) *Into Their Labours*. Granta Books, London.
FAO (1987) *The Paradigm of Communication in Development: from Knowledge Transfer to Community Participation – Lessons from the Grameen Bank, Bangladesh*. FAO, Rome.
Havelock, R.G. (1986) The knowledge perspective: definition and scope of a new study domain. In: Beal, G.M., Dissanayake, W. and Konoshima, S. (eds) *Knowledge Generation, Exchange, and Utilization*. Westview Press, Boulder, Colorado.
Hesse, M. (1978) Theory and value in the social sciences. In: Hookway, C. and Pettit, Ph. (eds) *Action and Interpretation. Studies in Philosophy of the Social Sciences*. Cambridge University Press, Cambridge.
Johnson, G.L. and Lard, C.F. (1961) Knowledge situations. In: *A Study of Managerial Processes of Midwestern Farmers*. State University Press, Ames, Iowa, pp. 39–54.
Leeuwis, C., Long, N. and Villarreal, M. (1991) Equivocations on knowledge systems theory: an actor-oriented critique. In: Kuiper, D. and Röling, N.G (eds) *Proceedings of the European Seminar on Knowledge Management and Information Technology*. Agricultural University, Wageningen, pp. 21–29.
Long, N. (1989) Knowledge, networks and power: discontinuities and accommodations at the interface. Draft paper prepared for the European Seminar on Knowledge Systems and Information Technology, Wageningen, 23–24 November.
Moreira, A.M.F. (1991) *O Processo de Aprendizagem no Grupo Doméstico: Um Estudo de Caso*. UTAD, Vila Real.

Portela, J. (1984) Investigadores e agricultores: tese, antítese e síntese. In: *Selecção das Comunicações da II Conferência Nacional dos Economistas, Lisboa*, Vol. I. Associação Portuguesa de Economistas, Lisbon, pp. 80–106.

Portela, J. (1988) Rural household strategies of income generation: a study of North-Eastern Portugal,1900–1987. Unpublished PhD thesis, University of Wales.

Portela, J. (1991a) Research and reductionism: have we pretty good conceptual tools? In: de Haan, H. and van der Ploeg, J.D. (eds) *Endogenous Regional Development in Europe – Theory, Method and Practice*. Proceedings of a Seminar held in Vila Real, November 4–5. European Commission, Brussels, pp. 45–62.

Portela, J. (1991b) The Terra Fria farming system: elements, practices and neglected research domains. In: de Haan, H. and van der Ploeg, J.D. (eds) *Endogenous Regional Development in Europe – Theory, Method and Practice*. Proceedings of a Seminar held in Vila Real, November 4–5. European Commission, Brussels, pp. 263–286.

Portcla, J. (1993) Agriculture is primordially what? Some comments on Frederick H. Buttel's keynote address – Agricultural change, rural society, and the state – prepared for presentation at the European Congress for Rural Sociology, Wageningen, August 2.

Röling, N.G. and Engel, P.G.H. (1991) IT from a knowledge system perspective: concepts and issues. In: Kuiper, D. and Röling, N.G. (eds) *Proceedings of the European Seminar on Knowledge Management and Information Technology*. Agricultural University, Wageningen, pp. 8–20.

Shaner, W.W. (1983) Linking extension with farming systems research. In: Claar, J.B. and Watts, L.H. (eds) *Knowledge Transfer in Developing Countries*, Proceedings of a Conference on International Extension at Steamboat Springs, July, pp. 45–54.

Sriskandarajah, N., Bawden, R.J. and Packham, R.G. (1989) Systems agriculture – a paradigm for sustainability. Paper presented at the Ninth Annual Farming Systems Research/Extension Symposium, Arkansas, October 9–11.

van der Ploeg, J.D. (1989) Knowledge systems, methaphor and interface: the case of potatoes in the Peruvian highlands. In: Long, N. (ed.) *Encounters at the Interface: a Perspective on Social Discontinuities in Rural Development*. Wageningen Studies in Sociology No. 27, Agricultural University, Wageningen.

van der Ploeg, J.D. (1992) The reconstitution of locality: technology and labour in modern agriculture. In: Marsden, T., Lowe, P. and Whatmore, S. (eds) *Labour and Locality*. David Fulton, London.

Warren, D.M. (1991) *Using Indigenous Knowledge in Agricultural Development*. World Bank Discussions Paper No. 127. World Bank, Washington, DC.

# 23

## Interaction Between Extension Services and Farmer Decision Making: New Issues and Sustainable Farming

### Niels Röling

### Introduction

Integrated pest management, common property resource management, sustainable natural resource management, low external input agriculture, ecological farming and social fences are all examples of efforts to cope with new emerging imperatives. They are leading to fundamental changes in extension practices, institutions, contexts and models. These are embedded in a wider debate about agricultural science in the post-Newtonian era.

The issues are highly relevant for FSR/E theory and practice (Lightfoot *et al.*, 1993). It is no longer sufficient to consider farmers as (i) primary producers or (ii) entrepreneurs, businessmen or farm managers. They must now also be regarded as (iii) managers of ecosystems. The change from (i) to (ii) has had major consequences for FSR/E thinking and practice; the change to (iii) is equally fundamental. For example, some of the key variables for the sustainable management of natural resources at the farm level can be controlled only by managing ecosystems at higher levels of aggregation, such as the irrigation block, polder, water catchment, catena, biotope, habitat, landscape, region, country or even the Earth itself. As we shall see, this involves accommodation and collective management by the stakeholders in the system, posing a challenge for researchers, extensionists and farmers.

The issues have important implications for the models which underpin decision making about investment, design, staffing, training, action-research and evaluation with respect to research extension.

# Learning How to Farm Sustainably

Recent studies at the farm level, both in Europe and in 'the south' (e.g. Somers and Röling, 1993, for 'integrated' arable farming in The Netherlands and Van de Fliert, 1993, for integrated pest management in irrigated rice in Indonesia) have suggested that fundamental changes accompany the move to more sustainable practices. These changes can be summarized as follows:

**1.** *The change cannot be understood as the adoption of innovations in Rogers' (1983) Diffusion of Innovations framework.* Instead, we are dealing with a complex learning process, consisting of a sequence of contingent steps. A typical example is provided by hard fruit producers in Zeeland. When the red spider mite had become resistant to pesticides, growers were compelled to introduce predatory mites into their orchards as a biological control. From then on they had to manage their orchards as perennial habitats for predatory mites and carry magnifying glasses to monitor this management. This change led to a host of other changes, in terms of using alternative pesticides, placing nest boxes for kestrels, etc.

**2.** *The learning process is calibrated by discontinuities.* After periods of gradual change, e.g. in the reduction of dosages of chemicals from the customary overdose to threshold doses, farmers encounter major hurdles. A typical example from integrated arable farming in The Netherlands (Röling, 1993a) is the change in potato cultivar which becomes necessary below a certain level of fungicide application.

**3.** *The learning process is fraught with uncertainty, as the reliance on customary practices, such as use of chemical inputs, is replaced by reliance on judgement.* Mistakes made early in the season are hard to redress later. Established risks become unhinged and it takes time for new risks to become known. This uncertainty is one reason why farmers moving towards integrated arable practices in the Netherlands claim they need guidance during the learning process and why they value joint learning in the context of groups of farmers in the same predicament. A question which is unsolved so far is whether all farmers have to move through the same learning process, or whether learning occurs faster in later phases of diffusion.

**4.** *Instead of discrete 'technologies,' we are dealing with a complex of interactive technologies, as farmers move from input-intensive to more knowledge-intensive management, and from component management to complex system management in which interaction effects are as important as the effects of individual interventions.* Instead of calendar-based routine decision making, farmers learn to take complex decisions, based on observation and knowledge about natural processes, requiring the weighing up of many factors. An example is the so-called 'thresholds' for spraying used in integrated pest management (IPM) in Indonesia (Röling and Van de Fliert, 1993; Van de Fliert, 1993). At first, these thresholds consisted of simple ratios of pests/predators per rice hill. Later, the concept of an 'economic threshold' was introduced, a complex equation comparing value of expected yield loss in the absence of spraying and cost of pesticide application. This threshold concept proved unmanageable for farmers. In the end, the IPM programme dropped the notion of a threshold and accepted whatever decision was made, as long as it was made on the basis of established principles and observation.

These developments lead to new concepts in agricultural research. The Experiment Station for Fruit in Wilheminadorp, Zeeland, is now setting up 'integrated systems research' in which the focus will be on managing the whole system. Explicit attention will be paid to interaction effects. The Fruit Growers Association is closely involved.

**5.** *Market forces seem incapable of providing the imperatives for moving to more sustainable practices, except for consumer pressures for 'cleaner' products.* Consumer pressures are, however, not very effective, especially as consumers are not involved in the struggle by farmers to clean up their act. In The Netherlands, agriculture continues to be a profitable industry (with some exceptions) but the Central Bureau of Statistics has recently calculated that farming's environmental costs are higher than its benefits to the nation in terms of employment, the contribution to the balance of payments, etc. In both Indonesia and The Netherlands, environmental legislation plays a key role in the shift to sustainable agriculture. The learning processes described occur within, and are accelerated by, a coercive policy context. As a consequence, information about policy measures and policy implementation becomes as important as technical information and information about market prices.

**6.** *Research in The Netherlands (Van der Ley and Proost, 1992) has shown that farmers accept policy measures because they removed 'free riders' if effectively implemented.* However, the fear remains of unfair competition with farmers in countries where comparable measures have not been implemented. None the less, the theoretical inconsistency between economic and ecological scenarios for farm development has been belied by Dutch farmers, who have demonstrated that it is possible to survive under integrated farming regimes. Wossink (1993) has calculated that trends in product prices and not environmental legislation are the main threat to farm continuity.

**7.** *In both Indonesia and The Netherlands the evidence is that the intensive learning process is experienced by farmers as exciting.* Their new-found expertise and management control are a source of pride and self-confidence.

# Facilitating Learning

Experience in Indonesia (Matteson *et al.*, 1992), Australia (Russell *et al.*, 1989) and The Netherlands has shown that conventional approaches to extension are not very effective when it comes to facilitating the learning processes involved in moving to more sustainable practices. In Indonesia, for example, an early effort to introduce IPM in irrigated rice through the regular extension service based on a local version of T & V (training and visit) proved an expensive failure. Later, deliberate application of principles of non-formal education proved more effective. 'Farmer Field Schools' trained groups of farmers throughout a full season in observation, recording, interpretation and complex decision making (Van de Fliert, 1993). The approach has now been proposed as the basis for general extension, as Indonesia moves into the post-green revolution phase. Further agricultural development cannot be expected from routine transfer of blanket recommendations and uniform packages of technology to farmers treated as the most lowly civil servants in a bureaucratic hierarchy. The IPM Field Schools have shown that future development rests on involving farmers as experts in their own right.

In The Netherlands, an experimental project to introduce integrated arable farming so far has shown that the conventional approach to extension, which relies on research-based expertise for impact, does not work. Instead of acting as experts themselves, extension workers must help farmers to become experts. This involves facilitation of learning processes in groups over time. The inability of extension workers to facilitate study clubs, formed around experimental integrated farms, has motivated a search for alternative approaches. One problem is that the recent privatization of the extension service forces staff to search for 'knowledge products' which can be sold to farmers. This pressure has emphasized the expert role of extension workers and the role of knowledge as a commodity. It is too early for solutions to have crystallized.

In all, the experience to date seems to show that the linear model (Kline and Rosenberg, 1986), according to which scientific research is the source of innovations, extension the instrument for their transfer and farmers the receivers and utilizers, is inappropriate. This is not too startling a conclusion for members of the Association of Farming Systems Research and Extension (AFSRE). However, the institutional contours of the alternatives have still to emerge, especially when it comes to methodologies, staff deployment, institution building and research linkage. Participatory technology development (PTD) (Chambers and Jiggins, 1987; Jiggins and De Zeeuw, 1992; Jiggins, 1994b) has provided important answers with respect to methodology and staff development. I shall return to institution building and research linkage later when discussing knowledge systems.

# The Interface Between Agroecosystems and Platforms for Decision Making

Agroecosystems can be considered at different levels of aggregation. At each level, one can speak of an interface between the perceived system and the platform for decision making about that system. At the farm level, the farm household (platform) interfaces with the farm (agroecosystem). A typical platform issue is accommodation of male and female interests in the use of farm resources. The recognition of the need for platforms at higher levels of aggregation is increasing. Two examples will be given, one of a success and one of a failure.

The successful example is the Australian Landcare movement (e.g. Campbell, 1992; Woodhill *et al.*, 1992). Enormous erosion problems have necessitated the formation of groups of stakeholders in water catchments who are facilitated to work together for the integral management of the catchments. The stakeholders must develop into a platform for collective learning and decision making about the catchment.

An example of how this 'facilitation' occurs is the development of the soil map of the catchment. Farmers meet on one of the properties to learn about the prevailing soil types. They dig soil pits, look at profiles and agree on the main soil taxonomies. These do not need to correspond to scientific soil types. The farmers return home to make a soil map of their own property, with the aid of a photo-mosaic of the property, acetate overlays to draw in soil units and other features, special pens, etc. The individual soil maps are digitized and read into a computer with GIS software. The program is used to produce one integrated soil map of the whole catchment. This map is again discussed with the farmers. As can be imagined, it has many mistakes, but in discussing and redrawing the map, farmers take ownership of the whole catchment and learn to see their own farm as part of it. In subsequent meetings, decisions are made, not only about the collective management of vulnerable soil types, but also about such issues as wildlife corridors.

That is the successful example. An example which is equally relevant but so far not successful is the management of subterranean water resources in The Netherlands. Unbelievable as it sounds, Holland is drying out. The reason is that various actors, such as farmers, drinking water companies, industries and others who utilize subterranean water have not been able to form a platform for its integral management (Van Duinhoven, 1993).

Other examples include common property resource management (e.g., McKean, 1992), the Yellowstone Area Coordination Committee (Keiter and Boyce, 1991) and United Nations Conference on Environment and Development (UNCED).

The examples show that sustainable natural resource management is not only a question of biophysical information and technical intervention. It requires accommodation among human actors (Long, 1984; Long and Long,

1992) who use the same natural environment with different purposes. These stakeholders are interdependent in that each affects the desired outcomes of the others. Therefore, environmental management involves collective 'agency' (the capacity to make a difference) at a platform of decision making which includes all stakeholders. Sustainable natural resource management, therefore, requires a *coupled system* between:

**1.** a 'hard' *agroecosystem* constructed according to biophysical science and managed on the basis of instrumental reasoning; and
**2.** a 'soft' *platform* constructed according to social insight and managed on the basis of strategic and communicative reasoning.

Sustainability can be considered as the emergent property of the coupled system. The key reason for constructing systems is that properties emerge at the system level which cannot be predicted from studying the components making up the system (Checkland, 1981). Hard scientists consider sustainability to be the emergent property of an agroecosystem in equilibrium, a point at which the carrying capacity is not exceeded (Jiggins, 1994a). Soft scientists or post-Newtonian biophysical scientists consider sustainability to be the emergent property of a soft learning system (e.g. Sriskandarajah *et al.*, 1991).

I propose that sustainability be considered the emergent property of the coupled system (Woodhill and Röling, in preparation; Röling, 1993b). This perspective raises many issues for discussion.

**1.** *The goodness-of-fit between perceived ecosystems and platforms for decision making.* Existing units for collective decision making, such as the household, prefecture, farmer association, car factory, province or nation, have not been set up for natural resource management and/or do not correspond to the system to be managed. A great challenge facing us today is to move from human organization for purposes of production, profit making, etc., to organization for natural resource management. Does the identification of an agroecosystem under threat affect the development of an appropriate platform? Can we learn to develop platforms fast enough to salvage the planet?

**2.** *The correspondence between agroecosystems identified as needing integral sustainable management and recommendation domains* (Jiggins, 1994b).

**3.** *The processes at the interface between hard systems and soft platforms.* Stakeholders must develop an information flow for the agroecosystem which allows them to learn about it and take concerted action. The work of hard scientists (interactive multiple goal planning models, GISs, and so on) can and does play a crucial role in this respect. However, it needs to be carefully studied. Other questions also arise. For example, stakeholders must learn from scratch about the ecosystem, agree on its boundaries, share concepts in order to discuss it and meaningfully decide about its sustainable management, develop new indicators for success and develop new methods of 'making things visible.' Such 'soft' sense making activities and their facilitation obviously require much attention in the near future.

**4.** *Increasing the level of social aggregation of platform–ecosystem coupling.* The level at which interdependence between stakeholders is recognized moves increasingly in a global direction. Actors and platforms must increasingly be considered as sub-assemblies (Koestler, 1967) of larger wholes. Moving up the level of aggregation means that diverse and conflicting objectives must be assembled into rich pictures and mutually accommodated to shared perspectives and values. Social dilemmas and ethical choices about end goals play a crucial role in these processes (Messick and Brewer, 1983).

**5.** *The interface between hard and soft scientists.* This is a crucial issue. In the author's university, it is solved by generating Interactive Multiple Goal Planning Models for land use planning (Fresco, 1993). These are computer simulation models which allow the calculation of alternative scenarios based on different 'goal functions' for the use of the same agroecosystem. The models are based on an integration of the 'hard' sciences and economics, to the extent that economics can fit human action into predictive formulae. However, the soft sciences cannot and do not want to be fitted into such models. They form an unrelated 'camp.' The major problem is that hard and soft sciences work from totally different epistemologies, with the former embracing positivist and even realist assumptions about the nature of human knowledge, while the latter take a constructivist position (Röling, 1993b). The coupled system could provide a fruitful area of discourse in the impasse.

## The Facilitation of Platform Processes

The subject of facilitation is, of course, of special interest to extension. How can one move stakeholders in an ecosystem from strategic to communicative reasoning (Habermas, 1984, 1987; Funtowicz and Ravetz, 1990)? How do they come to the joint appreciation that the sustainability of the agroecosystem in which they operate is a priority problem? How salient must that priority be to overcome inertia and self-interest? What is the experience with establishing a coercive framework? At what point does diversity among stakeholders require a coercive context? Can soft systems methodology (SSM), for joint learning of groups of corporate actors, as they move from joint problem appreciation to collective action (Checkland, 1981; Checkland and Scholes, 1990), be applied for platform development? What role does hard science play in such processes? And how do such processes affect hard science? PTD has shown how agronomy can be an interactive resource.

So far there is not much practical experience with platform processes. One exciting instance is the work of Wagemans (M. Wagemans, in preparation).

His professional experience has involved him intensively in implementation of spatial planning and environment legislation in The Netherlands. It is one of the hottest issues in a country which carries nearly 5% of the EC's population on 2% of the EC's land but produces around 15% of its pork, milk and potatoes, and manages to share with France the position of the second largest exporter of agricultural products by value after the USA. One area of conflict is a nature reserve, De Peel, under threat from surrounding intensive bioindustry (formerly animal production). Representatives of different directorates of two ministries, several communities, organizations such as the Limburg Landscape, farmers' organizations and other actors have wrangled for years about the future of the area, each defending its interests from entrenched positions, in a complex context of inconsistent policies, complex procedures, conflicting areas of jurisdiction and battles of competence involving the strategic use of communication (Wagemans, 1990). Wagemans is engaged is exploring ways of breaking through this congealed negotiation context to a 'context of creativity.'

## Knowledge Systems and Networks

The notion of the knowledge system emerged when the futility of looking only at farmers' 'indigenous' knowledge, or only at agricultural research, or only at extension, or even at all these in the absence of consideration of other actors, politics and power, became apparent (e.g., Lionberger and Chang, 1970; Rogers *et al.* 1976; Evenson *et al.*, 1979; Havelock, 1986; Röling, 1986, 1992; Röling and Engel, 1991; Dissanayake, 1992). The knowledge system construct focuses attention on subjective boundary judgement and deliberate consideration of the relevant actors in the perceived system, the integration, linkage and articulation between them, the forces that explain their coordination, the emergent properties of the system in terms of (failed) innovation and learning and finally the extent to which the relevant actors have been able to establish a joint mission (P. Engel, in preparation). An effective knowledge system is a platform for decision making by (institutional) actors about what Engel (in preparation) calls a 'theatre for agricultural innovation'.

Effective knowledge systems are underpinned by models which are widely shared among the actors involved. According to the conventional public sector model, the actors in the knowledge system calibrate the science–practice continuum in such a way that a super-conduit with booster stations is created between research and farmers. In more sophisticated models, 'user control' and marketing research (FSR) create a two-way circuit.

A knowledge system in which active farmer learning and experimenting groups are the key components of the system, provides a second entirely different model. Facilitators link the farmer groups into larger knowledge networks. In this perspective, research is an interactive resource and not the prime source of innovation. This second perspective on knowledge systems has been proposed as the most appropriate model for commercial innovation (Kline and Rosenberg, 1986) and is popular among NGOs, in FSR/E circles (e.g. Gubbels, 1993), in biological farming (U. Bader, in preparation), in US farmer learning groups, such as the 'Practical Farmers of Iowa', and, perhaps surprisingly, in the technologically advanced Dutch glasshouse sector. Study clubs are at the heart of the knowledge system serving this intensive sector (e.g., Leeuwis and Arkesteyn, 1991; Leeuwis, 1993).

The experience seems to suggest that the second perspective is the more appropriate for moving toward more sustainable practices. In The Netherlands, farmers learn about integrated arable farming in groups under intensive guidance over long periods. In Australia, farmers learn in landcare groups about sustainable catchment management. In Indonesia, Farmer Field Schools bring together groups of local farmers for season-long intensive learning under guidance. This tentative conclusion raises issues:

**1.** The optimal institutional arrangement for potentially large-scale implementation of learning groups. So far the focus has been on the groups themselves. Of special interest is the nature of the science linkage in such a set-up.
**2.** The methods for facilitation of groups and linkages and the training of extension workers for these tasks.
**3.** The role of policy and coercive instruments in the system.
**4.** The extent to which assisted farmer experimentation and local group learning can replace formal research and experimentation. Necessarily decentralized, highly segmented into specialized subsectors and locally specific, formal research might not be cost-effective or politically feasible.

# References

Bader, U. (in preparation) Learning processes in biological agriculture in Germany (provisional title). Doctoral Dissertation (in German), Department of Applied Psychology and Extension, University of Stuttgart Hohenheim, Stuttgart.

Baker, M. (ed.) (1994) *Grasslands for Our World, Proceedings of the XVII International Grasslands Congress.* SIR Publishing, Wellington, New Zealand.

Beal, G.M., Dissanayake, W. and Konoshima, S. (eds) (1986) *Knowledge Generation, Exchange and Utilisation.* Westview Press, Boulder, Colorado.

Campbell, A. (1992) *Taking the Long View in Tough Times: Landcare in Australia. Third Annual Report of the National Landcare Facilitator.* National Soil Conservation Programme, Canberra.

Chambers, R. and Jiggins, J. (1987) Agricultural research for resource-poor farmers. Part I: transfer-of-technology and farming systems research. Part II: a parsimonious paradigm. *Agricultural Administration and Extension* 27, 35–52 and 109–128.

Checkland, P. (1981) *Systems Thinking, Systems Practice.* Wiley, Chicester.

Checkland, P. and Scholes, J. (1990) *Soft Systems Methodology in Action.* Wiley, Chicester.

Denno, R.F. and Perfect, T.J. (eds) (1992) *Ecology and Management of Plant Hoppers.* Chapman and Hall, London.

Dissanayake, W. (1992) Knowledge, culture and power: some theoretical issues related to the agricultural knowledge and information system framework. *Knowledge and Policy* 5(1), 65–76.

Engel, P. (in preparation) Knowledge management in agriculture: a fundamental requirement for sustainable development. Dissertation, Agricultural University, Wageningen.

Evenson, R.E., Waggoner, P.E. and Ruttan, V.W. (1979) Economic benefits from research: an example from agriculture. *Science* 205, 1101–1107.

Fresco, L.O. (1993) From exploration of options for land use to integrated planning methods. Keynote address at the 75-year Anniversary Conference of the Wageningen Agricultural University, 'Future of the Land: Mobilising and Integrating Knowledge for Land Use Options,' August 22–25, 1993, Wageningen, The Netherlands (the paper will be published in the proceedings of the conference, Wiley, Chichester).

Funtowicz, S.O. and Ravetz, J.R. (1990) *Global Environmental Issues and the Emergence of Second Order Science.* CD-NA-12803-En-C, Report EUR 12803 EN, Commission for the European Communities, Directorate General Telecommunications, Information Industries and Innovation, Luxembourg.

Gubbels, P. (1993) *Peasant Farmer Organisation in Farmer-first Agricultural Development in West Africa: New Opportunities and Continuing Constraints.* Network Paper No. 40, ODI, Agricultural Administration (Research and Extension) Network, London.

Habermas, J. (1984) *The Theory of Communicative Action. Vol. 1: Reason and the Rationalisation of Society.* Beacon Press, Boston.

Habermas, J. (1987) *The Theory of Communicative Action. Vol. 2: Lifeworld and System. A Critique of Functionalist Reason.* Beacon Press, Boston.

Havelock, R.G. (1986) Modelling the knowledge system. In: Beal, G.M., Dissanayake, W. and Konoshima, S. (eds) *Knowledge Generation, Exchange and Utilisation.* Westview Press, Boulder, Colorado, pp. 77–105.

Jiggins, J.L.S. (1994a) *Changing the Boundaries: Women-centred perspectives on population and the environment.* Island Press, Washington, DC.

Jiggins, J.L.S. (1994b) From technology transfer to resource management. In: Baker, M. (ed.) *Grasslands for Our World.* SIR Publishing, Wellington, New Zealand.

Jiggins, J.L.S. and De Zeeuw, H. (1992) Participatory technology development in practice: process and methods. In: Reijntjes, C., Haverkort, B. and Waters-Bayer, A. (eds) *Farming for the Future: an Introduction to Low External Input Agriculture.* MacMillan, London, and ILEIA, Leusden, pp. 135–162.

Keiter, R.B. and Boyce, M.S. (1991) *The Greater Yellowstone Ecosystem: Redefining America's Wilderness Heritage.* Yale University Press, Boston.

Kline, S. and Rosenberg, N. (1986) An overview of innovation. In: Landau, R. and Rosenberg, N. (eds). *The Positive Sum Strategy. Harnessing Technology for Economic Growth.* National Academic Press, Washington, DC. pp. 275–306.

Koestler, A. (1967) *The Ghost in the Machine.* Penguin Arkana, London.

Landau, R. and Rosenberg, N. (eds) (1986) *The Positive Sum Strategy. Harnessing*

*Technology for Economic Growth.* National Academic Press, Washington, DC.

Leeuwis, C. (1993) Of computers, myths and modelling. The social construction of diversity, knowledge, information and communication technologies in Dutch agriculture and agricultural extension. Doctoral dissertation, Agricultural University. Wageningse Sociologische Reeks, Wageningen.

Leeuwis, C. and Arkesteyn, M. (1991) Planned technology development and local initiative: computer-supported enterprise comparisons among Dutch horticulturalists. *Sociologia Ruralis* 31 (2/3), 140–161.

Lightfoot, C., Pingali, P. and Harrington, L. (1993) Beyond romance and rhetoric: sustainable agriculture and farming systems research. *Agricultural Research and Extension Newsletter* 28 (July), 27–31. ODI, London.

Lionberger, H. and Chang, C. (1970) *Farm Information for Modernising Agriculture: The Taiwan System.* Praeger, New York.

Long, N. (1984) Creating space for change: a perspective on the sociology of development. *Sociologia Ruralis* 24, 168–184.

Long, N. and Long, A. (eds) (1992) *Battlefields of Knowledge: the Interlocking of Theory and Practice in Research and Development.* Routledge, London.

Matteson, P., Gallagher, K.D. and Kenmore, P.E. (1992) Extension and integrated pest management for planthoppers in Asian irrigated rice. In: Denno, R.F. and Perfect, T.J. (eds) *Ecology and Management of Plant Hoppers.* Chapman and Hall, London.

McKean, M.A. (1992) Success on the commons: a comparative examination of institutions                                                                              for common property resource management. *Journal of Theoretical Politics* 4 (3), 247–281.

Messick, D.M. and Brewer, M.B. (1983) Solving social dilemmas: a review. In: Wheeler, L. and Shaver, P. (eds) *Review of Personality and Psychology,* Vol. 4, pp. 11–44.

Rivera, W.M. and Gustafson, D.J. (eds) (1991) *Agricultural Extension: Worldwide Institutional Evolution and Forces for Change.* Elsevier, Amsterdam.

Rogers, E.M. (1983) *Diffusion of Innovations.* Free Press, New York.

Rogers, E.M., Eveland, J.D. and Dean, A.S. (1976) *Extending the Agricultural Extension Model.* Stanford University, Institute for Communication Research, Stanford, California.

Röling, N. (1986) Extension science: increasingly preoccupied with knowledge systems. *Sociologia Ruralis* 25, 269–290.

Röling, N. (1992) Emergence of knowledge systems thinking: the changing perception of the relationship between innovation, knowledge process, and configuration in the search for an effective diagnostic framework. *Knowledge and Policy* 5 (1), 42–64.

Röling, N. (1993a) Agricultural knowledge and environmental regulation: the Crop Protection Plan and the Koekoekspolder. *Sociologia Ruralis* 33 (2), 212–231.

Röling, N. (1993b) Platforms for decision making about eco-systems. Keynote address at the 75-year Anniversary Conference of the Wageningen Agricultural University, 'Future of the Land: Mobilising and Integrating Knowledge for Land Use Options,' August 22–25, 1993, Wageningen, The Netherlands (the paper will be published in the proceedings of the conference, Wiley, Chichester).

Röling, N. and Engel, P.G.H. (1991) The development of the concept of agricultural knowledge and information systems (AKIS): implications for extension. In:

Rivera, W.M. and Gustafson, D.J. (eds) *Agricultural Extension: Worldwide Institutional Evolution and Forces for Change.* Elsevier, Amsterdam. pp. 125–138.

Röling, N. and Van de Fliert, E. (in press) Transforming extension for sustainable agriculture: the case of integrated pest management in rice in Indonesia. *Agriculture and Human Values.*

Russel, D.B., Ison, R.L., Gamble, D.R. and Williams, R.K. (1989) *A Critical Review of Rural Extension Theory and Practice. Report to the Australian Wool Corporation.* University of Western Sydney, Hawkesbury.

Somers, B.M. and Röling, N. (1993) *Ontwikkeling van Kennis voor Duurzame Landbouw: een Verkennende Studie aan de Hand van Enkele Experimentele Projekten.* NRLO, The Hague.

Sriskandarajah, N., Bawden, R.J. and Packam, R.G. (1991) System agriculture: a paradigm for sustainability. Paper presented at the 9th Annual Farming Systems Research/Extension Symposium, University of Arkansas, Fayetteville, AR, October 9–11, 1989. *AFSRE Newsletter* 2 (3), 1–5.

Van de Fliert, E. (1993) Integrated pest management. Farmer Field Schools generate sustainable practices: a case study in Central Java evaluating IPM training. Doctoral dissertation, Agricultural University, Wageningen, WU Papers No. 93–3.

Van der Ley, H.A. and Proost, M.D.C. (1992) *Gewasbescherming met een Toekomst: de Visie van Agrarische Ondernemers: een Doelgroepverkennend Onderzoek ten Behoeve van Voorlichting.* Agricultural University, Department of Communication and Innovation Studies, Wageningen.

Van Duinhoven, G. (1993) Verdrogen tegen wil en dank. Deugdelijk beleid strandt op gebrek aan overleg. *LT Journaal* 12 (July), 7–9.

Wagemans, M. (1990) Analysis of the role of information in planning: the case of town and country planning. *Knowledge in Society* 3 (4), 72–90.

Wagemans, M. (in preparation) Creative contexts can break stalemates: a case study of platforms for natural resource management in the Netherlands (provisional title; in Dutch). Ministry of Agriculture Provincial Unit, Roermond.

Woodhill, J. and Röling, N. (in preparation) The second wing of the eagle. How soft science can help us learn our way to more sustainable futures. University of New South Wales, Hawkesbury, and Agricultural University, Wageningen.

Woodhill, J., Wilson, A. and McKenzie, J. (1992) Land conservation and social change: extension to community development. A necesary shift in thinking. Paper presented at the 7th International Soil Conservation Conference, Sydney, Australia, 27–30 September 1992.

Wossink, G.A.A. (1993) Analysis of future agricultural change. A farm economic approach applied to Dutch arable farming. Doctoral dissertation, Wageningen Agricultural University, Wageningen.

# 24

# PARTICIPATORY RESEARCH: WATER QUALITY AND CHANGES IN FARMING SYSTEMS

## Jacques Brossier and Eduardo Chia

## Introduction

Farming and agrarian systems research is oriented towards farmers and local operators and it is important to emphasize that researchers are not external to the system under study (principle of included third party) and that operators take part in the research. In French terminology, this is called recherche-action or action-research (AR). After Lewin (1947), Liu (1992) defines action-research as a fundamental research method used in the social sciences, where a desire for change converges with a research intention. It has a dual objective that consists of implementing a resolve for change and at the same time furthering fundamental knowledge in the social sciences. It is based on the combined work of all the parties involved. It is developed within an ethical framework that is negotiated and accepted by all (Liu, 1992; Vallerand, Chapter 26). In English scientific agricultural literature, the nearest equivalent concept seems to be the participatory approach which insists upon the association of insiders (farmers) with their knowledge from personal experience and outsiders (researchers) in designing and carrying out research: so research is built in real farm situations (Farrington and Martin, 1988). The terms action-research and participatory approach will both have similar meanings here.

Pollution resulting from agriculture is a complex phenomenon involving biotechnical, social and economic mechanisms and various social partner groups. It would appear that a systemic and participatory approach would be an appropriate method to deal with this matter.

# Presentation of the Problem

The request formulated by a company producing mineral water is the direct origin of this research (for more detailed information see Deffontaines *et al.*, 1993) (see Table 24.1). The mineral water emanating from a restricted area which is relatively well delimited (approximately 5000 ha according to hydrogeological studies) has a nitrates level which is on the increase. Since 1980, there has been a report of a slow but regular growth of nitrates in the water under the roots of a hydromineral watershed. Where do the nitrates come from? Above all from human activity: mainly from agriculture (soil leaching, manure heaps). Moreover, practically the whole area is devoted to agriculture and recent changes in systems of production (turning over of meadow land, development of corn, new technical methods) seem to be one of the main causes of the increase in the nitrates level; hence the question from the company to our research team: which changes in farming systems can slow the increase in the level of nitrates in drainage water seeping into the highest layer of the ground, and how can these changes be carried out? From the outset, the constraints were strict: no pesticides should be used, and a nitrates level lower than 10 mg $l^{-1}$ in the soil solution under the roots should be achieved.

To begin with, the contribution of traditional economic analysis to the study of environmental problems will be recalled, in particular those concerning nitrates and water quality. Then the research programme will be presented, followed by the participatory approach and selected results.

# What is the Economic Problem? Effect of Externality or Incompatible-use Goods

How can the problem of the increase in the level of nitrates in water emanating from agriculture be analysed? Certain researchers feel that the explanation lies in the externality concept: pollution is an external effect of farm activity. The possibility for a producer to use natural production factors without paying for them encourages him to use and abuse in his own interest. The field of study concerning external effects is about the interdependence between operators and commercial trade. For liberal economists, the external effects hinder market functioning and produce a distortion with respect to the optimum (Godard, 1984). The accepted way to suppress this distortion is to internalize the external costs by applying, for example, the Polluter Pays Principle (PPP).

Application of the PPP is almost impossible in the present case. On one hand, diffuse pollution exists due to several causes and also to heterogeneity of soil and substratum: identical farming practices can have different consequences according to their geographical location and to soil and climate conditions. On the other hand, one cannot speak of pollution or of the public

**Table 24.1.** Presentation of the problem.

A private company, in order to avoid an increase in the level of nitrates, wishes to take preventive measures concerning the farming practices of the perimeter.

Cause of the possible rise in nitrates: human activity including agriculture. Agriculture takes up practically the whole area and recent changes in farming systems (turning-over of meadow land, extension of corn, increase in fertilizers) seem to constitute a major cause of the rise in nitrates.

The company, wishing to prevent this increase, has asked INRA and the Chamber of Agriculture to propose some solutions.

The facts of the problem:
- a restricted area which is relatively well delimited: 5000 ha (diversity of soil);
- the actors involved (40 farmers, milk and cereal-gathering companies, farmers' organizations);
- milk (60,000 hl);
- cereals (8000 tonnes).

Compared with a traditional environmental problem, this is a particular case due to:
- major constraint arising from the nitrates level desired (10–15 mg $l^{-1}$);
- restricted area;
- the 'polluted' party is prepared to help the 'polluting' parties to curb nitrates leaching.

But one cannot speak of pollution as such, since the level is far below European standards. However, the private company could incur a prejudice with respect to its economic activity if water quality deteriorates due to intensive cropping practices.

domain in the legal sense. However, a private company could incur a prejudice since its economic activity is connected to water quality which could deteriorate as a result of farming practices (Brossier and Chia, 1990).

In fact, the resource subjected to externalities can be conceptualized as the space under the roots, which is an example of incompatible-use goods (Schmid, 1987). The farmer needs a place to keep amounts of non-utilized substances such as nitrates and the company also needs this underground space to 'stock' water. The institutional problem is to determine who owns this part of the subsoil which is destined for incompatible uses. Currently the farmers are the effective owners of the subsoil and use it to stock nitrates, up until the time when a better offer is made to them. Like any non-owner of a resource necessary to its production activity, the company is trying to buy land on the market so as to become the owner of this space under the roots.

This solution of land purchase appears to have limited prospects because, first, there have been few sellers of the land (at the end of 1993, only 20% of the whole surface was owned by the company) and also specifications are lacking together with a system for monitoring and control. The company probably would not need to have control of the entire area, but how much of it exactly? The heterogeneity of the soil and the uncertainty with regard to the movement of effluents and fluids rule out a precise response to this question at present. Therefore, the company has asked INRA to find a solution to make farming practices compatible with the desired level of water quality. The aim of the research undertaken by INRA is obviously to define the technical and economic details of these specifications, but more time is needed to implement the research.

## Research Programme

The question put to research is: which changes in farming practices and systems can be implemented, at one and the same time, to avoid an increase in the nitrates level, whilst maintaining competitive agriculture?

The research undertaken by INRA (see Fig. 24.1) is based on three main principles taken from systems modelling and the constructivist theory:

1. the holistic aspect of complex systems;
2. identification of interrelations between parties;
3. action-research approach in which the parties and the researchers are fully integrated in the process of research and change.

This project involves two branches of knowledge which must be associated. The first branch concerns the biotechnical and economic mechanisms held responsible for nitrogen leaks by localized agriculture. The simulation models generated are based on these mechanisms. The second branch of knowledge is the result of a collective approach to action-research involving all parties and includes the researchers themselves.

The general structure of the programme is based on an agrarian systems model, connecting the land with the operators and their activities. A diagram allows the main components to be identified. The hydrogeological, technical and socioeconomic aspects of the problem with their changes and interactions are taken into account and clarifies the negotiation necessary between the various partners involved (Fig. 24.1) (see also Deffontaines and Chia, 1992).

## Action-research

Each action-research project is specific and it is difficult to define a standard model [see Liu (1991) and Girin (1990) for basic principles and the main stages of action-research; see also Vallerand (Chapter 26) for further examples of action-research carried out by INRA–SAD]. In the present case, one of the

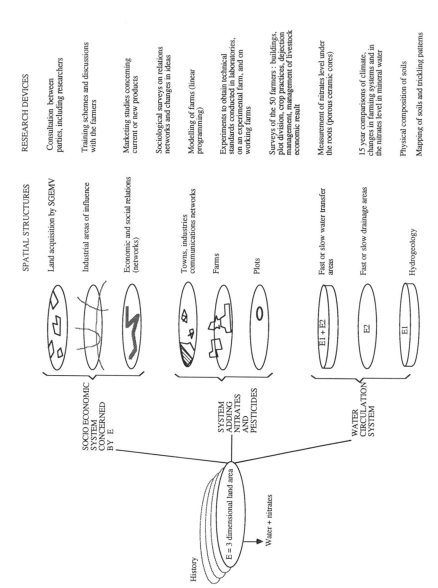

**Fig. 24.1.** Structure of the interdisciplinary research programme.

main particularities is that the request for changes (and therefore the funds needed for them) is made by a company, whereas the changes themselves concern other parties who are not particularly interested in them (or who possibly do not want them) and who are obviously not involved in funding the research. This action-research is the result of a plan for research formulated by a team and the desire of one party to change the activities of the other parties. One of the crucial points is to incorporate these parties in the action-research.

In order to illustrate this, the structure, the committees and teams, the partners and the scope of the negotiation are given below.

### Structure of this action-research

Figure 24.2 sets out the various operators involved in this AR. Three institutions have commissioned and are financing the research, and two of them are directly involved in it – these are the project managers who defined the general architecture of the programme. The project managers in the field leading the AR are INRA and the local Chamber of Agriculture.

Various committees and teams have been set up during the research programme. They answer a need for negotiation, arbitration, management and improvement of research performance (see Fig. 24.3).

#### Research management committee

This committee was called 4 + 1, because it was composed of the four team leaders plus the agricultural advisor hired by the research team to organize the contacts with the farmers. Its role is to determine responsibilities and

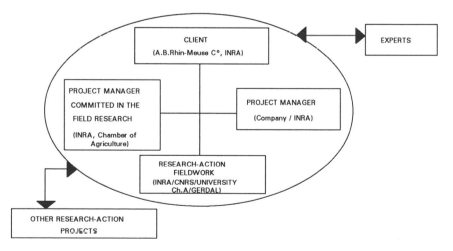

**Fig. 24.2.** Research-action system.

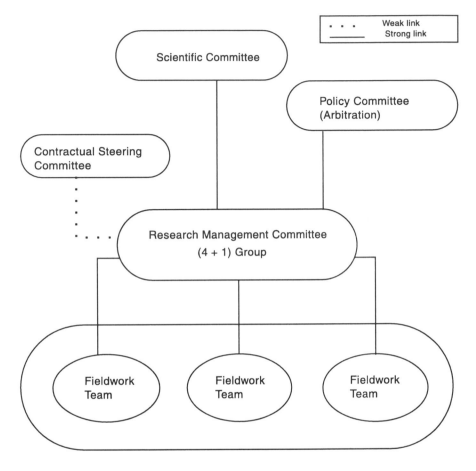

**Fig. 24.3.** Committees and teams.

activate research groups, fix priorities, manage the contacts and negotiate with various partners. At the end of the first stage in the programme, the advisor was hired by the mineral water company as manager of a new subsidiary in charge of contacts between the company and the farmers (these included contract negotiation and farm services to help farmers apply the technical aspects of the contract). This hiring was a source of difficulties in the relationship between INRA and the company, because the latter tried to push the research team into short-term expertise (preparation of files for Board of Trustees, for requesting subsidies, for direct farm negotiation, etc.).

## Contract steering committee

This was mandatory in the contract and brought clients and project managers together in order to ensure that the programme was carried out in accordance with the contract. Political conflicts with the Chamber of Agriculture prevented this committee from functioning well. In order to improve this situation, the INRA Board of Directors proposed to set up a *policy committee*, including the chairman of the Chamber of Agriculture, a Director of INRA, the Managing Director of the company and two representatives from the research team. This committee tried but had difficulties in settling the main political problems between the partners.

## Scientific committee

This committee is composed of renowned scholars in various disciplines relevant to the research but not involved in the research programme. Its two main objectives are scientific protection and openness. The scientific protection aspect ensures that the action and pressure of the clients are not an obstacle to either the scientific process or scientific progress, and helps the research team to keep a certain distance from the field. The scientific openness aspect is there to diversify the disciplines of the team, to specify scientific issues and find new ways of achieving scientific collaboration. The committee has proved to be an essential component of the research programme and its role is increasingly important.

## The main partners

The company is an international leader in the mineral water market. It is located in a rural area, where it is the main economic activity of the inhabitants.

The farms are family farms, managed by young farmers (about 40 years old). The farm families own two thirds of the land area. By French standards, the farm structure is good (87 ha) and so are economic efficiency and dynamism. The farming system is mainly based on cattle (milk), and cereals. The turnover of all farmers taken as a group represents about 2% of the company's turnover. Two dairy enterprises (private and cooperative) collect the milk. The other products are marketed mainly by the cooperatives.

## Negotiation

The negotiation covered:

- the programme (content, deadlines, partners, cost, etc.);
- the definition of the geographical perimeter;

- pollution limits (nitrates and pesticide constraints).

With reference to the last point, present knowledge on water circulation is not sufficient to allow the nitrates level in the under-roots zone to be set exactly to guarantee the 10 mg $l^{-1}$ level. Hence the research team wished to undertake research to clarify the connection. The company refused to finance this idea and asked the team to consider the 10 mg $l^{-1}$ level as the official target of the research. This solution is unsatisfactory and the issue remains under discussion between both parties. As far as pesticides are concerned (an even more difficult issue), the company refused to discuss this aspect and fixed a zero level for pesticides in the new technical proposals. Both objectives specified by the company have been accepted, being considered operational but temporary, in order to start up the programme.

Further, at the beginning of the negotiation the research team clearly stated that the objectives of the research were there not only to protect water resources but also to elaborate sustainable and economically efficient farming systems.

## Some Results

### *Modelling of the family-farm system* (Brossier *et al.*, 1992)

A double objective guided this research operation: on the one hand, creation of methodology and tools capable of testing the technical and economic consequences of the proposed changes, and on the other, economic analysis of the internal conditions (farms) and external conditions (organization, cooperation, partnership) for incorporating the costs of curbing pollution. With this action-research in view, the simulation model was an instrument in encouraging discussion. Making use of open and plausible interpretation of current and future situations, the discussions on the sensitivity of the results can help to define the issues at stake and the questions that need to be posed, by giving them an order of importance which can then be debated (Figs 24.4 and 24.5).

As shown, the two farmers in the simulation model find no satisfactory solutions. At the 10 mg $l^{-1}$ level, for example, the decrease in financial margins is more than FF100,000 for each farmer. When new technical and economic proposals (alfalfa, 20% price increase) are made, modelling shows that certain farming systems can be compatible with the demands of the company whilst giving returns comparable to those given by the current situation. Discussions on these figures showed that obtaining a similar gross margin is not sufficient for farmers to adopt these new systems. First, new investment is necessary, involving extra fixed costs and therefore lower income, and second, upheavals in farming systems and practices are not

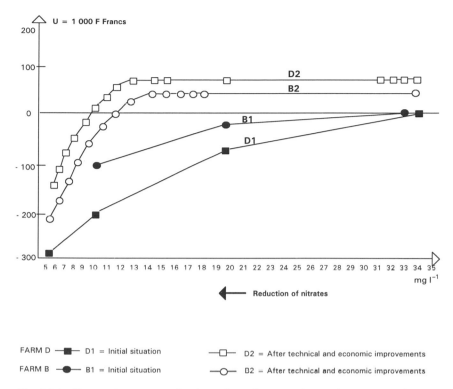

**Fig. 24.4.** Changes in gross margin of two farms in proportion to nitrates constraint.

justified if income remains comparable. A higher gross margin obtained by increased prices is then necessary.

Further, the model showed that the results were highly sensitive to variations in the annual nitrogen balance with respect to crop rotations and grassland. This sensitivity threshold is worth studying for two reasons: on the one hand, figures can sometimes be imprecise, leading to variations in margins; on the other, it indicates areas of research into the improvement of techniques. The discussion emphasizes the need for hypotheses to be clarified and also their degree of certainty. The research under way helps to illustrate this procedure. From a practical point of view, the recent debate on the constraint limit (10 mg l$^{-1}$ or more) using graphs showing marginal cost of the nitrogen constraint underlines the importance of negotiation between farmers and the company: what can the company do to help and how? A second programme under way (new contract) takes the above clarifications into consideration.

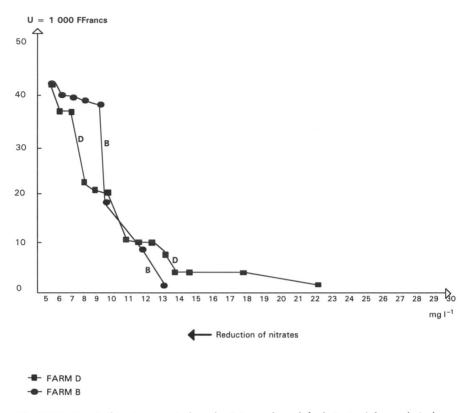

**Fig. 24.5.** Marginal cost − marginal productivity each mg l⁻¹ of nitrates (after technical and economic improvements).

## Consolidation of the project for change on the farms

Farmers on the perimeter have apparently no particular reason for adopting the proposals for technical change. Adoption of new practices by them depends as much on their individual situation as on the socioeconomic situation of which they are a part. If, from an individual point of view, it is advisable to make the farms as autonomous as possible, it is necessary for the related local structure to be very flexible so as to limit the technical, economic and social risks, because the project will cause much upheaval rather than just a change of production system. During a transitional phase, additional information will be needed by the farmers to help them master the new systems. Also, the technical and economic action should be backed up by a training system which will be implemented during the preliminary stage. Modelling enables the effects of the changes on the entire farm to be studied and analysed. However, one aspect of the problem that needs to be kept in mind is the collective dimension of local development. The negotiations between the various partners concern not only indemnity amounts and the new systems, but also monitoring and control devices.

### The role of INRA

The role of INRA in this research is to elaborate precise technical specifications for water circulation and for the development of less 'pollutive' crops, and to define a method for monitoring and control. However, the study of relationships creates a need for aids and devices that, although not unusual in research, imply the consideration of several disciplines and several levels of analysis: the research must deal with a multitude of factors from *bougies poreuses* (porous ceramic cores) to the common economic interests shared by the group (GIE). In addition, INRA is dealing with the project using an action-research procedure, and all the parties and the researchers are involved in the process of knowledge gathering and change.

We are therefore in the domain of objective-orientated research using a research and development technique. The demands of a research project of this kind are both legitimate and stimulating. Nevertheless, a risk is attached in undertaking research which needs to meet the demands of the company, the reservations of the agricultural organizations and the expectations of the farmers, all the more so because the problem has yet to be completely identified and defined. The research will help in this identification, gradually eliminating uncertainties and disagreements connected with time length, the information available and the changing projects of actor groups. This means accepting the need to adjust and even at times to steer the research as it progresses, with consideration given to the scientific limits set. The first step, as identified by Simon (Newell and Simon, 1972), is problem finding rather than problem solving and we hope we have supplied here the means to accomplish this.

## Conclusions

Entering into an active phase of the changes entails the implementation of this first set of proposals which, in view of current knowledge, appears to correspond best to the objectives set. The framework for the changes needs to be enlarged and further defined by the introduction of additional knowledge, by scientific monitoring and by negotiation and on-going evaluation devices, incorporated into the research programme. A second action-research has already been negotiated and is entitled *practice and theory of change*. The new action-research project has benefited from the difficulties encountered during the first stage.

We feel that a participatory approach is inescapable when dealing with complex issues such as those presented here. It is a frustrating and time-consuming process, requiring negotiation expertise, which is not generally recognized and valued in scientific circles, but is essential for research. The success of such an exercise depends on having partner groups who are also co-producers of the solutions, because the solutions cannot be imposed whatever their intrinsic technical qualities. In the present case, we think that implementation is proving both difficult and slow owing to a lack of farmer participation, so we are currently trying out new initiatives in order to increase their involvement.

Another important aspect of successful action-research is to put the various committees to good use. The first programme proved inadequate here, so we have ensured that in the second programme the steering committees function more efficiently and that more support is forthcoming from the scientific committee.

# References

Brossier, J., Benoit, M., Falloux, J.C., Gaury, F. and Pierre, Ph. (1992) Agricultural practices, underground water quality and research development project. Modelling of nitrogen constraint in several farms. XXIV EAAE Seminar. In: Loseby, M. (ed.) *The Environment and the Management of Agricultural Resources*. European Association of Agricultural Economists, Viterbo, pp. 201–216.

Brossier, J. and Chia, E. (1990) Pratiques agricoles et qualité de l'eau. Construction d'une recherche-développement dans le cas d'un périmètre hydrominéral. *Economie Rurale* 199, 6–13.

Deffontaines, J.P., Benoit, M., Brossier, J., Chia, E., Gras, F. and Roux, M. (1993) *Agriculture et Qualité des Eaux, Diagnostic et Propositions pour un Périmètre de Protection*. INRA, Paris, 336 pp.

Deffontaines, J.P. and Chia, E. (1992) Une recherche-action sur un système agraire soumis à des impératifs de qualité de l'eau. Résultats et bilans méthodologique. *Comptes Rendus de l'Academie d'Agriculture de France* 78 (7), 65–75.

Farrington, J. and Martin, A. (1988) *Farmer Participation in Agricultural Research: a Review of Concepts and Practices*. ODI Occasional Paper No. 9, ODI, London.

Girin, J. (1990) Analyse empirique des situations de gestion: éléments de théorie et de méthodes. In: Martinet, A.C. (ed.), *Epistémologie et Sciences de Gestion, Economica*, pp. 141–182.

Godard, O. (1984) Autonomie socio-économique et externalisation de l'environnement. La théorie néoclassique mise en perspective. *Economie Appliquée* 37 (2).

Lewin, K. (1947) Frontiers in group dynamics, I, II. *Human Relations* 1, 5–41 and 143–154.

Liu, M. (1992) Présentation de la recherche-action: définition, déroulement et résultats. *Revue Internationale de Systémique* 6, 293–311.

Newell, A. and Simon, H.A. (1972) *Human Problem Solving*. Prentice Hall, Englewood Cliffs, New Jersey.

Schmid, A. (1987) *Property, Power and Public Choice*, 2nd edn. Praeger, New York.

# 25

## THE ROLE OF FARMING SYSTEMS RESEARCH/EXTENSION IN GUIDING LOW INPUT SYSTEMS TOWARDS SUSTAINABILITY:
## An Agroecological Approach for Andalusia

*Eduardo Sevilla Guzmán and ISEC Team*

### Farming Systems Research and Agroecology as Strategies to Agricultural Technology Development

The term 'farming systems research' (FSR) is used to describe a range of activities with varied objectives and approaches that for many years have usually been associated with agricultural research. It was the uneven effects of the green revolution transfer of technology model of agricultural research and extension that prompted a focus on systems thinking and the development of a more client-sensitive systems approach to the prioritizing and implementation of research. This diversity of approaches in FSR has caused confusion over its role in agricultural development. Projects to devise new, often technically sustainable or economically optimal farming systems have come under the FSR umbrella (Gibbon, 1992).

In general, FSR introduces an interdisciplinary focus, including sociology and economy, a systems perspective and a more equal participation of researcher and farmer in the design of new technology in the research set-up. The approach is intended to overcome environmental and socioeconomic problems caused by standard agricultural technology generation. However, although in European countries conventional agricultural technology generation has also produced detrimental socioeconomic and environmental effects, few proposals for an alternative attitude towards agricultural technology design have been developed. As far as we know, only in The Netherlands (research on arable farming, Vereijken, 1992) and in Spain, France and The Netherlands (research on pumpkins, Groupe Expérimental Pluridisciplinaire, 1992) are on-farm research projects going on in organic agriculture, both financed by the EC.

It is necessary to distinguish between a technological answer to environmental problems and a methodological answer to the problems in the design process of agricultural technology. In Europe, the first answer has arisen from organic agriculture movements. This answer, however, has been small scale and until now has had only a limited projection into the agricultural sector. Although these movements question implicitly the design process of technology, the most substantial contribution to the second answer has come from FSR and participatory technology development (PTD) approaches as developed in the Third World and critiques on the philosophy of science developed from within the universities (Ploeg, 1987; Chambers *et al.*, 1989; Cornwall *et al.*, 1992; Scoones and Thompson, 1992).

Within FSR and PTD, there are a host of approaches. Merrill-Sands (1986) gives a highlighting view on the different types of FSR that had been carried out to that date. There is a huge variety of delimitations of the object and pretentions of research that leads her to speak about 'research with a farming systems perspective (FSP)' rather than about FSR. She distinguishes seven key concepts of FSR, to which the various 'perspectives' in various degrees adhere: farmer oriented, systems oriented, problem solving, interdisciplinary, complementary to commodity and disciplinary research, central role of on-farm experimentation, and farmer participation and feedback to on-station research. Gibbon (1992), who in his contribution to the first CAMAR seminar gave a broad overview of characteristics and weak and strong points of FSR, basically distinguishes the same features, adding a holistic perspective and a dynamic and iterative development of the research project. Cornwall *et al.* (1992) discuss the recent development of participatory methodologies.

In spite of all this, the FSR approach was pioneered by the international centres involved in developing and extending agricultural innovations to peasants in the Third World, especially in Latin America. In effect, the Centro Internacional de Mejoramiento de Maíz y Trigo (CIMMYT), Centro Agronómico Tropical de Investigación y Enseñanza (CATIE), Centro Internacional de la Papa (CIP) and Centro Internacional de Agricultura Tropical (CIAT) have been working in the last decade with this approach, which entails an understanding of what farmers are doing, why they have chosen their current practices and what is required for them to accept a new technology. Although these international centres have emphasized research efforts that encourage peasant participation, focus is still placed on increasing commodity production through high-yielding varieties accompanied by a set of chemical pesticides and fertilizers. Following Miguel Altieri, we think that although the participation of social scientists is novel in farming systems research programmes their efforts seem to be subordinated to the need expressed by plant breeders to understand why farmers are adopting the new varieties. In other words, the mission of social scientists in agricultural research seems constrained to overcome the social barriers that limit the adoption by peasants of the technology developed by centres (Altieri and Hecht, 1989).

The agroecological approach we are trying to implement in marginalized regions and social classes in Andalusia aims to improve subsistence production using new technologies of ecological farming to improve the welfare of these rural populations. To reconcile agricultural development with the needs and capacities of the peasants in the communities, we must account for their enormous diversity – in terms of ecology, population pressures, economic relations and social organization. Viewed from a strictly technological standpoint, this complexity is often missed. Agroecology, as a novel approach to agricultural development, facilitates the consideration of diversity by including in its criteria, along with increased production, biological stability, resource conservation, sustainability and equity. Such an approach would reinforce the ecological basis necessary to new agricultural systems.

Some Andalusian agroecological systems, such as the Alpujarra region or the dehesa areas, are very similar to those described by Altieri in Latin America: 'characterized by complex cropping systems which generally exhibit several ecological properties such as biological diversity, nutrient recycling capabilities, risk aversion, soil and water conservation features, pest suppressive potential, among others.'; thus, we concur with Altieri in saying: 'those desirable elements of traditional agriculture should be identified and retained in the course of agricultural modernization and used as starting points in any process of technology development' (Altieri, 1989).

## On-farm Research, Agroecology and Endogenous Development

On-farm research is a relatively new approach in agricultural technology development. Its roots lie in the Third World, where the green revolution provoked doubts about conventional technology generation. There on-farm research has been concieved as one of the central parts of FSR.

To approach the relationship between on-farm research and development, we first introduce the concept of 'social form of farming.' A social form of farming (SFF) is defined by 'the specific articulation of human labour, knowledge, the natural resources and the means of production aimed at, while transforming and consuming these resources, the production and reproduction of goods and necessary services, at every historical moment' (González de Molina and Sevilla Guzmán, 1992). What we need to do in the perspective of on-farm research in endogenous development is to scrutinize ways in which SFFs can be strengthened, building upon the elements of these SFFs. An important aspect is then the degree of control the articulating agent has over the changes brought upon his/her SFF. The pace, scale and nature of the generation of information and experiences in the development of the technology are hence crucial.

As Sumberg and Okali (1989) point out, an on-farm trial does not equal on-farm research. This depends very much on the degree to which the farmer has been involved in the set-up, management and implementation of the trial (see also Norman and Collinson, 1985). In our view, the key points of successful on-farm research lie in the process of definition of the problem to be solved and in the process of designing and implementing a new technology. In these two processes, we attribute vital importance to, on the one hand, a genuine farmer participation and on the other, to the embedment of the on-farm research in the rural context. We consider these elements crucial to the potential of on-farm research to contribute to endogenous development.

So far in mainstream OFR, farmers have only been part of the processes in an almost accidental way. It is striking, for example, that on-farm researchers such as Harrington *et al.* (1989) in an article that discusses on-farm client-oriented research (OFCOR), a 'subset of FSR,' as they themselves define it, involve the farmers only in the assessment phase of new technology. They then continue to argue that the farming participatory research approach (what we call here PTD) is a form of OFCOR, 'that was developed as a response to perceptions that normal cropping systems research or on-farm adaptive research are inefficient or inadequate when dealing with certain very complex kinds of technologies,' explaining complex technologies as 'those in which large numbers of decisions have to be made in defining an experimental treatment.' It is a rather cynical way of saying that when the real world is easy, science can do it alone, but if it becomes too complicated, science needs the help of farmers. To us, PTD is a form of on-farm research whose concept evolved through the 1980s and that stresses above all the importance of participation of the farmer in the diagnostic process of agricultural problems and in the design process of answers to them, for which it has generated a wide range of methodologies. It underlines the importance of local knowledge and, time and again, more than other approaches, stresses the need for a reversal of attitudes of scientists towards farmer agriculture and his or her knowledge (Chambers, 1989). This type of approach is known as 'farmers first' (Chambers *et al.*, 1989). We agree with this approach and our arguments are twofold. First, it has already frequently been demonstrated that farmers' farming (or local, traditional, indigenous farming as opposed to scientific farming) has a great agroecological validity, gained through years of experience and experimentation (Altieri, 1987). Through time, farmers have gained a profound knowledge on their environment and the possibilities and limitations of their land. Second, the farming activity is a holistic activity. For this reason, a farmer is better able to identify and assess the importance of the research items in the context of his household and overall rural development than is a researcher. Hence a farmer may cut across disciplinary biases that even the best intentioned researchers suffer from.

A basic assumption of our idea of farmer participation is the diversity of farming. Usually there is a richness of (incipient) answers to the problems present in the area that have been developed or tried out by the farmers themselves. Some have a fine-tuned management of green manures to restore soil fertility, others know how to make optimum use of scarce rainfall, another has succesfully developed terraces, others know how to anticipate cow diseases and some know well how to minimize labour costs. When the goal is a sustainable land use system in an endogenous development perspective, then the indicated way is to bring these answers together on one farm. This could be an experimental farm, or could be any of the farms of the interested farmers through an exchange of the information between them. Grillo Fernández (1990) speaks in this respect about 'horizontal diffusion', as opposed to the 'vertical diffusion' model of the transfer of technology from science to farmer. This 'revitalization of local knowledge' is one aspect of farmer participation. Another refers to the size and the type of the field trials. These should articulate with the farmer experimentation, and should be conceived in a dynamic and iterative way, close to the trial and error method farmers' manage in their own experiments. We think that the principal role of on-farm research in some cases may be that of a mere catalyst or encourager of farmer experiments. It is therefore important to note that a statistically adequate layout of a trial that may allow for extension to other zones is less important than a useful technique (Sumberg and Okali, 1989). However, from an agroecological perspective the main aspect of farmer research participation is to accept that people can, to at large extent, identify and modify their own solutions for their needs, within their cultural identity. Researchers should support farmers in order to increase their capacity to manage change in their farming systems. Agroecological participation aims to empower social groups to obtain greater access to and over resources and decision making (Haverkort *et al.*, 1991).

Another criticism that could be made of mainstream FSR is that it suffers mostly from an agricultural and productivist bias. Although 'the primary objective of FSR is to improve the well-being of individual farming families', it reduces the way to achieve this to 'increasing the productivity of their farming system' (Norman and Collinson, 1985). Usually this aim is already present at the onset of the research, and the research is then focused on the discovery of the 'causes' of the low production. However, agriculture may be not so central to the farmer as it is to the researcher: many farmers are involved in various rural activities. Although this, on the one hand, seemingly facilitates on-farm trials, as the farmer has other sources of income available, on the other hand he may not be willing to take risks with the little land he has. The size of the experiment should hence correspond to the farmers' ability to take risks.

What is questioned here is the position of the research project relative to the rural setting. The idea is not to adapt the region to the research project, but the other way around, to adapt the research project to the region. Scheuermeier (1988) also calls for this basic attitude in a very interesting approach termed 'approach development'. This implies that we conceive the development of technology as a learning process, in which objectives and methods should be continously readjusted in an iterative way. The farmer first approach also stresses this learning aspect (IDS Workshop, 1989a,b) but in our view fails to position agricultural technology generation adequately in the context of overall rural development. Also, links with other institutional activities should be taken into account, such as those of the local extension service and the development plans developed by the administration if they are really solutions for farmers' needs. For the agroecological approach it is very important to ensure the future development of the method and to create synergetic effects. The learning process at the same time implies that the research goes slowly forward, step by step.

## Does Ecological Farming Require a Different Approach?

Most of the recent research with an FSR perspective aims to contribute to 'sustainable' land use systems. A systems approach should guarantee this, since it would provide the research with a holistic view that enables one to assess the effect of changes in one element of the system (e.g. a modified sowing technique) along the interlinkages that exist. In reality, the systems approach is present to various differing extents, which is, according to Merrill-Sands (1986), one of the ambiguities of FSR. Harrington *et al.* (1989) emphasize especially the role that the system perspective plays in the structuring of the planning and evaluation process. Merrill-Sands then attributes great importance to the lack of precision in the definition of the boundaries of the system, whereas she considers this definition 'a fundamental step ... because it determines which factors are to be treated as endogenous variables and which as exogenous parameters' (p. 96). We believe, however, that too strict a definition may be in conflict with the learning and iterative aspects of the research. We propose to work with a range of variables and parameters that represent a shifting degree of variability, closer to a 'soft-systems approach' (Checkland, 1981). Moreover, we think that the real issue of sustainability refers mostly to the operationalization of the concept and to the level at which the systems approach is applied.

When we refer to a sustainable land use system, we speak about 'a system that minimizes the flows of inputs and products that proceed from non-renewable resources outside the production area and that at the same time maintains or augments the internal flows of matter, energy and information of this area, is compatible with or even impulses the social and cultural values of the rural communties and allows enough profitability to reach an adequate income without consuming its own future reproduction through an over-exploitation of the local natural resources'. In a European context we speak about ecological agriculture. In our view, then, the approach that stands closest to ours would be one of the PTD approaches, called low external input sustainable agriculture (LEISA) (Reijntjes *et al.*, 1992). It is based on agroecology and intends to deduce from ecology principles that can be applied to agriculture. Another important issue that we share with LEISA is the importance we attribute to drawing upon local agricultural knowledge and farming systems, since they mostly exihibit many facets of an organic system (Altieri, 1991; Remmers, 1993). Conway (1985) also uses the systems approach in a way more similar to ours. His contribution lies, in our view, in the way he operationalizes the systems concept. The approach presupposes a workshop environment that allows for multidisciplinarity and reduces professional biases. The analysis is made according to patterns discerned in time, space, flows and decisions, to be able finally to qualify the properties of the land use system (at various levels, including crop, farm, watershed and village), productivity, sustainability, stability and equitability, which are indicators of its performance.

It is necessary to stress the difference between ecological farming at farm level and ecological farming at landscape level, this being understood as the whole of social forms of farming in a biogeographic unit. On many current farms in Europe that claim to practice ecological farming, emphasis is laid on the substitution of conventional inputs with organic ones, reflected, e.g. in the definition the USDA uses for organic farming

> organic farming is a production system which avoids or broadly excludes the use of synthetic fertilizers, pesticides, growth regulators and additives in the concentrates. As far as possible, the organic farming systems are based on crop rotations, agricultural subproducts, manure, legumes plants, green manures, organic wastes, mineral rocks and biological pest control, in order to maintain the productivity of both soil and crop, to supply nutrients to the plants and to control insects, weeds and diseases
>
> (USDA, 1980)

and in some of the normative definitions of hallmark organizations for ecological agriculture (cf. definition of the Spanish Regulatory Board on Ecological Agriculture; CRAE, 1990). This interpretation of ecological farming, however, is not sustainable on a landscape level, where, as Lowrance *et al.* (1986) argue, 'the aggregated and synergic effects of economic and agricultural individual practices become visible.' [At the same time, this interpretation of ecological agriculture permits capitalist production structures to enter in ecological farming, whereas these, paradoxically, are at the heart of the current environmental crisis, as has been argued by González de Molina and Sevilla Guzmán (1993).] One farm may produce ecological horticultural products using animal manure purchased in the area, but if all farmers were to base their soil fertility on purchased manure, in many cases there would be not enough of it locally if there is no communication between the farmers, so that a dependence on nutrients from outside the area would be created. For this reason, the agroecological design of a farm should aim at developing a self-regulating capacity with respect to pest control and flows of nutrients and energy, while at the same time acknowledging the need for an adequate coordination of complementary activities of colleague farmers.

Hence the basic difference we attribute to on-farm research in ecological agriculture can be summarized as follows. First, the innovation should be based on the farmer-managed biotic and abiotic diversity of the agroecosystem, as the complexity of the agroecosystem is one of the bases of ecological farming. Second, it requires a systems approach operationalized at both farm and landscape levels, instead of at crop level as occurs in conventional FSR. Although FSR pretends to manage a systems perspective, in our view in many cases this perspective is reduced to cause–effect relationships that, despite the interdisciplinarity which might be involved, are modelled according to a preset and narrow-focused outcome: increased production. This, then, might be a valid approach, in some cases, for conventional farming, but it is not for ecological farming, where 'externalities' and long-term effects should be taken into account. Therefore, and this is the third feature that makes on-farm research in ecological agriculture different from on-farm research in conventional agriculture, the research objectives we would initially think of are not in terms of either increased commodity production or substitution of conventional by organic inputs, but refer to the performance of the 'social forms of farming' in a given area, in which the trade-off of the enhancement of certain system properties on others should be evaluated.

## How Ecological Agriculture Articulates with Endogenous Rural Development

Having established above some vital characteristics of the relationship of on-farm research (OFR) to ecological agriculture (EA) and endogenous rural development (ERD), the link between EA and ERD is, in our view, as follows.

ERD has been defined by the ISEC as 'the promotion and establishment of decentralized microeconomic and cultural activities that, with a strong component of local decision making, mobilize the population of a certain area to seek its well-being, defined by its folkloric cultural resources, through an optimal use of its own human and material resources' (López Calvo *et al.*, 1992). We perceive that ERD is an expression of the synergetic effects of activities that originate at the level of the SFF. At that level, and with respect to agriculture, we refer to activities that enhance:

**1.** the design of the agroecological diversity of the SFF [annual crops, trees, animals (both in temporal and in spatial sequences: rotations, plant associations, etc.) and ecological infrastructure (e.g. hedgerows)];
**2.** farmer control over the agricultural activity (with respect to external

inputs such as pesticides, fertilizers, financement, knowledge); and
**3.** an optimal use of local resources (flows of water and soil expressed as soil and water conservation, nutrient recycling and multiple land use).

These aspects could express themselves at a synergetic level as conservation and increase of environmental values and biodiversity (autochthonous species, ecosystem variety), uncontaminated production conditions that allow for a common commercialization strategy (e.g. as a cooperative) through a 'denomination of origin' of a 'quality product' and local nurseries of locally used crops. The multiple land use strategy and the ecological infrastructure allow for the recuperation of autonomous products (such as forest mushrooms, fruits and asparagus) (Acosta Naranjo, 1992) and traditional quality definitions. Multiple use suggests also the stabilization of farmer rents and employment opportunities. The optimum use of natural resources allows for the accumulation of water reserves and a reduction in nutrient losses.

It must be stressed, however, that the synergism is not produced automatically. This is a result of the articulation of the individual 'development projects' of the individual SFF, and of the articulation of these with the 'development projects' of the administrative and institutional research bodies (Ploeg, 1993). In this chapter we have discussed in which way OFR could contribute to this, and proposed farmer participation in the diagnosis and design process of new technology and an embedment in a rural context as two of the prerequisites. Here we could add that, as far as the contacts between research and farmer reality are concerned, regular study meetings between farmers, researchers and extension officers, field days and commonly undertaken field trips and community walks ( IDS Workshop, 1989c; Norman *et al.*, 1989; Vereijken, personal communication, cited in Remmers *et al.*, 1992a) could be valuable tools to enhance linkages among farmers and between farmers, research and extension.

# Conclusions

Several authors argue that, in general, FSR lacks explicit engagement with resource-poor farmers or peasants. The systems approach tends to depoliticize the research (Oasa, 1985) if no explicit attention is paid to the analysis of power relations. Thus, FSR will tend to reproduce existing power relations (Jackson, 1982). We try to overcome this problem by choosing a qualitative approach and by explicitly choosing to work with marginalized groups in marginalized regions. However, we acknowledge that in some cases there still exists a field of tension that we have not yet completely resolved.

Finally, we can summarize what we consider to be the basic characteristics of the ISEC approach in guiding low-input systems towards sustainability:

**1.** the main attention is given to the so-called 'marginalized' regions and rural social classes;

**2.** it is considered a learning process; it has a stepwise character, and we try to adapt the course of our project to the dynamic needs of the cases we study, instead of adjusting the rural reality to our project set-up;

**3.** the focus is on heterogeneity and diversity of farmers instead of on representativity;

**4.** for the last-mentioned reason our work is more qualitative than quantitative;

**5.** it intends to build upon locally existing agroecosystems and agricultural knowledge;

**6.** it intends to build upon locally existing forms of social organization;

**7.** it starts from a problem definition in a rural context: we try to avoid an agricultural bias;

**8.** the diagnosis of the present situation derives from an analysis with a historical perspective.

These eight characteristics are the fruit of the discusions held in our team so far and characterize the attitude in our studies. However, in all of the cases in which we intend to grow towards on-farm research (ISEC, 1992), they have been translated into locally adapted ways of working.

Currently, we work with two groups of agricultural land labourers ('jornaleros') and two group of small farmers in the dehesa and mountain agroecosystems. The groups of jornaleros both have a long history of struggle for land. However, they are different in their social structure, motivation and ideology. Both groups asked the ISEC to assist them with regard to ecological agriculture. The group in Villamartin (province of Cádiz) currently consists of nine persons who coherently work a farm of 6 ha. On-farm research there is already a fact; the goals and our role are clear. The focus is limited to the development of technology for that specific cooperative. In 1992 it was started with a small trial on ecological pumpkin growing; gradually the whole farm design will be the subject of discussions between ISEC and the cooperative (Avila Cano, 1992).

In the village of Marinaleda (province of Seville), the jornaleros acquired 1100 ha of land. Although 10 ha have already been worked in an ecological fashion since 1991, the use and management of the rest of the land is under continuous discussion. Among the approximately 180 members of the newly founded cooperative, there is a lack of clarity of goals and therefore our own role is sometimes not very clear. Both in Villamartin and in Marinaleda, it is difficult to build new agroecosystems upon traditional farming systems; the villages are set in areas with 'modern' agriculture, and the inherited agricultural knowledge of the jornaleros is of a fragmented nature (Amian Novales, 1992).

The third case concerns the Contraviesa, a mountainous region within the Alpujarra, south of Granada. The initial focus was a cooperative for ecological wine composed of almost 30 family farmers. However, it was strongly sensed that agricultural technology development there has much more sense if defined in a regional context. The on-farm research intends to bring together valuable solutions that the farmers have for different problems; the local agroecosystems are a valuable source for this. Efforts have been undertaken to establish a 'local working group', in which agronomic problems are discussed (Remmers, 1992).

The fourth case is the Dehesa agroecosystem. This second mountain case is focused on three villages, where a team made up of an anthropologist and an agronomist is carrying out a study concerning the 'dehesa', a complex agroecosystem that integrates livestock, forestry and agriculture with an important basis on traditional knowledge. In the last 40 years, it has suffered drastic social and economic transformations due to the introduction of the capitalist rationality. Because of this, the area is nowadays inmersed in a process of social and ecological degradation. Although we have not begun any experiments on on-farm research, the diversity of 'styles of farming' existing in the area has been recognized and the ancient ecological knowledge is being detected and characterized as grounds for making a future proposal for institutional action.

In all of the literature consulted emphasis is laid on the fact that there is no such thing as an 'ideal' model of agricultural research. No-one suggests that with on-farm research on-station research would become useless and without sense, and all stress the need for fundamental research. It is called 'complementarity of research' (IDS Workshop, 1989b), a 'toolbox approach to technology development' (Harrington *et al.*, 1989) or 'multiple source model' (Biggs, 1990). We agree with this point. None the less, as on-farm research is so new in Spain, there is still no institutional set-up to make the link between problems that remain unanswered in the field. For the moment, this is not the focus of our attention: the scale is too unbalanced in Andalusia. First, the farmers should speak.

# Acknowledgements

The authors have already carried out research on the same subject, part of which has necessarily been incorporated here, although obviously in a revised form (Sevilla Guzmán, 1991; Sevilla Guzmán and González de Molina, 1991a,b, 1993; ISEC, 1992; Remmers *et al.*, 1992). R. Acosta, I. Amian Novales, Jose Carlos Avila Cano, Gloria Guzmán Casado, Jesus Oarra Orellana, Gaston Remmers, Fernando Sanchez de Puerto and Juan Antonio Salas Mesa are part of the ISEC Research Team.

# References

Acosta Naranjo, R. (1992) The dehesa: arguments for a case study. In: *Proceedings of the CAMAR Seminar 'Endogenous Regional Development in Europe: Theory, Method and Practice,' Vila Real, Portugal, November 4–5 1991.* European Commission DG VI, Brussels, pp. 187–218.

Altieri, M.A. (1987) *The Scientific Basis of Agroecology.* Westview Press, Boulder, Colorado.

Altieri, M.A. (1989) Agroecology and rural development in Latin America. In: Altieri, M.A. and Hectht, S.B. (eds) *Agroecology and Small Farm Development.* CRC Press, Boston.

Altieri, M.A. (1991) ¿Porqué estudiar la agricultura tradicional? *Agroecología y Desarrollo* 1 (1) 25–36.

Altieri, M.A. and Hecht, S.B. (eds) (1989) *Agroecology and Small Farm Development.* CRC Press, Boston.

Amian Novales, I. (1992) Marinaleda: symbol and protagonist of the historical struggle for land among Andalusian agricultural day-workers. In: *Proceedings of the CAMAR Seminar 'Endogenous Regional Development in Europe: Theory, Method and Practice,' Vila Real, Portugal, November 4–5 1991.* European Commission DG VI, Brussels, pp. 171–186.

Archetti, E.P. and Skein, A. (1978) Peasants studies: an overview. In: Newby, H. (ed.) *International Perspectives in Rural Sociology.* Wiley, Chichester, pp. 107–127.

Avila Cano, J.C. (1992) Ecological horticulture in a 'latifundist' context: the cooperative experience of landless peasants in Andalusia (southern Spain). In: *Proceedings of the CAMAR Seminar 'Endogenous Regional Development in Europe: Theory, Method and Practice,' Vila Real, Portugal, November 4–5 1991.* European Commission DG VI, Brussels, pp. 95–131.

Biggs, S.D. (1990) A multiple source of innovation model of agricultural research and technology promotion. *World Development* 18 (11), 1481–1499.

Cernea, M.M., Coulter, J.K. and Russell, J.F.A. (1984) A two-way continuum for agricultural development. Research extension farmer. Paper presented at World Bank and UNDP Symposium, Washington, DC.

Chambers, R. (1989) Reversals, institutions and change. In: Chambers, R., Pacey, A. and Thrupp, L.A. (eds) *Farmer First: Farmer Innovation and Agricultural Research.* Intermediate Technology Publications, London.

Chambers, R., Pacey, A. and Thrupp, L.A. (eds) (1989) *Farmer First: Farmer Innovation and Agricultural Research.* Intermediate Technology Publications, London.

Checkland, P. (1981) Rethinking a systems approach. *Journal of Applied Systems Analysis* 8, 3–14.

Conway, G.R. (1985) Agroecosystem analysis. *Agricultural Administration* 20, 31–55.

Cornwall, A., Guijt, I. and Welbourn, A. (1992) Acknowledging process: challenges for agricultural research and extension methodology. Overview paper No. 2 of the IIED/IDA Workshop 'Beyond Farmer First: Rural People's Knowledge, Agricultural Research and Extension Practice,' University of Sussex, 27–29 October, p. 34.

CRAE (1990) *Reglamento y Normas Técnicas.* Ministerio de Agricultura, Pesca y Alimentación, Consejo Reguladorde la Agricultura Ecológica, Servicio de Extensión Agraria, Madrid.

Gibbon, D. (1992) Farming Systems Research for sustainable agriculture: the need for institutional innovation, participation and iterative approaches. In: *Proceedings of the CAMAR Seminar 'Endogenous Regional Development in Europe: Theory, Method and Practice,' Vila Real, Portugal, November 4–5 1991.* European Commission DG VI, Brussels, pp. 29–43.

Giner, S. and Sevilla Guzmán, E. (1977) The latifundio as a local mode of class domination: the andalusian case. *Iberian Studies* 6 (2) 47–58.

González de Molina, M. and Sevilla Guzmán, E. (1991a) Minifundio y gran propiedad agraria: estabilidad y cambio en la Alta Andalucía. In: Saavedra, P. and Vilclares, R. (eds) *Señores y Campesinos en la Península Ibérica, Siglos XVIII–XX.* Crítica, Barcelona, pp. 88–138.

González de Molina, M. and Sevilla Guzmán, E. (1991b) Movimiento jornalero y andalucismo histórico. In Berramedi, J. G. and Ramón Maíz (eds) *Los Nacionalismos en la España de la II República (Madrid:Siglo XXI).*

González de Molina, M. and Sevilla Guzmán, E. (1992) Una propuesta de diálogo entre socialismo y ecología: el neopopulismo ecológico. *Ecología Política* 3, 121–135.

González de Molina, M. and Sevilla Guzmán, E. (1993) Ecologia, campesinado e historia: para una reinterpretacion del dessarrollo del capitalismo en la agricutura. In: Sevilla Guzmán, E. and González de Molina, M. (eds) *Ecologia, Campesinado e Historia.* La Piqueta, Madrid, pp. 23–130.

Grillo Fernández, E. (1990) *Sistemas Campesinas de Investigación y Experimentación.* Documento de estudio No. 19, PRATEC, Lima, 19 pp.

Groupe Expérimental Pluridisciplinaire (1992) *Agronomic and Nutritional Research for the Valorization of Previously-grown Varieties of Pumpkin so as to Introduce Them onto the Organic Farming Market.* First Consolidated Progress Report to the EEC.

Harrington, L.W., Read, M.D., Garrity, D.P., Woolley, J. and Tripp, R. (1989) Approaches to on-farm client oriented research: similarities, differences and future directions. In: Sukmana, S., Amir, P. and Mulyadi, D.M. (eds) *Developments in Procedures for Farming Systems Research, Proceedings of an International Workshop, 13–17 March 1989, Puncak, Bogor, Indonesia.* Agency for Agricultural Research and Development.

Haverkort, B., Kamp, J. van der and Waters-Bayer, A. (eds) (1991) *Joining Farmers' Experiments. Experiences in Participatory Technology Development.* Intermediate Technology Publications, London.

IDS Workshop (1989a) Interactive research. In: Chambers, R., Pacey, A. and Thrupp, L.A. (eds) *Farmer First: Farmer Innovation and Agricultural Research.* Intermediate Technology Publications, London, pp. 100–105.

IDS Workshop (1989b) Final reflections about on-farm research methods. In: Chambers, R., Pacey, A. and Thrupp, L.A. (eds) *Farmer First: Farmer Innovation and Agricultural Research.* Intermediate Technology Publications, London, pp. 157–161.

IDS Workshop (1989c) Farmers' groups and workshops. In: Chambers, R., Pacey, A. and Thrupp, L.A. (eds) *Farmer First: Farmer Innovation and Agricultural Research.* Intermediate Technology Publications, London, pp. 122–126.

ISEC (1992) Ecological agriculture in Andalusia, Spain: preliminary results of four focusses of study. In: *Proceedings of the CAMAR Seminar 'Farm Household Strategies and Styles of Farming: Typologies for Designing Sustainable Agriculture'.* Vila Real, Portugal, 4–5 November 1991.

Jackson, M.A. (1982) The nature of 'soft' systems thinking: the work of Churman, Ackoff and Checkland. *Journal of Applied Systems Analysis* 9, 17–29.

López Calvo, L., Salas Mesa, J.A. and Sevilla Guzmán, E. (1992) Towards an empirical definition of the concept of human potential of endogenous development. Paper presented at the Second CAMAR Seminar 'Strengthening Endogenous Development Patterns in European Agriculture,' Chania, Crete, 20–22 October 1992.

Lowrance, R., Hendrix, P.F. and Odum, E.P. (1986) A hierarchical approach to sustainability. *American Journal of Alternative Agriculture* 1 (4), 169–173.

Merrill-Sands, D. (1986) Farming Systems Research: clarification of terms and concepts. *Experimental Agriculture* 22, 87–104.

Mintz, S. (1974) *Worker in the Cave.* Norton, New York.

Newby, H. (ed.) (1978) *International Perspectives in Rural Sociology.* Wiley, New York.

Newby, H. and Sevilla Guzmán, E. (1983) *Introducción a la Sociología Rural.* Alianza, Madrid.

Norman, D. and Collinson, M. (1985) Farming system research in theory and practice. In: Remenyi, J.V. (ed.) *Agricultural Systems Research for Developing Countries, Proceedings of an International Workshop held at Hawkesbury Agricultural College, Richmond, NSW, Australia.* ACIAR Proceedings Series, Canberra, pp. 16–30.

Norman, D., Baker, D., Heinrich, G., Jonas, C., Maskiara, S. and Worman, F. (1989) Farmer groups for technology development: experience in Botswana. In: Chambers, R., Pacey, A. and Thrupp, L.A. (eds) *Farmer First: Farmer Innovation and Agricultural Research.* Intermediate Technology Publications, London, pp. 136–146.

Oasa, E.K. (1985) Farming systems research: a change in form, but not in content. *Human Organization* 44 (3), 219–227.

Ploeg, J.D. van der (1987) *De Verwetenschappelijking van de Landbouwbeoefening.* Wageningse Sociologische Studies, No. 21, Agricultural University, Wageningen.

Ploeg, J.D. van der (1993) Over de betekenis van verscheidenheid. Inaugural lecture, 23 March 1993, Landbouwuniversiteit Wageningen, Wageningen.

Reijntjes, C., Haverkort, B. and Waters-Bayer, A. (1992) *Farming for the Future: an Introduction to Low-External-Input and Sustainable Agriculture.* ILEIA, Macmillan, London.

Remmers, G.G.A. (1992) Ecological wine making in a depressed mountainous region in southern Spain: a preliminary view on problems and prospects. In: *Proceedings of the CAMAR Seminar 'Endogenous Regional Development in Europe: Theory, Method and Practice,' Vila Real, Portugal, November 4–5 1991.* European Commission DG VI, Brussels, pp. 132–169.

Remmers, G.G.A. (1993) Agricultura tradicional y agricultura ecológica: vecinos distantes. *Agricultura y Sociedad,* 66, 201–220.

Remmers, G.G.A., Avila Cano, J.C. and Amian Novales, I. (1992a) *Investigación, Docencia y Desarrollo de la Agricultura Ecológica en Países Bajos: Informe de un Viaje de Estudio.* Documento interno, ISEC, Córdoba, 33 pp.

Remmers, G.G.A., Ávila Cano, J.C., Parra Orellana, J., Amián Novales, I. and Acosta Naranjo, R. (1992b) Some reflections on the design of on-farm research in ecological farming in Andalusia. Paper presented at the Second CAMAR–CERES seminar 'Strengthening Endogenous Development Patterns in European Agriculture,' Chania, Crete, 20–22 October 1992.

Scheuermeier, U. (1988) *Approach Development: a Contribution to Participatory Develop-*

*ment of Techniques Based on a Practical Experience in Tinau Watershed Project, Nepal.* Landwirtschaftliche Beratungszentrale, Lindau, Switzerland.

Scoones, I. and Thompson, J. (1992) Beyond farmer first: rural people's knowledge, agricultural research and extension practice: towards a theoretical framework. Overview paper No. 1 of the IIED/IDA Workshop 'Beyond Farmer First: Rural People's Knowledge, Agricultural Research and Extension Practice,' University of Sussex, 27–29 October, p. 29.

Sevilla Guzmán, E. (1977) Prólogo a la edición castellana. In: Galeski, B. (ed.) *Sociologia del Campesinado.* Penisula, Barcelona, pp. 5–19.

Sevilla Guzmán, E. (1980) Reflexiones Teórico sobre el concepto de latifundismo. In: de Barros, A. (ed.) *A Agricultura Latifundaria na Peninsula Iberica.* Instituto Gulbenkian de Ciencia, Oeiras, pp. 29–48.

Sevilla Guzmán, E. (1986a) Estructura social e identidad andaluza. In: Hernandez, F. and Mercadé, F. (eds) *Estructuras Sociales y Cuestión Nacional en España.* Ariel, Barcelona, pp. 261–300.

Sevilla Guzmán, E. (1986b) Nacionalismo andaluz y proceso autonómico: de la exaltación a la agonía. *Nación Andaluza* 6, 123–139.

Sevilla Guzmán, E. (1991) Hacia un desarrollo agroecológico desde el campesinado. *Política y Sociedad* 9, 57–72.

Sevilla Guzmán, E. and González de Molina, M. (1991a) Peasants knowledge in the old tradition of peasants studies. In: Tillman, H.J., Albrecht, H., Salas, M.A., Dhamothran, M. and Gottschalt, E. (eds) *Proceedings of the International Workshop: Agricultural Knowledge System and the Role of Extension,* 21–24 May 1991. Hohenheim University, Bad Boll, pp. 140–158.

Sevilla Guzmán, E. and González de Molina, M. (1991b) Ecosociología: algunos elementos para el análisis de la coevolución social y ecológica en la agricultura. *Revista Española de Investigaciones Sociológicas* 52, 7–45.

Sevilla Guzmán, E. and González de Molina, M. (eds) (1993) *Ecología, Campesinado e Historia.* La Piqueta, Madrid.

Sevilla Guzmán, E. and Heiser, K. (eds) (1988) *Anarquismo y Movimiento Jornalero en Andalucía.* Excmo Ayuntamiento de Córdoba, Córdoba.

Shanin, T. (ed.) (1971) *Peasants and Peasant Societies.* Penguin Books, Harmondsworth.

Sumberg, J. and Okali, C. (1989) Farmers, on-farm research and new technology. In: Chambers, R., Pacey, A. and Thrupp, L.A. (eds) *Farmer First: Farmer Innovation and Agricultural Research.* Intermediate Technology Publications, London, pp. 109–114.

Toledo, V.M. (1988) La sociedad rural, los campesinos y la cuestión ecológica. In: Zapeda Patterson, J.F. (ed.) *Las Sociedades Rurales Hoy.* Colegio de Midiocan, Mexico.

Toledo, V.M. (1992) What is ethnoecology? origins, scope and implications of a rising discipline. *Ethnoecology* 1 (1), 5–21.

Tripp, R. (ed.) (1991) *Planned Change in Farming Systems: Progress in On-farm Research.* Wiley, Chichester.

Wolf, E.R. (1971) *Peasant Wars in the Twentieth Century.* Faber and Faber, London.

USDA (1980) *Report and Recommendations on Organic Farming.* US Department of Agriculture, Washington DC, 64 pp.

Vereijken, P. (1992) Targeted innovation of technology for sustainable development of agriculture. Paper presented at the EC Workshop 'Potential and Limits of Organic Farming,' 17–19 September 1992, Louvaine-la-Neuve, Belgium.

# 26

## The Contribution of Action-research to the Organization of Agrarian Systems: Preliminary Results of Experiments under way in France

*François Vallerand*

> The organization, the organized thing, the product of this organization and the organizer are inseparable
>
> (P. Valery, 1920)

### Introduction

The emergence and development over the past few years of a specific branch of research on agrarian systems can be considered as the joint outcome of ongoing critical analysis in two areas, one pragmatic and agronomic and the other more general, cultural and epistemological. [Research on agrarian systems refers to both farming systems research (FSR) and farming systems research and extension (FSR/E), terms used in English-speaking research circles which cover several research fields, plus recherches/développement, the terms used in French-speaking circles and which is also polysemic. Albaladejo (1987), Pillot (1987) and Brossier (1988) in particular have analysed the common points and the large divergences between these different methodological fields.]

From the pragmatic point of view, repeated failure during the years 1950–1970 to transfer technology to agriculture led a number of people responsible for 'agricultural development' and a number of researchers to call into question the model known as the linear and univocal model for creation and diffusion of innovation in the rural sector. This work is well known (e.g. Chambers and Jiggins, 1987; Farrington and Martin, 1988; Gerber, 1991) and it is not necessary to go into it here except to correct a widely held idea: this critical analysis only applies to transfer programmes in developing countries (role of International Research Centres for specific productions). This diagnostic assessment of deficiency and inadequacy of research–transfer–producer relationships was in fact carried out almost simulataneously in Europe and in less developed countries (LDCs). In France, for example, as early as the 1960s a number of programmes concerning 'regional projects' were handled jointly by researcher–agronomists, livestock researchers, ecologists, economists, sociologists, and even ethnologists (the term regional agrarian systems had yet to be coined). During the course of this work, they were obviously in contact with producers, their 'reasons for doing what they do' (postulate of coherence) and their know-how. The concepts of 'practices', of 'crop management sequences', etc., which are the result of the above date from this period.

More generally, since the 1940s, an ever-spreading movement has cast doubt on the foundations of positivist epistemology and reductionism. Constructivist epistemology provides the basis for a number of new sciences which together deal with the complexity of 'objects', the interdependence between observing subject and observed object (system). The project consists of providing knowledge for managing these complex objects.

Europe is probably the part of the world in which the mutual interplay of these two innovative scientific research movements, applied and fundamental, is most likely to work in our area of interest, i.e. agrarian systems. For example, as early as 1979, French agronomic research (INRA) made modifications to its organization by creating the SAD, the department for research into Agrarian Systems and Development [see Bonnemaire (Chapter 2) for further analysis]. Systems modelling and management sciences provide the conceptual foundations. Scientific ambition also seeks to interconnect biotechnical and socioeconomic disciplines within 'transdisciplinary teams' (Piaget, 1970). Problems concerning the future (reconversion and sustainability) of several French agricultural areas provide the spheres of application.

The production of scientific knowledge with regard to such complex and constantly evolving objects, in which the researchers know full well that they are themselves among the actors, must be used, when it exists, but more often than not the need is to create specific research methodologies. Action-research is one such approach with which SAD teams are experimenting in several French projects. After describing what action-research consists of, three examples are presented and compared in order to present a first set of conclusions concerning this methodology.

# Action-research and Participatory Research

## *Emergence of the action-research concept*

The term 'action-research' (AR) was coined by Lewin (1947, quoted by Liu, 1992) to mean 'a fundamental research approach in the social sciences which is created by the convergence of a desire for change and a research intention.' This US researcher underlined two major aspects: first, the inherent unity between project implementation and the research approach, and second, the possibilities of carrying out fundamental research in the real world.

During this same period (World War II), two other European research teams, using different methods and stressing other aspects, reached the same conclusion concerning action-research as a research approach (Liu, 1992). The Curle team in the UK (Tavistock Clinic) underlined the role of research in encouraging users to learn about their 'capacity to transform certain aspects deemed to be unsatisfactory by the community.' The French school of institutional analysis (Dr Tosquelles, Hôpital Saint Alban) stresses the necessity for institutional inversion in order for users to promote change. It also considers that the domains of the subconscious and institutions should be studied by using the same methods since they are connected.

## *Constitutive elements of an action-research project*

For almost 50 years, a fair number of action-research projects have been carried out in different countries involving several disciplines. Educational research, sociology and hospitals in particular have used it more frequently than other disciplines. At the present time, diverse proposals that have been theorized to a greater or lesser extent are in existence. Our objective is not to analyse and discuss this work but to recall the probable constitutive elements of an action-research project.

Liu (1992) and Avenier (1992) propose the combination of the following elements:

- the convergence of a *desire for change* and a research intention;
- the *dual nature of the objective*, solve a problem and develop fundamental knowledge;
- an *ongoing long-term joint project* between researchers and users;
- a common *ethical framework* negotiated and accepted by all.

The general nature and the limits of these basic aspects will be investigated by comparative analysis of three projects.

## Participatory research and institutional interests at stake

If the work of Farrington and Martin (1988) summing up participatory agricultural research (PAR) is referred to, a major convergence between PAR and AR can be noted as far as the principles are concerned. They are founded in both cases on the intention to solve problems, confidence in the ability of users to produce and analyse information, refusal of the 'neutral value' concept of data and the training aspects of the process. The research objectives are identical. The authors point out, however, in their conclusions: 'as a general rule, farmer group participation is more rewarding than individual participation. To date, too few projects have involved groups, and those that do have had very diverse results.'

In order to set up research which corresponds more to social demand, investment is required in the emergence of local producer organizations and in their institutional back-up (Merrill-Sands and Collion, 1992).

The specificity of action-research, which is an extended form of participatory research, is to take into consideration without exception the social and institutional dimensions of the project for change as expressed by the users. When action-research is applied to agrarian systems, it is necessary to involve different groups of actors. In the light of the results presented below, this aspect will be re-examined in the discussions.

# Presentation of Three Case Studies

## Choice criteria

The SAD department is made up of five research units working on projects in several French regional areas (one to three per research team). [The term 'regional area' will not be discussed here. It refers to the problem of setting the limits of a local agrarian system for which the minimum requirements are a group of rural and agricultural activities, covering a fairly large area and which are subject to a management process (activity management), whilst enjoying a certain autonomy.] The common aim is systems modelling and its applications concerning agriculture (Brossier *et al.*, 1990).

In the continuing line of previous interdisciplinary research, our first projects (1980–1985) were clearly centred on the farm, its subsystems and its operation by the producers (farming systems in the strict sense of the word). This work continues today with a clearly defined objective, that is, aid for individual decision making with respect to farm management.

Since 1985, the research has also covered, more and more often, the subject of 'agricultural and rural development'. We deal with this as a process of successive stages in reorganization of regional agrarian systems or of production and processing system subsectors (local or regional). This process has major endogenous aspects.

Research functions change in nature and in complexity *vis-à-vis* such 'subjects.' Aid to individual action (decision making) should be replaced by aid to collective action and decision making. This work has logically led to teams or parts of teams involving themselves with certain regional development actor groups in order to grasp how the latter can be helped to solve a problem. The problem-solving procedure, in the form of aid to negotiation, is analysed by the researchers to be original and interesting from a methodological point of view. It should be noted that the teams are composed mainly of researchers who are competent in a particular biotechnical branch (agronomy, ecology, livestock research, technology) in addition to specialists in social sciences (economics, geography and less often sociology).

These research projects are recent and are usually still under way [several preliminary studies were made, in particular in the form of research '*in vivo*' concerning training of farmers in economic decision making (Brossier, 1980)]. Three examples have been chosen involving three different teams in order to present completely different action-research projects but which also bring out some common methodological aspects. First and foremost then, we practise action-research and put forward the hypothesis that a certain common basic methodology exists, currently under formulation, that the SAD research teams adapt according to the configuration of actors involved.

*Example A: Elaboration of an approach to acquire knowledge concerning the operation and diagnostic assessment of pastoral goat farming*

Area: southeastern France.

*General aspects of the problem addressed by the research*: the Mediterranean area is confronted from time to time with the problem of forest fires. Pastoral farming could fill several useful roles (enhancement of the environment). The pastoral farms have adopted specific operating methods which are not included in the available technical models. This absence of a model is a problem for those who are involved in the development of these farms and who need to consider including them in a development project.

*Action-research aspects of the problem*: gather knowledge concerning the operation of these pastoral goat farms.

*Users requesting research*: technician–consultants (working on livestock farming or pastoral farming) who are aware of the problem, wish to create a working group to acquire knowledge about these farms, in order to make their work more efficient. They wish to propose their ideas to aid the research project.

*Aspects relevant for the research*: emergence of think-tank with partner groups, production and organization of knowledge, fine tuning of methods relative to the operation.

*Partner groups*: technician–consultants of farm bureaux and pastoral farmers willing to participate.

*Nature of partnership*: co-steering of project by researchers and partner groups (activation committee).

*Duration*: start-up in 1985; the group was modified in 1990.

*Results*:

*For the users*: a regional frame of reference and a method for grasping production strategy (Napoleone, 1993).

*For research*: methodological principles for generalization in other situations (Napoléone and Prévost, 1989). Comparison is under way of the viewpoints of farmers, researchers and technician–consultants concerning herd management (Hubert *et al.*, 1993). This comparison is connected with the work presented by Papy in Chapter 18.

## *Example B: Modification of production systems used in a specific area in order to reduce the nitrogen content of commercialized mineral water springs*

*Area*: eastern France, Lorraine, Vittel basin.

*General aspects of the problem addressed by the research*: since the nitrate content of the commercialized spring water is increasing noticeably and regularly, Vittel enterprises have looked ahead. In order to preserve their market (less than 10 mg l$^{-1}$ and zero pesticides), this tendency needs to be modified and the causes of this increase need to be dealt with. The Société des Eaux de Vittel is looking for ways of greatly reducing nitrate percolation coming from the farms (about 40) in the catchment basin. Production systems have been modified over the past few decades: intensification of dairy cattle farming and corn crops, use of chemical fertilizers and spreading of manure on fields. Even though the Vittel enterprises are trying to buy available fields so as to impose their farming conditions, they have asked INRA–SAD to help them achieve these changes.

*Aspects relevant for the research*: for the team, in order to overcome this conflicting situation of incompatible uses, the emergence of dealing collectively with agrarian system changes, as an ongoing process and in partnership, is a methodological research project, the results of which are of great interest to the Water Agency which is participating in the financing.

*Type of partnership and plan of action*: for several months, INRA discussed the type of partnership to be established between the company (Société Vittel) and the research group. The principle consists of minority financing by the company (condition of independence) and participation of the third partner group: the farmers. A plan of action by degree of importance, monitoring and appraisal and mediation aspects were negotiated.

*Duration*: operation start-up in 1989; currently at the stage where a specification of practices generating less nitrates is being proposed to farmers.

*Results available*:

*For users*: frame of reference, simulation and technical specifications used as a basis for negotiation between the mineral water company and the farmers concerning changes in systems and practices.

*For research*: theorization under way (Brossier *et al.*, 1992; Deffontaines and Chia, 1992; Chia and Brossier, 1993; Deffontaines *et al.*, 1993).

### Example C: Organization of interprofessional group built around an Appellation d'Origine Contrôlée

*Area*: Corsica.

*General field of study*: livestock farming in Corsica is still highly pastoral. In spite of low physical productivity (per animal and per man), this activity endures because it involves manufacturing and marketing of original and often reputed products (ewe milk and goat milk cheeses, processed meat products). Development of this activity requires reorganization of system subsectors by product (milk-cheese, for example) built around modern utilization of this biotechnological and gastronomic heritage. Speciality certification (market segmentation) is one solution. All the actor groups in Corsican livestock farming are interested by this field of study concerning 'quality' and product specificity.

*Action-research field of study*: all those involved call for the contribution of research and appropriate public services in obtaining quickly the Appellation d'Origine Contrôlée (AOC) for the cheese called 'Brocciu', which is a specifically Corsican cheese. The main difficulty is that the Corsican dairy system subsector (14 million litres per year) involves three categories of processors (transforming milk into cheese): one industrial cheese manu-facturer, a dozen small dairy cottage industries and 400 livestock farmers producing their own 'farm cheese.' Each group processes about one third of the milk each. Even if each group calls for Brocciu certification, their points of view and interests are not at all the same.

*Aspects relevant for the research*: even if research can analyse afterwards how certifications are obtained and can find out, less easily, how they perform today, it does not know how to help reorganize a system subsector, in real time and giving consideration to its social interests. Action-research enables this methodological vacuum to be filled.

*Partner groups*: all those involved in the profession (farmers and dairy farmers). They have no common plan of action and require organization; one of the objectives is therefore to create an interprofessional group around this 'Appellation' project. Also, the regional directors of the appropriate public services must become partners.

*Type of partnership*: the research team must become a member of the future committee for supervising the 'Appellation' to be created by the union of the interprofessional group. This nascent union is to provide beforehand a framework for the partnership.

*Duration*: there have been several attempts to set up this project since 1980. Action-research was introduced in 1991 when the SAD team agreed to be involved in collective research for a strategy to include all categories of Brocciu producers in the same dynamic process.

*Results available*:

*For users*: a frame of reference for the product, an official request for 'Appellation,' schedule of conditions for inspection, internal regulations for the union for the protection of the AOC.

*Results available for research*: theorization under way concerning the dynamics of the relationships between technological heritage/quality/ ongoing social interaction (Casabianca *et al.*, 1993; Prost *et al.*, 1993; de Sainte Marie *et al.*, 1993).

# Comparative Analysis

Each action-research operation is a specific process during which, by nature, the points of view of the different partner groups evolve, in addition to their relationships. A comparative analysis of the three processes allows the essential phases of the approach, that we hold to be common, to be identified and described. The success of the partnership is highly dependent on operation start-up conditions, and on the ability of the research team in managing to produce pertinent information and in dealing with the consequences in the social sphere.

## Action-research operations start-up

### Source of request and desire for change

The examples below allow two situations and some variations to be differentiated.

#### CLIENT REQUESTS THE RESEARCH

The client is unable to solve a problem, and therefore makes the initial request. In order to ascertain if the problem is apt for an action-research operation, the research team must check the nature of the 'desire for change' and organize its hypotheses accordingly. Example B is significant since the farmers and not the client are expected to enact most of the changes.

#### NO CLIENT REQUEST

The agronomic research team is usually in contact with one or more local agrarian systems and institutions (decision makers) and is therefore aware of their concerns. Action-research operation start-up can take place using two procedures:

- Using coordination formalized around a common interest (example A). The partner groups and the research are considered at the same level:

transfer service researchers and technician–consultants are all involved in producing and diffusing information and knowledge. The aspect they all wish to change is to increase their ability to assume their respective social roles: to advise and guide the users, and create methods for the researchers.

•   Using interpretation of social needs (example C). The researchers and the other partner groups do not have the same type of organization. The initial problem is of a technical nature. Research can respond either in the form of disciplinary research or in the form of a service to users (adaptation of technology; research and development). Analysis of relationships and decision centres regarding this technical problem is usually already available thanks to the usual relationship (even if this is conflicting) between research, actor groups and agricultural development departments and institutions. The basic question to study is: on what grounds is research prepared to change its service status for that of an action-research partnership?

### Partnership formulization

#### Example B
Real negotiation with the client is required in order to lead to a formalized contract and plan of action (definition of the problem to solve, other actor groups involved or to bring in, schedule, financing, respective contributions, copyright of results, etc.). This almost always leads to the creation of an action-research steering committee and often to a management committee (budgetary in particular). Determination of the research plan of action necessarily includes, in addition to the client, the representatives of the other actor groups involved; in this particular case, the farmers who are required to carry out most of the changes.

#### Example A
In this case, action-research includes technician–consultants and a few producers. The group is strengthened by mutual trust and exchange of services rendered over a minimum of several years. The strength of the partnership and the duration of the coordination committee depend heavily on the degree of satisfaction of the different partner groups. This satisfaction is not only achieved owing to the results obtained (change in viewpoints of each actor group) but also owing to the procedures aiding problem comprehension.

#### Example C
Here, action-research develops with emerging collective structures. The desire for change calls existing institutions into question, even if this takes the form of a technical request. The partnership is, by definition, difficult to formalize because the institutions needing change are understandably reticent in

creating bonds with partner groups over whom they have little control. The mission of action-research is to give back-up to the development of socio-professional structures, still at an early stage, in cooperation with the public services (procedures recognizing a union for the protection of the certification). The research is organized within technical or scientific committees set up by this prefiguration. These consultative and regulative bodies are transformed over the course of time. Research needs to have a fundamental rationale, of an ethical nature (type, limits and conditions relative to institutional involvement) *vis-à-vis* the changes in structures which necessarily take place since this is the original objective.

### Project realization and management

*Elaboration of research subjects in the case of dual objectives*

In graphic terms, carrying out an action-research project is a series of successive loops (or better, a spiral around a time vector). Each loop is a succession of the following stages: elaboration of new hypotheses (even modifying the field of study), search for solutions and new diagnostic assessment in view of the results. In practice, the different loops overlap each other depending on how much knowledge has been acquired, which is never equivalent for all the tasks in hand.

Monitoring needs to be carried out of this series of hypotheses, results and intermediate diagnostic assessments, which each stage encompasses as a result of discussions between researchers and users. This monitoring should take the form of an action-research diary because it is an essential element for use in the creation of methodologies.

Our work is confined here to understanding how the main research subjects are identified collectively by researchers and users, and how they interconnect.

The fact that there is no symmetry between the users and the research team needs to be taken into consideration. At the beginning, the research team alone needs a subject (complex though it is) and a series of hypotheses on which effective methodologies will be used. At this stage, the user groups, on the other hand, only need solutions, and as quickly as possible.

Transformation into hypotheses of the initial question and general field of study specified at the beginning of the operation is a collective undertaking by users and the research team. The crux of the matter is the identification of the critical singular subject of the operation. In our opinion, this identification cannot be made quickly even with a certain action-research experience. Being certain that the right subject is pinpointed is much more important than rapid definition.

The following 'critical subjects,' for the three case studies, became apparent during the process:

*Example A*: modelling of functioning patterns of herds is not the subject but will be the product destined for the users; the subject is the learning process involved in solving a problem of this complexity.

*Example B*: the critical subject is not the nitrates content or the farming practices, but the multi-objective management of the space under the roots, which is both the pool of farmer productivity factors and the percolator of the run-off water. The action-research needs to result in procedures or even management structures compatible with these public goods.

*Example C*: the subject is neither Brocciu nor the 'Appellation,' but the creation of interprofessional group dynamics (two types of processors) which need to result in a union for the protection of the 'Appellation' or any other form of collective enhancement.

These critical subjects are only accessible to research through systems modelling and constructivist paradigms. We will proceed by distinguishing two groups of hypotheses: (H1) theses inherent to the operation since they are accepted by all to be the interpretation of a common field of study concerning the critical research subject; (H2) complementary hypotheses (or specific) – the function of the research is to change the viewpoints of the different actor groups concerning management of the critical subject; to do this, the research does not restrict the production of information and knowledge to one possible scenario, that proposed by actor groups, and it is necessary to open the field of possibilities by openly analysing other alternatives.

### EXAMPLE B

The research studies how farmers can obtain a satisfactory revenue whilst decreasing yield (limitation of inputs). These complementary hypotheses could be considered to be a waste of time by the user groups.

### *Operation management and problems of common ethic*

As the action-research process goes along, several phenomena need to be dealt with by the research team:

- the changing perception of actor groups concerning the image and competence of researchers;
- the change in research subjects that the researchers focus on;
- the production of information and researcher responsibility with respect to its differential appropriation by the different actor groups;
- research implication within a social structure which by necessity calls into question certain institutional aspects and affects the interests of power.

The actor groups know by experience that the problem they need to deal with is complex. They turn to researchers because the latter are considered to be rigorous and objective. Implicitly, the actor groups are asking the researchers to simplify reality and to give them results that are difficult to refute. This scientific production is supposed to reduce the tension endured by an individual (the case of the manager of a farm who is not satisfied with his own level of management) or by actor groups in a situation of potential conflict. The researcher is thus in a comfortable situation since he benefits from an air of scientific authority (knowledge, experimental approach) and from a certain distance respecting the actor groups and their fields. As the action-research process goes along, the actor groups quickly discover that the researcher cannot, or will not, propose ready-made solutions. He is neither an expert manager nor even an expert imparting all his authority and experience in the solutions he proposes. Brought in for problem solving, the partner groups discover instead a focus on reformulating questions (problem finding; Simon, 1969). The researcher comes down from his pedestal and can even turn into a hindrance when he refutes the reasons for and refuses to support the validity of certain questions that the actor groups want solved. This exercise of reformulation and modelling of phenomena and interests at stake is accepted little by little and often approved by the partner groups. The production of new information concerning judicious intermediate subjects and systematic recourse to the written word in formalizing the various points of view at a certain point in time give the researcher the status of author (Desroche, 1982). Lastly, research helps in constituting a 'collective actor group' (Vesperien, 1992) as in example A or in creating a 'negotiating area' (Crozier and Friedberg, 1977) as in examples B and C and finally validates the request for research. Given that the emergence of this collective actor group or of this negotiating area was a condition for engaging action-research, this creation would appear to be one of the criteria for recognizing and probably for evaluating a piece of action-research.

In order to advance the collective dynamics of problem information (review of knowledge, expansion of contents both quantitatively and qualitatively), and his own contribution, the researcher involved is temporarily led to separate certain intermediate research subjects. Understanding how they work will shed light and inform on certain of the critical subject's functions.

*Example A*: modelling the functioning patterns of herds leads the partner groups to pinpoint the critical periods of the milk production cycle of the different types of farm. Monitoring of certain livestock farms has enabled the essential mechanisms to be understood.

*Example B*: knowledge of soil behaviour and nitrates movements is an indispensable detour in informing the problem in general. This has led the research team to seek back-up in mobilizing the expertise of agronomists, pedologists and hydrologists. Similarly with regard to farm operation, linear programming simulations allow the economic consequences to be evaluated together with, in pollution and work organization terms, the changes in practices and production system proposed (giving up corn which is replaced by alfalfa, composting of animal manure).

*Example C*: knowledge of the product needing certification seems to be the first step in constituting the required files of application. The aim of the action-research operation is not to define the product (this concerns R & D). Elaboration of this frame of reference during the course of action-research can only be done using intermediate subjects that come up during the co-managed process. The research needs to adapt its methodologies and its experimental designs (on-farm trials). The intermediate subjects of this operation were successively: composition norms and variety between producers and over time; chemical composition as an indicator of fraudulent practices; and dynamics of microbial flora in the days immediately after manufacture (ultra-fresh product) taken as a basis for a minimum common indicator of quality guarantee.

The results generated during the detours do not generally satisfy any of the parties (including the researchers). In addition, the partner groups are not all able to appropriate the results for themselves so as to back up or refine their reasons and the defence of their interests.

*Example B*: analyses produced by the research are more easily used by the company than by the farmers; there is an asymmetry here which is a problem for the research.

*Example C*: creation of an analytical method (considered vital by professional groups and decision makers) for detecting fraud (consisting of adding industrial milk substitutes such as milk powder) has in fact put the ball in the court of the farmer producers. Certain producers who do not master inherited procedures well (excess heating) produce cheese of a questionable quality that the method excludes in the same way as that produced fraudulently. In practice, this means that those supporting 'authenticity' must also accept verification analyses. The same thing applies to the results concerning the microbial content of Brocciu after 7 and 14 days which obliges each producer to control his own process and to commit himself to respect the specifications. This means that the results obtained could, if the researcher diffused them, completely block the process integrating the various interests, and the negotiation. This could happen in two completely different ways, either through a lack or through an excess of discrimination between the interests of various actor groups. A lack in the sense that it is impossible to find one (or two) criteria that really discriminate between the true and the false; no-one can decide anything, everyone can do as he likes. An excess if one sole group has the means of appropriating the results then interpreting and using them to their exclusive advantage.

At one time or another, the action-research team can be confronted with managing certain crises resulting from changes in power games and interests. The image of research considered by some to act as a catalyst for development is, in our opinion, far removed from reality. Action-research necessarily changes the systems of actor groups. It not only creates a pseudo-community between researchers and actor groups, but also connects several types of actor groups over and above their usual institutional setting. This 'negotiation phase' obviously engenders reactions from the institutions concerned and from those in charge of them since their authority is called into question.

*Example B*: the negotiation being set up between farmers and companies has provoked reactions from the union structures which represent the farmers in the area and also directs transfer services (Chamber of Agriculture). These reactions have led to the creation of a political mediation committee.

*Example C*: the constitution of a collective actor group between the representatives of several types of processors and the general farming unions has proved difficult (several failed attempts).

It must not be forgotten that the institutional side of action-research holds that institutions are necessarily contested by users (natural tendency of all organized systems to close in on themselves). The objective for users is to remove the pressure of a constraint through collective action. This questions the 'inescapable' aspect of the constraint, this inescapable aspect that most institutions and opinion leaders have in many cases accepted for years. The approach is therefore fundamentally of a political nature since it affects viewpoints and social positions that are rooted in these viewpoints. These facts and arguments demonstrate why certain action-research operations cannot be finalized by exogenous research teams and/or who do not commit themselves over the long term. A certain in-culture is indispensable so that users do not use this 'foreign' aspect of the research as a pretext for not carrying through the measures of change. Excessive use of local researchers is as much of a problem as opening up the system. We feel that the importance of this indigenous/exogenous balance is completely ignored in the methodological debates concerning the different forms of FSR.

## Evaluation of Results

The research projects presented here constitute a sample of the action-research operations handled by the SAD. Given that they are practically all in progress, it is too soon to formulate many more management principles. It would be even more presumptuous to give any information concerning evaluation of results. This important methodological study on action-research as applied to French agriculture is under way and directed by our colleagues Albaladejo and Casabianca; it will be presented at a later date. We simply recall below certain basic aspects of this evaluation.

### *Results for users*

Action-research is evaluated at the outset for its ability to solve the problems that can come up when using a participatory and open approach, but on top of this it is evaluated for its learning capacity. The community as a whole acquires new knowledge and competence, both individual and collective, through participation in an iterative process requiring problems to be better defined before seeking solutions. This learning process reinforces confidence in undertaking other complex problems in the future. In certain cases, an action-research operation can lead to the emergence of a completely new collective structure which in turn changes the positions of the institutions.

Through these various types of end results, action-research is a factor of agrarian system sustainability.

### Research results

Research results fall into three categories: references, tools and knowledge of a methodological nature.

First, the success of an action-research operation must be distinguished from the production of methodological knowledge. An action-research operation can even be considered very successful (a solution to a problem is found and the users are satisfied with the contribution of research) without having contributed to research methodology itself. A second aspect of success concerning the social dimension is verification that research has been able to pull out of the operation having ensured user autonomy.

Besides specifically elaborated references, two other types of scientific results can be mentioned:

- Production of tools and methods defined during the operation. They can be used by actor groups in other situations [examples: diagnostic assessment method for goat herds (A); 'Bascule,' indicator of nitrate pollution risk (B); method for detecting additions of milk powder (C)].
- Production of methodology inherent to action-research requires specification on how to transcend local and contingent knowledge so as to obtain generative knowledge. This aspect is a deliberate decision that must be made by the research team at the outset.

## Conclusions

Each action-research operation, as it evolves, needs to keep the balance between the two aspects inherent to action: on the one hand, action is a powerful and irreplaceable means of understanding social systems which are not natural phenomena but are built up over the years; and on the other hand, the partnership that the operation requires causes the research team to lose part of its exteriority regarding the subjects to be informed.

Action-research can be likened to an aid to negotiation and often results in encouraging at least some of the actor groups of an agrarian system to reorganize, thus increasing the system's capacity to adapt to change (sustainability).

However, one must not overlook the fact that commitment to action-research is a choice of ethics on the part of the researcher: giving priority to increasing the capacity of the actor groups involved, to the detriment of a positivist rationale and of strict adherence to an experimental outline. This commitment thus qualifies for what Funtowicz and Ravetz (1990) call 'second-order science', i.e. science that informs about phenomena that build up, which are uncertain and which have major interests at stake, for which validation of results can only be achieved within constructivist epistemology.

## Acknowledgements

Not only has this contribution extensively used the results and reflections, some of which have yet to be published, of SAD colleagues who are working on the projects described here, but also I was able to benefit from their critical analysis and advice. I particularly thank C. Albaladejo, J. Brossier, F. Casabianca, E. Chia and Martine Napoleone.

## References

Albaladejo, C. (1987) Aménagement de l'espace rural et activités d'élevage dans des régions de petites exploitations. Thèse Université Grenoble I, Institut Géographie Alpine, 537 pp. (see pp. 13–54).

Avenier, M.-J. (1992) Recherche-action et épistémologies constructivistes, modélisation systémique et organisations socio-économiques complexes: quelques 'boucles étranges' fécondes. *Revue Internationale de Systémique* 6 (4), 390–403.

Brossier, J. (1980) De la recherche sur les décisions des agriculteurs à la formation économiques des agriculteurs. Pour la constitution de groupes de recherche-développement. *Economie Rurale* 136.

Brossier, J. (1988) Système et système de production; note sur ces concepts. *Cahiers des Sciences Humaines ORSTOM* 23 (3–4), 377–390.

Brossier, J., Vissac, B. and Lemoigne, J.-L. (1990) *Modélisation Systémique et Système Agraire; Décision et Organisation*. INRA, Paris, 365 pp.

Brossier, J., Benoit, M., Falloux, J.C., Gaury, F. and Pierre, Ph. (1992) Agricultural practices, underground water quality and research development project. Modelling of nitrogen constraint in several farms. In: Loseby, M. (ed.) *The Environment and the Management of Agricultural Resources*. European Association for Agro Economists, pp. 201–216.

Casabianca, F., de Sainte Marie, Ch., Santucci, P.M., Vallerand, F. and Prost, J.-A. (1994) Maitrise de la qualité et solidarité des acteurs; la pertinence des innovations dans les filières d'élevage en Corse. In: *Systèmes Agraires et Qualités: Techniques, Lieux et Acteurs*. INRA, Paris, in press.

Chambers, R. and Jiggins, J. (1987) Agricultural research for resource-poor farmers (two papers). *Agricultural Administration and Extension* 27, 35–52 and 109–128.

Chia, E. and Brossier, J. (1993) Qualité des eaux sous les racines et agriculture: une démarche de recherche-action. In: *Proceedings of the 2nd European Congress on Systems Science (Prague)*. Vol. IV, European Systems Science Union, pp. 1225–1234.

Crozier, M. and Friedberg, E. (1977) *L'Acteur et le Système*. Le Seuil, Paris.

Deffontaines, J.P. and Chia, E. (1992) Une recherche-action sur un système agraire soumis à des impératifs de qualité des eaux. Résultats et bilan méthodologique. *Comptes Rendus de l'Academie d'Agriculture de France* 78 (7), 65–75.

Deffontaines, J.P., Benoit, M., Brossier, J., Chia, E., Gras, E. and Roux, M. (1993) *Agriculture et Qualité des Eaux; Diagnostic et Proposition pour un Périmètre de Protection*. INRA, Paris, 334 pp.

Desroche, H. (1982) Les auteurs et les acteurs; la recherche coopérative comme recherche-action. In: *'Communautés', Archives de Sciences Sociales, de la Coopération et du Développement*, No. 59, pp. 39–64.

Farrington, J. and Martin, A. (1988) *La Participation des Agriculteurs dans la Recherche Agricole: Concepts et Pratiques*. Agricultural Administration Unit, Irregular Publication No. 9. Overseas Development Institute, London (translated by Side, D. (1990) CTA, Wageningen, 78 pp.).

Funtowicz, O. and Ravetz, J.R. (1990) *Global Environmental Issues and the Emergence of Second Order Science*. Direct General Science, Research and Development CD-NA-12803-En, Commission of the European Communities, Brussels, 24 pp.

Gerber, M. (1991) Participatory research and education for agricultural sustainability. Paper from Agro-ecology Program, University of Illinois College of Agriculture, Urbana-Champaign.

Hubert, B., Girard, N., Lasseur, J. and Bellon, S. (1993) Les systèmes d'élevage ovin préalpins: derrière les pratiques des conceptions modélisables. In: Landais, E. and Balent, G. (eds) *Pratiques d'Élevages Extensifs*. INRA, Versailles.

Liu, M. (1992) Présentation de la recherche-action, définition, déroulement et résultats. *Revue International de Systémique* 6, 293–312.

Merrill-Sands, D. and Collion M.-H. (1992) Making the farmers' voice count: issues and opportunities for promoting farmer-responsive. Paper presented at the 12th Annual FSR/E Symposium, Michigan State University, September 1992, Session 3.

Napoleone, M. (1993) *Des Parcours pour Chevriers – un Réseau Recherche-Développement Étudie les Élevages Caprins Laitiers qui Utilisent les Parcours*. Document INRA–SAD Avignon Région PACA, 143 pp.

Napoleone, M. and Prévost, F. (1989) Objectif d'élevage, stratégie alimentaire et utilisation du territoire en élevage caprin laiter. Paper presented at the FOA Seminar 'Systèmes de Production Caprins Méditerraéeens,' Corté, France.

Piaget, J. (1970) *Epistémologie des Sciences de l'Homme*. UNESCO, Geneva; republished by Gallimard, Paris (1977) NRF Idées.

Pillot, D. (1987) *Recherche-Développement et Farming System Research; Concepts, Approches et Méthodes*. Réseau R and D network, GRET, Paris, 41 pp.

Prost, J.-A., Casalta, E., de Sainte Marie, Ch., Maestrini, O. and Casabianca, F. (1992) *Exigences de Qualité et Normes Bactériologiques pour un Fromage A.O.C. Les Enjeux de la Définition d'une Date Limite de Consommation pour le Brocciu Frais*. INRA–LRDE, Corté, France, 19 pp.

Prost, J.-A., Casablanca, F., Casalta, E., Vallerand, F. and de Sainte Marie, Ch. (1994) La certification des produits, un levier pour le développement de l'élevage; La dynamique de l'Appellation d'Origine 'Brocciu corse.' In: *Systèmes Agraires et Qualités; Techniques, Lieux et Acteurs*. INRA, Paris, in press.

de Sainte Marie, Ch., Prost, J.-A., Casabianca, F., Casalta, E. (1993) La construction sociale de la qualité. *Economie Rurale* (à paraître dans Actes colloque 'La qualité dans l'agroalimentaire; enjeux économiques et objets scientifiques – Societé Française Economie rurale – Paris, October 1992).

Schmid, A. (1990) *Institutions et Emploi des Ressources sur le Plateau de Vittel*. Report prepared for INRA–SAD, Paris (translation, 13 pp).

Simon, H.A. (1969) *La Science des Systèmes, Sciences de l'Artificiel*. Translated from English (1974) L'Epi, Paris.

Vallerand, F., Casabianca, F., Santucci, P.M. and Bouche, R. (1992) Contribution of the concept of organisation for research-action upon mediterranean livestock farming systems. In: *Global Appraisal of Livestock Farming Systems and Study of Their Organisational Levels: Concepts, Methodology and Results*. EUR 14479, Commission of the European Communities, Luxembourg, pp. 21–44.

Vesperien, M.-R. (1992) La recherche-action de type stratégique. *Revue Internationale de Systémique* 6 (4), 351–364.

# =27=

## The Necessity, Theory and Reality of Developing Models of Farm Households

### Gareth Edwards-Jones and Murray McGregor

### Introduction

Agricultural systems research to date has tended to mimic the biological sciences by concentrating on the detail of either the individual production system or production from the whole farm system. As a result, the literature abounds with examples of individual crop, animal and whole farm models, which in many cases refer to a specific site, and therefore have limited utility (Loewer *et al.*, 1983; Guerrero *et al.*, 1984; Guetierrez-Aleman *et al.*, 1986; Doyle *et al.*, 1989; Sorensen, 1989; Lopez-Tirado and Jones, 1991). It is only recently that there has been an awakening to the fact that the further application of these models is limited by a suitable degree of understanding of the decision-making complex in which these models are set. Critical in this is the recognition that the farm household is the unit of decision making which determines the speed and level of uptake of new policies and/or technologies. It is these two factors which determine the ultimate cost–benefit of a policy or research outcomes.

As much of European agriculture is currently undergoing change at a level which is unprecedented in recent times, it has become increasingly important for policy makers to understand the reactions of farm businesses (and more specifically farm households) if they are to develop better policies and policy mechanisms. Models that mimic the decision-making processes of the farm-level decision-making unit (which may or may not be linked to biological process models) can help planning for change in two ways (Dent, 1991). The first is that such models would provide a useful mechanism to pre-screen the ways in which farm businesses would react to the new circumstances. The output from the models would, for example, permit the *ex ante* assessment of the likely way in which a farm business would respond to a new policy instrument or would permit a comparison of a possible policy scenario with another in terms of its economic and social benefits and costs. Second, farm-level decision-making models would also be useful for pre-screening potential new technologies (or changes in the physical environment such as a climate change) prior to expensive research, development and extension programmes being committed. This would allow decision makers to judge the relative merits of one research, development and extension programme against another.

A model which might accomplish these tasks would be required to mimic the behaviour of a farm household when exposed to a new policy and/or new technologies. Because, at the national level, which is the natural level of policy assessment, it would be impossible to model each individual business unit separately, any model would need to refer to a representative farm household or a defined group, and in addition it would also need to provide data about the behaviour of other members of the group in the widest sense. For instance, it may be interesting to understand the reaction of other household members in response to pressure on the household budget; would they be most likely to seek alternative employment off-farm, retrain or use their existing business skills to diversify the farming or non-farming activities on the property? The model would also have to be compatible with a classification system which would permit the identification of appropriate groups of farms. This classification would obviously need to go beyond current agroclimatic zoning to include sociocultural and economic factors. Finally, the model would have to be compatible with the method by which aggregation of group behaviour to regional or national level could occur.

This chapter initially discusses how successful the systems fraternity has been in developing suitable models of the farm household, and then examines the potential of future developments in this field.

## Historical Developments

Historically there have been three clear approaches to incorporating farm households in farm systems models, and the rationale of these approaches has often, but not exclusively, been derived from the discipline of the researcher developing the model. Thus, the first has generally been developed by economists, the second by sociologists, while the third involves a psychological–behaviourist approach.

The economics approach to farm household (or business) decision making has been built on the basis that the underlying objective of the farm decision-making complex is to maximize profits. A wide range of mathematical programming techniques which optimize a single objective function – with or without risk and uncertainty, and temporal aspects – have been reported in the literature (see, for example, Amir *et al.*, 1991; Ghadim *et al.*,

1991; Wossink *et al.*, 1992). In the main, these attempts at modelling have failed to capture the reality of decision making to a high degree of accuracy. This is due partly to the restrictions of the modelling framework adopted, but it is also the case that many of the decision-making models which have been developed have failed to predict adequately decisions because they make basic assumptions about rationality that are not upheld in the real world.

One criticism of these normative approaches is that they fail to recognize that other objectives such as job satisfaction and non-financial rewards from farming play a part in the overall behaviour of the decision-making complex. A general response to this has led to the expansion of the objective function to include socioeconomic factors. This has been achieved using multiple criteria decision-making methods (see, for example, Romero and Rehman, 1989; Flinn *et al.*, 1992; Piech and Rehman, 1993). However, much of the research that has been carried out using this wider multiple objective framework has used a definition of socioeconomics which is limited to those variables which are quantitative, readily accessible and easily structured (Skerratt *et al.*, 1991). Many important factors have been ignored as they are either too difficult to quantify in terms suitable for the modelling process being used ˙or alternatively, and more commonly, they have not even been recognized as important by the analyst. In addition, the majority of modelling work carried out has been hypothetical in nature and few real-life cases have been reported in the literature. This has meant that the crucial issues of the definition of objectives, and assignment of weights to individual objectives, to derive an overall objective function have been neglected.

The second broad approach has been the widening of the economics model by sociologists to include demographic variables such as age, education, marital status and number of children in the family (see, for example, Feder *et al.*, 1985; Nowak, 1987; Lynne *et al.*, 1988; Strauss *et al.*, 1991). The addition of these factors is said to increase the ability of these models to predict and model decisions; however, confirmation of this from the literature is sparse and the empirical modelling that has been reported has failed to explain more than 60% of actions at the best.

The third perspective on understanding and modelling farm decision making adopts a psychological–behaviourist approach. This is a relatively new approach and explicitly recognizes that farmers have multiple goals, and decisions are made that reflect the greatest satisfaction. To date, the approach has been limited to investigating farmers' perceptions of quality of life, farming values, satisfaction with farming and risk taking, generally without the credibility of well validated tests and often without reference to behaviour (Willock, personal communication). This approach could be improved by introducing personality and work-style factors in addition to cognitive ability tests and a closer correlation of attitudes with behaviour. However, the psychological variables such as perceptions, values and attitudes on their own are insufficient for a general model of decision making.

The decision-making process requires that the individual search and evaluate information before a choice can be made (Lindner, 1987). The path of the search and evaluation process will depend on the individual's ability and preferences based on past experience. Factors such as cognitive ability, personality and preferred style of working will have to be included in the model. However, decisions are also determined by a range of physical and financial factors, both endogenous and exogenous to the farm household (Doorman, 1991), and the existence of these renders the psychological–behaviourist approach unsuitable for use in isolation.

While each of these three modelling approaches has its own particular strengths, when used individually there is a definite need for a more holistic-oriented approach to modelling decision making and farm household behaviour. The most successful approach may well come from a fusion of the economic and psychological–behaviourist approaches.

## Computational Representation of Farm Household Models

Although identifying the appropriate modelling paradigm is a necessary first step to the practical implementation of farm household models, a second difficulty arises in attempting to represent this paradigm on the computer. The *raison d'être* of farm household models in the context discussed in the Introduction is as a simulation tool, and as such they are not intended to maximize output or optimize any objective function; rather, they aim to reveal the outcome of any given action and/or policy on the farm system as a whole. Given this aim, a first analysis would suggest that standard simulation techniques would seem the most appropriate tools to adopt for model construction. More detailed analysis, though, reveals that although standard simulation methods appear to be useful for biological modelling, in the socioeconomic situation this may not hold true.

Consider, for example, that biological simulation modellers can readily identify important variables, and through experimentation estimate parameter values. Further, relatively simple, numerical manipulation of these factors appears to provide adequate simulation of real systems. Thus, the important interactions of biological models can be represented mathematically, and these mathematical representations can be executed in standard computer languages such as FORTRAN and C. By comparison, developing models for socioeconomic systems poses severe problems: first, the subjects cannot be manipulated in a controlled manner, and all the data must come from observation; second, the important variables are difficult to identify; and third, it may not be possible to express these variables in a quantitative manner, e.g. feeling of stewardship, attitude to risk. Further complications arise because all members of a farm household may contribute to any overall decision, either explicitly or implicitly through their influence on other family members. In addition, each individual's response and relative influence may vary with situation. Consider, for example, a family composed of two adults and two teenage children. In times of relative wealth all the individuals within the household may respond to a given set of inputs in a unanimous way, and therefore the output of the household is simple to derive. If, however, in the next time period, the family is undergoing severe financial stress, all individuals may respond entirely differently to each other, and to the way they each responded in the previous time period, and therefore the structure of the decision becomes extremely difficult to predict.

In a recent study, we have attempted to tackle some of these problems through the adoption of programming techniques derived from artificial intelligence (Edwards-Jones *et al.*, 1994), and although this work points to some solutions to the problems discussed above, several others require more work. Further detail on these issues constitutes much of the subsequent discussion.

## Artificial Intelligence Techniques Suitable for Modelling Farm Households

### *Expert systems as techniques for modelling*

Of the range of artificial intelligence (AI) programming techniques, which include neural networks, machine learning, natural language processing and expert systems, it is the last which appear to hold most potential for modelling farm household decision making. Expert systems are computer programs which explicitly seek to emulate the decision-making process of human experts, and they have come to the fore within agriculture chiefly as advisory aids, where they emulate the performance of agricultural researchers and extension officers in recognizing and solving a variety of agricultural problems (Edwards-Jones and McGregor, 1992; Edwards-Jones, 1993).

The development of expert systems is based on the assumption that humans reach a decision by navigating through the search space associated with a problem by accessing a series of small and connected rules, each representing one specific decision point. The mechanisms used for this can be represented in computer code as a series of IF/THEN rules. Experience has shown that by linking a series of such rules (which may incorporate AND, OR and NOT operators within the rule structure) within a rule base, apparently simple rules can represent complex problems. Prior to representing these rules on a computer, it is necessary to extract them from the expert. This process, termed knowledge acquisition, often proves difficult and requires specially trained personnel to utilize a series of techniques, including informal interviews, formal interviews, hypothetical problem setting and observation of the expert performing problem-oriented tasks, in order to acquire the relevant knowledge.

Fortunately, all of these techniques are directly transferable from the development of expert systems to the development of simulation models of farm household decision making. Indeed, when applying any of the ideas associated with developing expert systems to modelling farmer decision making, all that is necessary is to treat the farmer (and other family members) as 'the expert.' Although this transfer is conceptually trivial, one major problem does arise from its adoption, that is, while there may be only one expert in any given area, there are many farmers, and as it is impossible to access the decision-making process of all farmers, some generalizations are necessary. Thus a generic decision-making framework is required which will represent all farmers within a given typology. The structure of this framework may be partially derived from primary data, utilizing the techniques of knowledge acquisition, but will probably be supplemented with secondary data from sociological sources.

### Techniques for representing social data on a computer

Although the existence of computer languages developed specifically for modelling human thinking and decision making greatly eases the task of modelling farm households, two further related computational techniques also have much to offer, particularly for representing psychological and social data. These are object-oriented and frame-based programming (Luger and Stubblefield 1989; Budd, 1991).

Object-oriented and frame-based programming, which seem set to herald a revolution in biological modelling (Judson, 1994), lend themselves to modelling any 'whole' which is composed of separate interacting parts. Thus a forest may be modelled as a series of interacting trees, each of which is composed of interacting branches, which in turn is composed of interacting leaves, which themselves are composed of interacting cells. This example emphasizes two of the main attractions of object-oriented programming, the transferability of code and inheritance.

Object-oriented code is transferable because, as opposed to traditional programs which have data structures and control structures to manipulate them, object-oriented programs are composed of objects, which contain both the data and their controls. The objects are therefore self-contained and can either be moved from program to program or alternatively be used many times in the same program. A second related feature of object-oriented languages is that they enable inheritance. Here any specified object (a child object) can take on the characteristics of any other object (the parent object). Thus in the forest example a general object may be a tree, and a child object may be an individual species of tree. Alternatively, if the model was based at a smaller spatial scale, the parent object may be a generalized cell, and child objects could be developed for different types of cell. These would inherit the basic characteristics of a cell, e.g. a cell wall, nucleus and cytoplasm, from the parent, but each cell type (child) may differ in their specific functions and response to stimuli.

The application of these techniques to modelling social systems becomes apparent if we assume that all individuals are basically structured in a similar manner, but the response of any given individual is a function of the specific characteristics of that individual. For example, in agriculture, the uptake response to a given environmental policy may be a function of each farmer's attitude to risk and his attitude to the environment. The latter, in turn, may be a function of age, level of general education, highest educational level at which environmental science was studied, religious beliefs, attitudes of other family members to the environment (e.g. parents, spouse and children), attitudes of colleagues to the environment and ambient environmental quality. The former characteristic, attitude to risk, is composed of an equally complex set of factors.

It is important to note that although many of the factors contributing towards a top-level response, i.e. attitude to the environment, may be fixed within a given individual, in fact the output response of that individual may vary according to the situation, for example, as the profitability of the farm business or stage in the family cycle vary. Therefore, when modelling the response of an individual to a stimulus, such as a new policy, it is important to include within the model other factors in the individual's life which may influence their decision in relation to that policy.

If the relationship between basic personal characteristics and higher order functions, such as attitude to risk or attitude to the environment, could be defined, then by forming an object 'farm family member' in the model, a series of 'child' objects could be formed in order to represent each member of the farm family. Modelling the farm family decision making would then require exposing each of the 'family member objects' first to their background situation (i.e. the farm, its business performance, the local environment, etc.) and then introducing a new stimulus and observing their interaction.

Fortunately, structuring these hierarchical relationships is made relatively simple if a frame-based approach to data structures is adopted. Here each basic characteristic of the object 'farm family member' would be represented by a slot, which in an object-oriented system would contain all relevant data, and controls for those data. These slots would be organized hierarchically in order to represent the overall object, 'farm family member,' and their influence on each other, defined by their respective controlling mechanisms. An example of a simple frame-based representation of a farmer is given in Fig. 27.1. This example concentrates on the characteristics discussed above, although clearly in different situations different characteristics would need to be included. For example, in developing countries, health and nutritional status may become much more important.

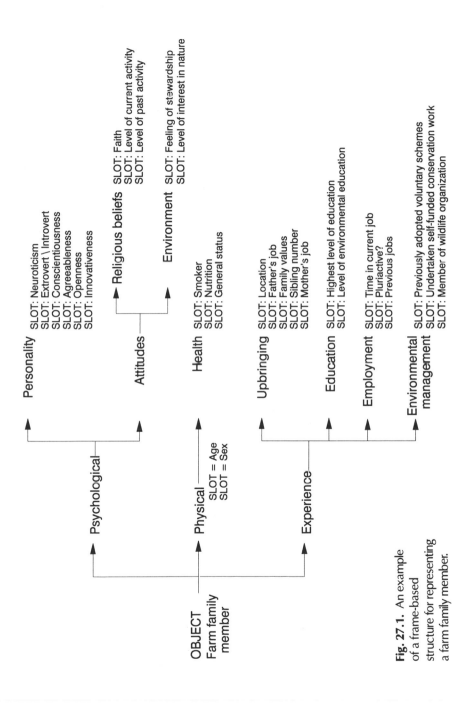

**Fig. 27.1.** An example of a frame-based structure for representing a farm family member.

*Summary comments on techniques and modelling approaches*

Object-oriented and frame-based programming techniques appear to be extremely useful for representing and holding data on individual members of farm families. Further, by utilizing techniques developed for expert systems it is possible first, to acquire the relevant knowledge to fill the slots in the frames, and second, through using rules to act upon the constituent slots in the 'farm family member,' to model the response to given stimuli, e.g. policy and new technologies.

Although, clearly, much basic psychological work is required before this type of model could be widely used, some progress may be achieved at a fairly gross level, simply by taking the data collected in previous studies and utilizing the results of the standard multivariate statistics in order to help structure the frames in an appropriate manner for incorporation into object-oriented programs. This approach was used during a recent study which utilized some of the ideas discussed above in order to investigate the possibility of integrating a farm household decision-making model with biological crop models for a farming system in Guatemala. Brief details of this model are given below.

# Structure of a Whole Farm Model for Subsistence Farmers in Guatemala

The farm system which has provided the focus for this work was that of subsistence farmers in the Jutiapa region of Guatemala. Typically, these farmers grow maize and beans, are dependent largely on family labour, use limited inputs to the crop and have restricted market opportunities (Thornton and Hoogenboom, 1990). This cropping pattern is reflected in the whole farm model, which utilizes the CERES maize model (Jones and Kiniry, 1986), the Beangro model (Hoogenboom *et al.*, 1990) and a fallow model (the fallow models are essentially the crop models, without the crop, and serve to simulate the soil nutrient dynamics during the fallow period, i.e. between harvest and the next sowing), run with local weather and soil data to simulate crop production. In order to represent better the whole farm system, these biological models are linked with two other modules, a family growth model and a farm-family decision model. Even this is a simplification of the real farm system, as no livestock are included and the models simulate the growth of crop monocultures rather than the reality of intercropping. These simplifications were acceptable within the project, as the work was largely exploratory in nature, aimed at identifying possible ways forward in whole farm modelling, and thus further agricultural complexities can be added at a future date if required.

## The family growth model

The family model is based around a Leslie matrix (Leslie, 1945). This matrix assumes that only four processes govern populations, immigration, emigration, births and deaths, and that the probability of any of these occurring over a given time period can be calculated and used to model fluctuations in the population over time. Thus the survival of individuals from the current time period to a future time period is specified probabilistically. These probabilities may vary with circumstance, and in the Guatemalan whole farm model they vary according to the age, sex and nutritive status of the individuals.

## The farm household decision-making model

The major outputs of the farm household decision-making model (FHDM) serve to act as the inputs into the crop models, they are calculated annually and include the variety to be sown, sowing density, plant spacing, sowing date and fertilizer strategy. In order to make these decisions, the FHDM also needs to assess the requirement and desirability of using credit, selling surplus food at local markets, the future nutritional requirements of the farm family and the relative taste and storage characteristics of the available varieties. The FHDM was developed in Prolog and the family's decisions are modelled using a series of rule bases. Throughout the decision-making process the model acts from the perspective of the farm family. Thus, inputs to the model are only those which would be available to farm families in Jutiapa, and similarly possible outputs or actions undertaken by the FHDM are also restricted to those which can be observed in the region. In addition to the decision-making rule bases, other routines monitor the family's financial transactions and the status of their available stores and also record the nutritional status of the family members. Further details on the structure and functioning of the model are available in Edwards-Jones *et al.* (1994).

## Running the model

On initiating the whole farm model (WFM), the family growth module is activated, and after simulating one year's family growth, the farm household decision-making model is activated. The outputs of this model relate to the crop production decisions of the household, and serve to act as the inputs to the crop models. Once initiated, the crop models run to their physiological maturity and then automatically trigger the fallow models. However, as the fallow models do not simulate plant growth, there is no natural end point to them, such as the physiological maturity which triggers the end of a simulation for the crop models; if left alone, therefore, the fallow models would run indefinitely. Clearly this is unacceptable, and within the WFM it is only necessary to run the fallow models up until the date of sowing the next crop.

However, as the date of sowing depends crucially on the weather conditions (and maybe on labour availability) in any particular year, the exact sowing date is not predictable from year to year.

In Jutiapa, sowing is timed to coincide with the annual rains, and this characteristic was used in the model to trigger the ending of the fallow models and to shift of control to the family growth model. Thus, the fallow models run until the soil moisture content reaches a stated threshold, and when this is exceeded the fallow models end and trigger the family growth model. The one slight difficulty with this approach is that occasionally the main rainy season is preceded by 'false' rains. Sowing during the false rains may lead to large-scale crop death, through poor germination, and it is therefore important to the farmers to sow crops only during the 'real' rains. In order to ensure that the model only sows during the real rain, the soil moisture threshold in the fallow model is set slightly higher than would be necessary in the absence of a 'false' rain phenomenon. This structure has proved robust and satisfactory for the current project, but it is not yet clear how the control of the modules could be manipulated in situations which do not have readily defined seasons.

### *Deficiencies and simplifications of the whole farm model*

The WFM described above was developed primarily to investigate the feasibility of integrating socioeconomic and biological models in a whole farm context and for this reason several issues were grossly simplified and future developments will require further developments in these areas. For example, further socio-logical work is needed on the relationship between nutrition and work capacity, on the distribution of food within the household during times of hardship, on the relative importance of the social (e.g. taste, storability and cookability) and agronomic characteristics (e.g. yield, pest resistance, seasonality) of crop varieties, on the relative importance of community, family and personal characteristics in influencing technology uptake and on the differential influence individual family members have on the final 'household' decision. In addition, further work is required on several technical aspects of the model, including an examination of the feasibility of representing each family member as a separate object in the model, the introduction of animals into the farm system, improving control over the fallow models and, eventually, linking a series of WFMs within a geographical information system (GIS).

## Prospects for Developing Integrated Social and Biological Farm Models in the European Situation

One of the attractions of modelling subsistence farm households in a developing country is the relative simplicity of the decision environment. It is assumed, for example, that survival is the overriding objective, that market access is direct to local outlets, that all labour is manual and that there is no national agricultural policy of relevance. Clearly, these assumptions are not valid in a European context, where farmers' objectives are multi-dimensional and often involve conflict between financial, environmental and social concerns, the markets are often distant and complex and the decision-making process is influenced considerably by both European Union (EU) and national policy on production and the environment. If the modelling approach described above is to be adopted for representing farm household decision making in whole farm systems in Europe, the following areas will need developing:

- *Biological models of agricultural production systems.* European scientists have developed a large number of biological models which would allow the development of at least a basic representation of the production processes involved in modelling a whole farm system. The major problem here is ensuring that the models utilized in a single system share the same protocols and are relevant to the region/environment in which they are to be used. In addition, very few of the models developed to represent production processes include adequate representations of the environmental implications of changes in the production system modelled. To be relevant to the current decision-making framework within Europe, this shortcoming would need to be rectified.
- *Understanding of the farm household decision-making complex.* Studies have begun in Scotland (involving the Scottish Agricultural College and the University of Edinburgh's Institute of Ecology and Resource Management and the Psychology Department, aimed at determining those factors which influence farm household decision making; this work is being funded by the Scottish Office Agriculture and Fisheries Department) to unravel the importance of farmer and farm household attitudes to their behaviour. The data produced by such studies will enable a detailed representation of the decision-making complex to be modelled as outlined above. Studies of the decision-making complex need to recognize that decisions about the farming system adopted will also require knowledge of responses to a range of policy mechanisms such as regulation, cross-compliance, subsidies and taxes.
- *Development of whole farm management modules.* Within the European context, any model of a whole farm system will need to be considerably more complex than that already developed for Guatemala. European whole farm models will need to integrate an array of biological models in order to represent the entire system, and these will need to be intimately linked with the decision-making model, which itself will be required to handle many more decision points than in the subsistence situation. A major requirement in the development of these models is to produce a

standard protocol which will allow data to be passed between the individual crop/animal models and the decision-making modules.

Despite these difficulties, the utility of a series of whole farm models for the European situation would be substantial, particularly in the areas of *ex ante* policy evaluation and the marketing of on-farm technology. Given the budget associated with the CAP, the first of these reasons alone would seem to be justification enough to develop this type of model. Should such a task be undertaken, it would seem that the frame-based approach, coupled with artificial intelligence programming techniques, would offer a suitable paradigm for modelling the decision making of individual members of farm households. Unfortunately, though, the major hurdle to the development of whole farm models in Europe may not be related to computational techniques, but rather may lie in our ignorance of the fundamental processes on-going within the farm household.

# References

Amir, I., Puech, J. and Granier, J. (1991) ISFARM: an integrated system for farm management: Part I – methodology. *Agricultural Systems* 35, 455–469.

Budd, T. (1991) *An Introduction to Object-oriented Programming.* Addison-Wesley, Reading, Massachusetts, 399 pp.

Dent, J.B. (1991) The potential for systems simulation in farming systems research? In: Penning de Vries, F., Teng, P. and Metselaar, K. (eds) *Systems Approaches for Agricultural Development, Proceedings of an International Symposium held at the Asian Institute of Technology, Thailand, 2–6 December.* Kluwer Academic, Dordrecht, pp. 325–340.

Doorman, F. (1991) A framework for the rapid appraisal of factors that influence the adoption and impact of new agricultural technology. *Human Organization* 50 (3), 235–244.

Doyle, C.J., Baars, J.A. and Bywater, A.C. (1989) A simulation model of bull beef production under rotational grazing in the Waikato region of New Zealand. *Agricultural Systems* 31, 247–278.

Edwards-Jones, G. (1993) Knowledge-based systems for crop protection: theory and practice. *Crop Protection* 12, 565–578.

Edwards-Jones, G. and McGregor, M.J. (1992) Expert systems in agriculture – a history of unfulfilled potential? In: *Proceedings of 4th International Congress for Computer Technology in Agriculture, Versailles, France, 1–3 June 1992.* Edinburgh School of Agriculture, Edinburgh, pp. 58–62.

Edwards-Jones, G., Dent, J.B., Morgan, O., McGregor, M.J. and Thornton, P.K. (1994) The integration of socio-economic data with biological crop models in a whole farm context. Unpublished report to IBSNAT, Hawaii.

Feder, G., Just, R.E. and Zilberman, D. (1985) Adoption of agricultural innovations in developing countries: a survey, *Economic Development and Cultural Change* 33, 225–298.

Flinn, J.C., Jayasuriya, S. and Knight, C.G. (1992) Incorporating multiple objectives in planning models of low-resource farmers. *Australian Journal of Agricultural Economics* 24 (1), 34–45.

Ghadim, A.A., Kingwell, R.S. and Pannell, D.J. (1991) An economic evaluation of deep tillage to reduce soil compaction on crop-livestock farms in Western Australia. *Agricultural Systems* 37, 291–307.

Guerrero, J.N., Wu, H., Holt, E.C. and Schake, L.M. (1984) Kleingrass growth and utilisation by growing steers. *Agricultural Systems* 13, 227–243.

Guetierrez-Aleman, N., de Boer, A.J. and Kehrbergm, E.W. (1986) A bio-economic model of small ruminant production in the semi-arid tropics of the Northeast region of Brazil: Part 2 – Linear programming applications and results. *Agricultural Systems* 19, 159–187.

Hoogenboom, G., Jones, J.W., White, J.W. and Boote, K.J. (1990) *BEANGRO V1.0: Dry Bean Crop Growth Simulation Model. User's Guide.* Agricultural Engineering Department and Agronomy Department, University of Florida, Gainesville.

Jones, C.A. and Kiniry, J.R. (1986) *CERES-Maize: a Simulation Model of Maize Growth and Development.* Texas A&M University Press, College Station, Texas.

Judson, O.P. (1994) The rise of the individual-based model in ecology. *Trends in Ecology and Evolution* 9, 9–14.

Leslie, P.H. (1945) On the use of matrices in certain population mathematics. *Biometrika* 33, 183–212.

Lindner, R.K. (1987) Adoption and diffusion of technology: an overview. In: Champ, B., Highley, E. and Remenyi, J. (eds) *Technological Change in Postharvest Handling of Grains in the Humid Tropics.* ACIAR, Canberra, pp. 144–151.

Loewer, O.J., Smith, E.M., Taul, K.L., Turner, L.W. and Gay, N. (1983) A body composition model for predicting beef animal growth. *Agricultural Systems* 10, 245–256.

Lopez-Tirado, Q. and Jones, J.G.W. (1991) A simulation model to assess primary production and use of *Bouteloua gracilis* grasslands, Part 1. Model structure and validation. *Agricultural Systems* 35, 189–208.

Luger, G.F. and Stubblefield, W.A. (1989) *Artificial Intelligence and the Design of Expert Systems.* Benjamin/Cummings, Redwood City, California.

Lynne, G.D., Shonkwiler, J.S. and Rola, L.R. (1988) Attitudes and farmer conservation behaviour. *American Journal of Agricultural Economics* 70, 12–19

Nowak, P.J. (1987) The adoption of agricultural conservation technologies: economic and diffusion explanations. *Rural Sociology* 52 (2), 208–220.

Piech, B. and Rehman, T. (1993) Application of multiple criteria decision-making methods to farm planning: a case study. *Agricultural Systems* 41 (3), 305–320.

Romero, C. and Rehman, T. (1989) *Multiple Criteria Analysis for Agricultural Decisions.* Developments in Agricultural Economics, Vol. 5, Elsevier, Amsterdam, 257 pp.

Skerratt, S., McGregor, M.J. and Sharma, R.A. (1991) Socio-economic evaluation of the Breadalbane Environmentally Sensitive Area: methodological issues. In: Loseby, M. (ed.) *The Environment and the Management of Agricultural Resources. Proceedings of the 24th Seminar of the European Association of Agricultural Economists, Viterbo, 24–26 January.* European Association for Agro Economists, Brussels, pp. 114–124.

Sorensen, J.T. (1989) A model simulating the production of dual purpose replacement heifers. *Agricultural Systems* 30, 15–34.

Strauss, J., Barbosa, M., Teixeira, S., Thomas, D. and Gomes, Jr, R. (1991) Role of education and extension in the adoption of technology: a study of upland rice and soybean farmers in Central–West Brazil. *Agricultural Economics* 5, 341–359.

Thornton, P.K. and Hoogenboom, G. (1990) Agrotechnology transfer using biological and socio-economic modelling in Guatemala. Unpublished report from the Edinburgh School of Agriculture and Department of Agricultural Engineering, University of Georgia, Athens, Georgia, 40 pp.

Wossink, G.A.A., Koeijer, T.J., Renkema, J.A. and de-Koeijer, T.J. (1992) Environmental–economic policy assessment: a farm economic approach. *Agricultural Systems* 39, 421–438.

# INDEX

typology 31, 114, 118, 190, 262
    farm 343

underdeveloped areas 23
underemployment 107, 111, 185
unemployment 65, 66, 111, 112, 166,
    189
utility 183, 211, 338, 350

village 68, 71–73, 111, 188, 194, 256,
    272, 275, 311, 314, 315

vocational identity 216

water
    catchment 173, 280
    management 136
    quality 146, 171, 173, 174,
        292–304
    resources 168, 173, 276, 284, 300

zones
    agroecological 7